# Consumer Demand in China

## About the Book and Authors

Because three-quarters of China's finished products are made for private consumption, changes in household income and expenditure exert a tremendous influence on the economy. This book provides a detailed overview of recent consumer trends in China. The data provide not only the best marketing information on China, but they are also a good measure of how successful China's economic reforms have been.

Using more than one hundred tables and graphs, the authors show differences between urban and rural income levels and changes in income distribution, spending patterns, commodity consumption, durable goods ownership, and housing. They discuss many of the underlying factors responsible for these changes; make comparisons between China's provinces; and explain the effect of income level, ethnic group, and geographic location on consumption patterns. All data are drawn exclusively from official Chinese sources, and many of the indicators have never appeared in English before.

Jeffrey R. Taylor is an economist with the U.S. Census Bureau's Center for International Research and professorial lecturer in Chinese studies at the Johns Hopkins University School of Advanced International Studies. Karen A. Hardee is a presidential management intern completing assignments at both the U.S. Bureau of the Census and the Agency for International Development.



# Consumer Demand in China

## A Statistical Factbook

Jeffrey R. Taylor
and Karen A. Hardee

Westview Press / Boulder and London

*Westview Special Studies on China*


---

This Westview softcover edition was manufactured on our own premises using equipment and methods that allow us to keep even specialized books in stock. It is printed on acid-free paper and bound in softcovers that carry the highest rating of the National Association of State Textbook Administrators, in consultation with the Association of American Publishers and the Book Manufacturers' Institute.

---

Published in 1986 in the United States of America by Westview Press, Inc.; Frederick A. Praeger, Publisher; 5500 Central Avenue, Boulder, Colorado 80301

Library of Congress Cataloging in Publication Data
Taylor, Jeffrey R., 1954- .
Consumer demand in China.
(Westview special studies on China)
Includes bibliographies.
1. Consumers--China--Statistics. 2. Consumption (Economics)--China--Statistics. I. Hardee, Karen A. II.Title. III. Series.
HC430.C6T39 1986 339.4'7'0951 86-19050
ISBN 0-8133-7310-7

Composition for this book was provided by the authors.
This book was produced without formal editing by the publishers.

Printed and bound in the United States of America

The paper used in this publication meets the requirements of the American National Standard for Permanence of Paper for Printed Library Materials Z39.48-1984.

6 5 4 3 2 1

# CONTENTS

# TABLES

## PART ONE
## CONSUMER DEMAND OVERVIEW AND ANALYSIS

## PART TWO
## STATISTICAL TABLES

### National Data
#### Sample and Household Size



#### Income and Wages

**Expenditures by General Categories**

**National Data**

**Expenditures by General Categories (continued)**



**Consumption of Individual Commodities**

**Retail Sales**

**National Data**
**Retail Sales (continued)**



**Ownership of Durable Goods**



**Housing**



**Provincial data**
**Income and Wages**

**Expenditures by General Categories**



**Consumption of Individual Commodities**

**Provincial Data**

**Consumption of Individual Commodities (continued)**



**Retail Sales**



**Ownership of Durable Goods**



**Price Indexes and Exchange Rates**

# CHARTS AND MAPS

## Charts

**Maps**

# PREFACE

This book evolved from a challenge to the authors to produce an easy-to-read factbook on consumer demand overseas that U.S. businesses would find useful, yet be rigorous enough to serve as a reference for scholars and government officials. China was chosen as the subject of this inquiry, increasing the complexity of the project several-fold because of problems in obtaining and interpreting the relevant statistics. To enliven matters still further, it was stipulated that the book be written within three months.

We hope that despite the haste in which this book was assembled, it meets the objectives set forth above. Our research was conducted at the U.S. Census Bureau's Center for International Research and sponsored by both the Center and its sister institution, the International Statistical Programs Center. The book was originally released as part of a U.S. Department of Commerce Country Marketing Report on China, which was published in January 1986.

Statistics cited in this book are the latest that were available as of November 1985. Readers interested in more current statistics on consumer demand in China are encouraged to consult Zhongguo tongji nianjian, 1985 [Statistical Yearbook of China, 1985] (December 1985), Zhongguo tongji zhaiyao, 1986 [Statistical Abstract of China] (July 1986), and Tongji yuebao [Statistical monthly]. A particularly detailed reference on rural consumers is Ge sheng, zizhiqu, zhixiashi nongmin shouru, xiaofei diaocha yanjiu ziliao huibian [Compilation of Survey and Research Materials on Peasant Incomes and Consumption in Each Province, Autonomous Region, and Independent Municipality] (1986). All of these publications are prepared by China's State Statistical Bureau and published in Beijing by Zhongguo tongji chubanshe [China Statistical Publishing House].

Empirical studies on consumer demand in China that have been published since we completed our research are most numerous in Chinese scholarly journals, but there are a few English-language publications as well. Readers may wish to consult a World Bank Staff Working Paper (number 755) by Li Xuezeng, Yang Shengming, and He Juhuang entitled, The Structure of China's Domestic Consumption. Also useful is a paper presented at the December 1985 meeting of the American Economic Association by Hu Teh-wei (Pennsylvania State University), Bai Jushan (Pennsylvania State University), and Shi Shuzhong (Nankai University) entitled "Household Expenditure Patterns in a Large Chinese City, 1982 and 1984."

To our colleagues in business, government, and academia, we extend the invitation to let this book serve not only as a reference, but as a stimulus for further research. Surely the largest collection of consumers in the world deserves no less.

Jeffrey R. Taylor
Karen A. Hardee

# ACKNOWLEDGMENTS

Many people assisted in the preparation of this book. Barbara Torrey, Karl Kindel, Judith Banister and Marie Argana offered comments and suggestions on draft versions of the book. Josephine Babbit and Yvonne Gist provided assistance in the preparation of tables and other production-related chores. Nina Pane-Pinto produced the original maps. Chinese calligraphy appearing in the book comes from the pen of Eric Yuan. Florence Yuan helped locate Chinese-language sources and verified numbers and romanization. Andrea Miles and Connie Woodard helped print, proofread, and photocopy the final tables. Richard Turnage and Al Ballinger graciously permitted us to use their computer equipment.

This research would not have been possible without the support of the Center for International Research and the International Statistical Programs Center of the U.S. Bureau of the Census. We are indebted to their generosity and their commitment to supporting quality research.

**Jeffrey R. Taylor**
**Karen A. Hardee**

## SELECTED EXCHANGE RATES AND PRICE INDEXES

| Year | Official exchange rate (yuan/dollar) | Cost of living index for staff and workers (1978=100) | Retail price index of of rural industrial products (1978=100) | General retail price index (1978=100) |
|---|---|---|---|---|
| 1978 | 1.684 | 100.0 | 100.0 | 100.0 |
| 1979 | 1.555 | 101.9 | 100.1 | 102.0 |
| 1980 | 1.498 | 109.5 | 101.0 | 108.1 |
| 1981 | 1.705 | 112.3 | 101.9 | 110.7 |
| 1982 | 1.893 | 114.4 | 103.5 | 112.8 |
| 1983 | 1.976 | 116.7 | 104.5 | 116.7 |
| 1984 | 2.320 | 119.9 | 107.7 | 117.7 |

Notes: Exchange rates shown are annual averages. The cost of living index for staff and workers includes list, negotiated, and market prices.

Sources: International Monetary Fund, International Financial Statistics Yearbook, 1985 (1985), p. 241.
State Statistical Bureau, Statistical Yearbook of China (1983), p. 455, and China: A Statistics Survey in 1985 (1985), p. 93.

PART ONE

# CONSUMER DEMAND OVERVIEW AND ANALYSIS

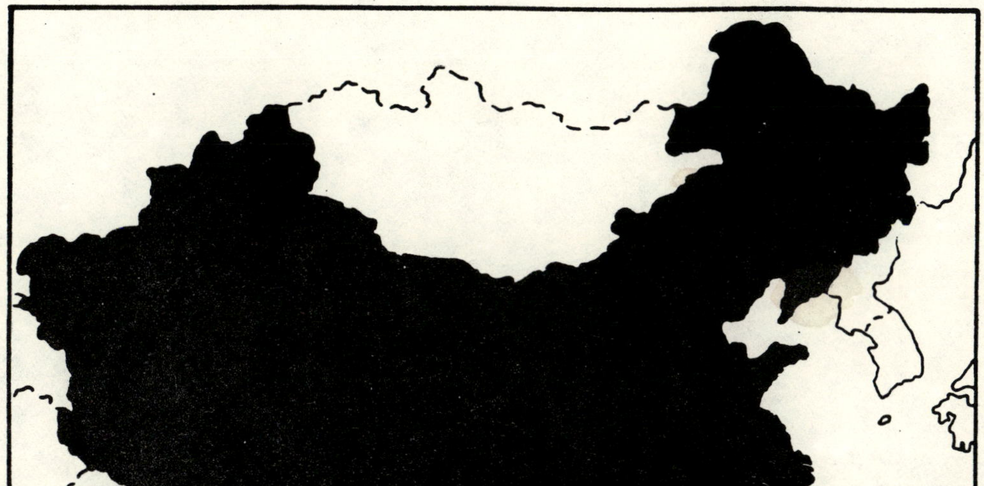

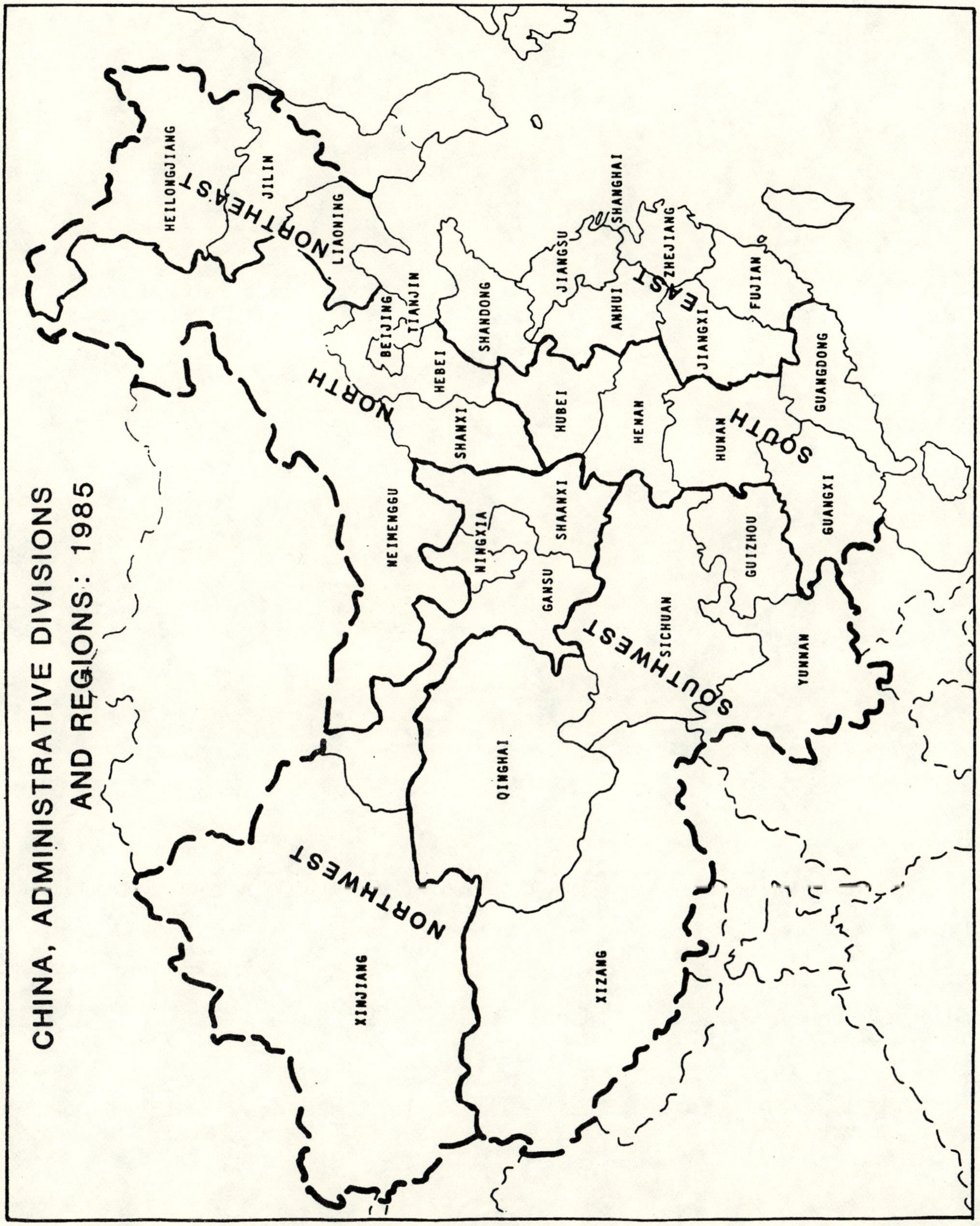
CHINA, ADMINISTRATIVE DIVISIONS
AND REGIONS: 1985
NORTHEAST
NORTH
EAST
SOUTH
SOUTHWEST
NORTHWEST
HEILONGJIANG
JILIN
LIAONING
BEIJING
TIANJIN
HEBEI
SHANXI
NEIMENGGU
SHANDONG
JIANGSU
SHANGHAI
ZHEJIANG
ANHUI
FUJIAN
JIANGXI
HENAN
HUBEI
HUNAN
GUANGDONG
GUANGXI
GUIZHOU
YUNNAN
SICHUAN
SHAANXI
NINGXIA
GANSU
QINGHAI
XINJIANG
XIZANG

MAP 1

# I. INTRODUCTION

**Understanding consumer demand trends in China is essential to a successful marketing strategy for both traders and investors.**

The vast majority of China's imports in recent years have been producer goods. Statistics from China's foreign trade departments indicate that in 1983, these goods constituted 79 percent of all imports. Why, given this reality, should individuals interested in business with China pay any attention to data on consumer incomes and demand for the country? After all, isn't China still a planned economy, where imports reflect government economic priorities far more than they reflect the preferences of individual consumers?

The market for exports of consumer goods to China is clearly very limited for now. Those who try to sell such commodities directly to China may well be frustrated. Still, an understanding of consumer income and expenditure trends for the country is essential to a successful marketing strategy for China, since consumer demand is the driving force behind demand for all commodities--including producer goods.

Private consumption makes up 70 percent of all final demand in China. When consumers increase their demand for food, this initially puts money in the pockets of agriculture and the food products industry (and to a limited extent, foreign grain companies). As agriculture and food products producers gear up to meet the increase in consumer demand, however, they put in increased orders with their suppliers, which includes a broader set of industries. These suppliers in turn increase their production to meet the rising orders from agriculture and the food products manufacturers, which increases the demand for inputs from a still broader array of industries. In this manner, increased demand for any consumer good multiplies throughout the economy, generating the demand for producer goods that most manufacturers are familiar with.

This is important because China is far more likely to rely on imports to help meet the derived demand for producer goods, than it is to meet the direct demand for consumer goods that started the whole process off. Therefore if one has an idea of consumer demand trends in China and can work backwards and identify the direct and indirect suppliers of these goods, one can get a fairly good idea of producer goods that China will be seeking from abroad in the future.

An example of this analysis is shown in chart 1. Consumer demand for food in China in the year 1990 was first projected. An

Chart 1.

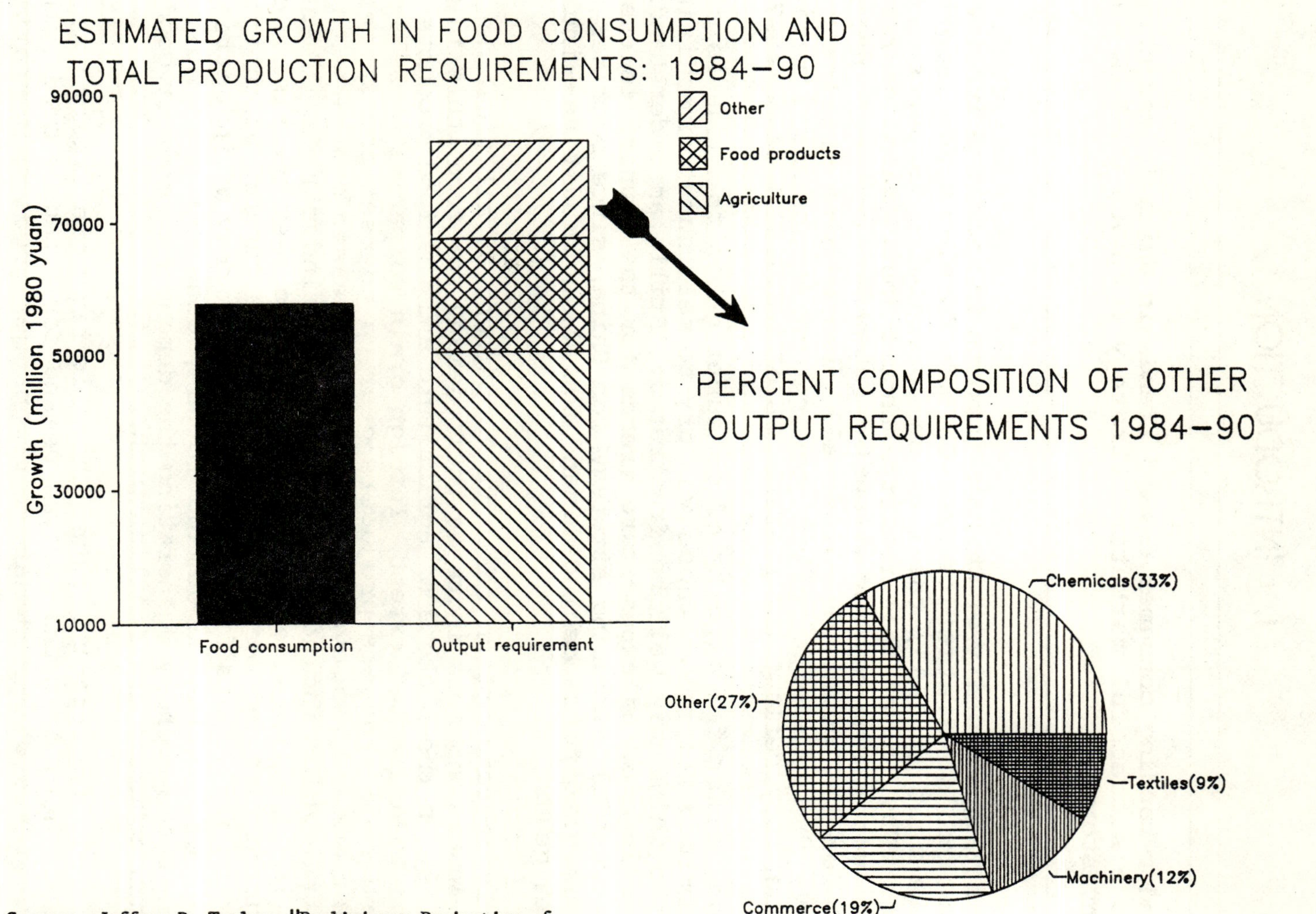


Source: Jeffrey R. Taylor, "Preliminary Projection of Consumer Demand for Food in China," U.S. Bureau of the Census, Center for International Research Staff Working Paper, 1985 (Pending).

estimate of imported foodstuffs was subtracted from the total, and the resultant increase in domestic demand was combined with an input-output table for China to calculate the direct and indirect supplies required from other sectors to meet this demand. This shows that a 57 million yuan increase in consumer demand for food would generate an estimated 82 million yuan increase in demand for the products of all sectors -- not just agriculture and the food products industry. Few would deny that this is useful marketing information.

There are more straightforward reasons for needing additional information on income and expenditure trends in China (such as for businessmen investing in Chinese joint ventures that produce consumer durables), but few more compelling than the above argument. It is simply sound marketing strategy for anyone doing business with China to understand the implications of these data. Knowing what these data mean has not been very easy in the past, however. China's personal income and consumer demand data are scattered in dozens of statistical references, many of which are untranslated, and all of which are difficult to obtain. It is for this reason that Consumer Demand in China: A Statistical Factbook was compiled.

The factbook consists of two parts. The first part provides an overview of China's consumers, their incomes, and the goods and services on which they spend their money. Urban-rural and interprovincial comparisons of incomes and expenditures are also made. The second part consists of a brief introduction to sources of data on Chinese consumer demand and incomes, and numerous detailed statistical tables from these sources. Except for an occasional conversion of monthly data to an annual basis, no adjustments have been made to the data presented in either part. This means that certain time series presented in the second part have gaps in them where data are still unavailable. Despite these omissions, the information assembled should go far in meeting most users' needs.

# II. CONSUMER PROFILE

**China has over one billion consumers, 68 percent of whom live in the countryside. Labor force participation rates are high and educational attainment low--particularly for women. The proportion of middle-aged and elderly people in the population is expected to rise substantially in the future.**

China's population is the largest in the world, with over 1 billion consumers. As shown in map 2, the country's population is distributed unevenly, with more than 95 percent of the people living on 40 percent of the land, mainly in the east. The most populous province, Sichuan, is located in the country's southwest region. Other heavily populated provinces include Henan, Shandong, Jiangsu, Guangdong, Hebei, and Anhui, all of which are in the eastern/coastal area (see table 1).

## URBAN/RURAL POPULATION

China is a predominantly rural, agrarian country. In 1984, 68 percent of the population lived in the countryside and, according to the 1982 census, 72 percent of all Chinese workers were engaged in agriculturally-related pursuits. Urban residency is regarded as a privilege with enormous legal and administrative implications, and population movements between urban and rural areas and even between cities of different sizes is strictly regulated by an elaborate household registration system.

Because of controls such as these, China's urban population has grown at a much slower rate than in other developing countries. Still, the urban portion of the population has increased sharply in recent years. In 1978, 18 percent of the population was classified as urban; by 1984, 32 percent of China's population lived in urban areas (see chart 2). This rapid increase reflects in part a broadening of the definition of urban residency, but is also due to economic policy changes favoring the growth of small cities and towns. Chinese economists estimate that 30 to 40 percent of China's farmers are underemployed, and see these towns as the prime vehicles for moving rural surplus labor into more productive nonagricultural jobs.

## AGE STRUCTURE

China's population is relatively young; an estimated 53 percent were under 25 years of age in 1985. As shown in chart 3, however,

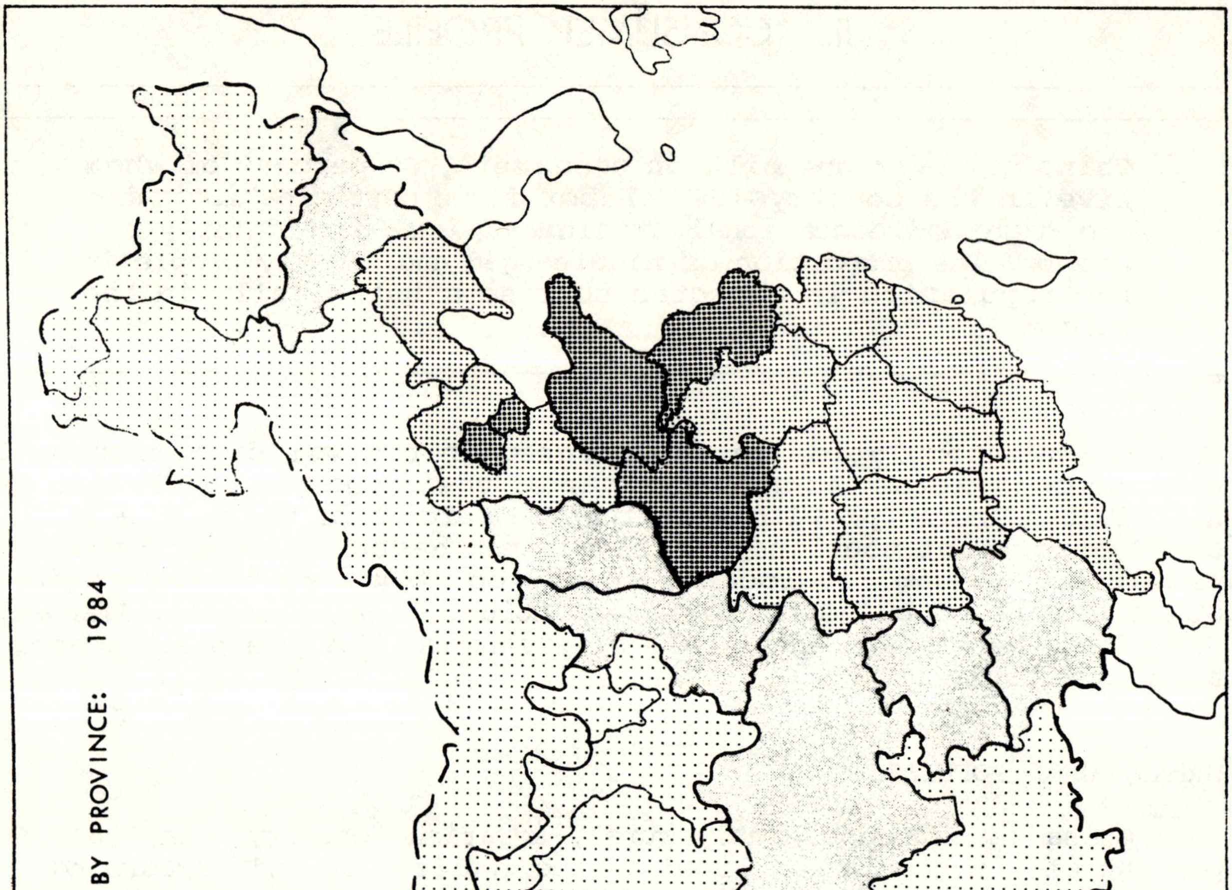
CHINA, POPULATION DENSITY, BY PROVINCE: 1984
Density
(per sq. km.)
0-99
100-199
200-399
400+

MAP 2

**Table 1. Population by Province, and Residence: 1984 (yearend, in millions, including military)**

| Province | Total | Urban | Rural |
|---|---|---|---|
| China.......... | 1,034.75 | 330.06 | 704.69 |
| North | | | |
| Beijing....... | 9.47 | 6.28 | 3.19 |
| Tianjin....... | 7.99 | 5.52 | 2.47 |
| Hebei......... | 54.70 | 15.11 | 39.76 |
| Shanxi........ | 26.00 | 14.53 | 11.47 |
| Neimenggu..... | 19.85 | 8.43 | 11.42 |
| Northeast | | | |
| Liaoning...... | 36.55 | 20.01 | 16.54 |
| Jilin......... | 22.84 | 12.56 | 10.28 |
| Heilongjiang.. | 32.95 | 16.92 | 16.03 |
| East | | | |
| Shanghai...... | 12.05 | 7.38 | 4.67 |
| Jiangsu....... | 61.71 | 13.96 | 47.75 |
| Zhejiang...... | 39.93 | 10.18 | 29.75 |
| Anhui......... | 51.03 | 9.15 | 41.88 |
| Fujian........ | 26.77 | 9.98 | 16.79 |
| Jiangxi....... | 34.21 | 7.61 | 26.60 |
| Shandong...... | 76.37 | 37.04 | 39.33 |
| South | | | |
| Henan......... | 76.46 | 12.28 | 64.18 |
| Hubei......... | 48.76 | 16.48 | 32.28 |
| Hunan......... | 55.61 | 12.88 | 42.73 |
| Guangdong..... | 61.66 | 16.02 | 45.64 |
| Guangxi....... | 38.06 | 14.34 | 23.72 |
| Southwest | | | |
| Sichuan....... | 101.12 | 18.60 | 82.52 |
| Guizhou....... | 29.32 | 8.54 | 20.78 |
| Yunnan........ | 33.62 | 8.78 | 24.84 |
| Xizang........ | 1.97 | .20 | 1.77 |
| Northwest | | | |
| Shaanxi....... | 29.66 | 11.01 | 18.65 |
| Gansu......... | 20.16 | 4.15 | 16.01 |
| Qinghai....... | 4.02 | 1.29 | 2.73 |
| Ningxia....... | 4.06 | 1.15 | 2.91 |
| Xinjiang...... | 13.44 | 5.44 | 8.00 |

Source: State Statistical Bureau, China: A Statistics Survey in 1985 (1985), p. 20.

Chart 2.

URBANIZATION IN CHINA: 1970 to 1984

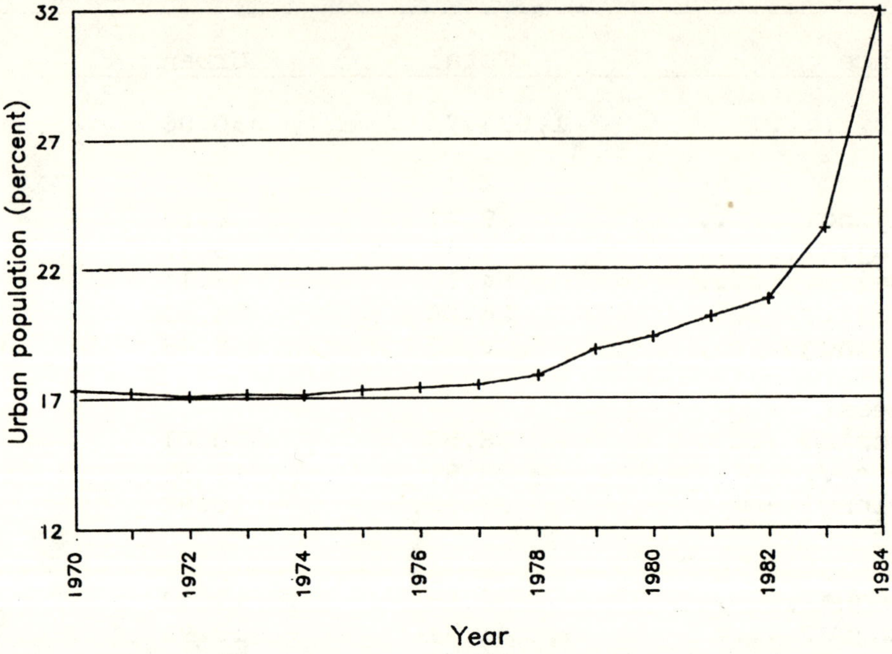


Source: State Statistical Bureau, China: A Statistics Survey in 1985 (1985), p. 19.

Chart 3.

POPULATION BY AGE: 1985 AND 2000

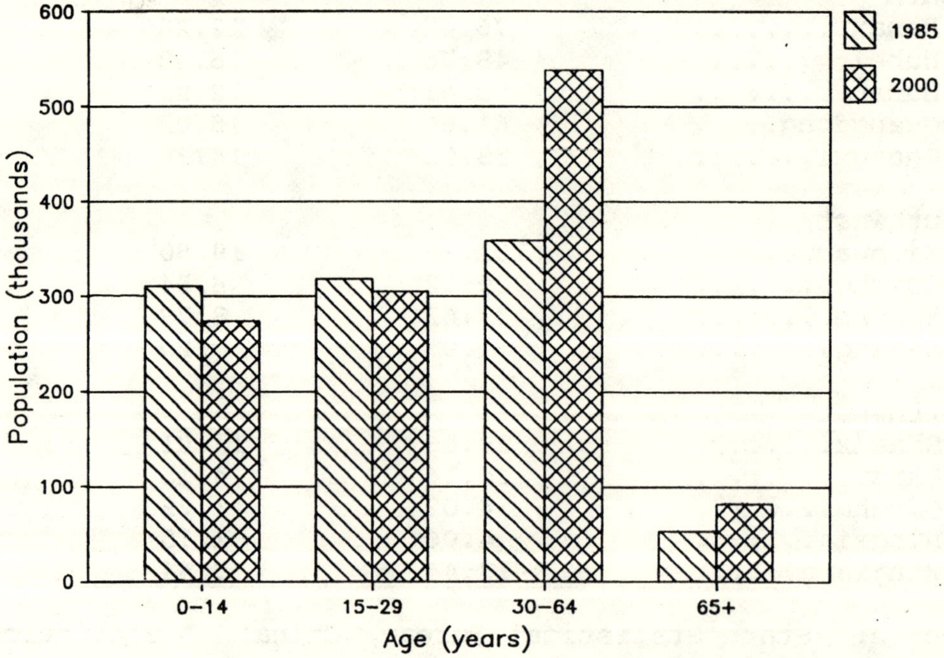


Source: Projections by the U.S. Bureau of the Census, Center for International Research.

the proportion of the population in their prime spending years (15 to 64 years of age) will increase dramatically by the year 2000. The estimated 65 percent share of total population held by this group in 1985 is expected to rise to 70 percent by the year 2000. The proportion of young people (0-14 years), on the other hand, will decrease by 23 percent, while the share of elderly people in the population will rise by 34 percent. These changes in the age composition of China's population could have a substantial effect on the composition of future retail sales.

## LABOR FORCE PARTICIPATION

Labor force participation rates are high in China, for both men and women. An estimated 90 percent of men and 74 percent of women over age 15 participated in the labor force at midyear 1982. These rates are high by international standards, as shown in table 2. Participation rates are particularly high for women compared to other countries, reflecting the important role women play in China's workforce. The 1982 census reported that 44 percent of the working population were women, although they tended to be concentrated in low-skill occupations.

## FAMILY STRUCTURE AND HOUSEHOLD SIZE

Families in China are slowly becoming smaller as couples have fewer children. Household income and expenditure surveys conducted for both urban and rural areas reflect this decline, although household size and family size cannot be strictly equated. The concept of an extended family, where several generations share the same living quarters, is still alive in China. This is particularly true in rural areas, where the size of one's household often exceeds the size of one's immediate family.

Households in urban areas have remained smaller by at least one person than those in rural areas since the income and expenditure surveys began in the 1950s. In 1984 household size was slightly more than 4 persons in urban areas and more than 5 persons in rural areas (table 3). Approximately 2.4 members of the urban households surveyed were employed in 1984, compared to an average of 1.6 workers per household in 1964. Increased employment participation in urban households combined with lower overall family size has reduced the number of persons supported by each urban worker from 3.4 persons in 1964 to 1.7 persons in 1984.

The trends in household composition are slightly different for rural areas. Workers per household in rural areas rose from 2.4 persons in 1965 to 2.9 persons in 1984. However, the average number of persons per household actually rose in rural areas from 1965 to 1984. Thus despite an increase in rural household employment

**Table 2. Estimated Labor Force Participation Rates for China and Other Areas (in percent)**

| Area | Both Sexes | Men | Women |
|---|---|---|---|
| China (1982, excluding Xizang).. | 82.1 | 89.6 | 74.1 |
| North America: | | | |
| United States (1982).......... | 64.0 | 76.6 | 52.6 |
| Europe: | | | |
| Germany (1982)................. | 53.4 | 70.0 | 38.9 |
| Great Britain (1981).......... | 62.6 | 78.6 | 48.1 |
| Italy (1982).................. | 47.4 | 66.6 | 29.9 |
| East Asia: | | | |
| Hong Kong (1981).............. | 66.8 | 82.5 | 49.5 |
| Japan (1982).................. | 62.7 | 79.3 | 47.0 |
| Korea, Republic of (1982)..... | 56.8 | 72.5 | 42.2 |
| Taiwan (1982)................. | 57.9 | 75.9 | 39.7 |
| South and Southeast Asia: | | | |
| Bangladesh (1979)............. | 53.8 | 88.9 | 3.8 |
| Indonesia (1980).............. | 58.1 | 80.4 | 37.1 |
| Malaysia, Peninsular (1979)... | 62.1 | 79.5 | 44.7 |
| Singapore (1982).............. | 63.4 | 81.5 | 45.2 |
| Thailand (1981)............... | 71.5 | 78.4 | 64.6 |
| Other: | | | |
| Soviet Union (1982)........... | 74.2 | 82.8 | 67.1 |

Note: Age groups included in the labor force participation rate calculations above are persons 10 years and over for Bangladesh, 14 and over for Korea and Italy, 15 and over for China, Hong Kong, Germany, Thailand, Singapore, Peninsular Malaysia, Indonesia, Taiwan and Japan, and 16 and over for the United States, Great Britain and the Soviet Union. Data are from the the latest available censuses, labor force surveys, household surveys, and official country estimates.

Source: Jeffrey R. Taylor, 1985, Employment and Unemployment in China (1985), p. 14.

**Table 3. Size and Employment Characteristics of China's Households, for Selected Survey Years: 1957 to 1984**

| Item | 1957 | 1964/1965 | 1984 |
|---|---|---|---|
| Rural: | | | |
| Persons per household... | 4.85 | 5.03 | 5.37 |
| Workers per household... | 2.33 | 2.35 | 2.87 |
| Persons supported by each worker.......... | 2.08 | 2.14 | 1.87 |
| Urban: | | | |
| Persons per household... | 4.73 | 5.30 | 4.04 |
| Workers per household... | 1.44 | 1.60 | 2.36 |
| Persons supported by each worker.......... | 3.29 | 3.40 | 1.71 |

Note: Data shown under 1964/1965 for rural households are for 1965; data for urban households are for 1964. All figures are from income and expenditure surveys of rural peasant households and urban staff and worker families.

Source: State Statistical Bureau, Statistical Yearbook of China 1983 (1983), pp. 492 and 499; and China: A Statistics Survey in 1985 (1985), pp. 99 and 100.

participation, the number of persons supported per worker has scarcely changed.

**EDUCATIONAL ATTAINMENT**

Levels of educational attainment in China are low. According to 1982 census data, 49 percent of all women aged 15 and over and 21 percent of all men in that age group are illiterate or semiliterate (see chart 4). Educational levels are higher for men than women in every age group, but the vast majority of individuals of both sexes do not progress beyond junior middle school.

Lower female educational levels are generally ascribed to the rural practice of withdrawing girls from school to work at home or in the fields. This practice reflects Chinese custom as well as the lack of comprehensive social insurance in rural areas. One's sons in China have traditionally been obligated to care for their parents in old age, yet daughters have been expected to give their full attention to the care of their husband's parents. This situation has established an almost irresistible incentive for parents to let their sons stay in school, for it improves their prospects of being well cared-for upon retirement. Given this tradition, the incentives for keeping daughters in school are considerably less.

Chart 4.

EDUCATIONAL ATTAINMENT, BY SEX, FOR PERSONS AGED 15 AND OVER: 1982

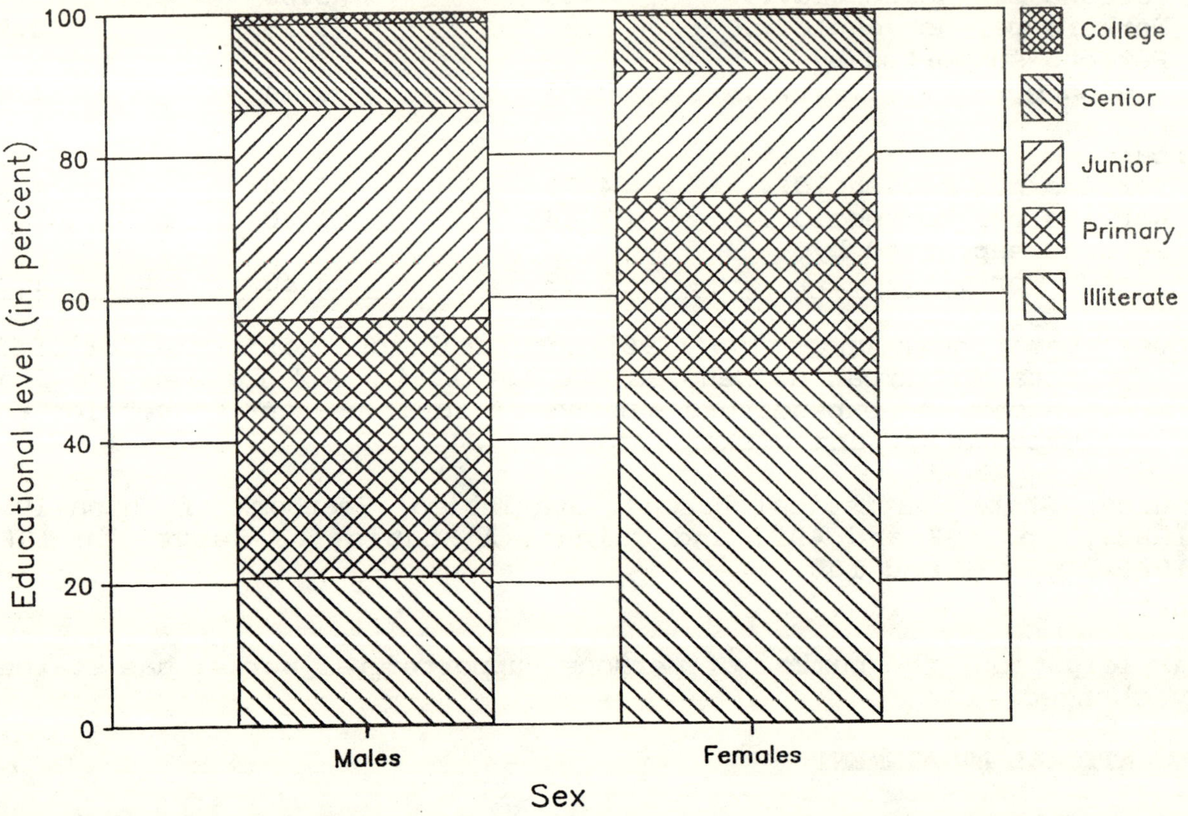


Source: Taylor, (1985), p. 20.

# III. INCOME, EXPENDITURE AND CONSUMPTION TRENDS AT THE NATIONAL LEVEL

**Urban and rural households are enjoying growing incomes in China. The standard of living in urban areas remains higher than in rural areas, but the gap is slowly narrowing.**

## WAGES AND INCOME

Income and wages are rising in China as a result of post-1978 economic reforms implemented to rejuvenate the economy and to raise living standards. Urban residents enjoy a higher standard of living than rural residents, though the gap has narrowed considerably in recent years as peasants have reaped the combined rewards of higher agricultural procurement prices, decollectivization, and implementation of the household responsibility system.

Comparisons between urban and rural areas should be made with caution. Although the household survey data for both areas may appear to be comparable, urban residents receive a wide array of income and consumption subsidies not available to peasants, including allowances for housing, food, transportation, and fuel. This means that even if urban and rural household survey data indicate similar consumption levels for a given commodity, the personal cost for peasants is still higher than the cost for urban residents.

Traditionally, China's income and expenditure surveys in urban areas have measured net per capita income for only the households of staff and workers who work in state-owned and collectively-owned enterprises. These data are not representative of the incomes of other urban households, particularly those households where family members are self-employed. Since only 3 percent of urban workers were classified as self-employed in 1984, their omission from current income and expenditure surveys is not a crippling defect. It is an omission that may become important in future years however, because self-employed workers are the fastest growing group in urban areas.

### Urban Wages and Income

**Nominal per capita urban incomes nearly doubled between 1978 and 1984, from 316 to 608 Yuan. Forms of compensation that reward greater efficiency, such as piece wages and bonuses, have risen from 3 percent of the wage bill in 1978 to 24 percent in 1984.**

The urban household survey gathers data on both total household income of staff and workers, and household income available for living expenses. The latter indicator is perhaps the most meaningful, for it excludes gifts and certain income subsidies that make comparisons with the rural survey data more difficult. Per capita income available for living expenses rose from 316 yuan in 1978 to 608 yuan in 1984 (these and other figures may be converted to U.S. dollars using the exchange rates printed on the inside cover). As shown in table 4, this yields a nominal average annual growth rate of 11.5 percent, compared to a real rate of growth of 8.2 percent.

**Table 4. Comparison of Urban and Rural Per Capita Incomes: 1978, 1983 and 1984**

| | | | | Annual average rate of growth (percent) | |
|---|---|---|---|---|---|
| Indicator | 1978 | 1983 | 1984 | 1978-83 | 1978-84 |
| Nominal per capita income (in yuan): | | | | | |
| Urban workers and staff.......... | 316 | 526 | 608 | 10.7 | 11.5 |
| Rural peasants........ | 134 | 310 | 355 | 18.3 | 17.6 |
| Real per capita income index (1978=100): | | | | | |
| Urban workers and staff.......... | 100.0 | 142.7 | 160.4 | 7.4 | 8.2 |
| Rural peasants........ | 100.0 | 198.4 | N/A | 14.7 | N/A |

N/A Data not available

Note: All statistics are from the urban or rural income and expenditure sample surveys. Because urban households receive substantial subsidies not generally available to peasants, these figures are not strictly comparable.

The real per capita income index for urban workers and staff in 1984 was estimated by applying the 12.5 percent real growth rate reported in the State Statistical Bureau's communique on fulfillment of the 1984 economic plan to the published index for 1983 of 142.7.

Sources: Part II, tables 5 and 17.

The rise in income has been accompanied by a shift in the distribution of income among households. In 1981, only 18 percent of worker and staff households had annual per capita incomes above 600 yuan (see chart 5). By 1984, fully 49 percent of worker and staff households were in this category. Rising urban prosperity is one reason for the shift in urban income distribution, but declining household size has also played an important role. Urban survey data for 1981 through 1984 suggest that there is an inverse relationship between household size and per capita income, as shown in chart 6. Since the average number of persons per worker and staff household fell from 4.2 persons in 1981 to 4.0 persons in 1984, a greater number of households were propelled into higher income brackets.

Urban wage data, broken down by sector, also cover only staff and workers in state-owned and collectively-owned units. Since 1984, wages for joint units (enterprises managed jointly by state and collective firms) have also been published. Jobs in state-owned enterprises have traditionally been among the highest paying in

Chart 5.

DISTRIBUTION OF ANNUAL URBAN INCOME BY INCOME GROUP: 1981 AND 1984

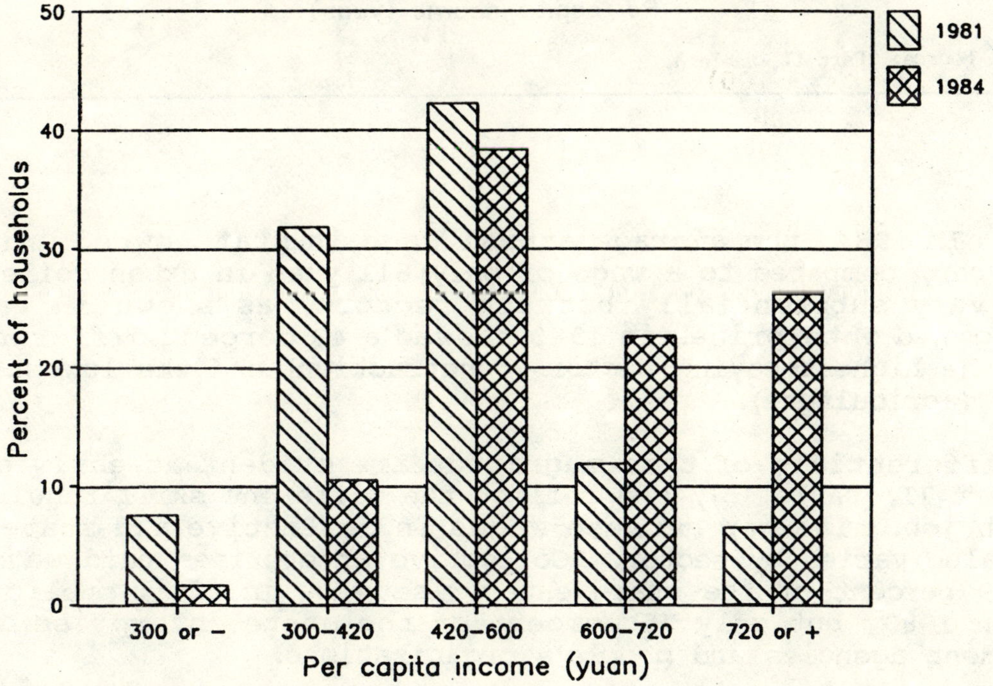


Source: Part II, table 7.

Chart 6.

PER CAPITA INCOME AND URBAN FAMILY SIZE: 1983

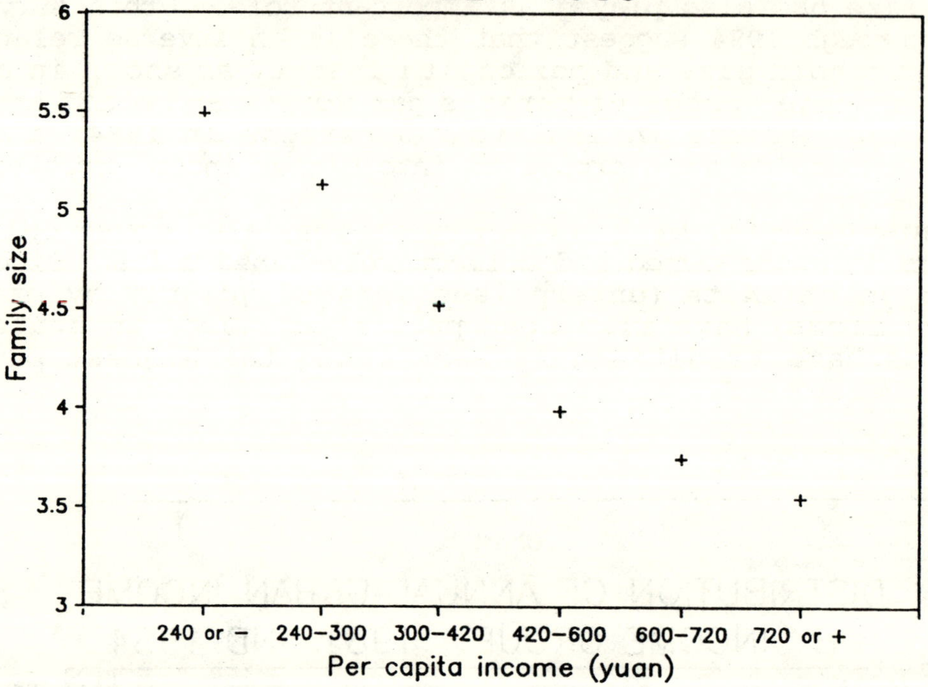


Source: Part II, table 3.

China. In 1984, the average annual wage in state-owned units was 1,034 yuan, compared to a wage of only 811 yuan in urban collectives. Wages vary substantially between sectors, as shown in table 5. State-owned enterprises in 1983 showed a 43 percent difference between the highest-paying sector (construction) and the lowest-paying sector (agriculture).

Differentials of this magnitude are evident as early as 1952 (see Part II, table 15), and reflect the different skill requirements of each job. The gap between wages in collective and state-owned units also varies by sector. Collective enterprises paid wages that were 89 percent of the state enterprise wage in civil public utilities in 1983, but only 75 percent of the state enterprise wage in government agencies and people's organizations.

Wages in state-owned enterprises rose by 87 percent between 1978 and 1984. Prior to 1978 both nominal and real wages in state-owned

Table 5. **Comparison of Wages in State-Owned and Collectively-Owned Enterprises, by Sector: 1983**

| Sector | State-owned enterprises | Collective-owned enterprises in cities and towns | Collective wages as a percent of state wages |
|---|---|---|---|
| Total...................... | 865 | 698 | 81 |
| Industry.................. | 878 | 684 | 78 |
| Construction and resources prospecting... | 1,023 | 844 | 83 |
| Agriculture, forestry, water conservancy, and meteorology......... | 713 | 555 | 78 |
| Transport, posts, and telecommunications...... | 959 | 787 | 82 |
| Commerce, catering, and service trades, and materials supply and marketing............... | 764 | 616 | 81 |
| Civil public utilities.... | 876 | 776 | 89 |
| Scientific research....... | 986 | 757 | 77 |
| Culture, education, public health and social welfare.......... | 861 | 685 | 80 |
| Banking and insurance..... | 820 | 688 | 84 |
| Government agencies and people's organizations.. | 927 | 696 | 75 |

Source: State Statistical Bureau, Statistical Yearbook of China 1984 (1984), p. 456.

enterprises plummeted because of the "Great Leap Forward" (1958-1962), and after a brief recovery, suffered almost 15 years of slow decline (see chart 7). The rapid increase after 1978 is a direct result of policies implemented by central authorities to raise living standards and establish incentives for more efficient work.

Precisely how total wages have been altered to establish these incentives can be seen from chart 8. Hourly wages, which are paid to workers regardless of the effort they put into their jobs, have declined from 85 percent of the total wage bill in 1978 to 59 percent

Chart 7.

AVERAGE AND REAL WAGES IN URBAN STATE-OWNED UNITS: 1952 TO 1983

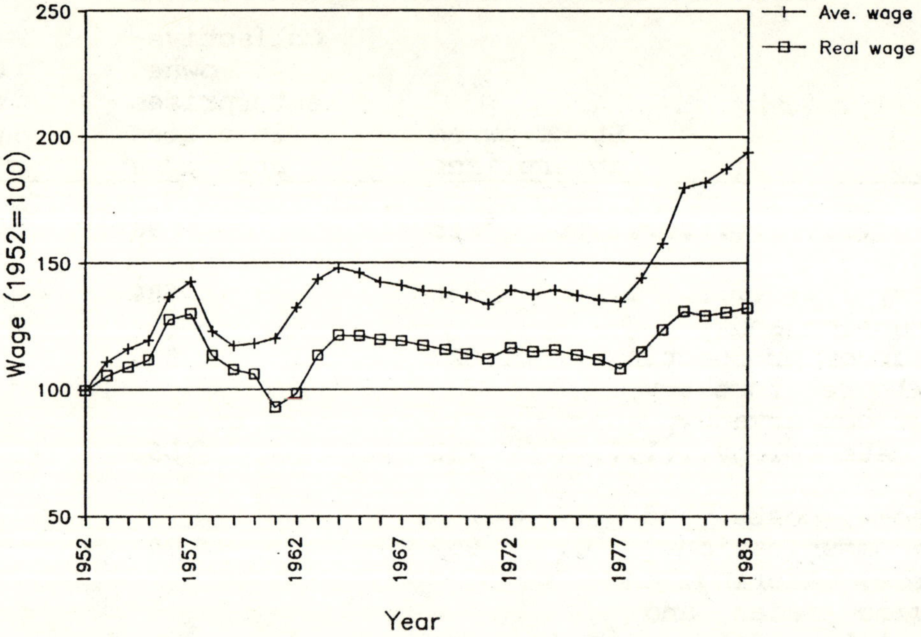


Source: Part II, table 15.

Source: Part II, table 10.

Chart 8.

COMPOSITION OF URBAN WAGES: 1978 AND 1984

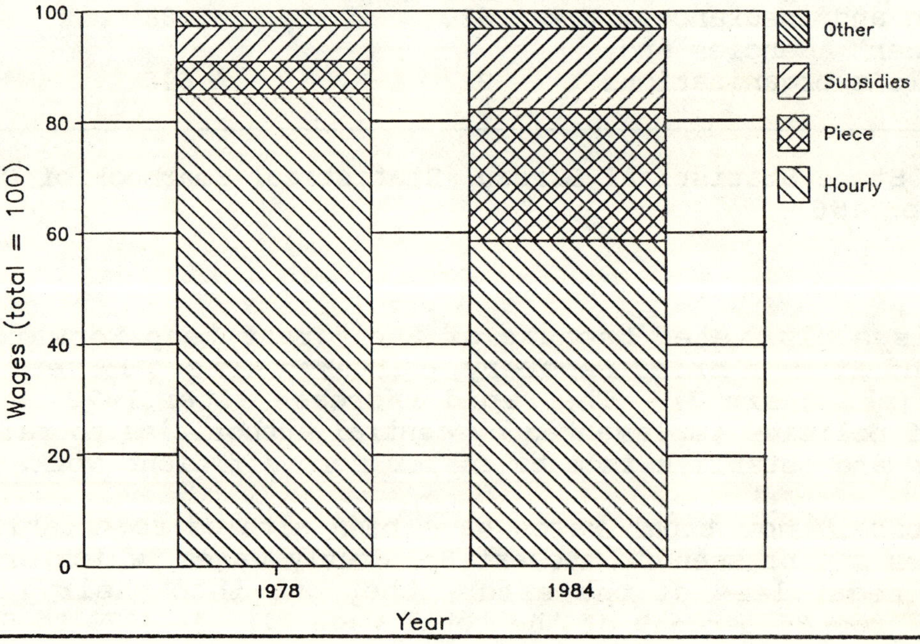

1984. Forms of compensation that reward greater efficiency, such as piece wages and bonuses, have risen on the other hand from 3 percent of the wage bill in 1978 to 24 percent in 1984.

**Rural Incomes**

---

**Rural incomes have skyrocketed in the past 7 years, rising by 1984 to two and one-half times their 1978 level. Households with per capita net incomes of 300 yuan and over rose from 7 percent in 1979 to 46 percent in 1983. Most of peasant income comes from sideline production, rather than from collective activities.**

---

National surveys of peasant household income and expenditures were conducted as early as 1954, and provide a wealth of information on rural incomes. The most commonly cited income statistic from these surveys is net income per capita, which is compared with urban per capita income available for living expenses in table 4. In 1984, average net per capita income for peasants was 355 yuan, more than two and one-half times as great as in 1978.

Despite this impressive growth, rural incomes were still substantially lower than the incomes of urban workers and staff in 1984. The gap has narrowed, however: per capita net income for peasants was 42 percent of per capita income for urban workers and staff in 1978, but rose to 58 percent by 1984.

The distribution of rural income has also shifted in recent years, as shown in chart 9. In 1979, only 7 percent of rural households had per capita net incomes of 300 yuan and over; by 1983 the number of households in that income group had risen to 46 percent.

Rising rural incomes are a direct result of agricultural reform measures first broached at the third plenary session of the Chinese Communist Party's 11th Central Committee in December 1978. These reforms have included substantially raising the prices farmers receive for their crops, reopening rural trade fairs, and most significantly, disbanding people's communes and replacing them with a system of individual household production contracts.

One byproduct of these reforms is that the bulk of peasant income now comes from sideline production (handicrafts, sewing, preparation of traditional medicines, etc.), instead of from collective activities. Income from sideline production was only 27 percent of per capita net peasant income in 1978, but rose to 80 percent of the total by 1984 (see chart 10).

Chart 9.

DISTRIBUTION OF ANNUAL PEASANT INCOME BY INCOME GROUP: 1979 AND 1983

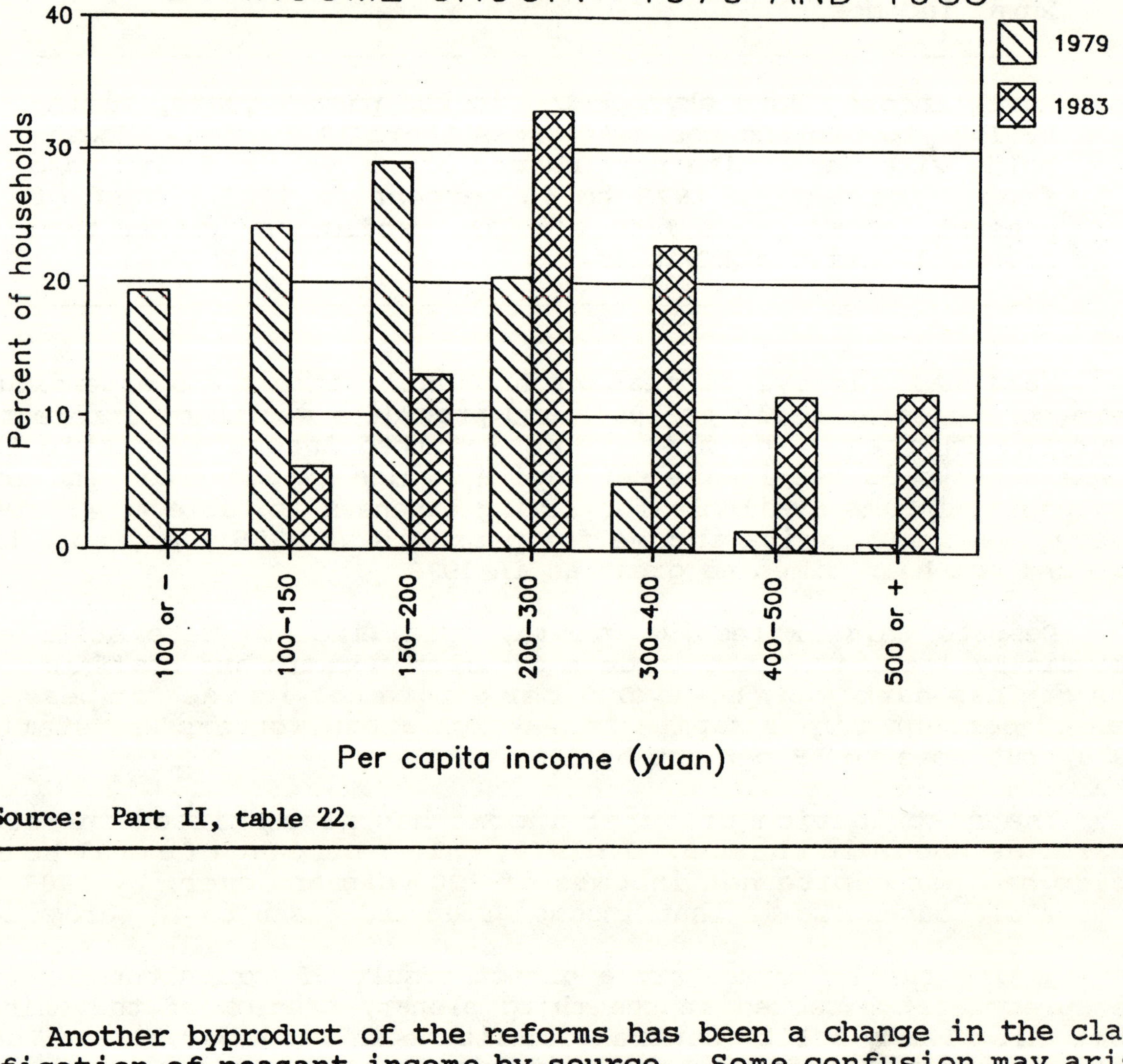


Source: Part II, table 22.

Another byproduct of the reforms has been a change in the classification of peasant income by source. Some confusion may arise from the fact that data for 1978 through 1983 are available in both classifications. Both the new and old classifications show net income from sideline activities, but the new classification for this sector is much broader than the old classification. For example, the old classification shows 1983 income from sideline production comprising 36 percent of total net income per capita, but the new classification indicates that 79 percent of peasant income came from this source. The figures used to produce chart 10 come from the new classification; readers interested in comparing the two sets data income by source data may wish to consult Part II, tables 18 and 19.

Chart 10.

# PEASANT INCOME BY SOURCE: 1978 and 1984

1978

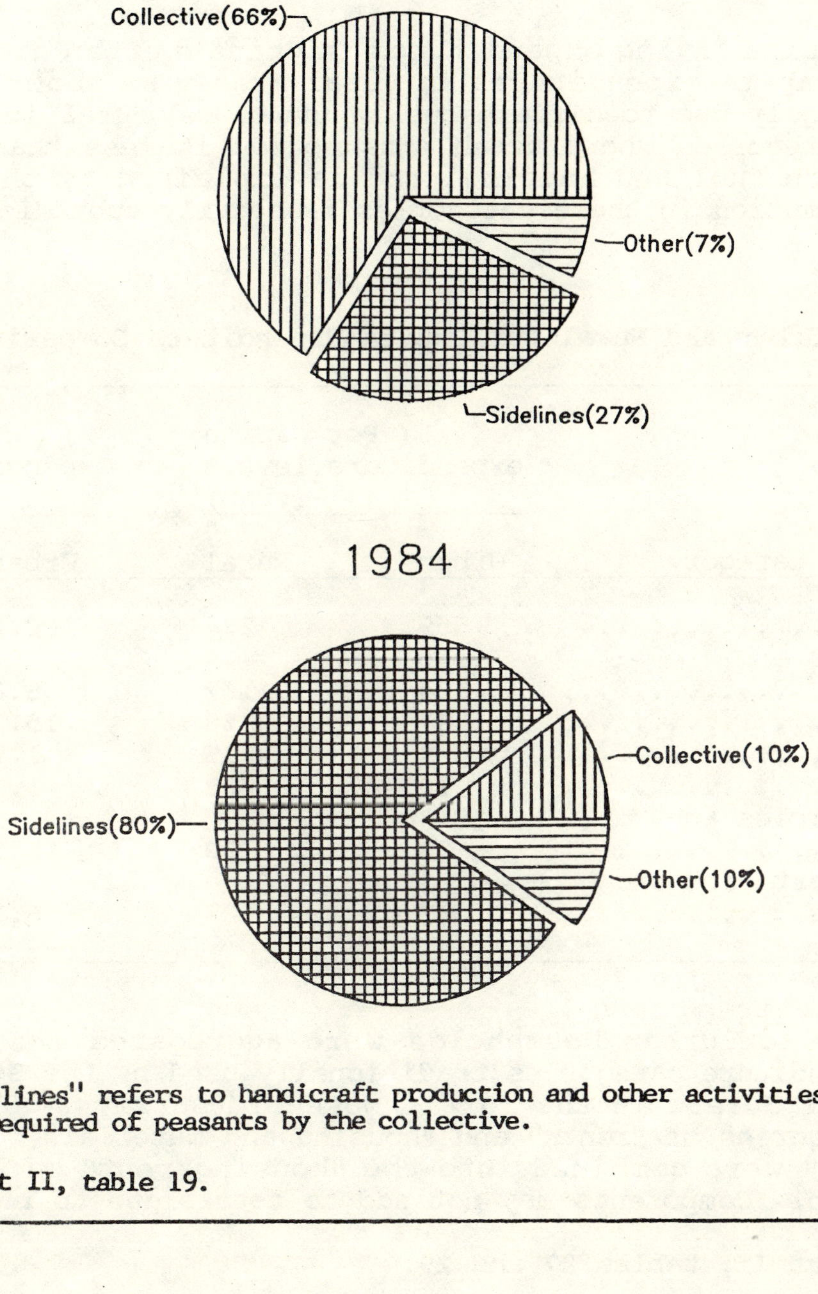


Note: "Sidelines" refers to handicraft production and other activities not required of peasants by the collective.

Source: Part II, table 19.

## LIVING EXPENDITURES

### Urban-Rural Expenditure Comparisons

**Per capita living expenditures in urban areas are far higher than in rural areas, however the growth of rural living expenditures is outpacing that in urban areas. The gap between urban and rural living standards is narrowing.**

Per capita living expenditures in China's urban areas far outstrip per capita expenditures in rural areas, as shown in table 6. This is largely due to differences in urban and rural income levels. The only categories where urban consumption is less than rural consumption are fuel and housing, and is explained by the fact that urban consumption in these categories is heavily subsidized.

**Table 6. Urban and Rural Per Capita Expenditure Comparisons: 1984**

| | Per capita expenditure levels (yuan) | | Per capita expenditure shares (percent) | |
|---|---|---|---|---|
| Expenditure category | Urban | Rural | Urban | Rural |
| Total.................... | 559 | 274 | 100.0 | 100.0 |
| Food.................... | 324 | 162 | 58.0 | 59.0 |
| Clothing................ | 87 | 28 | 15.5 | 10.3 |
| Fuel.................... | 9 | 15 | 1.7 | 5.5 |
| Housing................. | 11 | 32 | 1.9 | 11.7 |
| Daily articles and others................ | 91 | 30 | 16.3 | 11.1 |
| Cultural articles and services............. | 37 | 7 | 6.7 | 2.4 |

Note: Data for urban households were aggregated into the rural expenditure categories traditionally used by the State Statistical Bureau in the rural household surveys. Urban survey categories of "rents" and "housing and materials for construction" were combined into the "housing/rent" category shown above. Components may not add to totals due to rounding.

Source: Part II, tables 27 and 29.

Urban and rural expenditure patterns are strikingly similar for certain categories, despite the vast differences in disposable income of incomes of urban and rural residents. Individuals in both areas spend almost 60 percent of their incomes on food, and 10-15 percent of their incomes on clothing. Urban and rural expenditure shares differ more for other expenditure categories because of the effect of subsidies.

Rates of growth have also differed between expenditure categories for urban and rural consumers, as shown in table 7. Total per capita expenditures in rural households rose at an annual average rate of over 15 percent between 1978 and 1984. This is much higher than the rate of increase for urban households, but the gap between urban and rural living standards is still large.

**Table 7. Comparison of Urban and Rural Per Capita Expenditure Levels and Rates of Growth: 1978 and 1984**

| Expenditure category | Urban per capita expenditure levels (current yuan) | | Rural per capita expenditure levels (current yuan) | | Annual average growth rates, 1978-1984 (percent) | |
|---|---|---|---|---|---|---|
| | 1978 | 1984 | 1978 | 1984 | Urban | Rural |
| Total............ | 311 | 559 | 116 | 274 | 10.3 | 15.4 |
| Food.......... | 179 | 324 | 79 | 162 | 10.4 | 12.8 |
| Clothing....... | 42 | 87 | 15 | 28 | 12.8 | 11.5 |
| Fuel........... | 8 | 9 | 8 | 15 | 1.6 | 10.5 |
| Housing/Rent | 7 | 11 | 4 | 32 | 6.4 | 43.6 |
| Daily articles and others... | 49 | 91 | 8 | 30 | 11.0 | 25.8 |
| Cultural articles and services..... | 26 | 37 | 3 | 7 | 6.5 | 12.9 |

Note: Data for urban households were aggregated into the rural expenditure categories traditionally used by the State Statistical Bureau in the rural household surveys. Urban survey categories of "rents" and "housing and materials for construction" were combined into the "housing/rent" category shown above. The "housing and rents" portion of this category for 1978 had to be estimated, based on its 1982 share of urban per capita expenditure. Components may not add to totals because of rounding.

Sources: Part II, tables 27 and 29.

Rural expenditures increased at a faster rate than urban expenditures in almost every category between 1978 and 1984. The most dramatic increase in household expenditures for peasants has been for housing. Unlike urban residents, China's peasants own their living quarters and must pay full price for building materials. The spurt in housing investment is also understandable when one considers that other possible rural investments, such as in tools or draft animals, have been lost in the past because of collectivization. The right of peasants to own their own homes has always been maintained during these campaigns.

Rapid rates of growth are also shown for both urban and rural expenditures on "daily articles and other." This category includes expenses on books and magazines, bicycles, watches, televisions, radios, and articles for daily use. Such commodities are highly popular, and were not always plentiful in the past because of low investment allocations to the light industries producing them. At least part of the increase shown for this expenditure category can be attributed to the sudden unleashing of pent-up demand as more of these treasured commodities rolled off the production lines after 1978. Demand for these items is still strong, but consumers have grown more discriminating as such consumer goods have increased in availability.

### Expenditure Patterns by Income Group for Urban Households

Expenditure patterns often differ greatly between high and low income groups in many countries. Interestingly enough, this does not appear to be true for urban households in China. Despite the fact that in 1983 the lowest income group spent 230 yuan on per capita living expenses compared to 760 yuan spent by the highest income group, their expenditure patterns are quite similar (see chart 11). Higher income households did spend a lower proportion of their budget on food, medicine, and fuel, and more on leisure goods and sundries. In general, however, the differences are far less than one might see between income classes in other developing countries.

### Rising Purchases as a Percent of Total Rural Consumption

---

**The increasing tendency for China's rural households to purchase what they need rather than make it themselves is a marketing trend with enormous implications.**

---

In rural areas a significant proportion of consumption is self-produced. According to the rural household survey data, 41 percent of total consumption of goods (as opposed to services) in 1984 was

Chart 11.

URBAN HOUSEHOLD EXPENDITURE, BY INCOME: 1983

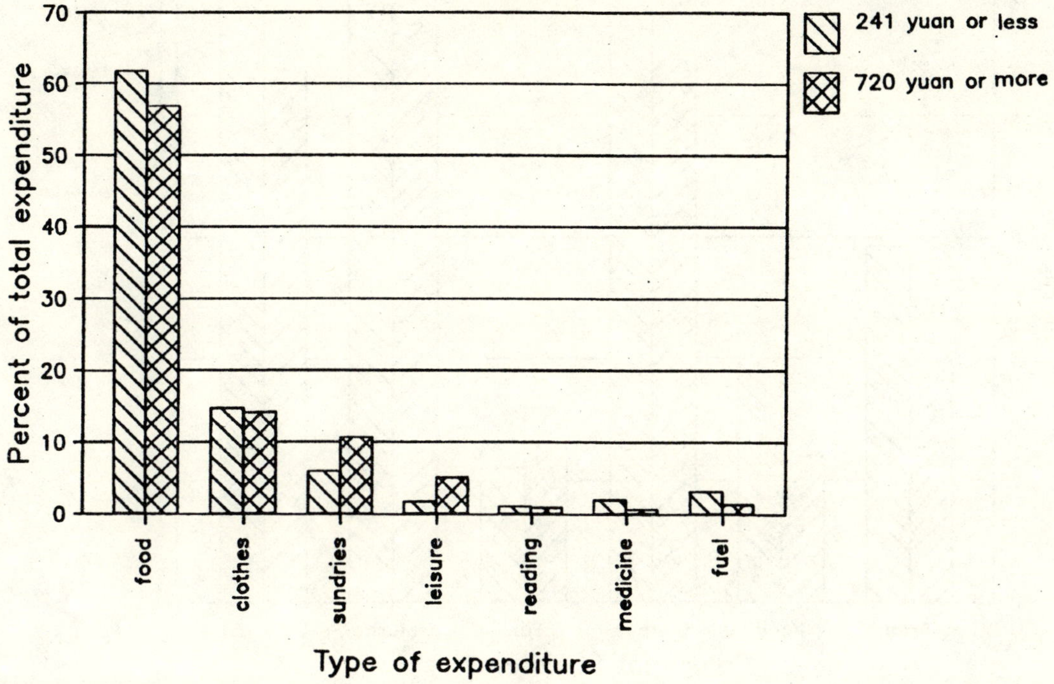


Source: Part II, table 27.

self-produced, compared to 60 percent in 1978. The vast majority of China's consumers are peasants (68 percent in 1984), and as noted above, their purchasing power has risen sharply in recent years. These factors, combined with the rising ratio of purchased commodities in peasants' consumption basket, point to exceptionally good prospects for retail sales in China.

As shown in chart 12, the proportion of total consumption that is purchased as opposed to self-produced varies greatly from sector to sector. The consumer goods comprising the daily use category top the list, with 99 percent of all expenditures purchased in 1984, and are closely followed by housing (98 percent) and clothing (98 percent). As noted above, rural consumption of the first two categories of goods grew faster than all others between 1978 and 1984. The only category registering a decline in the ratio of purchased goods to total consumption was fuel. This may represent a greater peasant reliance on biogas, foraged straw, or wood for fuels. Its effect on overall cash expenditures by peasants has in any event been negated by rising purchases of other commodities.

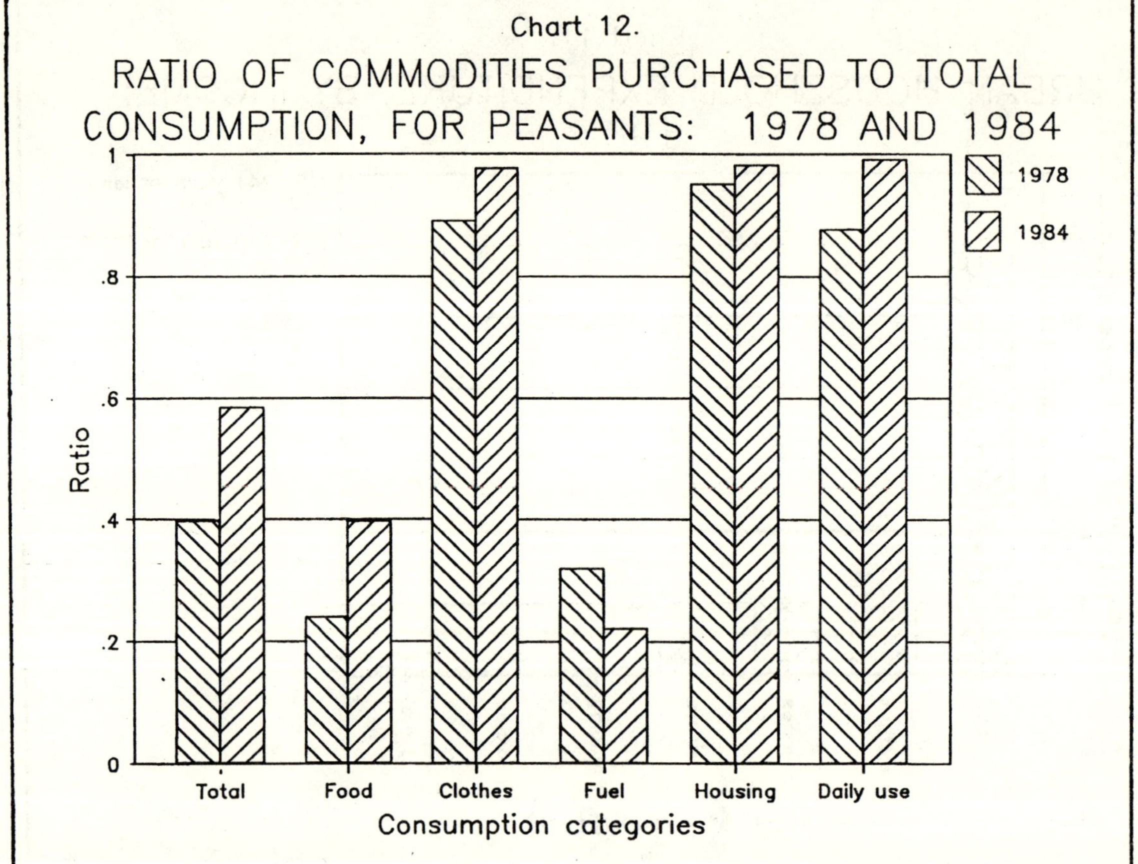


Source: Part II, table 31.

## CONSUMPTION OF SELECTED COMMODITIES

### Consumption of Food

---

**Urban and rural consumers are substituting fine grains for coarse grains, and have markedly increased their consumption of other foods. Increased imports of coarse grains and processed feeds may be required in the future to support the livestock necessary to meet rising consumer demand for animal products. Consumption growth in rural households has increased at a faster rate than in urban households for most major foodstuffs.**

---

#### Urban/Rural Comparisons

Food consumption is the single largest expenditure category in Chinese household budgets. As charts 13 and 14 show, per capita

Chart 13.

AVERAGE ANNUAL PER CAPITA CONSUMPTION OF GRAIN AND VEGETABLES, BY RESIDENCE: 1984

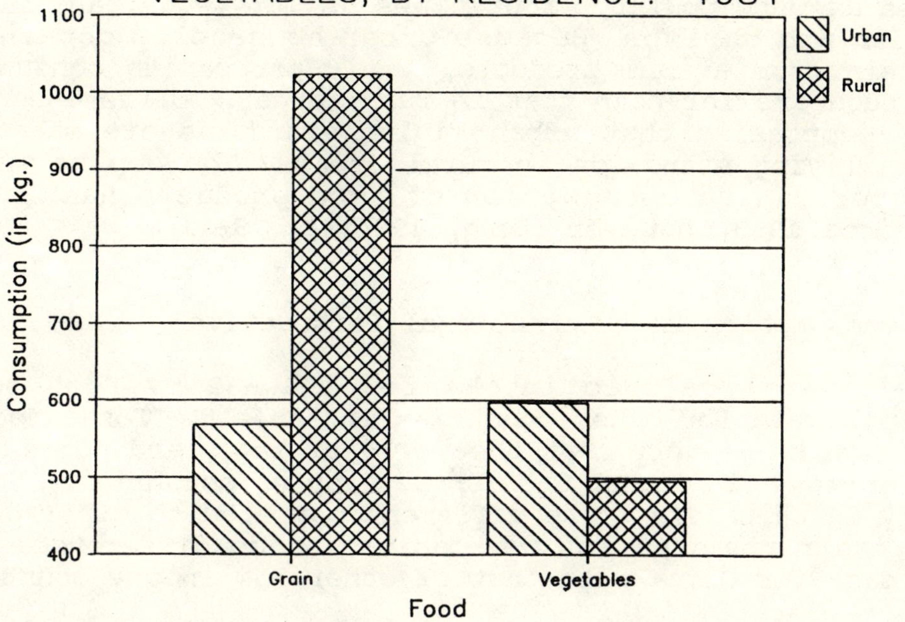


Source: Part II, tables 23 and 28.

Source: Part II, tables 23 and 28.

Chart 14.

AVERAGE ANNUAL PER CAPITA CONSUMPTION OF SELECTED FOODS, BY RESIDENCE: 1984

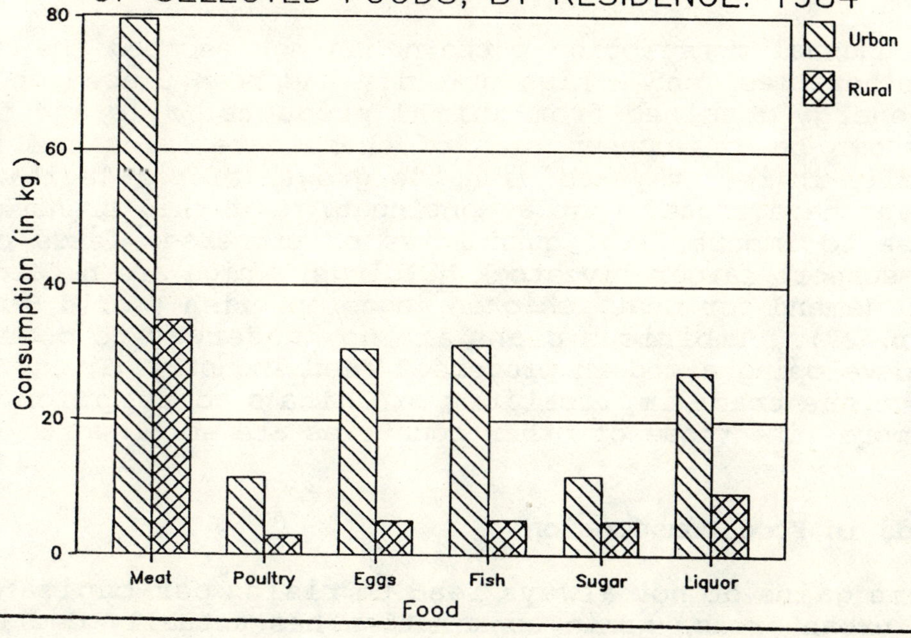

consumption levels for individual food items varies substantially between urban and rural areas. Higher urban incomes and access to a greater variety of food products enable urban households to consume almost twice as much meat, sugar, and liquor as rural households, three times as much poultry, four times as many eggs, and five times as much fish and shrimp. Because urban households obtain more of their protein from animal products, their per capita consumption of grains is much smaller than that in rural areas. Differences of this magnitude reemphasize that urban living standards are substantially higher than living standards in rural areas. The gap between urban and rural per capita consumption of food products has in general narrowed since 1983, however (Long, 1984, pp. 9-11).

### Food Consumption in International Perspective

China's total caloric intake for 1980-82 by food source is compared with data for other countries in table 8. Total food energy consumed in China is very near the world average, and higher than the averages for many Asian and for all developing countries. Sources of food energy in China are quite different compared to other countries, even when one normalizes for per-capita income differences and compares the data for China with that of other low income countries.

The proportion of food energy coming from grains generally declines as income rises, even within the low income country grouping. What is unusual about China is that for its estimated per-capita GNP, the proportion of food energy obtained from grain consumption is quite high. For example, China's per-capita GNP is higher than for India, yet India obtains 67 percent of its food energy from grains compared to 84 percent for China.

This unusual consumption pattern has not escaped the notice of Chinese authorities, and a high priority has been placed on increasing food energy obtained from animal products, oils and fats. As will be shown below, consumption of these categories has increased substantially in recent years with the growth of per-capita incomes. Some studies have argued that a continuation of this trend may force the Chinese to import large quantities of processed feeds or coarse grains to support larger livestock holdings, which are needed to meet the rising demand for meat, chicken, eggs and fish (World Bank, Annex 2, 1985, p. 27). Ambitious plans are now underway to counter this trend by developing a modern processed feed industry (Tuan, 1985, pp. 31-35), but the trade implications of China's consumption patterns becoming more like those of other countries are still worth watching.

### Trends in Food Consumption

Income gains do not always lead to rising per-capita consumption. In urban areas, grain consumption has actually declined from

Table 8. Per Capita Food and Nutrient Availability and Gross National Product Per Capita, for China and Selected Countries: Selected Years, 1977 to 1982

| | | Energy (Kcal/day) | | | | | | |
|---|---|---|---|---|---|---|---|---|
| | GNP per capita (in U.S. dollars) | | Source | | | Percent of total | | |
| Country | | Total | Grain | Animal | Oils and fats | Grain | Animal | Oils and fats |
| China............ | 300 | 2,548 | 2,145 | 148 | 102 | 84 | 6 | 4 |
| World average..... | N/A | 2,571 | 1,439 | 435 | 225 | 56 | 17 | 9 |
| Asia average...... | N/A | 2,251 | 1,580 | 196 | 125 | 70 | 9 | 6 |
| All developing.... | N/A | 2,260 | 1,531 | 205 | 134 | 68 | 9 | 6 |
| Industrial........ | N/A | 3,353 | 1,014 | 1,073 | 510 | 30 | 32 | 15 |
| Low Income: | | | | | | | | |
| Bangladesh...... | 140 | 1,796 | 1,563 | 62 | 54 | 87 | 3 | 3 |
| India........... | 260 | 1,919 | 1,294 | 93 | 136 | 67 | 5 | 7 |
| Nepal........... | 170 | 2,002 | 1,713 | 137 | 88 | 86 | 7 | 4 |
| Pakistan........ | 380 | 2,281 | 1,462 | 281 | 195 | 64 | 12 | 9 |
| Sri Lanka....... | 320 | 2,059 | 1,369 | 80 | 67 | 66 | 4 | 3 |
| Tanzania........ | 270 | 2,066 | 1,264 | 202 | 102 | 61 | 10 | 5 |
| Middle Income: | | | | | | | | |
| Brazil.......... | 2,170 | 2,259 | 1,156 | 421 | 184 | 45 | 16 | 7 |
| Egypt........... | 670 | 2,787 | 1,887 | 179 | 230 | 68 | 6 | 8 |
| Indonesia....... | 580 | 2,118 | 1,628 | 52 | 123 | 77 | 2 | 6 |
| Korea, Rep. of.. | 1,910 | 2,785 | 2,111 | 178 | 55 | 76 | 6 | 2 |
| Malaysia........ | 1,870 | 2,613 | 1,542 | 294 | 229 | 59 | 11 | 9 |
| Mexico.......... | 2,740 | 2,655 | 1,370 | 366 | 206 | 52 | 14 | 8 |
| Philippines..... | 820 | 2,216 | 1,498 | 216 | 108 | 68 | 10 | 5 |
| Thailand........ | 790 | 2,098 | 1,492 | 146 | 41 | 71 | 7 | 2 |
| Yugoslavia...... | 3,100 | 3,446 | 1,796 | 715 | 371 | 52 | 21 | 11 |
| Industrial: | | | | | | | | |
| Germany, FR..... | 12,300 | 3,382 | 1,796 | 1,318 | 618 | 53 | 39 | 18 |
| Japan........... | 10,050 | 2,946 | 1,438 | 547 | 284 | 49 | 19 | 10 |
| U.S.A........... | 13,160 | 3,578 | 719 | 1,312 | 583 | 20 | 37 | 16 |

NA Data not available
GNP Gross National Product

Note: Nutrient availability data for China are for 1980-82. For all other countries the data are for 1977. Grain includes rice, wheat, coarse grains, and tubers at one-fifth wet weight. Soybean and other pulse are not included in direct grain consumption figures.

Source: World Bank, 1985, China: Long Term Issues and Options, Annex 2: Agriculture to the Year 2000: Prospects and Options, p. 122; and The World Bank Atlas, no page number given.

its earlier levels, and growth has been modest in rural areas. The composition of grain consumption has radically changed, however, as higher incomes have enabled consumers to be more discriminating. As shown in chart 15, consumption of coarse grains (such as corn, sorghum, and millet) has dropped in rural households, while the demand for fine grains (wheat and rice) has risen. The same pattern is true for urban households as well.

Chart 16 shows consumption trends for other foodstuffs among urban and rural households. In urban households, annual average consumption growth between 1981-1984 was fastest for liquor (16 percent), followed by poultry (15 percent), vegetable oil (14 percent), and eggs (13 percent). In rural households, the annual average rate of increase in consumption between 1981 and 1984 was fastest for liquor and eggs (14 percent), followed by fish and shrimp (10 percent), poultry (9 percent), edible oil (8 percent) and meat (7 percent). Consumption of vegetables fell in urban households, and

Chart 15.

RURAL PER CAPITA GRAIN CONSUMPTION, BY TYPE OF GRAIN: 1978 TO 1984

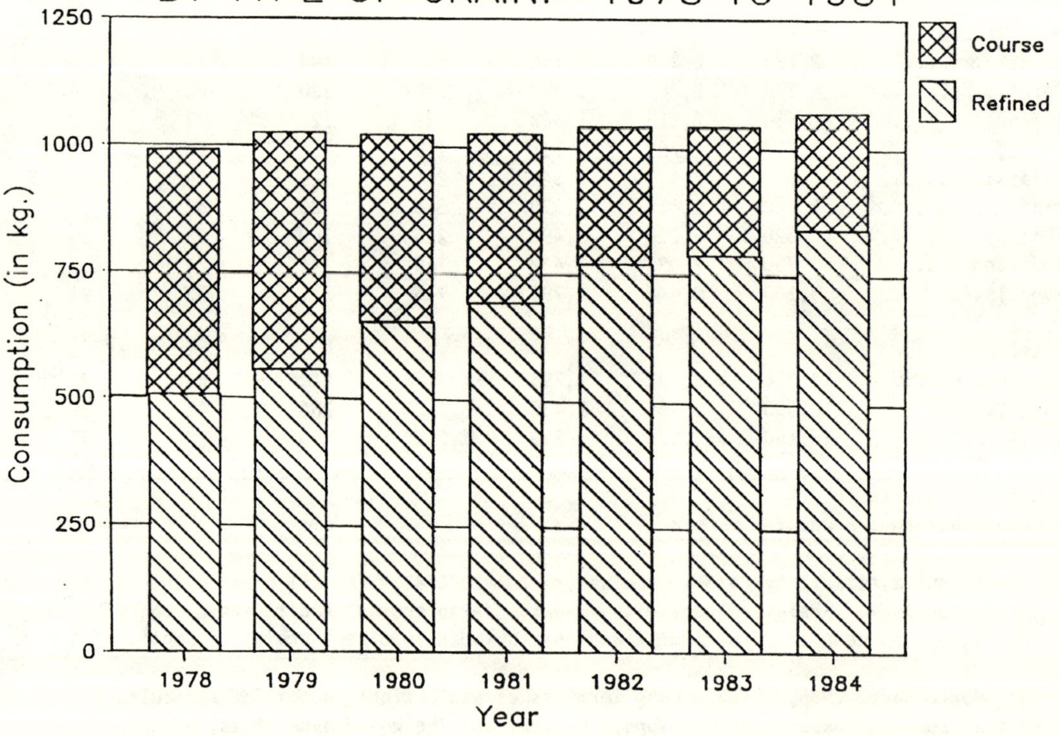


Source: Part II, table 38.

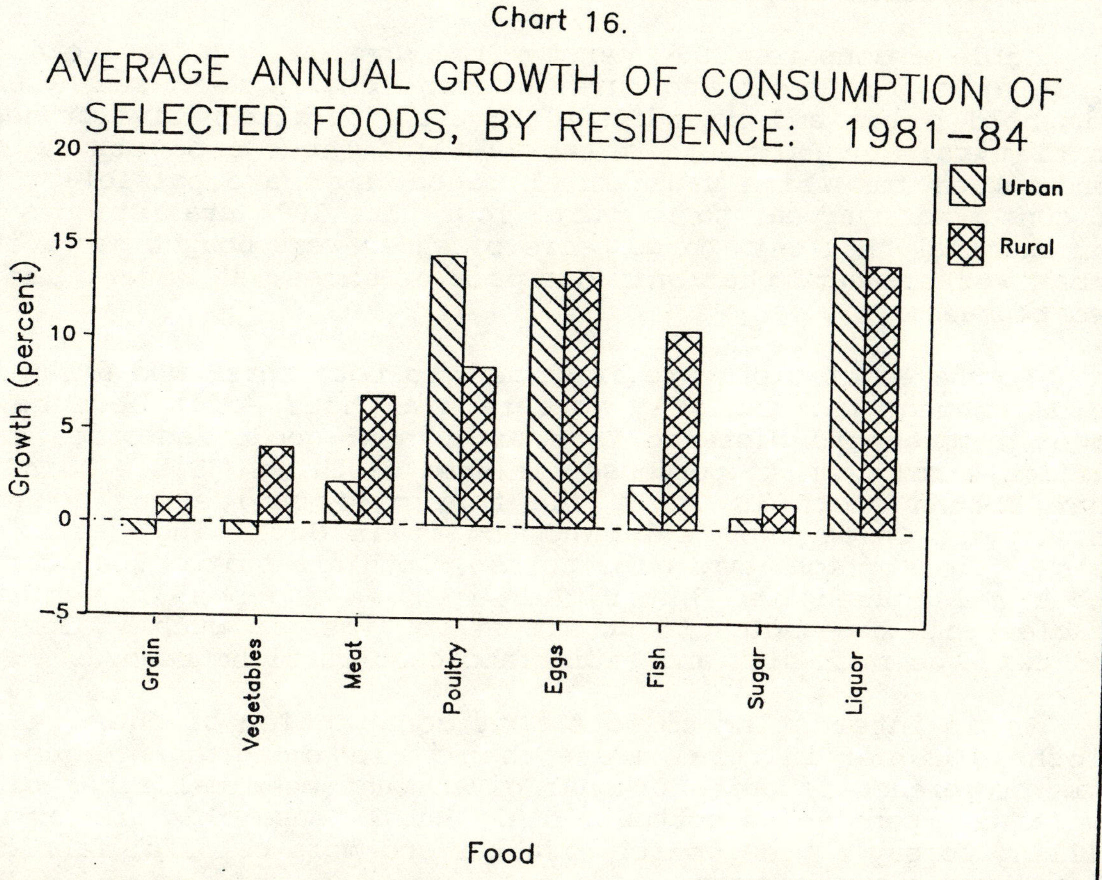

Source: Part II, tables 23 and 38.

grew modestly in rural households, though vegetable consumption even in rural areas has declined since 1978.

These figures indicate that consumption gains in general have been quite strong is recent years, particularly for non-grain foods. It is also clear that rural households have increased their consumption of almost every major foodstuff more rapidly in percentage terms than have urban households.

## Consumption of Nondurables

---

**General consumption of nondurable goods is low, particularly for rural consumers. Both urban and rural consumers are also shunning cotton clothing in favor of clothes produced from synthetics and other fabrics.**

---

**Urban/Rural Comparisons**

Table 9 compares 1984 per capita consumption of selected major nondurables for urban and rural households, as measured by China's household income and expenditure surveys (for alternative trade-based statistics, see Part II, tables 39-61). These products represent nondurables for which urban-rural comparisons are possible. Levels of consumption appear to be quite low. The 1984 statistics suggest, for example, that only three pairs of shoes were bought per every two urban workers, and that only one pair of shoes was bought per every two peasants.

Purchases of cloth are important to both rural and urban households, though particularly so for rural households because their lower incomes and distance from urban sewn-goods factories make it difficult for them to purchase finished clothing. Table 9 indicates that cotton cloth is still the fabric of choice for households throughout China though demand for it is declining, as is noted below. Consumption levels for cotton cloth are quite close for urban and rural households, but higher incomes and possible subsidies enable urban households to consume five times as much woolen fabric and twice as much silk and satin fabric as rural households.

It is interesting to note that consumption of chemical fiber cloth is higher in rural areas than it is among urban households. This preference is quite unusual given that chemical fiber cloth is twice as expensive as cotton cloth. Rural households are apparently willing to pay a premium for brighter and more colorful fabrics than those traditionally worn.

**Table 9. Annual Per Capita Consumption of Selected Nondurable Commodities, for Urban Worker and Staff Households and Rural Peasant Households: 1984**

| Commodity | Units | Urban Workers and Staff | Rural Peasants |
|---|---|---|---|
| Cloth: | | | |
| Cotton cloth.............. | meters | 3.00 | 2.82 |
| Chemical fiber cloth...... | meters | 1.95 | 2.48 |
| Woolen fabric............ | meters | 0.37 | 0.07 |
| Silk and satin fabric..... | meters | 0.49 | 0.24 |
| Knitting wool and knitwear.. | kg. | 1.10 | 0.18 |
| Shoes...................... | pairs | 1.64 | 0.57 |

Source: Part II, tables 35 and 38.

**Trends in Consumption**

Chart 17 compares average annual rates of growth for consumption of selected nondurables by urban and rural individuals. Consumption of cotton cloth is in rapid decline in both urban and rural areas; greater production of other fabrics has enabled substitution to take place. Substitution has followed very different paths in urban and rural areas, however. Urban consumers have increased their consumption of woolen fabric most rapidly, yet the data for rural consumers show consumption of chemical fiber cloth and silk and satin fabric growing at the most rapid rates. The reasons for these differences in consumption growth are unclear, though the improved availability of fabrics of all kinds in rural markets has undoubtedly played an important role.

Trends in clothing consumption overall are difficult to assess because of the paucity of data on rural clothing consumption. Growth rates from the urban and rural household surveys indicate that urban consumers increased their consumption of knitting wool and knitwear

Chart 17.

AVERAGE ANNUAL GROWTH OF PER CAPITA CONSUMPTION OF SELECTED NONDURABLES, BY RESIDENCE: 1981-84

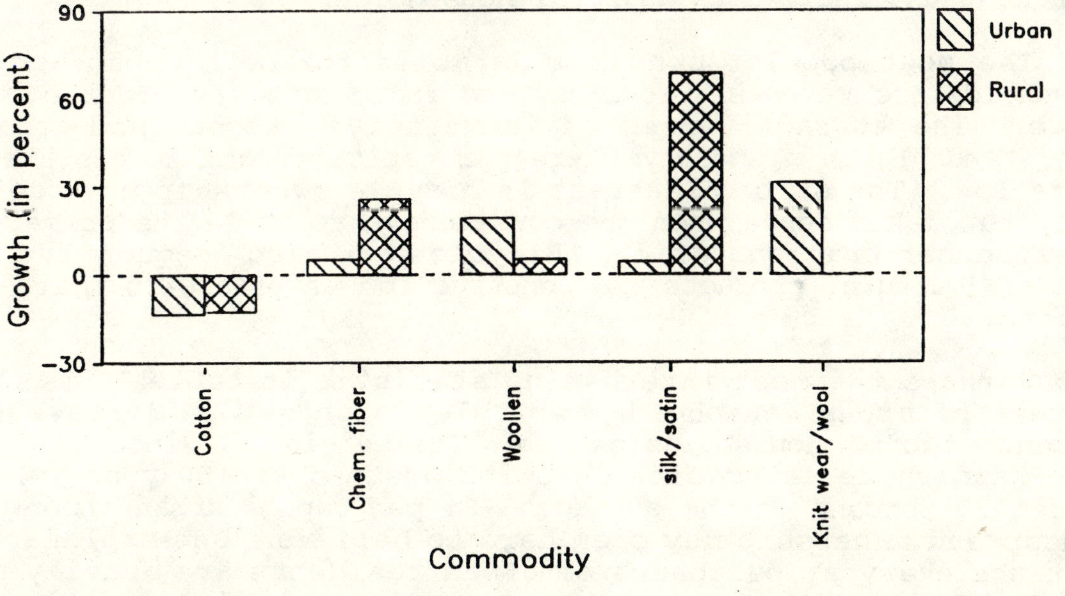


Source: Part II, tables 35 and 38.

at an annual average rate of 32 percent from 1981 to 1984, but that rural consumption growth was nil. Chart 18 compares rates of growth for selected urban clothing groups from 1981 to 1984. This chart indicates that consumption of cotton clothes is on the decline among urban households, and that demand for clothing from all other fabrics (especially silk and satin) is experiencing rapid growth.

## OWNERSHIP OF DURABLE GOODS

**Urban households have been larger consumers of durable goods in China, but rates of growth are now higher for rural households. 85 percent of urban households now own televisions, and television ownership among rural households is growing at an annual average rate of more than 100 percent.**

### Urban/Rural Comparisons

Table 10 compares 1984 urban and rural household survey data on ownership of durable consumer goods (alternative data may be found in Part II, table 73). Urban households have greater access to durable goods by virtue of location and income, thus their holdings of these commodities far outstrip ownership levels shown for rural areas. Urban households owned close to 12 times as many television sets, three times as many watches, and twice as many bicycles, sewing machines, and radio sets as rural households.

The most popular consumer durables for both urban and rural households are watches, bicycles, and radio sets, in order of importance. The attractiveness of inexpensive watches and radios is understandable in a society where per capita income levels are still quite low. The strong interest in bicycle ownership may seem unusual, but makes sense when one considers that it is the primary mode of passenger transportation. Bicycles are also frequently used to haul agricultural products and construction materials to their destinations.

Perhaps the most interesting statistic in table 10 is that 85 percent of urban households own television sets. Moreover, five percent of urban households own color televisions. Since the average black and white television in China costs over 450 yuan, which is almost 75 percent of the average 1984 per capita urban income, such widespread ownership may seem hard to believe. One explanation is that the everyday purchases of urban residents are heavily subsidized, allowing them to easily save for expensive durable goods. Another explanation is that the statistics refer to family rather than individual ownership of televisions. With an average of 2.4

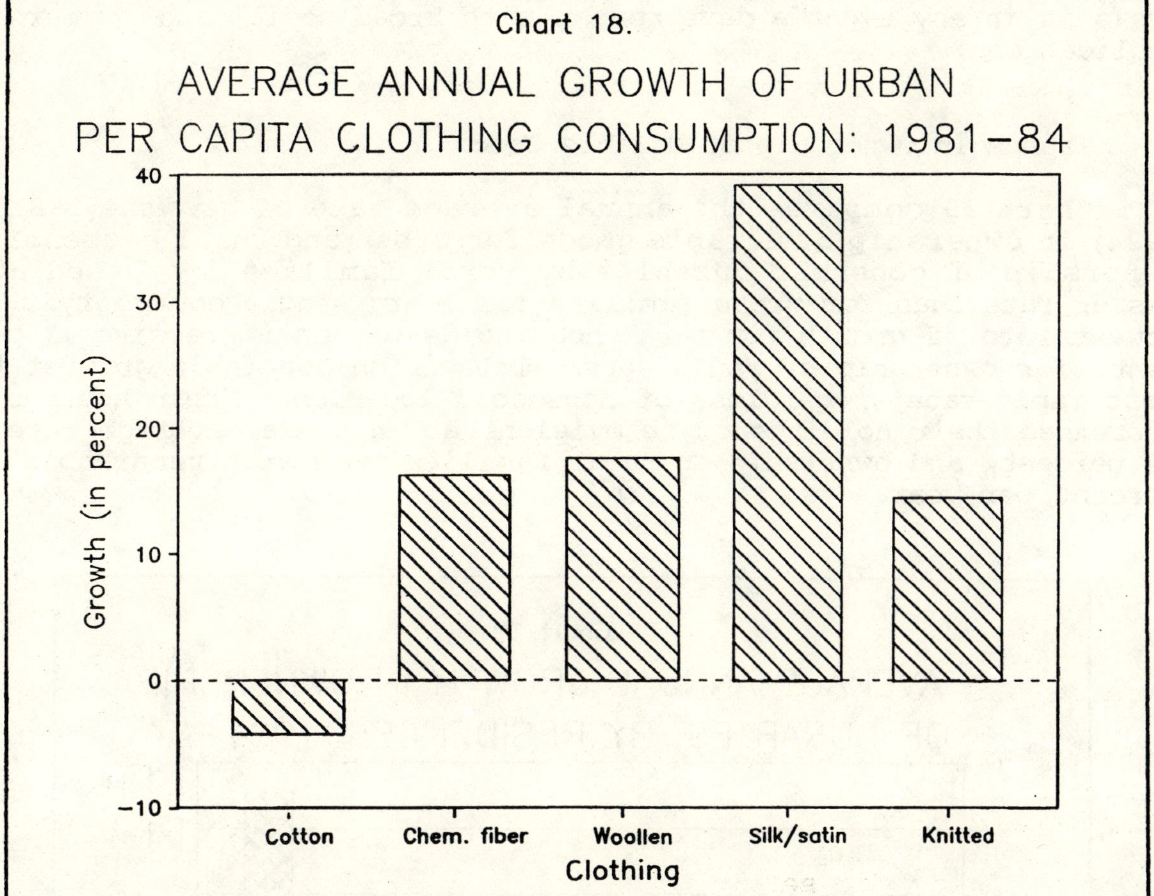


Source: Part II, table 35.

**Table 10. Comparison of Durable Good Ownership Per 100 Households, for Urban Worker and Staff Families and Peasant Families: 1984**

| Commodity | Urban Workers and Staff | Rural Peasants |
|---|---|---|
| Bicycles................. | 163 | 75 |
| Sewing machines.......... | 78 | 43 |
| Watches.................. | 283 | 109 |
| Radio sets............... | 103 | 61 |
| Televisions.............. | 85 | 7 |

Source: Part II, tables 69 and 72.

workers per household in urban areas, this makes it much easier to afford a television. Spreading ownership of televisions in urban areas is in any event a development with broad social and commercial implications.

### Trends in Ownership of Durable Goods

Chart 19 compares the annual average rate of growth (1981 to 1984) in ownership of durable goods for urban and rural households. Ownership of consumer durables by rural families increased at a faster rate than for urban families for every single commodity. The lowest rate of growth for rural households was an impressive 13 percent, for ownership of radio sets. Television ownership grew at the most rapid rate, regardless of household location. Urban households increased their holdings of televisions at an annual average rate of 14 percent, and ownership in rural families grew at a remarkable 103 percent per year.

Chart 19.

AVERAGE ANNUAL GROWTH IN OWNERSHIP OF DURABLES, BY RESIDENCE: 1981–84

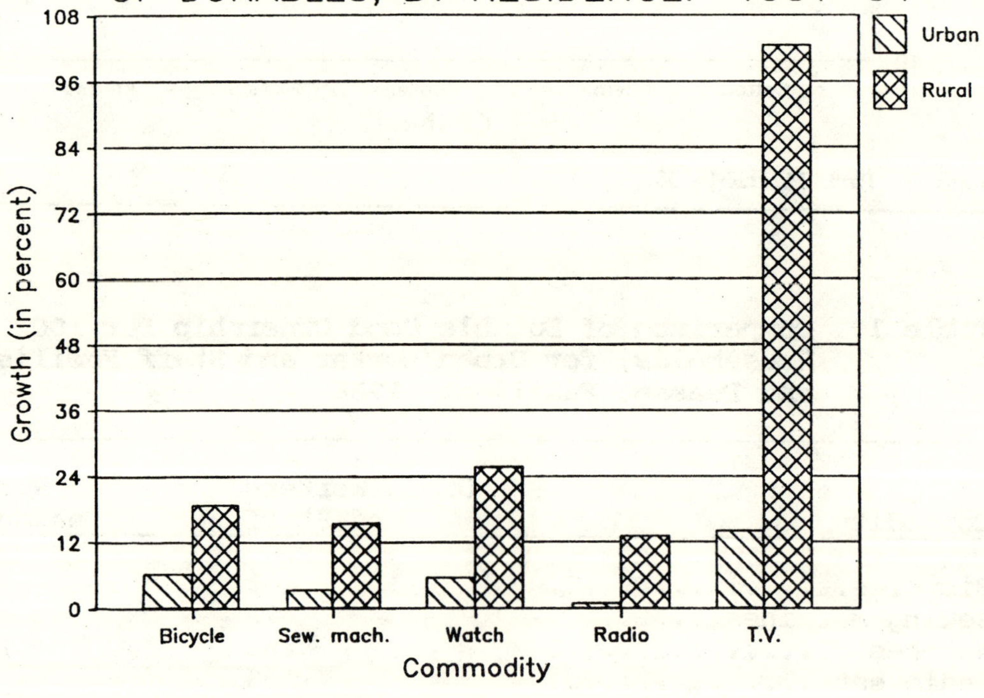


Source: Part II, tables 69 and 72.

The relatively slower growth rates in durable good ownership among urban households reflects both a change in preferences within certain commodity groups, and a growth in ownership of durables for which matching rural data are unavailable. For example, the slow growth in ownership of radio sets overall masks a substitution of old-fashioned valve radios for transistor radios. Ownership of valve radios in urban households actually declined by 4 percent each year on average between 1981 and 1984, while ownership of transistor radios grew by 4 percent.

Urban household survey data also show phenomenal growth in ownership of washing machines and refrigerators (85 percent and 145 percent annual average growth rates between 1981 and 1984, respectively), and of tape recorders and cameras. Ownership levels for these commodities are still low, however: only 3 percent of urban households owned refrigerators in 1984, and only 40 percent owned washing machines. The fastest rates of growth are nonetheless reserved for somewhat more sophisticated consumer durables in China's cities.

# IV. INTERPROVINCIAL COMPARISONS

## GEOGRAPHIC OVERVIEW

China is divided into 21 provinces, 5 autonomous regions and 3 municipalities. These areas are hereafter referred to as provinces, to simplify matters. As shown in map 1 (on page 2), these provinces can be divided into six regions. These regions include the North (encompassing Beijing, Tianjin, Hebei, Shanxi, and Neimenggu [Inner Mongolia]), the Northeast (Liaoning, Jilin, and Heilongjiang), the East (Shanghai, Jiangsu, Zhejiang, Anhui, Fujian, Jiangxi, and Shandong), the South (Henan, Hubei, Hunan, Guangdong, and Guangxi), the Southwest (Sichuan, Guizhou, Yunnan, and Xizang [Tibet]), and the Northwest (Shaanxi, Gansu, Qinghai, Ningxia, and Xinjiang).

The regions have different geographic and economic characteristics. The Northeast is the most heavily industrialized region, while the north is China's largest, but not most fertile, agricultural area. The East is prominent in both industry and agriculture, and contains some of China's most prosperous provinces and the important municipality of Shanghai. The South is semi-tropical, with both agricultural and mountainous areas. Guangdong, which contains most of China's new economic zones, is also located in the southern region. China's most populous province, Sichuan, is located in the Southwest. The Northwest has the lowest population density and the highest percentage of China's minority populations. Much of the area is desert or mountains.

Interprovincial comparisons show differences in income and wages, in living expenditure, and in consumption patterns. Including China's three municipalities in the discussion of provincial differences is somewhat misleading. By definition, these areas are highly urbanized, and urban residents are consistently better off than their rural counterparts for every economic indicator. This should be kept in mind throughout the following discussion.

## PROVINCIAL INCOME LEVELS

### Income Levels for Urban Households

**Per capita income levels for urban workers are highest in the Southern province of Guangdong. Surprisingly high income levels are also shown for workers in China's remote provinces, because of wage differentials granted as an inducement for working in less-developed areas.**

Interprovincial comparisons of 1983 per capita income available for living expenses in urban worker and staff households are shown in map 3. The highest per capita income by far is shown for Guangdong, which at 735 yuan is a full 209 yuan above the national average. Guangdong's relative prosperity is due to a variety of factors, including remarkable success in gaining a degree of autonomy from central control and promoting local growth, a tradition of commercial dynamism preceding 1949 in the province's major city of Guangzhou, the presence of two of China's four special economic zones, Shenzhen and Zhuhai and close proximity to Hong Kong. The three great municipalities of Shanghai, Tianjin and Beijing follow Guangdong in the per capita income ranking, which given their status as major industrial production centers is not unusual. Urban per capita income is lowest in Jiangxi, followed closely by Shanxi.

It is striking that per capita income levels in many of China's interior provinces generally regarded as poor approach and occasionally exceed income levels in the traditionally well-off coastal provinces. For example, workers and staff in landlocked Qinghai and Ningxia have slightly higher per capita incomes than workers in the coastal province of Jiangsu (500 yuan for the interior provinces vs. 498 yuan for Jiangsu in 1983). The reason for this is the practice of paying employees higher wages for agreeing to work in the harsher and less-developed regions of the country. When provinces are ranked according to average annual wages paid workers in state enterprises (see chart 20), it is clear that workers in relatively underdeveloped provinces (Xizang, Qinghai, Xinjiang, Gansu and Ningxia) are quite well-paid. Wages are higher than per capita income, of course, because not all household members work.

It is not altogether certain that higher wages for workers in remote provinces gives them greater purchasing power. Many popular consumer goods are difficult to buy in these provinces because of transportation problems. Shortages in these provinces may force personal saving to be higher than consumers would prefer were markets better developed.

### Income Levels for Rural Households

---

**Per capita incomes for rural workers are highest in China's municipalities and coastal provinces. These areas are either in close proximity to China's largest markets or have the most favorable farming conditions.**

---

Differences in rural per capita net income are considerably larger than differences in per capita incomes for urban workers. The highest rural per capita income shown for any province in 1983 was 2.6 times as high as the lowest income shown (563 yuan in Shanghai,

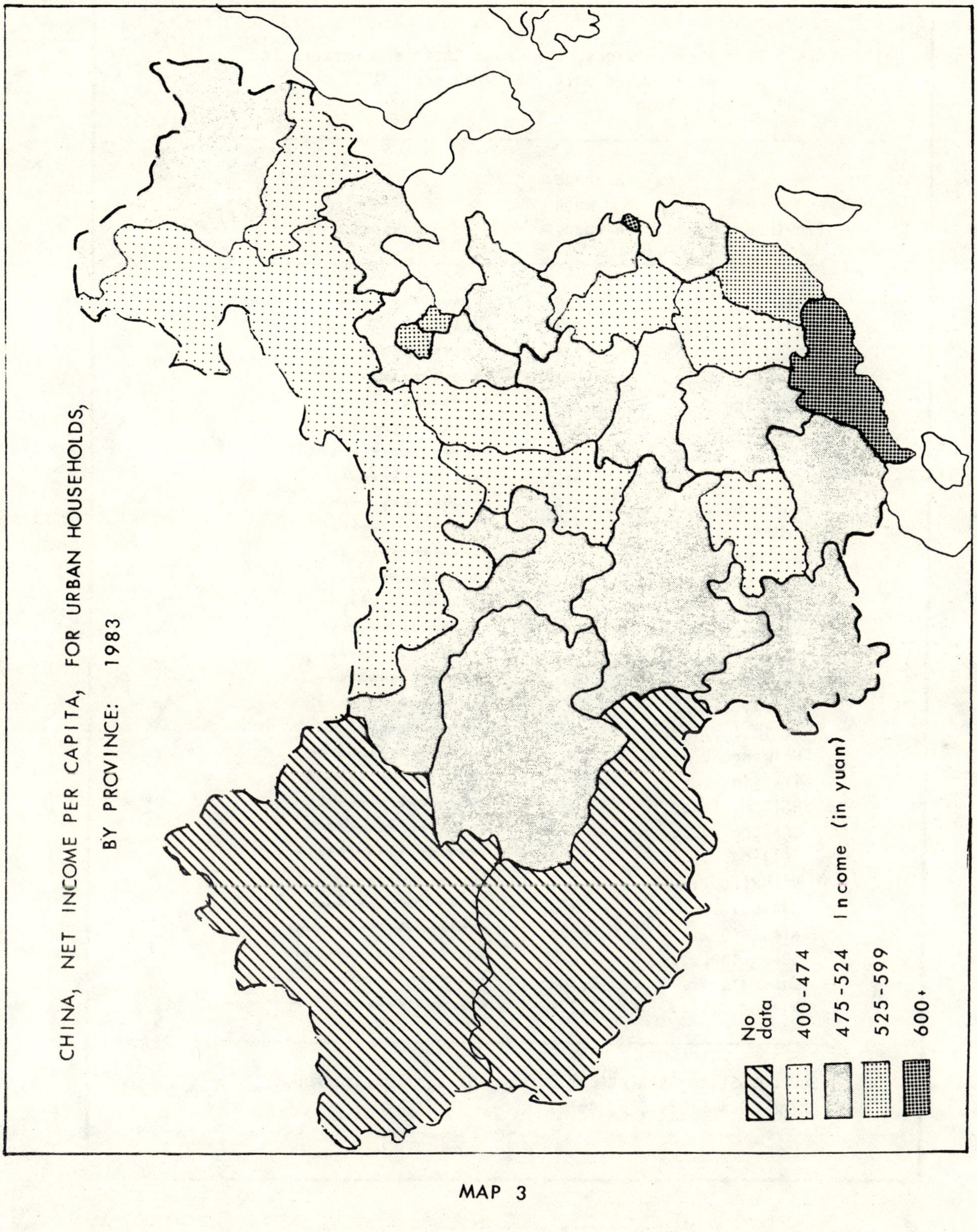
CHINA, NET INCOME PER CAPITA, FOR URBAN HOUSEHOLDS,
BY PROVINCE: 1983
No data
400-474
475-524
525-599
600+
Income (in yuan)

MAP 3

Chart 20. Average Wages, for Urban Staff and Workers in State-Owned Units, By Province: 1983 (In Yuan)

| Province | Average wage (in yuan) | Ranking |
|---|---|---|
| Jiangsu....... | 768 | *************** |
| Jiangxi....... | 774 | *************** |
| Hubei......... | 781 | *************** |
| Anhui......... | 791 | *************** |
| Zhejiang...... | 797 | *************** |
| Hunan......... | 803 | **************** |
| Henan......... | 805 | **************** |
| Guangxi....... | 810 | **************** |
| Shandong...... | 818 | **************** |
| Hebei......... | 824 | **************** |
| Sichuan....... | 827 | **************** |
| Guizhou....... | 830 | **************** |
| Liaoning...... | 852 | ***************** |
| Yunnan........ | 857 | ***************** |
| Shaanxi....... | 857 | ***************** |
| Fujian........ | 861 | ***************** |
| Shanxi........ | 868 | ***************** |
| Jilin......... | 881 | ***************** |
| Neimenggu..... | 902 | ****************** |
| Tianjin....... | 916 | ****************** |
| Heilongjiang.. | 930 | ****************** |
| Shanghai...... | 935 | ****************** |
| Beijing....... | 964 | ******************* |
| Ningxia....... | 970 | ******************* |
| Gansu......... | 973 | ******************* |
| Xinjiang...... | 998 | ******************* |
| Guangdong..... | 1,022 | ******************** |
| Qinghai....... | 1,302 | ************************** |
| Xizang........ | 1,397 | *************************** |

Source: State Statistical Bureau, Statistical Yearbook of China 1984 (1984), p. 457.

compared to 213 in Gansu), compared to a high/low ratio of 1.8 for interprovincial comparisons of urban income. As shown in map 4, net incomes are highest for rural residents of coastal provinces and the municipal regions of Shanghai, Beijing, and Tianjin. These areas are either close to major consumption centers, or possess the best soils, water resources, and climates in China. Given these attributes, their residents' ability to earn more money than peasants elsewhere in China is understandable.

High net incomes for peasants in the Northeastern provinces of Liaoning and Jilin are particularly noteworthy. These provinces are important producers of grains, especially coarse grains. Grain yields in both provinces have dramatically risen as a result of post-1979 increases in procurement prices, the implementation of the household responsibility system, and much better-than-average weather conditions. High income levels are the offspring of this happy marriage of circumstances. Whether or not this will continue is debatable, however. Weather patterns in the northeast will eventually return to normal, and central authorities have drastically cut the amount of grain they will purchase at guaranteed prices in an effort to reduce overproduction. These factors do not augur well for rural incomes in the northeast. On the other hand, internal demand for the coarse grains produced by these provinces may increase as rising consumer preferences for animal products create a higher derived demand for animal feedstuffs. The net effect of these developments on future living standards is difficult to predict.

Also noteworthy are the relatively low per capita net income levels for peasants in Gansu, Shanxi, and Guizhou. Shanxi's low standing compared to other provinces is often overlooked, despite the fact that it ranks third lowest out of all provinces in peasant net income, and second lowest in urban per capita income. Gansu and Guizhou are similar to Shanxi in rural income levels, but are otherwise quite different. Both are predominantly agrarian, whereas most of Shanxi's population lives in urban areas (although Shanxi's high degree of urbanization is largely due to a recent administrative change reclassifying small towns from rural to urban status). Income levels in both Gansu and Guizhou are low because of poor soils, isolation from markets, and limited access to chemical fertilizers and farm machinery. Government policies have attempted to assist these poorer areas, but growth potential in Gansu and Guizhou is still severely constrained by basic lack of natural resources.

## PROVINCIAL LIVING EXPENDITURES

**Differences in provincial living expenditures can be attributed to a variety of factors, including differing income levels, regional tastes and access to consumer goods.**

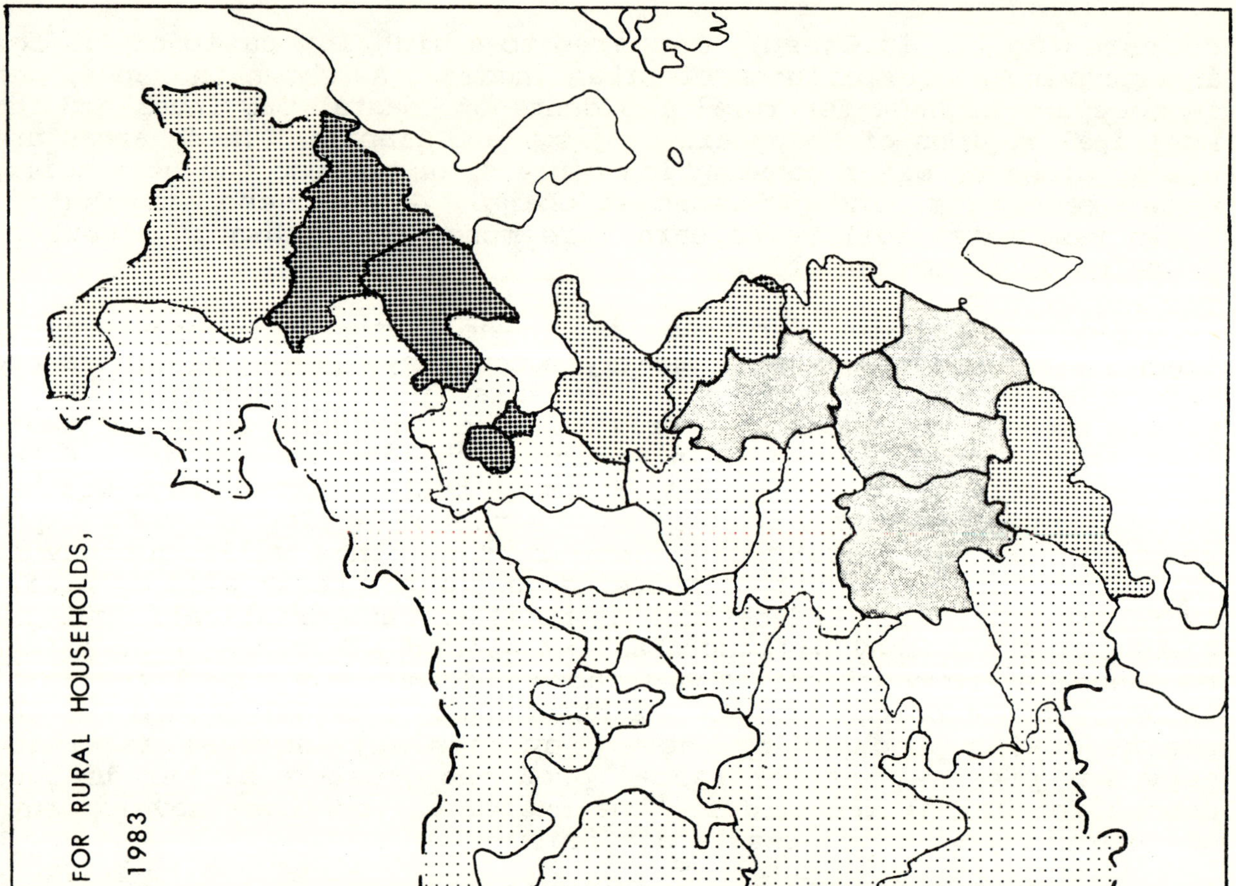
CHINA, NET INCOME PER CAPITA, FOR RURAL HOUSEHOLDS,
BY PROVINCE: 1983
Income (in yuan)
No data
200-249
250-299
300-349
350-399
400+

MAP 4

As noted earlier, both rural peasant and urban worker and staff households participate in income and expenditure surveys. The only provincial expenditure data currently available on a comprehensive basis are from the rural household survey, however. Interprovincial comparisons of the components of rural household expenditures are discussed below. These comparisons concentrate on the proportion of total expenditures devoted to consumption of food, clothing, and other commodities. Consumption level comparisons are not made here, for the simple reason that the findings are obvious: high income provinces consume more per capita in every expenditure group than low income provinces, with rare exception. Readers interested in interprovincial comparisons of consumption levels should consult Part II, tables 79-81.

### Food Expenditures

The proportion of total expenditures devoted to food consumption tends to decline as income rises, according to 1983 expenditure data for peasant households. Peasants in Shanghai, the wealthiest province, spent 47 percent of their budgets on food, whereas peasants in Gansu, the poorest province, spent 64 percent of their household budget on food. The inverse relation between food budget shares and total expenditures is plotted in chart 21 and confirms that Engel's Law holds for China, as it generally holds for the rest of the world.

Another pattern shown by the provincial data is that the share of total food expenditures devoted to the purchase of nonstaple foods (meat, processed foods, outside meals, etc.) rises with income. Again, taking the highest and lowest income provinces as our points of comparison, nonstaple food consumption as a percent of food consumption is 69 percent for Shanghai, but only 28 percent for Gansu. The relationship between these two indicators for all provinces in 1983 is plotted in chart 22. This expenditure pattern is important, because it suggests that rural households will demand more animal products as their incomes rise. As earlier noted, this could create a situation where China is a net importer of coarse feedgrains and processed animal feeds.

### Clothing Expenditure

Clothing expenditures are a major proportion of rural household budgets in China. In 1983, 11 percent of rural household expenses were devoted to clothing purchases. This expenditure share varies from province to province, though less according to per capita income than according to regional considerations. For example, clothing's expenditure share averages 13 percent in the North, and 11-15 percent in the Northeast, and 11-19 percent in the Northwest. These regions are quite a bit colder than the South, where clothing expenditures drop as low as 6 percent of total expenditures in Guangdong.

Chart 21.

PERCENT OF BUDGET SPENT ON FOOD, BY INCOME AND PROVINCE: 1983

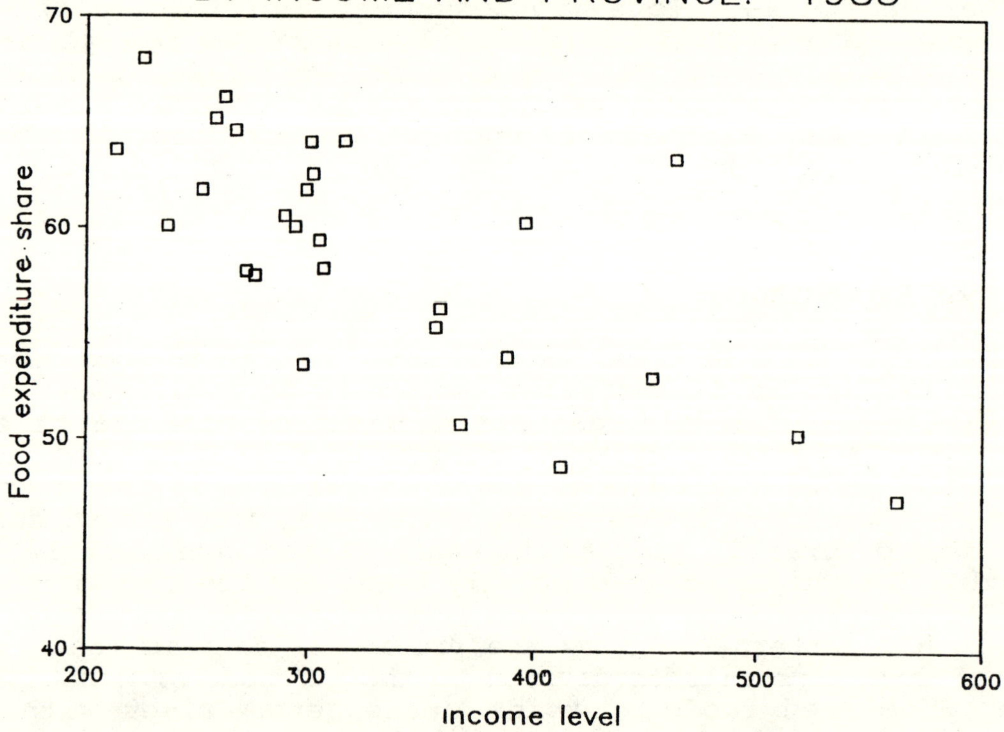


Note: Each point on the graph represents a province, excluding those for which data are not available.

Source: Part II, table 81.

Clothing consumption may also be influenced by concentrations of minority nationalities in certain provinces. The highest clothing shares are shown for Xinjiang (19 percent), a majority of whose population is made up of Muslim minority groups, and Qinghai (16 percent), which has large numbers of Hui muslims and Tibetans. Both provinces are also quite cold much of the year, however. The importance of ethnicity should thus not be overestimated.

**Housing Expenditure**

In 1983, the proportion of peasant household expenditures de-

Chart 22.

RELATION OF FOOD BUDGET SPENT ON NONSTAPLE FOODS TO INCOME LEVEL, BY PROVINCE: 1983

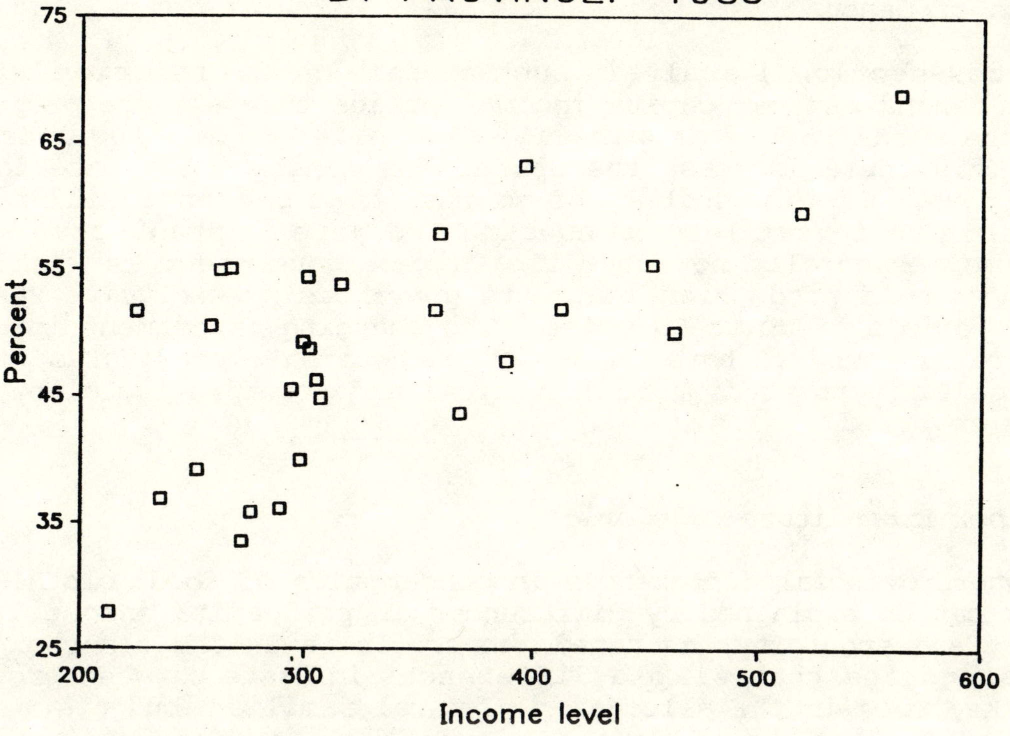


Note: Each point on the graph represents a province, excluding those for which data are not available.

Source: Part II, table 81.

voted to housing was 11 percent for China overall. This makes housing the third largest of major consumption categories. Its importance to peasant families and the rural economy overall in recent years has been much greater than this expenditure share indicates, however. Between 1978 and 1984, peasant families increased their per capita housing expenditures at an average annual rate of 44 percent--higher than for any other consumption category. Floor space added between 1978 and 1984 was actually greater than all rural housing constructed in the thirty years preceding 1978.

The reason given most frequently for the phenomenal growth in rural housing demand is that rural incomes have risen dramatically since 1978, and that the income elasticity of demand for housing for peasant families is very high. As chart 23 shows, there is similarly a strong positive relationship between provincial income levels and the share of total expenditures devoted to housing. Data for the richest and poorest provinces in 1983 bear this out: 30 percent of household expenditures by Shanghai's peasants were for housing, compared to a 5 percent expenditure share for the considerably poorer peasants of Gansu.

Cross-sectional analysis such as this on the relation between housing demand and per capita income implies that a large proportion of future rural income growth will be applied to housing construction. This could increase the demand for construction materials in rural areas. It is possible, of course, that peasants will find it preferable to invest less in housing and more in productive assets over time, especially now that the Chinese government is willing to write household production contracts guaranteeing exclusive resource use for periods of up to 50 years. The changing investment incentive structure is bound to have an effect on housing expenditures, though it is too early to predict if historical and interprovincial patterns will be reversed.

**Other Expenditure Categories**

Interprovincial differences in consumption of food, clothing and housing can be explained by differences in per capita income levels, weather, and ethnicity, as noted above. It is in the other expenditure categories that simple differences in taste between provinces play a key role in the allocation of rural families' budgets.

For example, Shandong province was ranked eighth in per capita peasant net income in 1983, but second in the share of total expenditures on daily use articles (12 percent of the budget, compared to a national average of 7 percent). The effect of tastes on the rural family budget share for cultural and recreational goods is even more striking. High-income Beijing led the nation in 1983 with a 3.2 percent budget share for this category (compared to a national average of .9 percent), but higher-income Shanghai peasants spent only 0.8 percent of their budgets on these goods. Ningxia followed Beijing in the percent of household expenditures devoted to cultural and recreational goods (2.7 percent), though it ranked only 19th in 1983 per capita peasant net income. Also interesting are provincial differences in the share of rural household budgets devoted to culture and services. Leading the list in this category for 1983 was Heilongjiang, which ranked 7th in per capita peasant net income, and the surprising second-place runner-up was Qinghai, which ranked 4th from the bottom in per capita net income.

These unusual rankings of household budget share may be due primarily to differences in tastes, but the role that prices may play

Chart 23.

PERCENT OF BUDGET SPENT ON HOUSING, BY INCOME AND PROVINCE: 1983

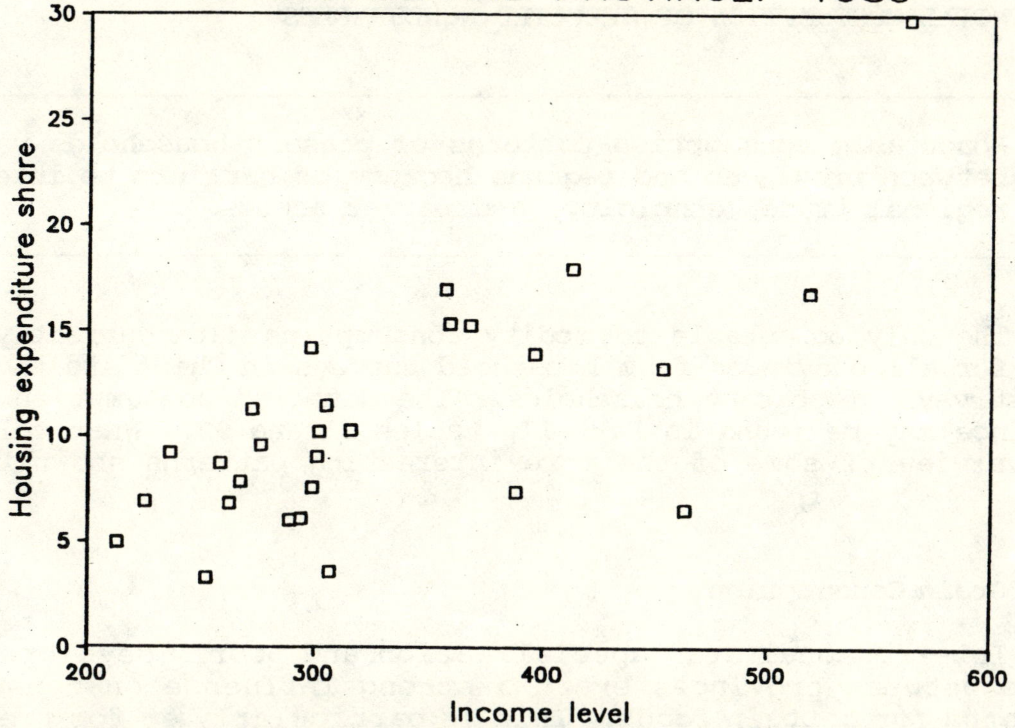


**Note:** Each point on the graph represents a province, excluding those for which data are not available.

**Source:** Part II, table 81.

should be acknowledged. Chinese pricing authorities set unified national prices for many manufactured goods, but prices are allowed to deviate from these norms by a specified percentage rate for most consumer goods. Recent price reform initiatives have moreover given merchants the freedom to set their prices based on supply and demand conditions for a number of commodities, particularly those sold at rural trade fairs.

Prices for identical commodities can thus vary from province to province, and these price differences can be maintained because poor transportation links hinder efforts by enterprising marketing agents to truck commodities in from regions where prices are lower. Lack of detailed price information from each of China's provinces precludes a formal test of the impact these differences may have on expenditure patterns, though the interregional price differences undoubtedly affect consumer demand.

## PROVINCIAL CONSUMPTION OF SELECTED NONDURABLES

**Nondurable consumption patterns of peasant households vary between provinces and regions because of barriers to inter-regional trade, ethnicity, and market access.**

The only nondurable commodity consumption data currently available for all provinces from household surveys in China are those from the surveys of peasant households. The detailed consumption data by province may be found in Part II, tables 91 and 92. What follows is an overview of some of the more interesting patterns shown by these data.

### Grain Consumption

Interregional crop specialization and poorly developed trade links between provinces exert a strong influence on consumption patterns for certain foods. This is particularly so for grain consumption, as shown in charts 24 through 26. In the North, where wheat production is dominant, wheat consumption levels are almost twice the national average, but rice consumption is much lower. In the South and East, wheat consumption is substantially below the national average (except in Henan and Shandong, which are major wheat producers), but consumption of rice, of which the two regions are major producers, is quite high by national standards. Finally, in the Northeast, consumption of the locally abundant coarse grains is almost three times the national average. In short, provincial grain consumption tends to be correlated with what is available close at hand. The same is true for other commodities as well, particularly for consumption of fish and shrimp.

### Ethnicity and Commodity Consumption

National-level data indicate that pork is the meat of choice in peasant households, but the pattern is quite different in provinces with large Muslim populations. Qinghai, Ningxia and Xinjiang are home to many of the Hui and Uigher minorities, and their status as Muslims is reflected in their higher than average consumption of beef. Peasants in Qinghai and Xinjiang also drink between 16 and 30

Chart 24.

PER CAPITA REGIONAL CONSUMPTION OF WHEAT COMPARED TO THE NATIONAL AVERAGE CONSUMPTION: 1983

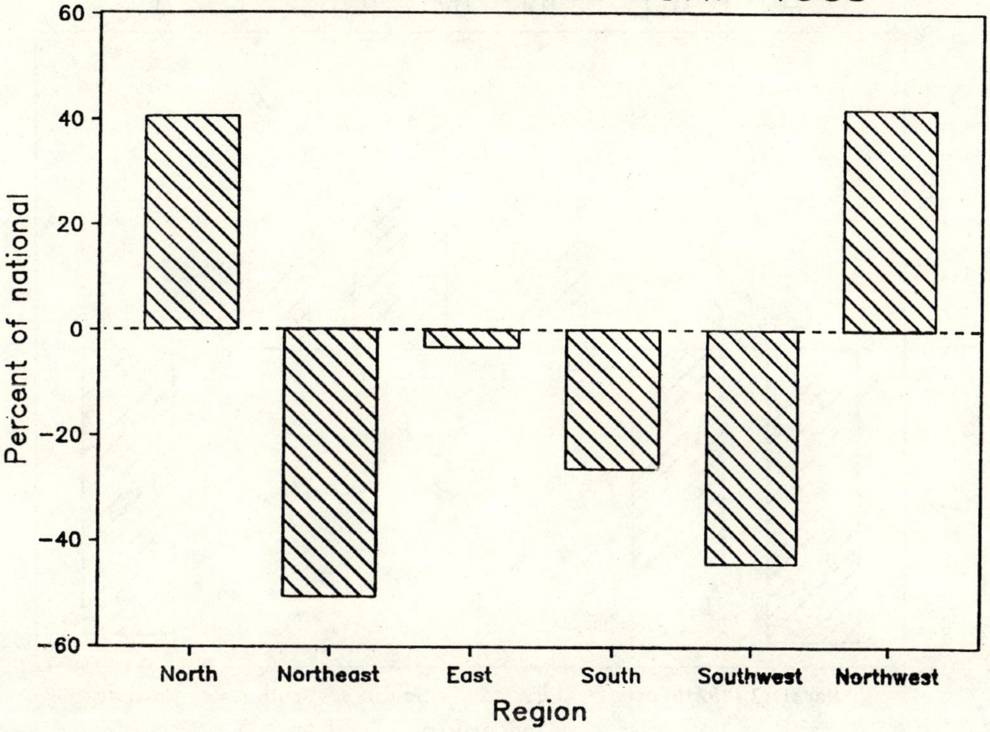


Source: Part II, table 92.

times as much milk, 5 to 8 times as much tea, and much less liquor than the average Chinese peasant.

### Chicken and Egg Consumption

Consumption patterns for chickens and eggs across provinces show a high degree of specialization. Simultaneous above-average consumption levels for both chickens and eggs occurs in Tianjin and the eastern provinces of Shanghai, Jiangsu, Zhejiang and Anhui. Consumption in other areas tends to favor either one of the two products, but not both. In Beijing, for example, per capita egg consumption by rural households in 1983 was almost 3 times the national average, but consumption of chicken was 66 percent of the national consumption level. In Guangxi, chicken consumption was almost three times the national average, but consumption of eggs was only 38 percent of the

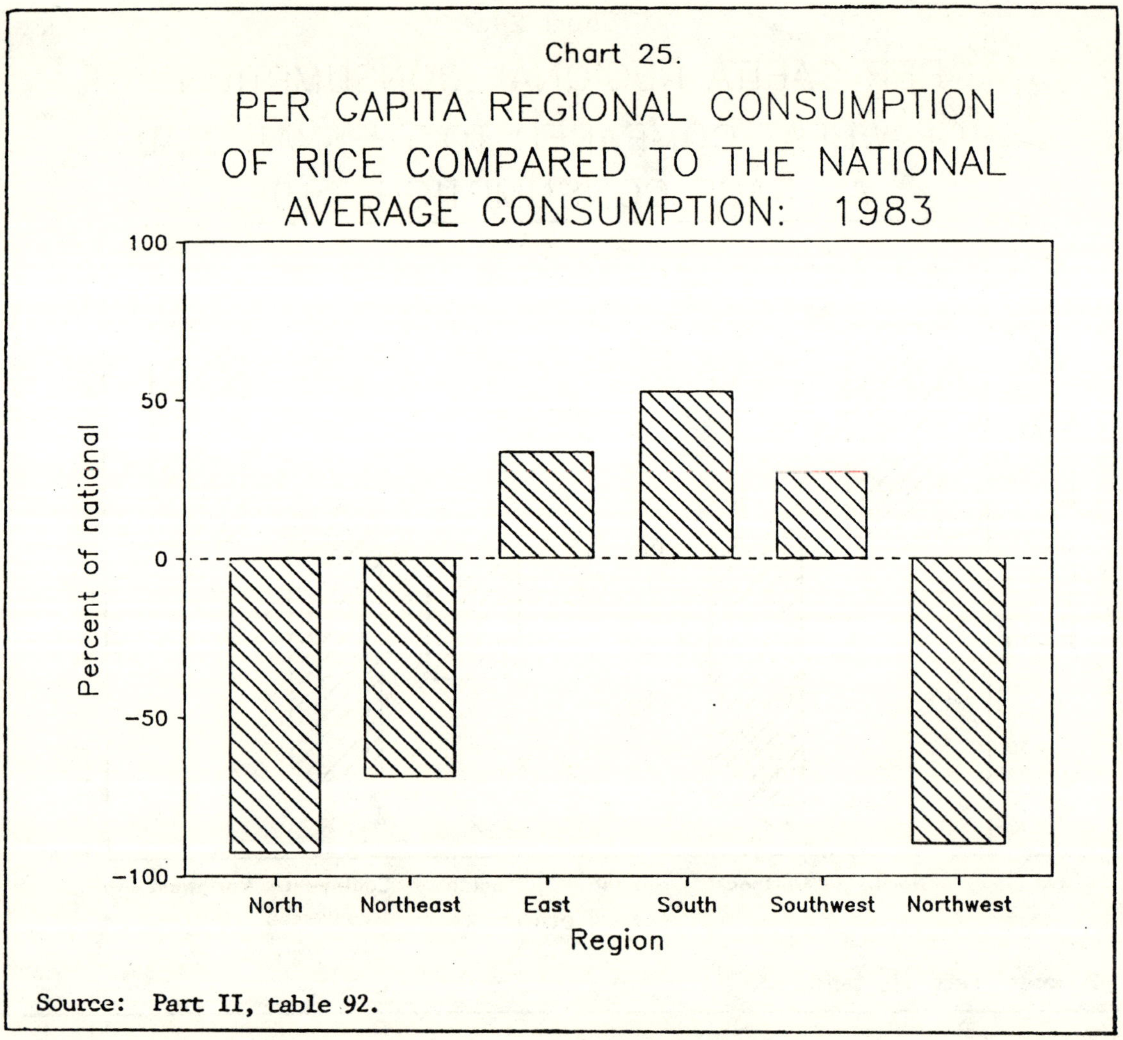


national level. The patterns shown by Beijing and Guangxi are not atypical, and suggest that there may be substantial interregional trade in poultry products.

### Consumption of Processed Goods

Processed commodities, such as sugar, cigarettes, and candy are not uniformly available throughout China because of transportation and distribution problems. The 1983 rural household survey data thus show consumption of these commodities to be highest for peasants living in the municipal areas of Beijing, Tianjin, and Shanghai, and for peasants living in the relatively well-developed eastern region of the country.

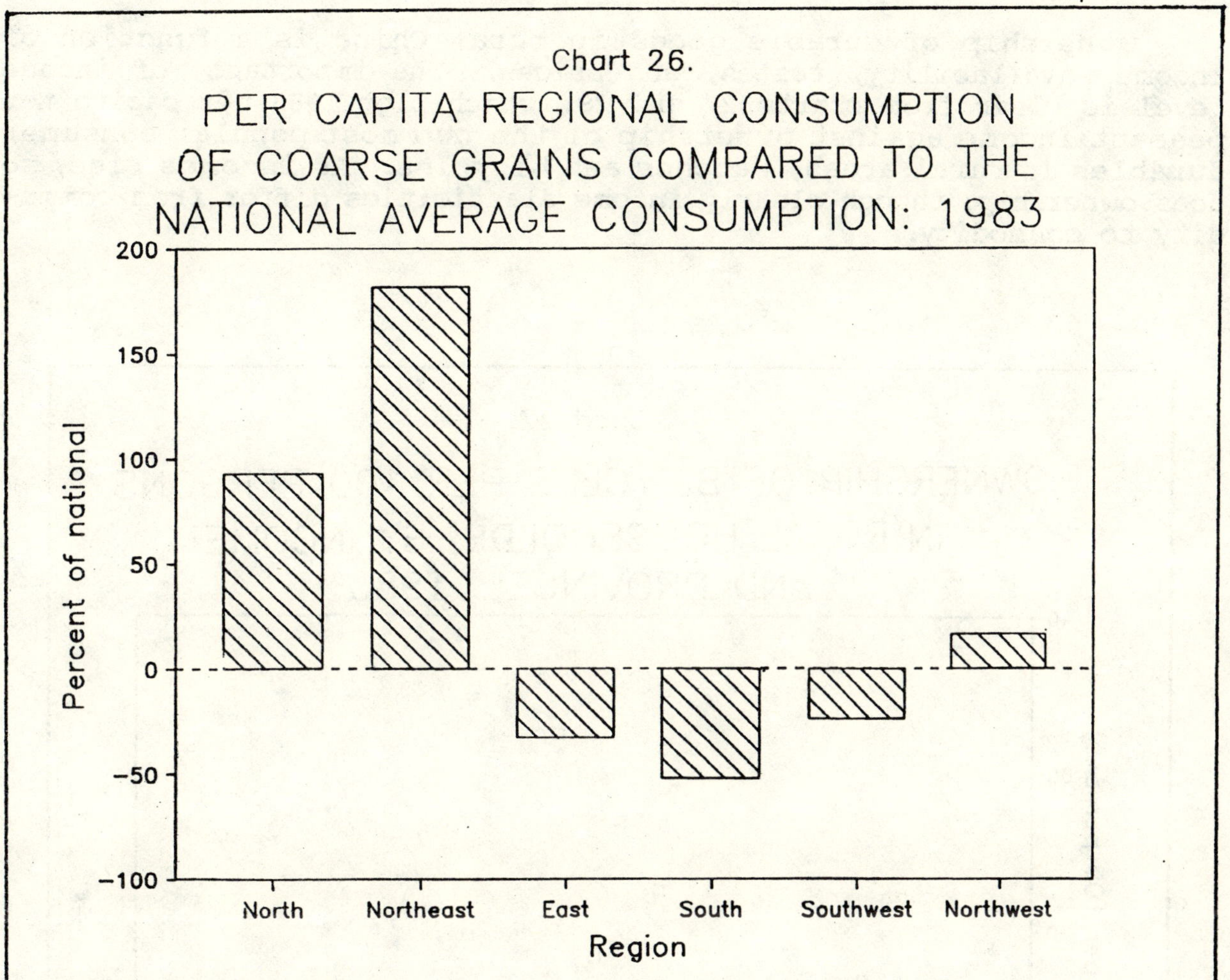


Source: Part II, table 92.

**OWNERSHIP OF DURABLE GOODS BY PROVINCE**

---

**Peasants closest to China's large municipalities have the greatest access to durable goods, and thus the highest ownership levels. Income levels and tastes also play important roles in interprovincial differences in ownership of durable goods.**

---

As was the case with household expenditure and commodity consumption data, the only comprehensive survey figures on durable good ownership by province are from the rural household surveys. These figures are listed in Part II tables 98 and 99, and discussed below.

### Factors Influencing Durable Good Ownership

Ownership of durable goods in rural China is a function of income, availability, tastes, and prices. The importance of income level is clear from charts 27 and 28, which plot 1983 per capita net peasant income against ownership of the two most popular consumer durables in rural areas, watches and bicycles. As incomes rise, so does ownership, though clearly income elasticities differ from commodity to commodity.

Chart 27.

OWNERSHIP OF BICYCLES PER 100 PERSONS IN RURAL HOUSEHOLDS, BY INCOME AND PROVINCE: 1983

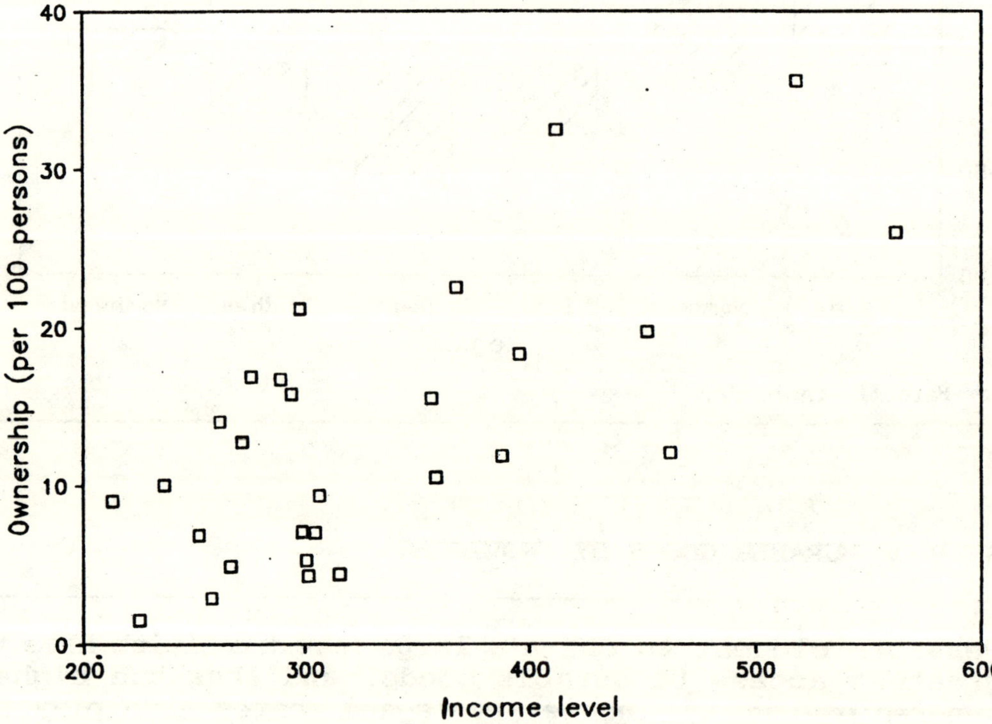


Note: Each point on the graph represents a province, excluding those for which data are not available.

Source: Part II, table 99.

Chart 28.

OWNERSHIP OF WATCHES PER 100 PERSONS IN RURAL HOUSEHOLDS, BY INCOME AND PROVINCE: 1983

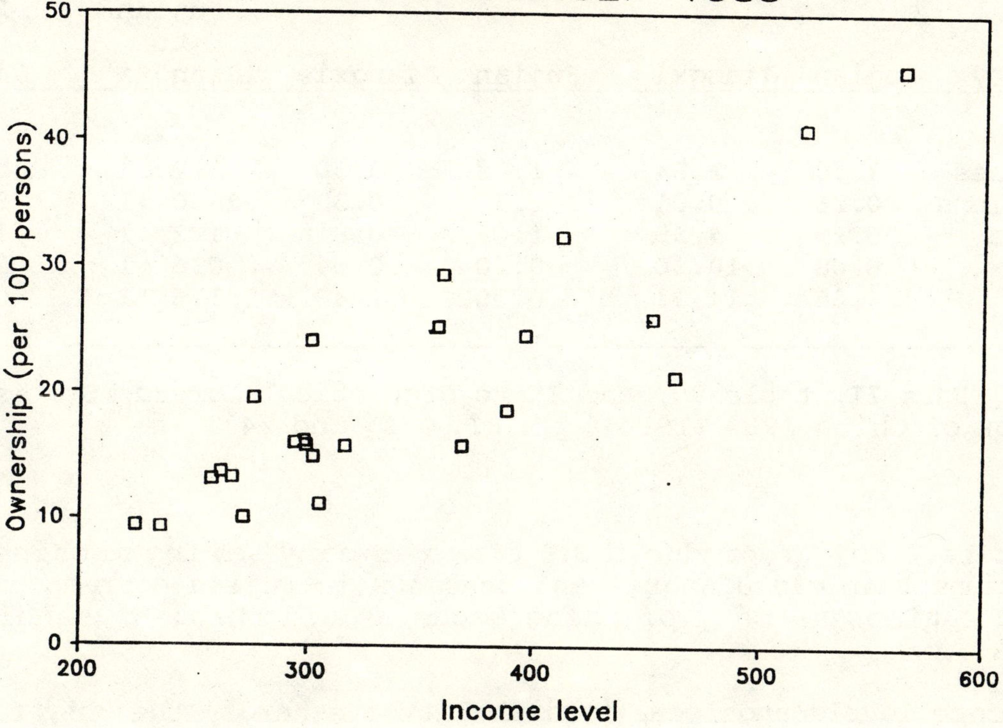


Note: Each point on the graph represents a province, excluding those for which data are not available.

Source: Part II, table 99.

Marketing and transport links between provinces are not well established for all commodities, which greatly influences the availability of consumer durables throughout China. Where local production levels of consumer durables are relatively low, households may find their consumption of these goods restricted, even if their income levels would support higher ownership levels. For example, Fujian and Jiangxi provinces have virtually identical per capita income levels (301 and 302 yuan in 1983, respectively), but as shown in table 11, differ markedly in ownership levels for selected durable goods. The relatively higher ownership levels for sewing machines, televisions and bicycles in Fujian appear to be related to their greater availability, as reflected in provincial production

**Table 11. Comparison of Durable Good Ownership and Production in Fujian and Jiangxi: 1983**

| Commodity | Ownership per 100 peasants: Fujian | Ownership per 100 peasants: Jiangxi | Local production per 100 residents: Fujian | Local production per 100 residents: Jiangxi | Ownership ratio: Fujian to Jiangxi | Production ratio: Fujian to Jiangxi |
|---|---|---|---|---|---|---|
| Sewing machines | 7.44 | 2.34 | 1.08 | 0.30 | 3.2 :1 | 3.2 :1 |
| Televisions | 0.26 | 0.01 | 1.37 | 0.38 | 26.0 :1 | 3.6 :1 |
| Bicycles | 5.29 | 4.30 | 1.01 | 0.81 | 1.2 :1 | 1.2 :1 |
| Radios | 6.08 | 10.30 | 0.70 | 0.64 | 0.6 :1 | 1.1: 1 |
| Watches | 24.06 | 14.91 | 0.00 | 1.49 | 1.6 :1 | 0.0: 1 |

Source: Part II, table 99, and State Statistical Bureau, Statistical Yearbook of China 1984 (1984), pp. 81, 239, and 241.

statistics. Fujian produced 3.6 times as many sewing machines per 100 persons than did Jiangxi, and peasants in Fujian correspondingly owned 3.2 times as many of these goods as did rural households in Jiangxi.

Income levels and local availability are hardly the only factors explaining provincial differences in ownership of durable goods. Differences in tastes and prices also play a role. This is evident from table 11, which indicates that peasants in Fujian apparently own more watches on average than do peasants in Jiangxi, despite the fact that Jiangxi produces watches while Fujian evidently does not, and income levels in the two provinces are similar. Radio ownership in the two provinces is also difficult to explain on the basis of income and availability criteria. Analyzing the relative impact of prices and tastes on durable good ownership is beyond the scope of this book, but interprovincial differences in consumer demand are clearly affected by these factors.

### Ownership Levels by Province and Commodity

According to 1983 rural household survey data, peasants in Shanghai, Beijing and Tianjin own far more consumer durables than do peasants in most other provinces (see Part II, table 99). Peasants in these municipalities have better access to retail outlets selling consumer durables, and also have higher-than-average incomes that enable purchase of such goods to fit more easily into their budgets.

There is also a north-south dichotomy in ownership of selected durable goods; peasants in the North, Northeast, and East own more than the national average of most commodities than do their counterparts in the South, Southwest, and Northwest. Guangdong, in the South, is an exception.

1983 statistics indicate that there are 12 bicycles for every 100 individuals in rural areas. Peasants in Beijing have three times the national average, while peasants in Tianjin and Shanghai have more than twice the national average. Bicycle ownership in the Southwest is less than one-half the national average. Ownership of sewing machines is more evenly distributed between provinces; peasants in Shanghai again have over twice the national average of 7 sewing machines per 100 persons, while peasants in Guizhou come in last with ownership levels that were only 29 percent of national levels. Peasants in the North, Northeast, and East own more radios than average; radio ownership among their comrades in the South, Southwest, and Northwest is significantly lower.

The popularity of wristwatch ownership is evident from 1983 statistics. The lowest ownership level shown for this commodity is in Shaanxi, where 9 percent of all individuals owned watches, compared to a high of 46 percent owned by peasants in Shanghai. Television ownership among rural families is quite rare outside urbanized areas. Television ownership could be claimed by fewer than 1 percent of rural residents in 1983. The highest ownership levels are shown for Beijing, which at 9 televisions per 100 persons is more than 10 times the national average. Tape recorders are another popular, but hard-to-find item in rural areas. Peasants in Beijing and Guangdong held just over 1 tape recorder per 100 persons in 1983, but this was still 5 times the national average. Finally, electric fan ownership appeals most to peasants in warmer climates; ownership in the east and south is well above the national average, whereas ownership among northern peasants is below average in all but the high-income municipalities of Beijing and Tianjin.

# V. THE FUTURE

**Per capita consumption may double by the year 2000, according to econometric projections. High and rising savings rates also suggest that there is substantial repressed demand in China. These findings suggest that China is embarking on a period of strong growth in consumer demand.**

What are the growth prospects for consumer demand in China? If recent history is any guide, the prospects are no less than outstanding. Rates of growth in personal income and consumption of almost every kind of consumer good have skyrocketed since 1978. Although this is exciting news, market researchers know through painful experience that a backward glance at past trends is rarely sufficient in itself to predict future patterns of consumption. Stronger analytical techniques are required to shed light on this subject.

One way in which consumer demand prospects can be more rigorously analyzed is by constructing a formal econometric model of private consumption. A number of models have been constructed for China within the past year, including efforts by Song and Liu (1984), and the World Bank (1985). The technical merits of each model will not be discussed here; estimation techniques used by each author are somewhat different, and are mentioned in the body of their reports. What is important is that each study concludes that growth rates for consumer demand are excellent. As shown in table 12, in the near term (to 1990) both studies do not forsee the possibility of annual average growth rates in per capita consumption falling below 4.5 percent. In the long term (1990-2000), the World Bank projects that annual average growth in consumption should not fall below 4 percent, and may exceed 5 percent. This projection does not rule out the possibility of growth averaging 4.7 percent from now through the end of the century, which means that per capita consumption levels in China could actually double by the year 2000.

Another way of analyzing consumer demand prospects in China is to assess the extent of repressed demand by examining savings rates and their trends. Chart 29 shows that Chinese households save a very high proportion of their incomes: 20 percent for rural residents, 12 percent for urban residents, and an estimated 12 percent for the country overall. Moreover, these savings rates have risen sharply from 1981 to 1983. It is not unusual in societies with undeveloped consumer credit markets to see high savings rates (consumers must save to buy expensive consumer durables, rather than pay for them on installment) but it is notable for already high savings rates to rise. This strongly suggests that the output of consumer goods in China has not kept pace with growth in demand. Put another way, this

Table 12. Comparison of Alternative Projections of Growth in Per Capita Consumption

| Study | Projected annual average growth in per capita consumption (in percent) | |
|---|---|---|
| | 1980's to 1990 | 1990 to 2000 |
| Song and Liu (1) | N/A | N/A |
| Urban households | 4.6 - 5.5 | N/A |
| Rural households | 4.9 - 5.6 | N/A |
| World Bank (2) | 4.5 - 6.4 | 4.1 - 5.3 |

Notes: (1) "1980's to 1990" data are for the period 1982 to 1990.
(2) "1980's to 1990" data are for the period 1981 to 1990. Per capita consumption was calculated here by dividing household consumption by population levels.

Sources: Song and Liu (1984), p. 35; and World Bank (1985), Annex 4, pp. 34-47.

means that as more consumer goods come onto the market, Chinese consumers may liquidate part of their savings to acquire items previously in short supply -- in addition to consuming their usual bundle of commodities. Precisely when jumps in demand like this will occur in China is difficult to say; it is important from a marketing standpoint that they can occur at all.

In summary, China appears to be headed for a period of strong growth in consumer demand. Will foreign businesses be able to reap any of the benefits of this growth? Given China's aversion to spending its hard-earned foreign exchange on consumer goods, it is unlikely that those who seek to export these commodities to China will see much gain. On the other hand, exporters of machinery for manufacturing consumer goods, and suppliers of direct and indirect inputs to China's consumer products industries may be able to benefit from the explosion in demand. Finally, foreign investors in China may see the greatest benefit of all. Chinese authorities have been reluctant to allow joint ventures the right to compete with domestic enterprises in internal markets, but have made exceptions when the investment is a net earner of foreign exchange. Meeting this criterion is difficult for many overseas investments, but may be worth the cost for those interested in staking a claim in China's growing consumer market.

Chart 29.

ESTIMATED SAVINGS RATE, FOR CHINA: 1981 AND 1983

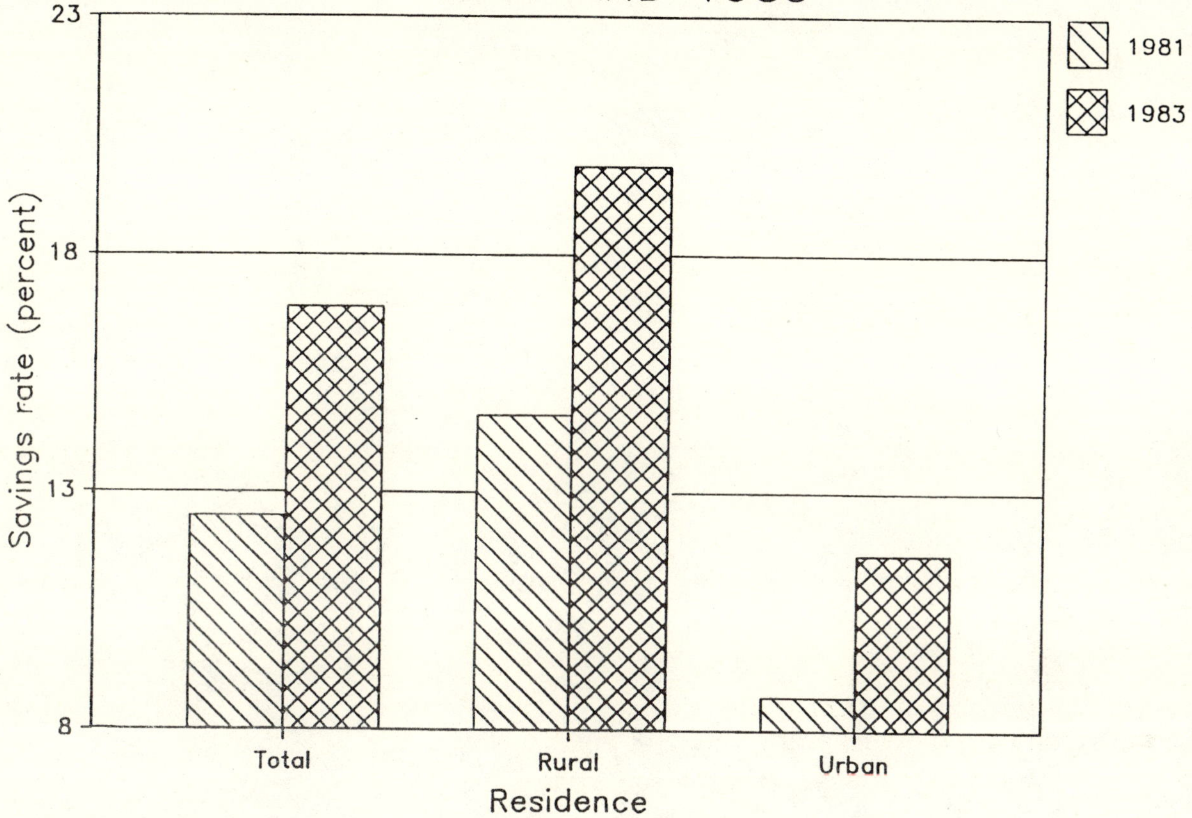


Savings rates were calculated for household income and expenditure survey data.

PART TWO

# STATISTICAL TABLES

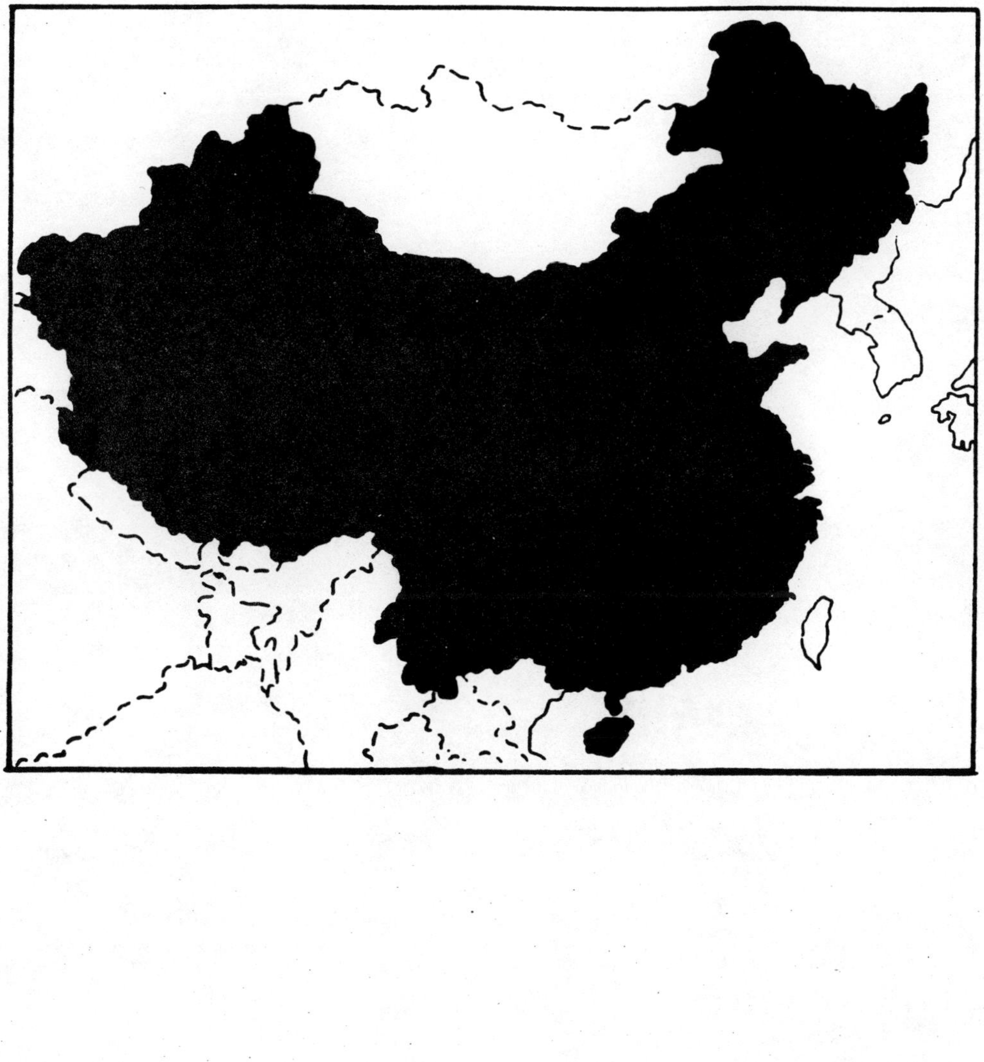

# VI. NOTE ON THE DATA

## Sample Surveys of Household Income and Expenditure

Most of the information discussed in Part I come from China's sample surveys of household income and expenditure. Unless mentioned otherwise in footnotes, all the tables in Part II are also from these surveys. China has gathered information of this sort on urban and rural households since the 1950s (Chen, 1967, pp. 89-92). Both the rural and the urban surveys were suspended in the mid 1960s and were resumed in the mid and late 1970s.

The rural sample survey is formally referred to by the State Statistical Bureau as the "Peasants' Family Budget Survey" (State Statistical Bureau, 1985, The Present..., pp. 16-17). It is designed to obtain data on production, trade, consumption, and investment by peasant households. The survey covered 31,375 households in 1984. Households are selected using a three-stage stratified and systematic sampling scheme, where counties are first selected from each province, production teams are then selected from the counties, and households are finally selected from the production teams. Stratified sampling techniques are used to select the survey units from a list of all households ranked by per capita distributed income. A sampling interval is calculated from cumulative population figures and the number of samples, and units falling in the midpoint of each interval are selected for inclusion in the survey. Once a household is in the sample, it is likely to remain there for years. Respondents are requested to maintain a daily log of expenditures in addition to account books of income and expenditure as well as production information.

Two additional points are worthy of note on the rural household survey. First, the sample size is determined to yield data representative of households for each province overall; data representative of subprovincial areas (counties, townships, etc.) can be obtained only if the provincial statistical authorities increase the sample size at their own expense. A number of provinces have invested their own funds to obtain this more detailed information. Second, Chinese statisticians admit that selection of communes for the survey does not strictly accord with the principles of random sampling, but assert that the impact has not been significant (Tuan and Crook, 1983, p. 55).

Urban income and expenditure survey data published to date include only the households of workers and staff employed in state and collective enterprises and institutions. This means that the families headed by retirees and self-employed workers are not included -- an estimated 4 to 5 percent of all urban households (Li,

1985, p. 1.1-8). The State Statistical Bureau began efforts in July 1984 to broaden the urban survey to include these households without wage-earners, but no statistics have yet appeared from this broader survey (Tan, 1984, p. 3).

The urban survey gathers data on family size and composition, employment, income, expenditure on goods and services, possession of durable goods, and housing. A three stage sampling procedure is used (State Statistical Bureau, 1985, The Present..., pp. 13-15). In the first stage, cities are selected by dividing more than 200 cities into three strata according to size, subdividing the cities in each stratum into six additional substrata according to administrative region, and finally within each region the cities are ranked according to average wages of workers and staff. In the second stage, enterprises and institutions within the cities are selected according to the distribution of total employment. Finally, households are selected from the enterprises and institutions. Sample sizes have varied; in 1984 the sample contained 12,500 households, compared to 9,020 households in 1982. As in the rural survey, households employ the diary technique to keep track of expenditures. The sampling method used is a variant of stratified and systematic sampling techniques.

Despite obvious attempts to improve the urban household surveys throughout the 1980's, there are a few problems. First, as noted earlier, the published data exclude households having no wage earners. Second, the sample households tend to stay fixed for years, which affects the representativeness of the data over time. Finally, the survey is designed to gather statistics that are representative of worker and staff households for the nation as a whole. Data representative for individual provinces can only be obtained if the provincial statistical authorities increase the number of households sampled, at their own expense. Though many provinces have done this, there are still a few holdouts. Because of this, the State Statistical Bureau has yet to publish provincial data from the urban household survey. Per capita income data from this survey are available for most provinces from other sources, however.

Though many of the expenditure categories in the urban and rural household surveys appear the same, the two sets of data are not strictly comparable. Urban residents receive a wide array of income, consumption, and housing subsidies not available to rural residents (Lardy, 1983, pp. 163-165). As such, consumption levels for urban residents are in a sense artificially high, and not strictly representative of what they would be in the absence of external support.

### Data Comparability Problems

There are two sources for the statistics used in this report on consumption and ownership of durable goods. Much of the data comes from the household income and expenditure surveys, but the State Statistical Bureau publishes additional statistics on per capita consumption and durable good ownership that appear to be independent of the household survey data. So as to avoid confusion, the non-household survey data have been clearly noted in each table in Part II.

Consumption and durable good ownership statistics from the sample surveys and from other official sources cannot be simply substituted for one another to describe demand trends in China. Discrepancies between the two sets of data exist regarding per capita consumption of grain, liquor, cigarettes, sugar and coal. Consumption statistics for pork, on the other hand, are virtually the same in both sources. The reasons for these differences are not clear, but readers should be aware that comparability problems exist.

Table 1. Sample Size and Household Size in Urban Household Surveys: Selected Years, 1957 to 1984

| Item | 1957 | 1964 | 1978 | 1980 1st Qtr | 1980 4th Qtr | 1981 | 1982 | 1983 | 1984 |
|---|---|---|---|---|---|---|---|---|---|
| Number of households surveyed.......... | 5,900 | 3,537 | N/A | 86,955 | 7,962 | 8,715 | 9,020 | 9,060 | 12,500 |
| Average number of persons per household......... | 4.37 | 5.30 | 4.48 | 4.48 | 4.30 | 4.24 | 4.14 | 4.06 | 4.04 |
| Average number of employees per household.......... | 1.33 | 1.56 | 2.18 | 2.47 | 2.35 | 2.40 | 2.39 | 2.38 | 2.36 |
| Number of persons supported by each employee (including his- or herself).... | 3.29 | 3.40 | 2.06 | 1.81 | 1.83 | 1.77 | 1.73 | 1.71 | 1.71 |

NA Data not available

Source: Ma Hong, Zhongguo jingji shidian [Economic Events of Modern China], (1982), p. 576; State Statistical Bureau, Statistical Yearbook of China 1983 (1983), p. 492; China: A Statistics Survey in 1985 (1985), p. 99; Xue Muqiao, et al., eds, Zhongguo jingji nianjian 1981 [Economic Yearbook of China 1981] (1981), p. VI-25; and Hu Qiaomu, et al., Encyclopedic Yearbook of China 1981 (1981), p. 543.

Table 2. Sample and Household Size in Urban Household Surveys, by Income Group: 1980 to 1983

| Item | | Per Capita Monthly Income Group (in Yuan) | | | | | | | | |
|---|---|---|---|---|---|---|---|---|---|---|
| | All households | 15.00 and below | 15.01-25.00 | 20 and below | 20.01-25.00 | 25.01-35.00 | 35.01-50.00 | 50.01-60.00 | 50.01 and above | 60.01 and above |
| Number of households surveyed: | | | | | | | | | | |
| 1980, 1st quarter...... | 86,955 | 1,826 | 18,608 | N/A | N/A | 32,173 | 26,261 | N/A | 8,087 | N/A |
| 1981.................. | 8,715 | N/A | N/A | 179 | 476 | 2,772 | 3,685 | 1,037 | N/A | 566 |
| 1982.................. | 9,020 | N/A | N/A | 83 | 332 | 2,312 | 4,095 | 1,281 | N/A | 917 |
| 1983.................. | 9,060 | N/A | N/A | 55 | 269 | 1,841 | 4,218 | 1,488 | N/A | 1,189 |
| Average number of persons per household: | | | | | | | | | | |
| 1980, 1st quarter...... | 4.48 | 5.30 | 5.03 | N/A | N/A | 4.60 | 4.18 | N/A | 3.53 | N/A |
| 1981.................. | 4.24 | N/A | N/A | 5.60 | 5.22 | 4.66 | 4.00 | 3.70 | N/A | 3.20 |
| 1982.................. | 4.14 | N/A | N/A | 5.88 | 5.22 | 4.62 | 4.02 | 3.80 | N/A | 3.34 |
| 1983.................. | 4.06 | N/A | N/A | 5.49 | 5.13 | 4.52 | 3.99 | 3.75 | N/A | 3.55 |
| Average number of employees per household: | | | | | | | | | | |
| 1980, 1st quarter...... | 2.47 | 1.31 | 1.98 | N/A | N/A | 2.37 | 2.85 | N/A | 3.01 | N/A |
| 1981.................. | 2.39 | N/A | N/A | 1.63 | 1.96 | 2.18 | 2.43 | 2.79 | N/A | 2.69 |
| 1982.................. | 2.39 | N/A | N/A | 1.17 | 1.93 | 2.12 | 2.37 | 2.78 | N/A | 2.79 |
| 1983.................. | 2.38 | N/A | N/A | 1.78 | 1.96 | 2.12 | 2.33 | 2.59 | N/A | 2.82 |
| Percent of employment per household: | | | | | | | | | | |
| 1980, 1st quarter...... | 55.13 | 24.72 | 39.36 | N/A | N/A | 51.52 | 68.18 | N/A | 85.27 | N/A |
| 1981.................. | 56.37 | N/A | N/A | 29.11 | 37.55 | 46.78 | 60.75 | 75.41 | N/A | 84.06 |
| 1982.................. | 57.73 | N/A | N/A | 29.08 | 36.97 | 45.89 | 58.96 | 73.16 | N/A | 83.53 |
| 1983.................. | 58.62 | N/A | N/A | 32.42 | 38.21 | 46.90 | 58.40 | 69.07 | N/A | 79.44 |
| Number of persons supported by each employee: | | | | | | | | | | |
| 1980, 1st quarter...... | 1.81 | 4.05 | 2.54 | N/A | N/A | 1.94 | 1.47 | N/A | 1.17 | N/A |
| 1981.................. | 1.77 | N/A | N/A | 3.44 | 2.66 | 2.14 | 1.65 | 1.33 | N/A | 1.19 |
| 1982.................. | 1.73 | N/A | N/A | 3.44 | 2.70 | 2.18 | 1.70 | 1.37 | N/A | 1.20 |
| 1983.................. | 1.71 | N/A | N/A | 3.08 | 2.62 | 2.13 | 1.71 | 1.45 | N/A | 1.26 |

NA Data not available

Source: Renmin ribao [People's Daily], December 31, 1980, p. 1; State Statistical Bureau, Statistical Yearbook of China 1981 (1982), p. 428; Statistical Yearbook of China 1983 (1983), p. 493; Statistical Yearbook of China 1984 (1984), p. 466; and Summary of World Broadcasts, FE/6616/C/1, January 7, 1981.

Table 3. Distribution of Households in Urban Household Surveys, by Income Group: 1980 to 1983

| Item | Per Capita Monthly Income Group (in Yuan) | | | | | | | | | |
|---|---|---|---|---|---|---|---|---|---|---|
| | All households | 15.00 and below | 15.01-25.00 | 20 and below | 20.01-25.00 | 25.01-35.00 | 35.01-50.00 | 50.01-60.00 | 50.01 and above | 60.01 and above |
| Number of households surveyed: | | | | | | | | | | |
| 1980, 1st quarter...... | 100 | 2 | 21 | N/A | N/A | 37 | 30 | N/A | 9 | N/A |
| 1981.................. | 100 | N/A | N/A | 2 | 5 | 32 | 42 | 12 | N/A | 6 |
| 1982.................. | 100 | N/A | N/A | 1 | 4 | 26 | 45 | 14 | N/A | 10 |
| 1983.................. | 100 | N/A | N/A | 1 | 3 | 20 | 47 | 16 | N/A | 13 |
| Average number of persons per household: | | | | | | | | | | |
| 1980, 1st quarter...... | 100 | 118 | 112 | N/A | N/A | 103 | 93 | N/A | 79 | N/A |
| 1981.................. | 100 | N/A | N/A | 132 | 123 | 110 | 94 | 87 | N/A | 75 |
| 1982.................. | 100 | N/A | N/A | 142 | 126 | 112 | 97 | 92 | N/A | 81 |
| 1983.................. | 100 | N/A | N/A | 135 | 126 | 111 | 98 | 92 | N/A | 87 |
| Average number of employees per household: | | | | | | | | | | |
| 1980, 1st quarter...... | 100 | 53 | 80 | N/A | N/A | 96 | 115 | N/A | 122 | N/A |
| 1981.................. | 100 | N/A | N/A | 68 | 82 | 91 | 102 | 117 | N/A | 113 |
| 1982.................. | 100 | N/A | N/A | 49 | 81 | 89 | 99 | 116 | N/A | 117 |
| 1983.................. | 100 | N/A | N/A | 75 | 82 | 89 | 98 | 109 | N/A | 118 |
| Percent of employment per household: | | | | | | | | | | |
| 1980, 1st quarter...... | 100 | 45 | 71 | N/A | N/A | 93 | 124 | N/A | 155 | N/A |
| 1981.................. | 100 | N/A | N/A | 52 | 67 | 83 | 108 | 134 | N/A | 149 |
| 1982.................. | 100 | N/A | N/A | 50 | 64 | 79 | 102 | 127 | N/A | 145 |
| 1983.................. | 100 | N/A | N/A | 55 | 65 | 80 | 100 | 118 | N/A | 136 |
| Number of persons supported by each employee: | | | | | | | | | | |
| 1980, 1st quarter...... | 100 | 224 | 140 | N/A | N/A | 107 | 81 | N/A | 65 | N/A |
| 1981.................. | 100 | N/A | N/A | 194 | 150 | 121 | 93 | 75 | N/A | 67 |
| 1982.................. | 100 | N/A | N/A | 199 | 156 | 126 | 98 | 79 | N/A | 69 |
| 1983.................. | 100 | N/A | N/A | 180 | 153 | 125 | 100 | 85 | N/A | 74 |

NA Data not available

Source: Renmin ribao [People's Daily], December 31, 1980, p. 1; State Statistical Bureau, Statistical Yearbook of China 1981 (1982), p. 428; Statistical Yearbook of China 1983 (1983), p. 493; Statistical Yearbook of China 1984 (1984), p. 466; and Summary of World Broadcasts, FE/6616/C/1, January 1, 1981.

Table 4. Sample and Household Size in Rural Household Surveys: Selected Years, 1954 to 1984

| Item | 1954 | 1956 | 1957 | 1965 | 1978 | 1979 | 1980 | 1981 | 1982 | 1983 | 1984 |
|---|---|---|---|---|---|---|---|---|---|---|---|
| Number of households surveyed............. | 15,432 | 14,172 | 17,378 | 11,632 | 6,095 | 10,282 | 15,914 | 18,529 | 22,775 | 30,427 | 31,375 |
| Number of permanent residents in the households surveyed... | N/A | N/A | 84,279 | N/A | 34,961 | 58,153 | 88,090 | 101,998 | 124,286 | 165,131 | 168,446 |
| Average number of permanent residents per survey household.. | 4.69 | 4.86 | 4.85 | 5.03 | 5.74 | 5.66 | 5.54 | 5.5 | 5.46 | 5.43 | 5.37 |
| Average number of able-bodied and semi-able bodied laborers per household............ | N/A | N/A | 2.33 | 2.35 | 2.27 | 2.38 | 2.45 | 2.53 | 2.58 | 2.84 | 2.87 |
| Average number of persons supported by each able-bodied laborer.............. | N/A | N/A | 2.08 | 2.14 | 2.53 | 2.38 | 2.26 | 2.17 | 2.12 | 1.91 | 1.87 |

NA Data not available

Source: Guojia tongji ju, Woguo nongmin shenghuo de juda bianhua [State Statistical Bureau, Great Changes in the Lives of China's Peasants] (1984), p. 55; State Statistical Bureau, Statistical Yearbook of China 1983 (1983), p. 499; and China: A Statistics Survey in 1985 (1985), p. 102.

Table 5. Current and Constant Price Income Data for Urban Households: 1978 to 1984

| Indicator | 1978 | 1979 | 1980 | 1981 | 1982 | 1983 | 1984 |
|---|---|---|---|---|---|---|---|
| Current price annual income available for living expenses per capita (yuan): | | | | | | | |
| Original series (1)........ | 316 | N/A | 444 | 463 | 500 | N/A | N/A |
| Revised series (2)......... | 316 | N/A | N/A | N/A | 494 | 526 | 608 |
| Constant price index of income available for living expenses per capita (1978=100): | | | | | | | |
| Original series (1)........ | 100.0 | N/A | 128.5 | 130.8 | 138.3 | N/A | N/A |
| Revised series (2)......... | 100.0 | N/A | N/A | N/A | 136.8 | 142.7 | 160.4 |

NA Data not available

Note: (1) 1980 current and constant price net income figures are calculated from absolute increases and percentage growth rates reported in the State Statistical Bureau's communique on fulfillment of the 1981 social and economic plan. All other data are from the 1981 and 1983 Statistical Yearbook of China.

(2) The 1982 and 1984 constant price increases are calculated from real growth rates listed in the State Statistical Bureau's communique on fulfillment of the 1983 and 1984 social and economic plans. All other data are from the 1984 Statistical Yearbook of China, and China: a Statistical Survey in 1985.

Source: Guojia tongji ju, [State Statistical Bureau], Zhongguo tongji zhaiyao, 1984 [Statistical Abstract of China 1984] (1984), p. 124; Renmin ribao (People's Daily], April 30, 1982, p. 4; State Statistical Bureau, Statistical Yearbook of China 1981 (1982), p. 421; Statistical Yearbook of China, 1983 (1983), p. 483; Statistical Yearbook of China 1984 (1984), p. 462; China: A Statistics Survey in 1985 (1985), pp. 99 and 124; Xue Muqiao, et al., eds. Zhongguo jingji nianjian 1982 [Economic Yearbook of China 1982] (1982), and p. VIII-61; Zhongguo jingji nianjian 1983 [Economic Yearbook of China 1983] (1983), p. III-40.

Table 6. Per Capita Income and Expenditure Indicators for Urban Staff and Workers: Selected Years, 1957 to 1984 (in yuan)

| | | | | 1980 | | | | | |
|---|---|---|---|---|---|---|---|---|---|
| Item | 1957 | 1964 | 1978 | 1st Qtr. | 4th Qtr. | 1981 | 1982 | 1983 | 1984 |
| Monthly income...... | 21.13 | 20.29 | N/A | 35.80 | 42.80 | 41.70 | 44.61 | 47.74 | 55.01 |
| Income available for living expenditure...... | 19.62 | 18.92 | 26.33 | 32.68 | 37.70 | 38.17 | 41.21 | 43.83 | 50.63 |
| Other income...... | 1.51 | 1.37 | N/A | 3.12 | 5.10 | 3.53 | 3.40 | 3.91 | 4.38 |
| Monthly living expenditure........ | 18.50 | 18.39 | 25.93 | N/A | N/A | 38.07 | 39.25 | 42.16 | 46.62 |

NA Data not available

Note: Income available for living expenses is that portion of income available to cover the daily expenditure of the household. It is equal to total household income minus supporting expenses and subsidies reported by survey respondents.

Source: Li Chengrui, "Statistical Reporting on the Impact of China's Economic Policies of Recent Years on People's Income and Consumption," (1985), pp. 1.1-9; Renmin ribao [People's Daily], April 30, 1982, p. 4; State Statistical Bureau, Statistical Yearbook of China 1984 (1984), p. 462; China: A Statistics Survey in 1985 (1985), pp. 94 and 99; and Xue Muqiao, et al., eds., Zhongguo jingji nianjian 1981 [Economic Yearbook of China 1981] (1982), p. VI-25.

Table 7. Distribution of Monthly Per Capita Income Available for Living Expenses for Urban Staff and Workers, by Income Group: Selected Years, 1964 to 1984 (in percent)

| Income group | 1964 | 1980 1st qtr. | 1981 | 1982 | 1983 | 1984 |
|---|---|---|---|---|---|---|
| 15 Yuan and below... | N/A | 2.10 | N/A | N/A | N/A | N/A |
| 15 - 25 Yuan........ | N/A | 21.40 | N/A | N/A | N/A | N/A |
| 20 Yuan and below... | 59.74 | N/A | 2.05 | .92 | .61 | { 1.67 |
| 20 - 25 Yuan........ | 17.19 | N/A | 5.46 | 3.68 | 2.97 | { |
| 25 - 35 Yuan........ | 16.03 | 37.00 | 31.81 | 25.63 | 20.32 | 10.52 |
| 35 - 50 Yuan........ | 5.77 | 30.20 | 42.29 | 45.40 | 46.56 | 38.89 |
| 50 - 60 Yuan........ | { 1.27 | { 9.30 | 11.90 | 14.20 | 16.42 | 22.67 |
| 60 Yuan and over.... | { | { | 6.49 | 10.17 | 13.12 | 26.25 |

NA Data not available

Note: Income available for living expenses is that portion of income available to cover the daily expenditure of the household. It is equal to total household income minus supporting expenses and subsidies reported by survey respondents.

For 1978,1983 and 1984 income distribution by population rather than household, see Li Chengrui, "Statistical Reporting on the Impact of China's Policies of Recent Years on People's Income and Consumption," (1985), p. 1.1-10, and Li Chengrui, "Economic Reform Brings Better Life" (1985) p. 15. These data were excluded because they appear to be inconsistent with the data shown above for matching years.

Source: State Statistical Bureau, Statistical Yearbook of China 1984, (1984), p. 462; China: A Statistics Survey in 1985 (1985) p. 99; and Renmin Ribao [People's Daily], December 30, 1980, p.1.

Table 8. Current and Constant Price Average Wage Data, for Staff and Workers, by Ownership System: 1978 to 1984

| Unit and wage | 1978 | 1979 | 1980 | 1981 | 1982 | 1983 | 1984 |
|---|---|---|---|---|---|---|---|
| Current price average wage level (yuan): | | | | | | | |
| All units............ | 614 | 668 | 762 | 772 | 798 | 826 | 974 |
| State-owned units.... | 644 | 705 | 803 | 812 | 836 | 865 | 1,034 |
| Collectively-owned units............... | 505 | 542 | 624 | 642 | 671 | 698 | 811 |
| Constant Price Average wage growth index (1978=100): | | | | | | | |
| All units............ | 100.0 | N/A | N/A | 111.9 | 113.6 | 115.3 | 130.5 |
| State-owned units.... | 100.0 | 107.6 | 113.9 | 112.3 | 113.5 | 115.1 | N/A |
| Collectively-owned units............... | 100.0 | N/A | N/A | N/A | N/A | 118.4 | N/A |

NA Data not available

Note: Constant price wage index for all units in 1984 was calculated as a 13.2 percent increase over the 1983 reported figure, based on information in the State Statistical Bureau's Communique on fulfillment of China's 1984 Social and Economic Plan. The constant price wage index series for staff and workers in state-owned units was rebased from 1952=100 to 1978=100.

Source: Ma Hong, Zhongguo jingji shidian [Economic Events of Modern China] (1982), p. 572; State Statistical Bureau, Statistical Yearbook of China 1981 (1982), pp. 429 and 431; Statistical Yearbook of China 1983 (1983), pp. 483 and 485; Statistical Yearbook of China 1984 (1984), pp. 455 and 460; and China: A Statistics Survey in 1985 (1985), p. 124.

Table 9. Composition of Annual Average Wage of Urban Staff and Workers, by Ownership System: 1978 to 1984 (in yuan)

| Unit and wage | 1978 | 1979 | 1980 | 1981 | 1982 | 1983 | 1984 |
|---|---|---|---|---|---|---|---|
| **All Staff and Workers:** | | | | | | | |
| Average wage............ | 614.0 | 668.0 | 762.0 | 772.0 | 798.0 | 826.0 | 974.0 |
| Bonuses, piece rate wages and above quota payments.......... | 12.1 | 50.4 | 69.4 | N/A | 98.6 | 106.8 | 160.0 |
| Bonuses................ | 11.6 | 47.8 | 65.6 | 73.8 | 81.5 | N/A | N/A |
| Piece rate wages, and above quota payments.............. | .5 | 2.6 | 3.8 | N/A | 17.1 | N/A | N/A |
| Basic wage, subsidies, and other.... | 601.9 | 617.6 | 692.6 | N/A | 699.4 | 719.0 | 814.0 |
| **Staff and Workers in State-Owned Units:** | | | | | | | |
| Average wage............ | 644.0 | 705.0 | 803.0 | 812.0 | 836.0 | 865.0 | 1,034.0 |
| Bonuses, piece rate wages and above quota payments.......... | 15.5 | 55.6 | 77.9 | N/A | 104.2 | 111.7 | N/A |
| Bonuses................ | 14.8 | 52.2 | 73.1 | 82.9 | 90.8 | N/A | N/A |
| Piece rate wages, and above quota payments.............. | .7 | 3.4 | 4.8 | N/A | 13.4 | N/A | N/A |
| Basic wage, subsidies, and other.... | 628.5 | 649.4 | 725.1 | N/A | 731.8 | 753.3 | N/A |
| **Staff and Workers in Collectively-Owned Units:** | | | | | | | |
| Average wage............ | 505.0 | 542.0 | 624.0 | 642.0 | 671.0 | 698.0 | 811.0 |
| Bonuses, piece rate wages and above quota payments.......... | N/A | 32.4 | 40.5 | N/A | 80.2 | 91.0 | N/A |
| Bonuses................ | N/A | 32.4 | 40.5 | 44.3 | 51.3 | N/A | N/A |
| Piece rate wages, and above quota payments.............. | N/A | .0 | .0 | .0 | 28.9 | N/A | N/A |
| Basic wage, subsidies, and other.... | N/A | 509.6 | 583.5 | N/A | 590.8 | 607.0 | N/A |

NA Data not available

Source: State Statistical Bureau, Statistical Yearbook of China 1983 (1983), p. 485; Statistical Yearbook of China 1984 (1984), p. 455; and China: A Statistics Survey in 1985 (1985), p. 97.

Table 10. Composition of Total Wage Bill of Staff and Workers in State-Owned Work Units: 1978 to 1984 (in percent)

| Item | 1978 | 1979 | 1980 | 1981 | 1982 | 1983 | 1984 |
|---|---|---|---|---|---|---|---|
| Total wage bill..... | 100.0 | 100.0 | 100.0 | 100.0 | 100.0 | 100.0 | 100.0 |
| Time wage......... | 85.0 | 75.5 | 69.8 | 67.2 | 64.4 | 63.5 | 58.5 |
| Piece rate wage... | .8 | 2.5 | 3.2 | 5.5 | 7.6 | 8.5 | 9.5 |
| Of which above-quota wage....... | .1 | N/A | .6 | 1.1 | 1.6 | 1.8 | 2.1 |
| Bonuses........... | 2.3 | 7.5 | 9.1 | 10.2 | 10.9 | 11.1 | 14.4 |
| Subsidies......... | 6.5 | 8.8 | 14.1 | 14.0 | 14.1 | 14.1 | 14.5 |
| Overtime.......... | 2.0 | 2 | 1.6 | 1.6 | 1.5 | 1.3 | 1.5 |
| Additional wage... | 2.9 | 2.4 | 1.5 | 1.0 | .9 | .7 | |
| Other............. | .5 | 1.3 | .7 | .5 | .6 | .8 | 1.6 |

NA Data not available

Source: State Statistical Bureau, Statistical Yearbook of China 1984 (1984), p. 461; and China: A Statistics Survey in 1985 (1985), p. 98.

Table 11. Average Annual Wages of All Staff and Workers, by Sector: 1980 to 1983 (in yuan)

| Sector | 1980 | 1981 | 1982 | 1983 |
|---|---|---|---|---|
| Total...................... | 762.1 | 772.2 | 797.5 | 825.6 |
| Industry................. | 784.1 | 788.0 | 801.9 | 819.0 |
| Construction and resources prospecting............ | 870.2 | 890.9 | 927.7 | 968.9 |
| Agriculture, forestry, water conservancy, and meteorology........ | 628.2 | 645.8 | 667.8 | 702.1 |
| Transport, posts, and telecommunications..... | 841.0 | 846.3 | 883.5 | 909.2 |
| Commerce, catering, and service trades, and materials supply and marketing... | 690.2 | 699.2 | 708.8 | 727.1 |
| Civil public utilities.. | 761.3 | 785.6 | 807.4 | 859.2 |
| Science research........ | 851.6 | 857.4 | 859.9 | 983.2 |
| Culture, education, public health and social welfare......... | 704.9 | 726.7 | 816.8 | 844.5 |
| Banking and insurance... | 717.2 | 745.0 | 765.5 | 761.5 |
| Government agencies and people's organizations.......... | 800.5 | 813.7 | 822.4 | 921.3 |

Note: The annual average wages of all staff and workers were derived by dividing the total staff and worker wage bill by the number of employees in state-owned and collectively-owned units. The breakdown of number of employees by state- and collectively-owned units was calculated by dividing the total wage bill from the respective ownership type by the average wage for that type of enterprise.

Source: State Statistical Bureau, Statistical Yearbook of China 1981 (1981), p. 432; Statistical Yearbook of China 1983 (1983), p. 487; and Statistical Yearbook of China 1984 (1984), p. 465.

Table 12. Average Annual Wages of Staff and Workers, by Sector and Ownership System: 1980 to 1983
(in yuan)

| Sector | State-owned units | | | | Collective-owned units in cities and towns | | | |
|---|---|---|---|---|---|---|---|---|
| | 1980 | 1981 | 1982 | 1983 | 1980 | 1981 | 1982 | 1983 |
| Total.................... | 803 | 812 | 836 | 865 | 624 | 642 | 671 | 698 |
| Industry................ | 854 | 852 | 864 | 878 | 622 | 644 | 659 | 684 |
| Construction and resources prospecting............ | 923 | 948 | 982 | 1023 | 714 | 738 | 794 | 844 |
| Agriculture, foresty, water conservancy, and meteorology........ | 636 | 654 | 676 | 713 | 489 | 515 | 544 | 555 |
| Transport, posts, and telecommunications..... | 906 | 909 | 934 | 959 | 696 | 703 | 764 | 787 |
| Commerce, catering, and service trades, and materials supply and marketing... | 723 | 736 | 745 | 764 | 570 | 578 | 595 | 616 |
| Civil public utilities.. | 789 | 803 | 823 | 876 | 642 | 695 | 727 | 776 |
| Science research........ | 856 | 860 | 863 | 986 | 605 | 686 | 651 | 757 |
| Culture, education, public health and social welfare......... | 729 | 749 | 835 | 861 | 528 | 553 | 648 | 685 |
| Banking and insurance... | 760 | 787 | 797 | 820 | 623 | 635 | 679 | 688 |
| Government agencies and people's organizations.......... | 807 | 819 | 827 | 927 | 561 | 615 | 642 | 696 |

Source: State Statistical Bureau, Statistical Yearbook of China 1981 (1982), p. 433, Statistical Yearbook of China, 1983 (1983), p. 487; Statistical Yearbook of China, 1984 (1984), p. 456.

Table 13. Average Annual Wage of Staff and Workers in State-Owned Enterprises, by Sector: 1952 to 1983
(In Yuan)

| Year | Average wage of all sectors | Industry | Con-struction and resources pros-pecting | Agri-culture, forestry, water conservancy, meteorology | Trans-port, posts and tele-commu-nications | Commerce, catering, and service trades, and supply and marketing of materials | Civil public utilities | Science culture, education, and public health | Banking and insurance | Government agencies, and people's organiz-ations |
|---|---|---|---|---|---|---|---|---|---|---|
| 1952... | 446 | 515 | 564 | 375 | 583 | 360 | 634 | 368 | 458 | 376 |
| 1953... | 496 | 576 | 591 | 433 | 643 | 381 | 650 | 392 | 498 | 423 |
| 1954... | 519 | 597 | 612 | 459 | 648 | 403 | 672 | 422 | 521 | 451 |
| 1955... | 534 | 600 | 612 | 461 | 645 | 443 | 610 | 448 | 532 | 479 |
| 1956... | 610 | 674 | 698 | 498 | 746 | 490 | 661 | 548 | 586 | 597 |
| 1957... | 637 | 690 | 744 | 501 | 752 | 529 | 651 | 580 | 613 | 631 |
| 1958... | 550 | 526 | 595 | 471 | 673 | 489 | 642 | 557 | 586 | 639 |
| 1959... | 524 | 514 | 554 | 411 | 627 | 454 | 589 | 542 | 583 | 631 |
| 1960... | 528 | 538 | 581 | 365 | 618 | 449 | 564 | 519 | 543 | 615 |
| 1961... | 537 | 560 | 596 | 362 | 620 | 455 | 582 | 519 | 553 | 605 |
| 1962... | 592 | 652 | 705 | 392 | 702 | 494 | 631 | 542 | 559 | 626 |
| 1963... | 641 | 720 | 775 | 421 | 760 | 550 | 672 | 574 | 604 | 658 |
| 1964... | 661 | 741 | 765 | 433 | 782 | 581 | 683 | 596 | 614 | 688 |
| 1965... | 652 | 729 | 730 | 433 | 774 | 579 | 687 | 598 | 624 | 684 |
| 1966... | 636 | 689 | 644 | 428 | 755 | 570 | 697 | 583 | 620 | 660 |
| 1967... | 630 | 701 | 672 | 426 | 754 | 563 | 696 | 578 | 620 | 681 |
| 1968... | 621 | 689 | 654 | 419 | 740 | 561 | 667 | 577 | 630 | 681 |
| 1969... | 618 | 683 | 661 | 418 | 734 | 561 | 660 | 564 | 611 | 680 |
| 1970... | 609 | 661 | 650 | 419 | 709 | 553 | 660 | 555 | 588 | 678 |
| 1971... | 597 | 635 | 662 | 426 | 709 | 539 | 655 | 554 | 604 | 668 |
| 1972... | 622 | 650 | 714 | 423 | 723 | 585 | 702 | 598 | 616 | 679 |
| 1973... | 614 | 640 | 715 | 436 | 714 | 568 | 680 | 582 | 602 | 659 |
| 1974... | 622 | 648 | 710 | 483 | 713 | 571 | 675 | 582 | 629 | 661 |
| 1975... | 613 | 644 | 704 | 460 | 699 | 562 | 639 | 574 | 609 | 645 |
| 1976... | 605 | 634 | 696 | 459 | 684 | 555 | 621 | 566 | 602 | 636 |
| 1977... | 602 | 632 | 695 | 459 | 677 | 552 | 623 | 559 | 622 | 635 |
| 1978... | 644 | 683 | 748 | 492 | 733 | 587 | 652 | 582 | 643 | 662 |
| 1979... | 705 | 758 | 814 | 548 | 808 | 641 | 694 | 620 | 675 | 690 |
| 1980... | 803 | 854 | 923 | 636 | 906 | 723 | 789 | 741 | 760 | 807 |
| 1981... | 812 | 852 | 948 | 654 | 909 | 736 | 803 | 759 | 787 | 819 |
| 1982... | 836 | 864 | 982 | 676 | 934 | 745 | 823 | 837 | 797 | 827 |
| 1983... | 865 | 878 | 1,023 | 713 | 959 | 764 | 876 | 873 | 820 | 927 |

Source: State Statistical Bureau, Statistical Yearbook of China 1984 (1984), p. 459.

Table 14. Annual Average Wage of Staff and Workers in State-Owned Units, by Industrial Sector: Selected Years, 1952 to 1983 (in yuan)

| Industry | 1952 | 1957 | 1963 | 1977 | 1978 | 1979 | 1980 | 1981 | 1982 | 1983 |
|---|---|---|---|---|---|---|---|---|---|---|
| Total............... | 515 | 690 | 720 | 632 | 683 | 758 | 854 | 852 | 864 | 878 |
| Metallurgy........ | 563 | 773 | 759 | 650 | 717 | 815 | 930 | 921 | 931 | 956 |
| Electricity....... | 685 | 817 | 698 | 613 | 660 | 735 | 855 | 857 | 868 | 883 |
| Coal.............. | 504 | 793 | 822 | 735 | 810 | 908 | 1,008 | 1,025 | 1,062 | 1,083 |
| Petroleum......... | 632 | 923 | 882 | 682 | 763 | 864 | 964 | 971 | 1,017 | 1,067 |
| Chemicals......... | 637 | 677 | 685 | 578 | 619 | 698 | 802 | 806 | 827 | 853 |
| Machinery......... | 585 | 734 | 720 | 615 | 667 | 733 | 822 | 818 | 829 | 845 |
| Building materials | 406 | 613 | 682 | 593 | 641 | 705 | 805 | 811 | 845 | 858 |
| Forest products... | 536 | 768 | 793 | 772 | 813 | 866 | 958 | 989 | NA | 996 |
| Food products..... | 441 | 574 | 585 | 551 | 605 | 663 | 760 | 775 | 779 | 784 |
| Textiles (1)...... | 534 | 663 | 719 | 605 | 653 | 723 | 810 | 788 | 776 | 774 |
| Paper............. | 477 | 537 | 655 | 600 | 649 | 723 | 798 | 782 | 787 | 800 |
| Other (2)......... | NA | NA | NA | 643 | 625 | 706 | 808 | 782 | NA | NA |

NA Data not available.

Note: (1) Excludes clothing.
(2) Includes production of coke, clothing, leather, and cultural and educational products.

Source: Guojia tongji ju, Zhongguo gongye de fazhan [State Statistical Bureau, The Development of China's Industry] (1984), p. 99; Statistical Yearbook of China 1984 (1984), p. 459; United Nations, Industrial Statistics Yearbook, 1981, Vol. I, (1984), pp. 51-52; and Industrial Statistical Yearbook 1982, Vol. I, (1985), pp. 105-106.

Table 15. Average Annual Wage of Staff and Workers in State-Owned Work Units, and Current and Constant Price Wage Indexes: 1952 to 1984

| | Average wage (current yuan) | Wage Index (1952 = 100) Nominal index | Constant price index |
|---|---|---|---|
| 1952....... | 446 | 100 | 100 |
| 1953....... | 496 | 111 | 106 |
| 1954....... | 519 | 116 | 109 |
| 1955....... | 534 | 120 | 112 |
| 1956....... | 610 | 137 | 128 |
| 1957....... | 637 | 143 | 130 |
| 1958....... | 550 | 123 | 114 |
| 1959....... | 524 | 118 | 108 |
| 1960....... | 528 | 118 | 106 |
| 1961....... | 537 | 120 | 93 |
| 1962....... | 592 | 133 | 99 |
| 1963....... | 641 | 144 | 114 |
| 1964....... | 661 | 148 | 122 |
| 1965....... | 652 | 146 | 122 |
| 1966....... | 636 | 143 | 120 |
| 1967....... | 630 | 141 | 120 |
| 1968....... | 621 | 139 | 118 |
| 1969....... | 618 | 139 | 116 |
| 1970....... | 609 | 137 | 114 |
| 1971....... | 597 | 134 | 112 |
| 1972....... | 622 | 140 | 117 |
| 1973....... | 614 | 138 | 115 |
| 1974....... | 622 | 140 | 116 |
| 1975....... | 613 | 137 | 114 |
| 1976....... | 605 | 136 | 112 |
| 1977....... | 602 | 135 | 109 |
| 1978....... | 644 | 144 | 115 |
| 1979....... | 705 | 158 | 124 |
| 1980....... | 803 | 180 | 131 |
| 1981....... | 812 | 182 | 129 |
| 1982....... | 836 | 187 | 131 |
| 1983....... | 865 | 194 | 133 |
| 1984....... | 1,034 | 232 | 154 |

NA Data not available

Source: State Statistical Bureau, Statistical Yearbook of China 1984 (1984), p. 460, and China: A Statistical Survey in 1985 (1985), p. 97.

Table 16. Labor Insurance and Welfare Funds Paid by State-Owned Units: Selected Years, 1952 to 1984

| Year | Labor insurance and welfare funds (million yuan) | Percent of total wage bill |
|---|---|---|
| 1952......... | 9.5 | 14.0 |
| 1957......... | 27.9 | 17.9 |
| 1962......... | 28.3 | 13.2 |
| 1978......... | 66.9 | 14.3 |
| 1979......... | 92.1 | 17.4 |
| 1980......... | 116.0 | 18.4 |
| 1981......... | 132.4 | 20.0 |
| 1982......... | 153.8 | 21.7 |
| 1983......... | 179.6 | 24.0 |
| 1984......... | 210.4 | 23.9 |

Source: State Statistical Bureau, Statistical Yearbook of China 1984 (1984), p. 461; and China: A Statistics Survey in 1985 (1985), p. 98.

Table 17. Current and Constant Price Rural Per Capita Income Indicators: 1978, 1983 and 1984

| Indicator | 1978 | 1983 | 1984 | Annual average growth rate (percent) 1978-1983 | 1978-1984 |
|---|---|---|---|---|---|
| Current price net per capita peasant income (yuan)...... | 133.57 | 309.77 | 355.33 | 18.3 | 17.7 |
| Constant price index of net per capita income (1978=100).. | 100.00 | 198.40 | N/A | 14.7 | 15.0 |

NA Data not available

Source: State Statistical Bureau, Statistical Yearbook of China, 1984 (1984), p. 453 and 471; and Li Chengrui, "Economic Reform Brings Better Life," Beijing Review, Vol. 28, No. 29, July 22, 1985, p. 17; and State Statistical Bureau, China: A Statistics Survey in 1985 (1985), p. 102.

Table 18. Annual Net Per Capita Income for Peasants, by Source, (Old Definition): Selected Years, 1949 to 1984 (in Yuan)

| Income by source | 1949 | 1952 | 1954 | 1956 | 1957 | 1965 | 1978 | 1979 | 1980 | 1981 | 1982 | 1983 | 1984 |
|---|---|---|---|---|---|---|---|---|---|---|---|---|---|
| Average net income.......... | 43.80 | 57.00 | 64.14 | 72.92 | 72.95 | 107.20 | 133.57 | 160.17 | 191.33 | 223.44 | 270.11 | 309.77 | 355.33 |
| Income from the collective.. | N/A | N/A | 2.43 | 45.47 | 43.40 | 63.17 | 88.53 | 101.97 | 108.37 | 116.20 | 142.84 | 169.47 | N/A |
| Distributed from basic administrative unit...... | N/A | N/A | N/A | N/A | N/A | N/A | 84.06 | 94.10 | 94.77 | 98.87 | 126.95 | 149.86 | N/A |
| Directly received from commune and brigade enterprises............. | N/A | N/A | N/A | N/A | N/A | N/A | 3.01 | 4.55 | 5.94 | 7.62 | 8.97 | 11.92 | N/A |
| From public welfare funds.................... | N/A | N/A | N/A | N/A | N/A | N/A | .12 | .29 | .30 | .40 | .43 | .74 | N/A |
| From collectively provided awards.......... | N/A | N/A | N/A | N/A | N/A | N/A | .15 | 1.01 | 1.69 | 2.00 | 1.43 | 1.54 | N/A |
| Other income............. | N/A | N/A | N/A | N/A | N/A | N/A | 1.19 | 2.02 | 5.67 | 7.31 | 5.06 | 5.41 | N/A |
| Income from household sideline production........ | N/A | N/A | 56.39 | 17.02 | 21.46 | 33.29 | 35.79 | 44.00 | 62.55 | 84.52 | 102.80 | 112.13 | N/A |
| From farming and forestry products.... | N/A | N/A | N/A | N/A | N/A | N/A | 15.15 | 15.29 | 21.93 | 28.82 | 32.08 | 34.88 | N/A |
| From raising livestock, poultry, and small animals................. | N/A | N/A | N/A | N/A | N/A | N/A | 12.01 | 19.00 | 25.71 | 33.03 | 35.14 | 38.81 | N/A |
| From household handicrafts............. | N/A | N/A | N/A | N/A | N/A | N/A | 1.42 | 1.76 | 2.87 | 3.75 | 4.43 | 5.71 | N/A |
| From gathering, fishing, and hunting..... | N/A | N/A | N/A | N/A | N/A | N/A | 5.19 | 3.90 | 5.80 | 6.16 | 8.43 | 6.88 | N/A |
| Other income............. | N/A | N/A | N/A | N/A | N/A | N/A | 2.02 | 4.05 | 6.24 | 12.76 | 22.72 | 25.85 | N/A |
| From construction, transport, and production labor....... | N/A | N/A | N/A | N/A | N/A | N/A | N/A | N/A | N/A | 10.72 | 18.63 | 20.01 | N/A |
| Commerce, catering, and service income..... | N/A | N/A | N/A | N/A | N/A | N/A | N/A | N/A | N/A | .76 | 2.52 | 3.08 | N/A |
| Other household sideline income........ | N/A | N/A | N/A | N/A | N/A | N/A | N/A | N/A | N/A | 1.28 | 1.57 | 2.76 | N/A |
| Other non-borrowing income.. | N/A | N/A | 5.32 | 10.43 | 8.09 | 10.74 | 9.25 | 14.20 | 20.41 | 22.72 | 24.47 | 28.17 | N/A |

NA Data not available

Note: Other non-borrowing income refers to money in cash and kind remitted by persons working away from home and allowances for living expenses, subsidies for work on public projects, and support for disabled servicemen, or other persons.

Source: Guojia tongji ju, Woguo nongming shenghuo de juda bianhua [State Statistical Bureau, Great Changes in the Lives of China's Peasants] (1984), pp. 57, 60, and 62; and State Statistical Bureau, China: A Statistics Survey in 1985 (1985), p. 102.

Table 19. Annual Net Per Capita Income for Peasants, by Source (New Definition): Selected Years, 1978 to 1984

| Income by source | 1978 | 1983 | 1984 |
|---|---|---|---|
| Total net income (yuan)....... | 133.57 | 309.77 | 355.33 |
| Income from unified management of the collective............ | 88.53 | 36.06 | 35.33 |
| Income from local economic associations...... | .00 | .88 | 2.85 |
| Income from household sideline production........ | 35.79 | 244.66 | 285.44 |
| Other non-borrowing income.. | 9.25 | 28.17 | 31.71 |
| Distribution of all Sources of income (percent).......... | 100.00 | 100.00 | 100.00 |
| Income from unified management of the collective............ | 66.30 | 11.60 | 10.00 |
| Income from local economic associations...... | .00 | .30 | .80 |
| Income from household sideline production........ | 26.80 | 79.00 | 80.30 |
| Other non-borrowing income.. | 6.90 | 9.10 | 8.90 |

NA Data not available

Source: State Statistical Bureau, China: A Statistics Survey in 1985 (1985), p. 102.

Table 20. Annual Net Per Capita Income for Peasants, by Activity: 1978 to 1983

| Activity | 1978 | 1979 | 1980 | 1981 | 1982 | 1983 |
|---|---|---|---|---|---|---|
| Total income (yuan)....... | 133.57 | 160.17 | 191.33 | 223.44 | 270.11 | 309.77 |
| Income from production.. | 122.86 | 142.24 | 166.39 | 194.51 | 237.15 | 272.91 |
| Agricultural production........... | 113.47 | 128.37 | 149.62 | 170.58 | 203.65 | 221.77 |
| Non-agricultural production........... | 9.39 | 13.87 | 16.77 | 23.93 | 33.50 | 51.14 |
| Income from other activities............. | 10.71 | 17.93 | 24.94 | 28.93 | 32.96 | 36.86 |
| Distribution of income by activity (percent).... | 100.00 | 100.00 | 100.00 | 100.00 | 100.00 | 100.00 |
| Income from production.. | 91.98 | 88.81 | 86.96 | 87.05 | 87.80 | 88.10 |
| Agricultural production........... | 84.95 | 80.15 | 78.20 | 76.34 | 75.40 | 71.59 |
| Non-agricultural production........... | 7.03 | 8.66 | 8.76 | 10.71 | 12.40 | 16.51 |
| Income from other activities............. | 8.02 | 11.19 | 13.04 | 12.95 | 12.20 | 11.90 |

Note: Income from agricultural production refers to net income from farming, forestry animal husbandry, sideline occupations, and fisheries. Income from non-agricultural production refers to net income from work in rural industry, construction, transport, commerce, and catering. Income from other activities includes cash income and income in kind from persons working away from home, income received from the collective accumulation and public welfare funds, and income from the state budget.

Source: Guojia tongji ju, Woguo nongmin shenghuo de juda bianhua [State Statistical Bureau, Great Changes in the Lives of China's Peasants] (1984), p. 59.

Table 21. Annual Net Per Capita Income for Peasants, Cash and in Kind: 1978 to 1983 (in yuan)

| Income | 1978 | 1979 | 1980 | 1981 | 1982 | 1983 |
|---|---|---|---|---|---|---|
| Total income.................. | 133.57 | 160.17 | 191.33 | 223.44 | 270.11 | 309.77 |
| Income in kind............. | 69.69 | 75.66 | 78.21 | 70.23 | 85.63 | 95.05 |
| Cash income................. | 63.88 | 84.51 | 113.12 | 153.21 | 184.48 | 214.72 |
| From collective activities.............. | 25.53 | 32.29 | 36.45 | 42.00 | 46.43 | 37.82 |
| From sale of household sideline products........ | 26.73 | 35.41 | 48.61 | 69.80 | 89.15 | 119.11 |
| From construction, transport, and production services...... | 2.98 | 4.92 | 8.77 | 16.51 | 19.85 | 25.54 |
| From commerce, catering other services........... | .00 | .00 | .00 | .72 | 2.49 | 4.15 |
| Other non borrowing income.................. | 8.64 | 11.89 | 19.29 | 24.18 | 26.56 | 28.10 |

Source: Guojia tongjiju, Woguo nongmin shenghuo de juda bianhua [State Statistical Bureau, Great Changes in the Lives of China's Peasants] (1984), pp. 59 and 65.

Table 22. Distribution of Annual Net Income Per Capita for Peasant Households, By Income Group: 1978 to 1983 (In percent)

| Income group | 1978 | 1979 | 1980 | 1981 | 1982 | 1983 |
|---|---|---|---|---|---|---|
| 100 Yuan or less... | 33.3 | 19.3 | 9.8 | 4.7 | 2.7 | 1.4 |
| 100 - 150 Yuan..... | 31.7 | 24.2 | 24.7 | 14.9 | 8.1 | 6.2 |
| 150 - 200 Yuan..... | 17.6 | 29.0 | 27.1 | 23.0 | 16.0 | 13.1 |
| 200 - 300 Yuan..... | 15.0 | 20.4 | 25.3 | 34.8 | 37.0 | 32.9 |
| 300 - 400 Yuan..... | 2.4 | 5.0 | 8.6 | 14.4 | 20.8 | 22.9 |
| 400 - 500 Yuan..... | | 1.5 | 2.9 | 5.0 | 8.7 | 11.6 |
| 500 Yuan or more... | | .6 | 1.6 | 3.2 | 6.7 | 11.9 |

Source: Guojia tongji ju, Guanghui de sanshiwu nian 1949-1984 [State Statistical Bureau, Thirty Five Glorious Years 1949-1984] (1984), p. 171.

Table 23. Annual Per Capita Living Expenditure for Urban Staff and Workers: Selected Years, 1957 to 1984
(In yuan)

| Item | 1957 | 1964 | 1978 | 1981 | 1982 | 1983 | 1984 |
|---|---|---|---|---|---|---|---|
| Total living expenditure..... | 222.00 | 220.68 | 311.16 | 456.84 | 471.00 | 505.92 | 559.44 |
| Expenditure on commodities.............. | 190.68 | 188.40 | 279.60 | 420.36 | 432.12 | 464.04 | 514.32 |
| Food.................... | 129.72 | 130.68 | 178.92 | 258.84 | 276.24 | 299.52 | 324.24 |
| Grain................. | 50.52 | 49.44 | N/A | 59.16 | 60.72 | 61.56 | 63.12 |
| Non-staple food........ | 59.52 | 62.16 | N/A | 140.28 | 150.96 | 166.08 | 180.96 |
| Tobacco, liquors, and tea.............. | 8.88 | 7.80 | N/A | 23.16 | 24.84 | 26.76 | 30.36 |
| Other foods............ | 10.80 | 11.28 | N/A | 36.24 | 39.72 | 45.12 | 49.80 |
| Clothing................. | 26.64 | 24.24 | 42.24 | 67.56 | 67.68 | 73.56 | 86.88 |
| Articles for daily use... | 16.92 | 13.20 | 26.16 | 43.68 | 43.44 | 45.72 | 50.64 |
| Articles for cultural life and recreation..... | | 2.40 | | 25.92 | 21.72 | 20.76 | 24.60 |
| Books, newspapers, and magazines.......... | 1.32 | 2.52 | 16.08 | 4.32 | 4.20 | 4.92 | 5.88 |
| Medical products......... | 4.08 | 4.08 | 3.12 | 2.76 | 2.88 | 3.12 | 3.36 |
| Fuels.................... | 8.64 | 9.36 | 8.40 | 8.88 | 8.76 | 8.76 | 9.24 |
| Construction materials... | | | | | 2.04 | 2.40 | 2.88 |
| Other commodities........ | 3.36 | 1.92 | 4.68 | 8.40 | 5.16 | 5.28 | 6.60 |
| Non-commodity expenditure.............. | 31.32 | 32.28 | 31.56 | 36.48 | 38.88 | 41.88 | 45.12 |
| Rent..................... | 5.16 | 5.76 | 6.00 | 6.36 | 7.08 | 7.68 | 7.80 |
| Water and power.......... | 3.24 | 3.84 | 4.20 | 4.44 | 5.04 | 5.76 | 6.24 |
| Child care............... | 2.88 | 3.48 | N/A | 2.76 | 2.76 | 2.40 | 2.52 |
| Transportation........... | | | | 6.12 | 6.60 | 6.96 | 7.56 |
| Post and tele-communications.......... | 5.28 | 3.84 | 5.20 | .48 | .60 | .60 | .72 |
| School fees.............. | 1.44 | 2.76 | | 2.64 | 2.76 | 3.24 | 4.44 |
| Cultural life and recreation.............. | 2.40 | 1.56 | 4.68 | 2.88 | 2.40 | 2.28 | 2.16 |
| Gas...................... | | | | | .96 | .96 | .84 |
| Services and repairs.... | | | | | 5.76 | 6.72 | 7.32 |
| Medical treatment........ | 10.92 | 11.04 | 11.48 | 10.80 | 1.56 | 1.68 | 1.56 |
| Other non-commodity...... | | | | | 3.36 | 3.60 | 3.96 |

NA Data not available

Source: Li Chengrui, "Economic Reform Brings Better Life," Beijing Review, No. 29, July 22, 1985, p. 18; State Statistical Bureau, Statistical Yearbook of China 1984 (1984), p. 463; and China: A Statistics Survey in 1985 (1985), p. 100.

Table 24. Distribution of Annual Per Capita Living Expenditure for Urban Staff and Workers: Selected Years, 1957 to 1984
(In percent)

| Item | 1957 | 1964 | 1978 | 1981 | 1982 | 1983 | 1984 |
|---|---|---|---|---|---|---|---|
| Total living expenditure..... | 100.00 | 100.00 | 100.00 | 100.00 | 100.00 | 100.00 | 100.00 |
| Expenditure on commodities.............. | 85.89 | 85.37 | 89.86 | 92.01 | 91.75 | 91.72 | 91.93 |
| Food..................... | 58.43 | 59.22 | 57.50 | 56.66 | 58.65 | 59.20 | 57.96 |
| Grain.................. | 22.76 | 22.40 | N/A | 12.95 | 12.89 | 12.17 | 11.28 |
| Non-staple food........ | 26.81 | 28.17 | N/A | 30.71 | 32.05 | 32.83 | 32.35 |
| Tobacco, liquors, and tea.............. | 4.00 | 3.53 | N/A | 5.07 | 5.27 | 5.29 | 5.43 |
| Other foods............ | 4.86 | 5.11 | N/A | 7.93 | 8.43 | 8.92 | 8.90 |
| Clothing................. | 12.00 | 10.98 | 13.58 | 14.79 | 14.37 | 14.54 | 15.53 |
| Articles for daily use... | { 7.62 | 5.98 | 8.41 | 9.56 | 9.22 | 9.04 | 9.05 |
| Articles for cultural life and recreation..... | | 1.09 | | 5.67 | 4.61 | 4.10 | 4.40 |
| Books, newspapers, and magazines........... | .59 | 1.14 | { 5.17 | .95 | .89 | .97 | 1.05 |
| Medical products......... | 1.84 | 1.85 | 1.00 | .60 | .61 | .62 | .60 |
| Fuels.................... | 3.89 | 4.24 | 2.70 | 1.94 | 1.86 | 1.73 | 1.65 |
| Construction materials... | | | | | .43 | .47 | .51 |
| Other commodities........ | { 1.52 | { .87 | { 1.50 | { 1.84 | 1.10 | 1.04 | 1.18 |
| Non-commodity expenditure.............. | 14.11 | 14.63 | 10.14 | 7.99 | 8.25 | 8.28 | 8.07 |
| Rent..................... | 2.32 | 2.61 | 1.93 | 1.39 | 1.50 | 1.52 | 1.39 |
| Water and power.......... | 1.46 | 1.74 | 1.35 | .97 | 1.07 | 1.14 | 1.12 |
| Child care............... | 1.30 | 1.58 | N/A | .60 | .59 | .47 | .45 |
| Transportation........... | | | | 1.34 | 1.40 | 1.38 | 1.35 |
| Post and tele-communications........... | { 2.38 | { 1.74 | { 1.67 | .11 | .13 | .12 | .13 |
| School fees.............. | .65 | 1.25 | | .58 | .59 | .64 | .79 |
| Cultural life and recreation.............. | 1.08 | .71 | { 1.50 | .63 | .51 | .45 | .39 |
| Gas...................... | N/A | N/A | N/A | N/A | .20 | .19 | .15 |
| Services and repairs..... | | | | | 1.22 | 1.33 | 1.31 |
| Medical treatment........ | { 4.92 | { 5.00 | { 3.69 | { 2.37 | .33 | .33 | .28 |
| Other non-commodity...... | | | | | .71 | .71 | .71 |

NA Data not available

Note: Percent distribution of per capita living expenditures were derived by dividing the components of living expenditures by the total living expenditure for each year, multiplied by 100.

Source: Li Chengrui, "Economic Reform Brings Better Life," Beijing Review, No. 29, July 22, 1985, p. 18. State Statistical Bureau, Statistical Yearbook of China 1984 (1984), p. 463; and China: A Statistics Survey in 1985 (1985), p. 100.

Table 25. Per Capita Urban Worker and Staff Living Expenditures, by Income Group: 1982
(In yuan)

| Type of expenditure | Average | Per Capita Monthly Income Group (in Yuan) 20 and below | 20.01-25.00 | 25.01-35.00 | 35.01-50.00 | 50.01-60.00 | 60.01 and above |
|---|---|---|---|---|---|---|---|
| Total living expenditure...... | 471.00 | 227.64 | 269.04 | 362.04 | 473.52 | 598.92 | 742.08 |
| Expenditure on commodities.. | 432.12 | 209.28 | 244.44 | 330.84 | 434.52 | 552.36 | 681.12 |
| Food..................... | 276.24 | 143.64 | 171.96 | 220.32 | 277.44 | 340.20 | 409.68 |
| Grain.................. | 60.72 | 52.56 | 51.84 | 55.20 | 60.96 | 67.32 | 76.92 |
| Non-staple food......... | 150.96 | 66.72 | 88.08 | 119.40 | 150.60 | 188.16 | 227.16 |
| Tobacco, liquors, tea... | 24.84 | 12.84 | 14.52 | 17.40 | 24.60 | 34.20 | 41.64 |
| Other foods............ | 39.72 | 11.52 | 17.52 | 28.32 | 41.28 | 50.52 | 63.96 |
| Clothing................. | 67.68 | 29.28 | 33.24 | 48.72 | 68.64 | 93.00 | 115.92 |
| Articles for daily use.... | 43.44 | 11.64 | 16.08 | 27.00 | 42.24 | 64.32 | 84.00 |
| Articles for cultural life and recreation...... | 21.72 | 7.08 | 9.12 | 15.00 | 23.52 | 26.28 | 34.68 |
| Books, newspapers, and magazines................ | 4.20 | 2.04 | 2.40 | 3.72 | 4.20 | 4.80 | 6.72 |
| Medicine and medical articles................ | 2.88 | 4.80 | 2.04 | 2.76 | 2.64 | 2.76 | 3.60 |
| Fuel..................... | 8.76 | 8.04 | 6.84 | 8.04 | 8.76 | 9.96 | 11.52 |
| Construction materials and other commodities........ | 7.20 | 2.76 | 2.76 | 5.28 | 7.08 | 11.04 | 15.00 |
| Expenditure on non-commodities........... | 38.88 | 18.36 | 24.60 | 31.20 | 39.00 | 46.56 | 60.96 |
| Rent..................... | 7.08 | 2.76 | 4.80 | 5.64 | 6.96 | 9.12 | 11.40 |
| Water and power........... | 5.04 | 3.00 | 3.48 | 4.20 | 4.92 | 6.00 | 7.56 |
| School fees............... | 2.76 | 3.36 | 3.12 | 3.60 | 2.76 | 1.68 | 1.20 |
| Child care............... | 2.76 | .48 | 1.68 | 2.52 | 3.24 | 1.80 | 1.20 |
| Transportation............ | 6.60 | 3.48 | 3.36 | 4.56 | 6.48 | 8.88 | 11.04 |
| Posts and tele-communication............ | .60 | .24 | .24 | .36 | .48 | .96 | 1.44 |
| Cultural life and recreation.............. | 2.40 | .96 | 1.32 | 1.80 | 2.40 | 3.00 | 3.72 |
| Other services............ | 11.64 | 4.08 | 6.60 | 8.52 | 11.76 | 15.12 | 23.40 |

Note: Other services includes gas, services and repairs, medical treatment, and other noncommodity expenses.

Source: State Statistical Bureau, Statistical Yearbook of China 1983 (1983), p. 494.

Table 26. Distribution of Per Capita Urban Worker and Staff Living Expenditures, by Income Group: 1982 (In percent)

| Type of expenditure | | Per Capita Monthly Income Group (in Yuan) | | | | | |
|---|---|---|---|---|---|---|---|
| | Average | 20 and below | 20.01-25.00 | 25.01-35.00 | 35.01-50.00 | 50.01-60.00 | 60.01 and above |
| Total living expenditure...... | 100.00 | 100.00 | 100.00 | 100.00 | 100.00 | 100.00 | 100.00 |
| Expenditure on commodities.. | 91.75 | 91.93 | 90.86 | 91.38 | 91.76 | 92.23 | 91.79 |
| Food..................... | 58.65 | 63.10 | 63.92 | 60.86 | 58.59 | 56.81 | 55.21 |
| Grain.................. | 12.89 | 23.09 | 19.27 | 15.25 | 12.87 | 11.24 | 10.37 |
| Non-staple food......... | 32.05 | 29.31 | 32.74 | 32.98 | 31.80 | 31.42 | 30.61 |
| Tobacco, liquors, tea... | 5.27 | 5.64 | 5.40 | 4.81 | 5.20 | 5.71 | 5.61 |
| Other foods............ | 8.44 | 5.06 | 6.51 | 7.82 | 8.72 | 8.44 | 8.62 |
| Clothing................. | 14.37 | 12.86 | 12.36 | 13.46 | 14.50 | 15.53 | 15.62 |
| Articles for daily use.... | 9.22 | 5.11 | 5.98 | 7.46 | 8.92 | 10.74 | 11.32 |
| Articles for cultural life and recreation...... | 4.61 | 3.11 | 3.39 | 4.14 | 4.97 | 4.39 | 4.67 |
| Books, newspapers, and magazines............... | .89 | .90 | .89 | 1.03 | .89 | .80 | .91 |
| Medicine and medical articles................ | .61 | 2.11 | .76 | .76 | .56 | .46 | .49 |
| Fuel..................... | 1.86 | 3.53 | 2.54 | 2.22 | 1.85 | 1.66 | 1.55 |
| Construction materials and other commodities........ | 1.53 | 1.21 | 1.03 | 1.45 | 1.50 | 1.84 | 2.02 |
| Expenditure on non-commodities........... | 8.25 | 8.07 | 9.14 | 8.62 | 8.24 | 7.77 | 8.21 |
| Rent..................... | 1.50 | 1.21 | 1.78 | 1.56 | 1.47 | 1.52 | 1.54 |
| Water and power.......... | 1.07 | 1.32 | 1.29 | 1.16 | 1.04 | 1.00 | 1.02 |
| School fees.............. | .59 | 1.48 | 1.16 | .99 | .58 | .28 | .16 |
| Child care............... | .59 | .21 | .62 | .70 | .68 | .30 | .16 |
| Transportation........... | 1.40 | 1.53 | 1.25 | 1.26 | 1.37 | 1.48 | 1.49 |
| Posts and tele-communication............ | .13 | .11 | .09 | .10 | .10 | .16 | .19 |
| Cultural life and recreation.............. | .51 | .42 | .49 | .50 | .51 | .50 | .50 |
| Other services........... | 2.47 | 1.79 | 2.45 | 2.35 | 2.48 | 2.52 | 3.15 |

Note: Other services includes gas, services and repairs, medical treatment, and other noncommodity expenses. Components may not add to totals due to rounding.

Source: State Statistical Bureau, Statistical Yearbook of China 1983 (1983), p. 494.

Table 27. Per Capita Urban Worker and Staff Living Expenditures, by Income Group: 1983 (In Yuan)

| Type of expenditure | | Per Capita Monthly Income Group (in Yuan) | | | | | |
|---|---|---|---|---|---|---|---|
| | Average | 20 and below | 20.01-25.00 | 25.01-35.00 | 35.01-50.00 | 50.01-60.00 | 60.01 and above |
| Total living expenditure...... | 505.92 | 230.16 | 282.00 | 371.76 | 487.08 | 614.04 | 759.60 |
| Expenditure on commodities.. | 464.04 | 210.24 | 259.08 | 340.68 | 447.00 | 564.48 | 696.60 |
| Food...................... | 299.52 | 142.08 | 178.92 | 227.16 | 290.64 | 355.80 | 432.60 |
| Grain.................... | 61.56 | 45.12 | 54.00 | 56.28 | 61.20 | 66.48 | 71.04 |
| Non-staple food......... | 166.08 | 71.28 | 90.24 | 120.72 | 159.12 | 200.64 | 252.96 |
| Tobacco, liquors, tea... | 26.76 | 10.92 | 14.64 | 19.32 | 25.92 | 32.40 | 40.92 |
| Other foods............ | 45.12 | 14.76 | 20.04 | 30.84 | 44.40 | 56.28 | 67.68 |
| Clothing................. | 73.56 | 34.08 | 38.28 | 52.80 | 71.52 | 92.16 | 107.52 |
| Articles for daily use.... | 45.72 | 13.68 | 19.44 | 28.44 | 42.72 | 59.16 | 81.60 |
| Articles for cultural life and recreation...... | 20.76 | 3.96 | 6.48 | 12.96 | 19.08 | 28.68 | 38.40 |
| Books, newspapers, and magazines................ | 4.92 | 2.52 | 3.36 | 3.84 | 4.80 | 5.88 | 6.84 |
| Medicine and medical products................ | 3.12 | 4.44 | 2.04 | 2.28 | 2.88 | 3.60 | 4.80 |
| Fuel..................... | 8.76 | 7.20 | 7.20 | 7.92 | 8.76 | 9.12 | 10.44 |
| Construction materials and other commodities........ | 7.68 | 2.28 | 3.36 | 5.28 | 6.60 | 10.08 | 14.40 |
| Expenditure on non-commodities............ | 41.88 | 19.92 | 22.92 | 31.08 | 40.08 | 49.56 | 63.00 |
| Rent...................... | 7.68 | 3.12 | 3.96 | 5.64 | 7.32 | 9.00 | 11.64 |
| Water and power........... | 5.76 | 2.64 | 3.48 | 4.20 | 5.16 | 6.60 | 9.96 |
| School fees............... | 3.24 | 3.48 | 3.60 | 3.96 | 3.48 | 2.64 | 2.04 |
| Child care................ | 2.40 | 2.52 | 1.80 | 2.04 | 2.76 | 2.64 | 2.04 |
| Transportation............ | 6.96 | 2.16 | 2.52 | 4.08 | 6.36 | 9.24 | 11.64 |
| Posts and tele-communications........... | .60 | .24 | .24 | .36 | .60 | .84 | 1.20 |
| Cultural life and recreation.............. | 2.28 | .72 | .96 | 1.68 | 2.16 | 2.64 | 3.36 |
| Other services............ | 12.96 | 5.04 | 6.36 | 9.12 | 12.24 | 15.96 | 21.12 |

Note: Other services includes gas, services and repairs, medical treatment, and other noncommodity expenses.

Source: State Statistical Bureau, Statistical Yearbook of China 1984 (1984), p. 467.

Table 28. Distribution of Per Capita Urban Worker and Staff Living Expenditures, by Income Group: 1983 (In percent)

| Type of expenditure | Per Capita Monthly Income Group (in Yuan) | | | | | | |
|---|---|---|---|---|---|---|---|
| | Average | 20 and below | 20.01-25.00 | 25.01-35.00 | 35.01-50.00 | 50.01-60.00 | 60.01 and above |
| Total living expenditure...... | 100.00 | 100.00 | 100.00 | 100.00 | 100.00 | 100.00 | 100.00 |
| Expenditure on commodities.. | 91.72 | 91.35 | 91.87 | 91.64 | 91.77 | 91.93 | 91.71 |
| Food...................... | 59.20 | 61.73 | 63.45 | 61.10 | 59.67 | 57.94 | 56.95 |
| Grain................. | 12.17 | 19.60 | 19.15 | 15.14 | 12.56 | 10.83 | 9.35 |
| Non-staple food......... | 32.83 | 30.97 | 32.00 | 32.47 | 32.67 | 32.68 | 33.30 |
| Tobacco, liquors, tea... | 5.29 | 4.74 | 5.19 | 5.20 | 5.32 | 5.28 | 5.39 |
| Other foods............ | 8.92 | 6.41 | 7.11 | 8.30 | 9.12 | 9.17 | 8.91 |
| Clothing................. | 14.54 | 14.81 | 13.57 | 14.20 | 14.68 | 15.01 | 14.15 |
| Articles for daily use.... | 9.04 | 5.94 | 6.89 | 7.65 | 8.77 | 9.63 | 10.74 |
| Articles for cultural life and recreation........... | 4.10 | 1.72 | 2.30 | 3.49 | 3.92 | 4.67 | 5.06 |
| Books, newspapers, and magazines................ | .97 | 1.09 | 1.19 | 1.03 | .99 | .96 | .90 |
| Medicine and medical products................. | .62 | 1.93 | .72 | .61 | .59 | .59 | .63 |
| Fuel...................... | 1.73 | 3.13 | 2.55 | 2.13 | 1.80 | 1.49 | 1.37 |
| Construction materials and other commodities......... | 1.52 | .99 | 1.19 | 1.42 | 1.36 | 1.64 | 1.90 |
| Expenditure on non-commodities........... | 8.28 | 8.65 | 8.13 | 8.36 | 8.23 | 8.07 | 8.29 |
| Rent...................... | 1.52 | 1.36 | 1.40 | 1.52 | 1.50 | 1.47 | 1.53 |
| Water and power........... | 1.14 | 1.15 | 1.23 | 1.13 | 1.06 | 1.07 | 1.31 |
| School fees............... | .64 | 1.51 | 1.28 | 1.07 | .71 | .43 | .27 |
| Child care................ | .47 | 1.09 | .64 | .55 | .57 | .43 | .27 |
| Transportation............ | 1.38 | .94 | .89 | 1.10 | 1.31 | 1.50 | 1.53 |
| Posts and tele-communication............ | .12 | .10 | .09 | .10 | .12 | .14 | .16 |
| Cultural life and recreation............... | .45 | .31 | .34 | .45 | .44 | .43 | .44 |
| Other services............ | 2.56 | 2.19 | 2.26 | 2.45 | 2.51 | 2.60 | 2.78 |

Note: Other services includes gas, services and repairs, medical treatment, and other noncommodity expenses. Components may not add to totals due to rounding.

Source: State Statistical Bureau, Statistical Yearbook of China 1984 (1984), p. 467.

Table 29. Annual Per Capita Total Living Expenditure for Peasants: Selected Years, 1954 to 1984
(In Yuan)

| Item | 1954 | 1956 | 1957 | 1965 | 1978 | 1979 | 1980 | 1981 | 1982 | 1983 | 1984 |
|---|---|---|---|---|---|---|---|---|---|---|---|
| Total living expenditure.... | 59.57 | 66.63 | 70.86 | 95.11 | 116.06 | 134.51 | 162.21 | 190.81 | 220.23 | 248.29 | 273.80 |
| Expenditures on commodities............. | 57.95 | 64.88 | 69.63 | 92.53 | 112.90 | 130.81 | 157.95 | 186.17 | 215.30 | 242.81 | 267.27 |
| Food................... | 40.86 | 45.40 | 46.59 | 65.11 | 78.59 | 86.03 | 100.19 | 113.83 | 133.20 | 147.24 | 161.52 |
| Staple foods.......... | NA | NA | NA | NA | 51.33 | 55.36 | 60.56 | 61.07 | 70.74 | 75.04 | NA |
| Non-staple food....... | NA | NA | NA | NA | 24.67 | 27.86 | 35.27 | 41.50 | 47.85 | 53.69 | NA |
| Other food and outside meals........ | NA | NA | NA | NA | 2.59 | 2.81 | 4.36 | 11.26 | 14.61 | 18.51 | NA |
| Other food......... | NA | NA | NA | NA | NA | NA | NA | NA | NA | 15.81 | NA |
| Outside meals...... | NA | NA | NA | NA | NA | NA | NA | NA | NA | 2.70 | NA |
| Clothes................. | 7.79 | 8.84 | 9.52 | 10.00 | 14.74 | 17.64 | 19.99 | 23.57 | 24.77 | 27.65 | 28.33 |
| Fuel.................... | 3.92 | 5.01 | 7.11 | 7.90 | 8.28 | 8.34 | 9.66 | 10.59 | 12.36 | 13.47 | 15.04 |
| Housing................. | 1.23 | 1.35 | 1.49 | 2.69 | 3.67 | 7.66 | 12.80 | 18.67 | 22.58 | 27.56 | 32.12 |
| Daily articles and others................ | 4.15 | 4.28 | 4.92 | 6.83 | 7.62 | 11.14 | 15.31 | 19.51 | 22.39 | 26.89 | 30.26 |
| Daily articles........ | NA | NA | NA | NA | NA | NA | NA | NA | NA | 18.43 | NA |
| Cultural and recreational goods... | NA | NA | NA | NA | NA | NA | NA | NA | NA | 2.17 | NA |
| Books, newspapers and periodicals...... | NA | NA | NA | NA | NA | NA | NA | NA | NA | 0.81 | NA |
| Medical and health products...... | NA | NA | NA | NA | NA | NA | NA | NA | NA | 3.65 | NA |
| Other................. | NA | NA | NA | NA | NA | NA | NA | NA | NA | 1.83 | NA |
| Costs for cultural activities and services.. | 1.62 | 1.75 | 1.23 | 2.58 | 3.16 | 3.70 | 4.26 | 4.64 | 4.93 | 5.48 | 6.53 |

NA Data not available

Source: Guojia tongji ju, Woguo nongmin shenghuo de juda bianhua [State Statistical Bureau, Great Changes in the Lives of China's Peasants] (1984), pp. 67, 69, and 72-74; and China: A Statistics Survey in 1985 (1985), p. 103.

Table 30. Distribution of Annual Per Capita Total Living Expenditure for Peasants: Selected Years, 1954 to 1984 (In percent)

| Item | 1954 | 1956 | 1957 | 1965 | 1978 | 1979 | 1980 | 1981 | 1982 | 1983 | 1984 |
|---|---|---|---|---|---|---|---|---|---|---|---|
| Total living expenditure.... | 100.00 | 100.00 | 100.00 | 100.00 | 100.00 | 100.00 | 100.00 | 100.00 | 100.00 | 100.00 | 100.00 |
| Expenditures on commodities............. | 97.28 | 97.37 | 98.26 | 97.29 | 97.28 | 97.25 | 97.37 | 97.57 | 97.76 | 97.79 | 97.62 |
| Food.................. | 68.59 | 68.14 | 65.75 | 68.46 | 67.71 | 63.96 | 61.77 | 59.66 | 60.48 | 59.30 | 58.99 |
| Staple foods.......... | N/A | N/A | N/A | N/A | 44.23 | 41.16 | 37.33 | 32.01 | 32.12 | 30.22 | N/A |
| Non-staple food....... | N/A | N/A | N/A | N/A | 21.26 | 20.71 | 21.74 | 21.75 | 21.73 | 21.62 | N/A |
| Other food and outside meals........ | N/A | N/A | N/A | N/A | 2.23 | 2.09 | 2.69 | 5.90 | 6.63 | 7.45 | N/A |
| Other food......... | N/A | N/A | N/A | N/A | N/A | N/A | N/A | N/A | N/A | 6.37 | N/A |
| Outside meals...... | N/A | N/A | N/A | N/A | N/A | N/A | N/A | N/A | N/A | 1.09 | N/A |
| Clothes................ | 13.08 | 13.27 | 13.43 | 10.51 | 12.70 | 13.11 | 12.32 | 12.35 | 11.25 | 11.14 | 10.35 |
| Fuel................... | 6.58 | 7.52 | 10.03 | 8.31 | 7.13 | 6.20 | 5.96 | 5.55 | 5.61 | 5.43 | 5.49 |
| Housing................ | 2.06 | 2.03 | 2.10 | 2.83 | 3.16 | 5.69 | 7.89 | 9.78 | 10.25 | 11.10 | 11.73 |
| Daily articles and others | 6.97 | 6.42 | 6.94 | 7.18 | 6.57 | 8.28 | 9.44 | 10.22 | 10.17 | 10.83 | 11.05 |
| Daily articles....... | N/A | N/A | N/A | N/A | N/A | N/A | N/A | N/A | N/A | 7.42 | N/A |
| Cultural and recre-ational goods...... | N/A | N/A | N/A | N/A | N/A | N/A | N/A | N/A | N/A | .87 | N/A |
| Books, newspapers and periodicals..... | N/A | N/A | N/A | N/A | N/A | N/A | N/A | N/A | N/A | .33 | N/A |
| Medical and health products..... | N/A | N/A | N/A | N/A | N/A | N/A | N/A | N/A | N/A | 1.47 | N/A |
| Other............... | N/A | N/A | N/A | N/A | NA | N/A | N/A | N/A | N/A | .74 | N/A |
| Costs for cultural activities and services.. | 2.72 | 2.63 | 1.74 | 2.71 | 2.72 | 2.75 | 2.63 | 2.43 | 2.24 | 2.21 | 2.38 |

NA Data not available

Note: Percent distribution of per capita living expenditures were derived by dividing the components of living expenditure by the total living expenditure for each year, and multiplying it by 100.

Source: Guojia tongji ju, Woguo nongmin shenghuo de juda bianhua [State Statistical Bureau, Great Changes in the Lives of China's Peasants] (1984), pp. 67, 69, and 72-74; and China: A Statistics Survey in 1985 (1985), p. 103.

Table 31. Percent of Goods Purchased to Total Per Capita Consumption, for Peasants: 1978 to 1984

| Item | 1978 | 1979 | 1980 | 1981 | 1982 | 1983 | 1984 |
|---|---|---|---|---|---|---|---|
| Living expenditure........ | 39.7 | 44.5 | 50.4 | 56.1 | 56.5 | 58.8 | 58.6 |
| Food............. | 24.1 | 25.8 | 31.1 | 36.6 | 38.0 | 40.2 | 39.7 |
| Clothes........... | 89.0 | 91.6 | 98.1 | 98.6 | 98.4 | 98.2 | 97.7 |
| Fuel.............. | 31.9 | 32.4 | 28.7 | 25.1 | 22.7 | 22.4 | 22.1 |
| Housing........... | 95.1 | 95.6 | 88.8 | 94.2 | 96.1 | 97.8 | 98.3 |
| Daily articles and others....... | 87.7 | 88.9 | 96.3 | 98.2 | 98.7 | 99.0 | 99.3 |

Source: State Statistical Bureau, Statistical Yearbook of China 1983 (1983), p. 501; and China: A Statistics Survey in 1985 (1985), p. 103.

Table 32. Annual Per Capita Expenditure for Peasants: Purchased Expenditures and Self-Provided Expenses: 1978 to 1984 (In Yuan)

| Commodity | 1978 | 1979 | 1980 | 1981 | 1982 | 1983 | 1984 |
|---|---|---|---|---|---|---|---|
| Food.................... | 78.59 | 86.03 | 100.19 | 113.83 | 133.20 | 147.24 | 161.52 |
| Self-provided......... | 59.68 | 63.86 | 69.06 | 72.13 | 82.59 | 88.10 | 97.40 |
| Purchased............. | 18.91 | 22.17 | 31.13 | 41.70 | 50.61 | 59.14 | 64.12 |
| Percent purchased...... | 24.06 | 25.77 | 31.07 | 36.63 | 38.00 | 40.17 | 39.70 |
| Clothing................ | 14.74 | 17.64 | 19.99 | 23.57 | 24.77 | 27.65 | 28.33 |
| Self-provided......... | 1.62 | 1.48 | .38 | .32 | .41 | .51 | .65 |
| Purchased............. | 13.12 | 16.16 | 19.61 | 23.25 | 24.36 | 27.14 | 27.68 |
| Percent purchased...... | 89.01 | 91.61 | 98.10 | 98.64 | 98.34 | 98.16 | 97.70 |
| Fuel.................... | 8.28 | 8.34 | 9.66 | 10.59 | 12.36 | 13.47 | 15.04 |
| Self-provided......... | 5.64 | 5.64 | 6.89 | 7.93 | 9.56 | 10.46 | 11.72 |
| Purchased............. | 2.64 | 2.70 | 2.77 | 2.66 | 2.80 | 3.01 | 3.32 |
| Percent purchased...... | 31.88 | 32.37 | 28.67 | 25.12 | 22.65 | 22.35 | 22.10 |
| Housing................. | 3.67 | 7.66 | 12.80 | 18.67 | 22.58 | 27.56 | 32.12 |
| Self-provided......... | .18 | .34 | 1.44 | 1.08 | .88 | .61 | .55 |
| Purchased............. | 3.49 | 7.32 | 11.36 | 17.59 | 21.70 | 26.95 | 31.57 |
| Percent purchased...... | 95.10 | 95.56 | 88.75 | 94.22 | 96.10 | 97.79 | 98.30 |
| Articles for daily life, and other.............. | 7.62 | 11.14 | 15.31 | 19.51 | 22.39 | 26.89 | 30.26 |
| Self-provided......... | .94 | 1.24 | .56 | .36 | .29 | .26 | .21 |
| Purchased............. | 6.68 | 9.90 | 14.75 | 19.15 | 22.10 | 26.63 | 30.05 |
| Percent purchased...... | 87.66 | 88.87 | 96.34 | 98.15 | 98.70 | 99.03 | 99.30 |

Note: The components of expenditure for 1984 were reconstructed using data from tables 29 and 31.

Source: Guojia tongji ju, Woguo nongmin shenghuo de juda bianhua [State Statistical Bureau, Great Changes in the Lives of China's Peasants] (1984), pp. 67 and 70; and State Statistical Bureau, China: A Statistics Survey in 1985 (1985), p. 103.

Table 33. Purchased and Self-Produced Consumption Per Capita, for Peasants: 1983

| Item | Total (in yuan) | Purchased (in yuan) | Self-produced (in yuan) | Purchased as a percent of total |
|---|---|---|---|---|
| Total living expenditure.... | 248.29 | 148.30 | 99.99 | 59.73 |
| Expenditures on commodities............. | 242.81 | 142.87 | 99.94 | 58.84 |
| Food.................... | 147.24 | 59.14 | 88.10 | 40.17 |
| Staple foods.......... | 75.04 | 11.97 | 63.07 | 15.95 |
| Non-staple food....... | 53.69 | 29.84 | 23.85 | 55.58 |
| Other food and outside meals........ | 18.51 | 17.33 | 1.18 | 93.63 |
| Other food......... | 15.81 | 14.63 | 1.18 | 92.54 |
| Outside meals...... | 2.70 | 2.70 | .00 | 100.00 |
| Clothes................. | 27.65 | 27.14 | .51 | 98.16 |
| Fuel.................... | 13.47 | 3.01 | 10.46 | 22.35 |
| Housing................. | 27.56 | 26.95 | .61 | 97.79 |
| Daily articles and others................ | 26.89 | 26.63 | .26 | 99.03 |
| Daily articles........ | 18.43 | 18.27 | .16 | 99.13 |
| Cultural and recreational goods... | 2.17 | 2.16 | .01 | 99.54 |
| Books, newspapers and periodicals...... | .81 | .81 | .00 | 100.00 |
| Medical and health products...... | 3.65 | 3.63 | .02 | 99.45 |
| Other................. | 1.83 | 1.76 | .07 | 96.17 |
| Costs for cultural activities and services.. | 5.48 | 5.43 | .05 | 99.09 |

Source: Guojia tongji ju, Woguo nongmin shenghuo de juda bianhua [State Statistical Bureau, Great Changes in the Lives of China's Peasants] (1984), pp. 72-74, and 78-80.

Table 34. Average Annual Consumption Per Capita, in Current and Constant Prices, by Residence: 1952 to 1984
(In yuan)

| Year | Consumption (in current prices) | | | Consumption Index (1952=100 in constant prices) | | |
|---|---|---|---|---|---|---|
| | All residents | Agri-cultural | Non agri-cultural | All Residents | Agri-cultural | Non agri-cultural |
| 1952........ | 76 | 62 | 148 | 100.0 | 100.0 | 100.0 |
| 1953........ | 87 | 69 | 181 | 107.7 | 103.2 | 115.0 |
| 1954........ | 89 | 70 | 183 | 108.2 | 104.4 | 115.0 |
| 1955........ | 94 | 76 | 188 | 115.1 | 113.4 | 117.9 |
| 1956........ | 99 | 78 | 197 | 120.0 | 115.0 | 123.7 |
| 1957........ | 102 | 79 | 205 | 122.9 | 117.1 | 126.3 |
| 1958........ | 105 | 83 | 195 | 124.9 | 120.0 | 120.1 |
| 1959........ | 97 | 65 | 210 | 112.9 | 94.7 | 123.1 |
| 1960........ | 103 | 68 | 217 | 106.2 | 90.4 | 108.6 |
| 1961........ | 114 | 82 | 225 | 99.4 | 92.0 | 93.3 |
| 1962........ | 117 | 88 | 226 | 103.9 | 98.8 | 96.6 |
| 1963........ | 116 | 90 | 222 | 114.5 | 106.8 | 113.7 |
| 1964........ | 120 | 95 | 234 | 121.6 | 114.1 | 126.5 |
| 1965........ | 125 | 100 | 237 | 132.4 | 124.8 | 136.8 |
| 1966........ | 132 | 106 | 244 | 138.2 | 130.9 | 141.3 |
| 1967........ | 137 | 111 | 251 | 143.5 | 136.8 | 145.3 |
| 1968........ | 132 | 106 | 250 | 138.5 | 130.4 | 144.5 |
| 1969........ | 135 | 108 | 255 | 141.9 | 133.9 | 148.7 |
| 1970........ | 140 | 114 | 261 | 147.6 | 141.4 | 152.0 |
| 1971........ | 142 | 116 | 267 | 149.2 | 142.4 | 156.3 |
| 1972........ | 147 | 116 | 294 | 153.4 | 141.7 | 171.8 |
| 1973........ | 155 | 123 | 306 | 161.4 | 150.3 | 178.1 |
| 1974........ | 155 | 123 | 314 | 161.0 | 149.0 | 181.7 |
| 1975........ | 158 | 124 | 324 | 163.9 | 150.9 | 187.3 |
| 1976........ | 161 | 125 | 340 | 166.9 | 151.4 | 195.7 |
| 1977........ | 165 | 124 | 361 | 168.4 | 150.9 | 202.0 |
| 1978........ | 175 | 132 | 383 | 177.0 | 157.5 | 212.9 |
| 1979........ | 197 | 152 | 406 | 188.8 | 168.4 | 221.8 |
| 1980........ | 227 | 173 | 468 | 207.1 | 184.8 | 238.0 |
| 1981........ | 249 | 194 | 487 | 222.2 | 203.3 | 241.6 |
| 1982........ | 267 | 212 | 500 | 234.0 | 218.5 | 243.3 |
| 1983........ | 290 | 235 | 523 | 251.1 | 239.5 | 249.4 |
| 1984........ | 327 | 265 | 584 | 278.5 | 267.8 | 271.1 |

Note: Consumption levels are calculated by dividing personal consumption (in the available portion of national income) by the mean population of each year. Data are not obtained from household income and expenditure surveys.

Source: State Statistical Bureau, Statistical Yearbook of China 1984 (1984), p. 454; and China: A Statistical Survey in 1985 (1985), p. 95.

Table 35. Per Capita Purchase of Major Commodities, for Urban Staff and Workers: Selected Years, 1957 to 1984
(In physical units)

| Item | Unit | 1957 | 1964 | 1981 | 1982 | 1983 | 1984 |
|---|---|---|---|---|---|---|---|
| Grain (1)............... | jin | 334.32 | 311.52 | 290.88 | 289.11 | 288.96 | 284.16 |
| Fine grains............ | jin | N/A | N/A | N/A | N/A | 219.84 | 220.80 |
| Coarse grains.......... | jin | N/A | N/A | N/A | N/A | 18.36 | 14.52 |
| Fresh vegetables......... | jin | 218.28 | 260.64 | 304.68 | 318.16 | 330.00 | 298.08 |
| Edible vegetable oil..... | jin | 8.40 | 4.44 | 9.60 | 11.55 | 13.08 | 14.16 |
| Pork..................... | jin | 13.44 | 16.44 | 33.84 | 33.69 | 36.00 | 34.20 |
| Beef and mutton.......... | jin | 2.40 | | 3.36 | 3.63 | 3.72 | 5.52 |
| Poultry.................. | jin | 2.40 | .96 | 3.84 | 4.51 | 5.16 | 5.76 |
| | | | | | | | |
| Tea...................... | jin | N/A | N/A | 1.10 | 4.20 | 3.60 | 4.32 |
| Fresh fruit and melons... | jin | N/A | N/A | N/A | N/A | 54.24 | 64.20 |
| Fresh fruit........... | jin | N/A | N/A | 42.50 | 32.30 | 34.90 | N/A |
| Dried Fruit.............. | jin | N/A | N/A | N/A | N/A | 4.80 | 6.60 |
| Pastries................. | jin | N/A | N/A | N/A | N/A | 8.28 | 8.16 |
| Fresh Milk............... | jin | N/A | N/A | N/A | N/A | 9.24 | 10.32 |
| Candy.................... | jin | N/A | N/A | 2.80 | 2.50 | 2.50 | 2.52 |
| | | | | | | | |
| Fresh eggs............... | jin | 6.58 | 4.08 | 10.44 | 11.75 | 13.80 | 15.24 |
| Fish and shrimp.......... | jin | 15.24 | 9.36 | 14.52 | 15.33 | 16.20 | 15.60 |
| Sugar.................... | jin | 2.88 | 3.24 | 5.76 | 5.59 | 5.52 | 5.88 |
| Liquor................... | jin | 5.03 | 1.99 | 8.70 | 8.95 | 10.68 | 13.56 |
| White liquor........... | jin | N/A | N/A | N/A | N/A | 4.20 | 4.68 |
| Other liquor........... | jin | N/A | N/A | N/A | N/A | 6.48 | 8.88 |
| Cigarettes............... | pack | 27.72 | 23.52 | 35.88 | 31.86 | 33.48 | 34.08 |
| | | | | | | | |
| Cotton cloth............. | meter | 7.20 | 3.75 | 4.64 | 4.24 | 5.21 | 3.00 |
| Chemical fiber cloth..... | meter | N/A | N/A | 1.67 | 2.00 | 2.26 | 1.95 |
| Woollen fabric........... | meter | .05 | .08 | .22 | .24 | .31 | .37 |
| Silk and satin cloth..... | meter | .09 | .18 | .43 | .41 | .45 | .49 |
| | | | | | | | |
| Cotton clothes........... | piece | .66 | .41 | .47 | .46 | .46 | .41 |
| Chemical fibre clothes... | piece | N/A | N/A | .73 | .83 | 1.04 | 1.14 |
| Woollen fabric clothes... | piece | .04 | .03 | .11 | .11 | .14 | .18 |
| Silk and satin clothes... | piece | .01 | .01 | .02 | .01 | .03 | .05 |
| Knitted garments......... | piece | N/A | .56 | 1.15 | 1.36 | 1.59 | 1.73 |
| Knitting wool and woollen knitwear........ | jin | N/A | N/A | .24 | .36 | .38 | .55 |

NA Data not available One jin = 0.5 kg.

Table 35. Per Capita Purchase of Major Commodities, for Urban Staff and Workers: Selected Years, 1957 to 1984--continued
(In physical units)

| Item | Unit | 1957 | 1964 | 1981 | 1982 | 1983 | 1984 |
|---|---|---|---|---|---|---|---|
| Shoes.................... | pair | N/A | N/A | N/A | N/A | 1.58 | 1.63 |
| Rubber shoes........... | pair | N/A | N/A | N/A | N/A | .24 | .23 |
| Cloth shoes............ | pair | N/A | N/A | N/A | N/A | .52 | .51 |
| Plastic shoes.......... | pair | N/A | N/A | N/A | N/A | .31 | .27 |
| Leather shoes.......... | pair | .23 | .15 | .46 | .48 | .51 | .62 |
| Soap..................... | bar | N/A | 5.92 | 10.20 | 8.78 | 9.72 | 10.32 |
| Toilet soap (2).......... | bar | N/A | .57 | 1.68 | 1.90 | 1.92 | 2.01 |
| Laundry soap............. | jin | N/A | N/A | N/A | N/A | 1.42 | 1.68 |
| Thermos bottle........... | jin | N/A | N/A | N/A | N/A | .05 | .05 |
| Liquified petroleum gas.. | jin | N/A | N/A | N/A | N/A | 8.13 | 6.82 |
| Coal..................... | jin | 549.24 | 570.96 | 480.00 | 459.00 | 458.52 | 509.64 |

NA Data not available One jin = 0.5 kg.

Note: Data are from sample surveys of household income and expenditure of urban staff and workers in state-owned and collective units.

(1) Components of grain consumption do not add to the total. Total consumption is the average of the sum of coarse and fine grain consumption for each quarter, rather than the sum of the annual averages of components.

(2) Data for 1983 consumption differ in the Statistical Yearbook of China 1984, and Tongji yuebao. The figure published in the former source is used for that year.

Source: State Statistical Bureau, Statistical Yearbook of China 1984 (1984), p. 465; and Guojia tongji ju, Guanghuai de sanshi wu nian 1949-1984 [State Statistical Bureau, Thirty-Five Glorious Years 1949-1984] (1984), p. 168; and Tongji yuebao [Statistics Monthly], No. 1, July 1985, pp. 81-84.

Table 36. Per Capita Purchase of Major Commodities, by Income Group, for Urban Staff and Workers: 1982
(In physical units)

| Item | Unit | Average | Per Capita Monthly Income Group (in Yuan) | | | | | |
|---|---|---|---|---|---|---|---|---|
| | | | 20 and below | 20.01-25.00 | 25.01-35.00 | 35.01-50.00 | 50.01-60.00 | 60.01 and above |
| Grain.................... | jin | 289.11 | 280.86 | 272.97 | 278.22 | 281.56 | 310.64 | 352.62 |
| Fresh vegetables......... | jin | 318.16 | 247.91 | 277.62 | 292.35 | 313.90 | 362.50 | 425.31 |
| Edible vegetable oil..... | jin | 11.55 | 7.92 | 9.40 | 10.42 | 11.50 | 13.09 | 15.01 |
| Pork..................... | jin | 33.69 | 13.30 | 19.67 | 27.67 | 33.48 | 43.12 | 51.81 |
| Beef and mutton.......... | jin | 3.63 | 2.06 | 2.07 | 2.74 | 3.80 | 4.59 | 5.37 |
| Poultry.................. | jin | 4.51 | .40 | 1.34 | 2.59 | 4.58 | 5.97 | 7.96 |
| Fresh eggs............... | jin | 11.75 | 3.34 | 6.03 | 9.06 | 12.26 | 14.85 | 17.83 |
| Fish and shrimp.......... | jin | 15.33 | 5.66 | 8.20 | 12.24 | 15.63 | 18.80 | 21.98 |
| Sugar.................... | jin | 5.59 | 2.61 | 3.69 | 4.72 | 5.56 | 6.50 | 7.53 |
| Liquor................... | jin | 8.95 | 3.34 | 5.21 | 6.54 | 8.86 | 12.26 | 13.82 |
| Cigarettes............... | pack | 31.86 | 19.37 | 22.88 | 22.51 | 31.85 | 41.71 | 52.52 |
| Cotton cloth............. | meter | 12.71 | 8.12 | 9.70 | 11.34 | 12.71 | 14.80 | 17.41 |
| Chemical fiber cloth..... | meter | 2.00 | .64 | 1.02 | 1.61 | 2.05 | 2.65 | 2.70 |
| Woollen fabric........... | meter | .24 | .01 | .06 | .12 | .24 | .38 | .61 |
| Silk and satin cloth..... | meter | .41 | .04 | .14 | .24 | .40 | .67 | .85 |
| Cotton clothes........... | piece | .46 | .36 | .34 | .43 | .48 | .44 | .50 |
| Chemical fibre clothes... | piece | .83 | .42 | .42 | .67 | .86 | 1.07 | 1.27 |
| Woollen fabric clothes... | piece | .11 | .01 | .05 | .05 | .11 | .18 | .26 |
| Silk and satin clothes... | piece | .01 | N/A | N/A | .01 | .01 | .04 | .04 |
| Knitted garments......... | piece | 1.36 | .84 | .91 | 1.22 | 1.40 | 1.43 | 1.86 |
| Knitting wool and woollen knitwear........ | jin | .36 | .12 | .12 | .24 | .36 | .48 | .48 |
| Leather shoes............ | pair | .48 | .20 | .24 | .36 | .52 | .60 | .70 |
| Soap..................... | bar | 8.78 | 8.42 | 7.58 | 8.11 | 8.93 | 9.63 | 9.66 |
| Toilet soap.............. | bar | 1.90 | .64 | .99 | 1.42 | 1.94 | 2.32 | 3.04 |
| Coal..................... | jin | 459.00 | 493.00 | 395.00 | 439.00 | 455.00 | 495.00 | 584.00 |

NA Data not available
1 jin = 0.5 kg.

Note: Data are from sample surveys of household income and expenditures of urban staff and workers in state-owned and collective units.

Source: State Statistical Bureau, Statistical Yearbook of China 1983, (1983), p. 496.

Table 37. Per Capita Purchase of Major Commodities, by Income Group, for Urban Workers and Staff: 1983
(In physical units)

| Item | Unit | Average | Per Capita Monthly Income Group (in Yuan) | | | | | |
|---|---|---|---|---|---|---|---|---|
| | | | 20 and below | 20.01-25.00 | 25.01-35.00 | 35.01-50.00 | 50.01-60.00 | 60.01 and above |
| Grain.................... | jin | 288.96 | 241.68 | 276.60 | 273.24 | 286.20 | 302.16 | 311.16 |
| Fresh vegetables......... | jin | 330.00 | 216.96 | 295.08 | 311.40 | 332.16 | 345.60 | 341.04 |
| Edible vegetable oil..... | jin | 13.08 | 9.48 | 11.04 | 11.76 | 13.20 | 14.04 | 14.04 |
| Pork..................... | jin | 36.00 | 17.04 | 20.76 | 28.56 | 35.04 | 42.24 | 45.96 |
| Beef and mutton.......... | jin | 3.72 | 1.68 | 2.40 | 2.76 | 3.60 | 4.56 | 4.80 |
| Poultry.................. | jin | 5.16 | .96 | 1.20 | 2.88 | 4.68 | 7.08 | 9.60 |
| Fresh eggs............... | jin | 13.80 | 4.44 | 6.84 | 10.32 | 14.16 | 16.32 | 16.80 |
| Fish and shrimp.......... | jin | 16.20 | 4.80 | 6.96 | 10.80 | 15.24 | 20.40 | 26.40 |
| Sugar.................... | jin | 5.52 | 2.88 | 3.48 | 4.20 | 5.28 | 6.36 | 7.08 |
| Liquor................... | jin | 10.68 | 2.76 | 4.68 | 7.56 | 10.44 | 13.44 | 15.00 |
| Cigarettes............... | pack | 33.48 | 18.24 | 22.44 | 25.92 | 33.00 | 40.20 | 46.20 |
| Cotton cloth............. | meter | 5.21 | 3.74 | 3.78 | 4.76 | 5.07 | 5.93 | 6.19 |
| Chemical fiber cloth..... | meter | 2.26 | 1.51 | 1.54 | 1.91 | 2.37 | 2.66 | 2.80 |
| Woollen fabric........... | meter | .31 | .10 | .09 | .14 | .29 | .48 | .58 |
| Silk and satins.......... | meter | .45 | .07 | .11 | .24 | .42 | .66 | .78 |
| Cotton clothes........... | piece | .46 | .35 | .31 | .37 | .46 | .48 | .42 |
| Chemical fibre clothes... | piece | 1.04 | .57 | .54 | .80 | 1.05 | 1.23 | 1.14 |
| Woollen fabric clothes... | piece | .14 | .04 | .04 | .07 | .14 | .21 | .24 |
| Silk and satin clothes... | piece | .03 | .01 | .01 | .02 | .03 | .04 | .05 |
| Knitted garments......... | piece | 1.59 | .77 | .89 | 1.28 | 1.60 | 1.78 | 2.00 |
| Knitting wool and woollen knitwear........ | jin | .38 | .15 | .15 | .25 | .38 | .48 | .54 |
| Leather shoes............ | pair | .51 | .21 | .24 | .39 | .52 | .60 | .66 |
| Soap..................... | bar | 9.72 | 9.00 | 6.36 | 9.84 | 10.08 | 9.84 | 8.64 |
| Toilet soap.............. | bar | 1.92 | .60 | .96 | 1.44 | 1.92 | 2.40 | 2.76 |
| Coal..................... | jin | 458.52 | 468.60 | 462.84 | 480.48 | 466.44 | 450.12 | 465.36 |

1 jin = 0.5 kg.

Note: Data are from sample surveys of household income and expenditure of staff and workers in state-owned and collective units.

Source: State Statistical Bureau, Statistical Yearbook of China 1984, (1984), p. 469.

Table 38. Per Capita Consumption of Major Commodities, for Peasants: Selected Years, 1954 to 1984
(In physical units)

| Item | Unit | 1954 | 1956 | 1957 | 1965 | 1978 | 1979 | 1980 | 1981 | 1982 | 1983 | 1984 |
|---|---|---|---|---|---|---|---|---|---|---|---|---|
| Grain.................. | jin | 443.47 | 493.00 | 454.00 | 453.00 | 496.00 | 513.00 | 511.00 | 512.00 | 520.00 | 519.81 | 533.00 |
| Refined wheat and rice............ | jin | 190.15 | 252.00 | 220.13 | 226.00 | 254.01 | 278.86 | 325.84 | 344.83 | 383.68 | 392.51 | 418.00 |
| Wheat............ | jin | N/A | N/A | N/A | N/A | N/A | N/A | N/A | N/A | N/A | 260.37 | N/A |
| Rice............. | jin | N/A | N/A | N/A | N/A | N/A | N/A | N/A | N/A | N/A | 132.14 | N/A |
| Coarse grain......... | jin | 253.32 | 241.00 | 233.87 | 227.00 | 241.99 | 234.14 | 185.16 | 167.17 | 136.32 | 127.30 | N/A |
| Vegetables............. | jin | 141.32 | 182.00 | 204.50 | 260.00 | 283.00 | 262.00 | 254.00 | 248.00 | 264.00 | 261.90 | 280.00 |
| Edible oil............. | jin | 2.53 | 3.06 | 3.17 | 2.98 | 3.94 | 4.76 | 4.97 | 6.25 | 6.86 | 7.05 | 7.93 |
| Vegetable oil......... | jin | 2.22 | 2.49 | 2.50 | 2.19 | 2.59 | 3.03 | 2.80 | 3.78 | 4.14 | 4.38 | N/A |
| Animal oil........... | jin | .31 | .57 | .67 | .79 | 1.35 | 1.73 | 2.17 | 2.47 | 2.72 | 2.67 | N/A |
| Meat.................. | jin | 9.18 | 8.44 | 9.06 | 9.62 | 11.51 | 13.01 | 15.49 | 17.41 | 18.10 | 19.93 | 21.24 |
| Pork................. | jin | 7.39 | 6.21 | 6.89 | 7.68 | 10.34 | 12.15 | 14.53 | 16.34 | 16.72 | 18.59 | N/A |
| Beef and mutton....... | jin | 1.79 | 2.23 | 2.17 | 1.94 | 1.17 | .86 | .96 | 1.07 | 1.38 | 1.34 | N/A |
| Cows and goats milk..... | jin | N/A | N/A | N/A | N/A | N/A | N/A | N/A | N/A | N/A | 1.33 | N/A |
| Poultry................. | jin | N/A | N/A | N/A | N/A | .50 | .63 | 1.31 | 1.41 | 1.56 | 1.63 | 1.80 |
| Fresh eggs............. | jin | 1.63 | 1.37 | 1.61 | 1.70 | 1.59 | 1.79 | 2.39 | 2.50 | 2.85 | 3.14 | 3.68 |
| Fish and shrimp........ | jin | 2.72 | 2.46 | 2.20 | 2.56 | 1.68 | 1.39 | 2.19 | 2.56 | 2.63 | 3.17 | 3.47 |
| Sugar.................. | jin | .81 | .91 | .94 | 1.30 | 1.46 | 1.60 | 2.12 | 2.49 | 2.37 | 2.51 | 2.60 |
| Liquor.................. | jin | 1.67 | .99 | 1.04 | 1.26 | 2.44 | 2.83 | 3.78 | 4.64 | 5.46 | 6.39 | 6.95 |
| Cigarettes............. | pack | N/A | N/A | N/A | N/A | N/A | N/A | N/A | 15.00 | 18.87 | 19.89 | N/A |
| Tea.................... | jin | N/A | N/A | N/A | N/A | N/A | N/A | N/A | .44 | .43 | .44 | N/A |
| Fruit.................. | jin | N/A | N/A | N/A | N/A | N/A | N/A | N/A | N/A | N/A | 1.61 | N/A |
| Candy.................. | jin | N/A | N/A | N/A | N/A | N/A | N/A | N/A | N/A | N/A | 6.04 | N/A |
| Cotton cloth ........... | chi | N/A | N/A | N/A | N/A | 16.90 | 15.60 | 12.89 | 12.62 | 11.83 | 9.53 | 8.47 |
| Cotton ................ | jin | N/A | N/A | N/A | N/A | .79 | .89 | .76 | .66 | .77 | .79 | .84 |
| Chemical fibre cloth.................. | chi | N/A | N/A | N/A | N/A | 1.24 | 2.18 | 2.81 | 3.70 | 4.59 | 7.01 | 7.43 |
| Woollen fabric.......... | chi | N/A | N/A | N/A | N/A | .07 | .17 | .18 | .18 | .12 | .16 | .21 |
| Silk and satins......... | chi | N/A | N/A | N/A | N/A | .06 | .15 | .17 | .15 | .16 | .21 | .72 |
| Knitting wool and woollen knitwear....... | jin | N/A | N/A | N/A | N/A | .04 | .07 | .09 | .09 | .08 | .08 | .09 |
| Rubber. gym, and leather shoes.......... | pair | N/A | N/A | N/A | N/A | .32 | .14 | .51 | .19 | .48 | .49 | .57 |

NA Data not available
1 jin = 0.5 kg.
1 chi = 1/3 meter

Note: (Data are from sample surveys of household income and expenditure of peasants)

Source: State Statistical Bureau, Statistical Yearbook of China 1984, (1984), p. 474; China: A Statistics Survey in 1985 (1985), p. 104; and Guojia tongji ju, Guanghuai de sanshiwu nian 1949-1984 [State Statistical Bureau, Thirty-Five Glorious Years 1949-1984] (1984), p. 168.

Table 39. Total and Per Capita Consumption of Grain, by Residence: 1952 to 1984
(Data refer to grain traded)

| Year | Total consumption (in 100 million jin) | | | Per capita consumption (in jin) | | |
|---|---|---|---|---|---|---|
| | China | Urban | Rural | China | Urban | Rural |
| 1952..... | 2,244.1 | 333.7 | 1,910.4 | 395.34 | 480.70 | 383.44 |
| 1953..... | 2,286.5 | 357.3 | 1,929.2 | 394.14 | 484.47 | 380.99 |
| 1954..... | 2,333.1 | 379.2 | 1,953.9 | 392.75 | 472.41 | 380.31 |
| 1955..... | 2,408.5 | 359.0 | 2,049.5 | 396.53 | 428.81 | 391.37 |
| 1956..... | 2,534.0 | 378.0 | 2,156.0 | 408.58 | 400.51 | 410.03 |
| 1957..... | 2,583.5 | 392.0 | 2,191.5 | 406.12 | 392.00 | 408.76 |
| 1958..... | 2,584.8 | 432.8 | 2,152.0 | 396.46 | 371.09 | 401.99 |
| 1959..... | 2,471.8 | 522.8 | 1,949.0 | 373.18 | 401.78 | 366.19 |
| 1960..... | 2,171.2 | 532.5 | 1,638.7 | 327.24 | 385.17 | 311.99 |
| 1961..... | 2,093.4 | 465.8 | 1,627.6 | 317.57 | 358.97 | 307.42 |
| 1962..... | 2,188.2 | 426.2 | 1,762.0 | 329.25 | 367.67 | 321.13 |
| 1963..... | 2,242.9 | 427.8 | 1,815.1 | 329.29 | 379.71 | 319.30 |
| 1964..... | 2,536.9 | 467.9 | 2,069.0 | 363.91 | 400.09 | 356.62 |
| 1965..... | 2,630.6 | 516.3 | 2,114.3 | 365.67 | 421.30 | 354.25 |
| 1966..... | 2,797.0 | 492.3 | 2,304.7 | 379.14 | 411.52 | 372.87 |
| 1967..... | 2,812.8 | 495.1 | 2,317.7 | 372.36 | 398.50 | 367.22 |
| 1968..... | 2,695.2 | 474.3 | 2,220.9 | 347.61 | 377.69 | 341.80 |
| 1969..... | 2,772.0 | 487.9 | 2,284.1 | 347.77 | 383.15 | 341.05 |
| 1970..... | 3,065.8 | 538.7 | 2,527.1 | 374.43 | 403.58 | 368.75 |
| 1971..... | 3,165.9 | 559.7 | 2,606.2 | 376.53 | 398.90 | 372.05 |
| 1972..... | 2,974.5 | 579.2 | 2,395.3 | 345.02 | 411.92 | 331.98 |
| 1973..... | 3,380.2 | 592.6 | 2,787.6 | 383.14 | 416.09 | 376.79 |
| 1974..... | 3,379.9 | 593.2 | 2,786.7 | 375.28 | 409.39 | 368.74 |
| 1975..... | 3,493.7 | 615.8 | 2,877.9 | 381.03 | 418.51 | 373.87 |
| 1976..... | 3,543.7 | 643.0 | 2,900.7 | 380.56 | 424.03 | 372.10 |
| 1977..... | 3,626.7 | 681.6 | 2,945.1 | 384.14 | 420.95 | 376.52 |
| 1978..... | 3,741.0 | 700.0 | 3,041.0 | 390.92 | 410.58 | 386.66 |
| 1979..... | 4,015.5 | 740.0 | 3,275.5 | 414.05 | 421.51 | 412.40 |
| 1980..... | 4,199.4 | 773.0 | 3,426.4 | 427.62 | 427.76 | 427.59 |
| 1981..... | 4,361.4 | 799.1 | 3,562.3 | 438.35 | 431.46 | 439.93 |
| 1982..... | 4,546.1 | 825.7 | 3,720.4 | 450.92 | 434.58 | 454.72 |
| 1983..... | 4,738.3 | 860.1 | 3,878.2 | 464.46 | 443.35 | 469.41 |
| 1984..... | N/A | N/A | N/A | 502.70 | 478.69 | 508.34 |

NA Data not available
One jin = 0.5 kg

Note: Data are not from the household income and expenditure surveys, nor necessarily consistent with the survey data.

Source: Guojia tongji ju, Zhongguo maoyi wujia tongji ziliao, 1952-1983, [State Statistical Bureau, Trade and Price Statistics, 1952-1983] (1984), p. 27, China: A Statistics Survey in 1985 (1985), p. 96; and Tongji [Statistics], Vol. 8, 1985, p. 48.

Table 40. Total and Per Capita Consumption of Edible Vegetable Oil, by Residence: 1952 to 1984

| Year | Total consumption (in 100 million jin) | | | Per capita consumption (in jin) | | |
|---|---|---|---|---|---|---|
| | China | Urban | Rural | China | Urban | Rural |
| 1952..... | 23.8 | 7.1 | 16.7 | 4.19 | 10.23 | 3.35 |
| 1953..... | 23.4 | 7.9 | 15.5 | 4.03 | 10.71 | 3.06 |
| 1954..... | 21.4 | 7.5 | 13.9 | 3.60 | 9.34 | 2.71 |
| 1955..... | 26.7 | 8.7 | 18.0 | 4.40 | 10.39 | 3.44 |
| 1956..... | 31.8 | 9.6 | 22.2 | 5.13 | 10.17 | 4.22 |
| 1957..... | 30.2 | 10.3 | 19.9 | 4.84 | 10.30 | 3.71 |
| 1958..... | 30.8 | 10.6 | 20.2 | 4.72 | 9.09 | 3.77 |
| 1959..... | 29.8 | 10.5 | 19.3 | 4.50 | 8.07 | 3.63 |
| 1960..... | 24.8 | 9.8 | 15.0 | 3.74 | 7.09 | 2.86 |
| 1961..... | 18.1 | 7.0 | 11.1 | 2.75 | 5.39 | 2.10 |
| 1962..... | 14.4 | 5.7 | 8.7 | 2.17 | 4.92 | 1.59 |
| 1963..... | 15.3 | 6.9 | 8.4 | 2.25 | 6.12 | 1.48 |
| 1964..... | 19.3 | 8.7 | 10.6 | 2.77 | 7.44 | 1.83 |
| 1965..... | 24.7 | 11.8 | 12.9 | 3.43 | 9.63 | 2.17 |
| 1966..... | 26.0 | 12.6 | 13.4 | 3.52 | 10.53 | 2.16 |
| 1967..... | 26.6 | 12.3 | 14.3 | 3.52 | 9.90 | 2.26 |
| 1968..... | 25.0 | 11.4 | 13.6 | 3.22 | 9.08 | 2.09 |
| 1969..... | 25.3 | 11.6 | 13.7 | 3.17 | 9.11 | 2.04 |
| 1970..... | 26.3 | 11.3 | 15.0 | 3.21 | 8.47 | 2.19 |
| 1971..... | 27.6 | 11.9 | 15.7 | 3.28 | 8.48 | 2.24 |
| 1972..... | 28.7 | 12.4 | 16.3 | 3.33 | 8.82 | 2.25 |
| 1973..... | 29.2 | 12.4 | 16.8 | 3.31 | 8.71 | 2.27 |
| 1974..... | 30.8 | 12.9 | 17.9 | 3.42 | 8.90 | 2.37 |
| 1975..... | 31.6 | 13.7 | 17.9 | 3.45 | 9.31 | 2.33 |
| 1976..... | 29.7 | 14.0 | 15.7 | 3.19 | 9.23 | 2.01 |
| 1977..... | 29.4 | 13.4 | 16.0 | 3.11 | 8.28 | 2.05 |
| 1978..... | 30.5 | 14.0 | 16.5 | 3.19 | 8.21 | 2.10 |
| 1979..... | 37.9 | 17.5 | 20.4 | 3.91 | 9.97 | 2.57 |
| 1980..... | 45.2 | 19.7 | 25.5 | 4.60 | 10.90 | 3.18 |
| 1981..... | 58.5 | 25.5 | 33.0 | 5.88 | 13.77 | 4.08 |
| 1982..... | 71.3 | 34.0 | 37.3 | 7.07 | 17.89 | 4.56 |
| 1983..... | 82.1 | 38.7 | 43.4 | 8.05 | 19.95 | 5.25 |
| 1984..... | N/A | N/A | N/A | 9.39 | 22.15 | 6.38 |

NA Data not available
One jin = 0.5 kg.

Note: Data are not from the household income and expenditure surveys, nor necessarily consistent with the survey data.

Source: Guojia tongji ju, Zhongguo maoyi wujia tongji ziliao, 1952-1983 [State Statistical Bureau, Trade and Price Statistics, 1952-1984] (1984), p. 28, China: A Statistics Survey in 1985 (1985), p. 96; and Tongji [Statistics], Vol. 8, 1985, p. 48.

Table 41. Total and Per Capita Consumption of Pork, by Residence 1952 to 1984

| Year | Total consumption (In 100 million jin) | | | Per capita consumption (in jin) | | |
|---|---|---|---|---|---|---|
| | China | Urban | Rural | China | Urban | Rural |
| 1952..... | 67.1 | 12.4 | 54.7 | 11.83 | 17.84 | 10.99 |
| 1953..... | 70.3 | 14.9 | 55.4 | 12.12 | 20.20 | 10.94 |
| 1954..... | 71.4 | 16.3 | 55.1 | 12.01 | 20.29 | 10.72 |
| 1955..... | 60.0 | 16.2 | 43.8 | 9.88 | 19.30 | 8.37 |
| 1956..... | 57.8 | 15.8 | 42.0 | 9.32 | 16.75 | 7.99 |
| 1957..... | 64.6 | 18.0 | 46.6 | 10.15 | 17.95 | 8.70 |
| 1958..... | 68.1 | 18.7 | 49.4 | 10.45 | 16.06 | 9.22 |
| 1959..... | 40.8 | 13.0 | 27.8 | 6.16 | 9.97 | 5.22 |
| 1960..... | 20.3 | 7.5 | 12.8 | 3.06 | 5.42 | 2.44 |
| 1961..... | 18.6 | 4.5 | 14.1 | 2.82 | 3.49 | 2.66 |
| 1962..... | 29.5 | 8.8 | 20.7 | 4.43 | 7.58 | 3.77 |
| 1963..... | 58.2 | 18.6 | 39.6 | 8.54 | 16.55 | 6.97 |
| 1964..... | 78.3 | 25.3 | 53.0 | 11.23 | 21.60 | 9.13 |
| 1965..... | 90.4 | 25.4 | 65.0 | 12.57 | 20.73 | 10.89 |
| 1966..... | 103.9 | 30.8 | 73.1 | 14.08 | 25.75 | 11.83 |
| 1967..... | 104.0 | 29.6 | 74.4 | 13.77 | 23.82 | 11.79 |
| 1968..... | 101.8 | 29.3 | 72.5 | 13.13 | 23.33 | 11.16 |
| 1969..... | 94.1 | 26.8 | 67.3 | 11.81 | 21.05 | 10.05 |
| 1970..... | 98.5 | 28.7 | 69.8 | 12.03 | 21.50 | 10.19 |
| 1971..... | 118.1 | 31.4 | 86.7 | 14.05 | 22.38 | 12.38 |
| 1972..... | 130.3 | 35.2 | 95.1 | 15.11 | 25.03 | 13.18 |
| 1973..... | 134.6 | 38.4 | 96.2 | 15.26 | 26.96 | 13.00 |
| 1974..... | 138.1 | 41.5 | 96.6 | 15.33 | 28.64 | 12.78 |
| 1975..... | 139.8 | 43.9 | 95.9 | 15.25 | 29.84 | 12.46 |
| 1976..... | 137.4 | 42.0 | 95.4 | 14.76 | 27.70 | 12.24 |
| 1977..... | 136.8 | 41.7 | 95.1 | 14.49 | 25.75 | 12.16 |
| 1978..... | 146.8 | 46.7 | 100.1 | 15.34 | 27.39 | 12.73 |
| 1979..... | 187.4 | 61.1 | 126.3 | 19.32 | 34.80 | 15.90 |
| 1980..... | 219.1 | 68.6 | 150.5 | 22.31 | 37.96 | 18.78 |
| 1981..... | 220.4 | 62.9 | 157.5 | 22.15 | 33.96 | 19.45 |
| 1982..... | 237.0 | 66.7 | 170.3 | 23.51 | 35.11 | 20.81 |
| 1983..... | 251.9 | 70.0 | 181.9 | 24.69 | 36.08 | 22.02 |
| 1984..... | N/A | N/A | N/A | 26.03 | 37.42 | 23.35 |

NA Data not available
One jin = 0.5 kg.

Note: Data are not from household income and expenditure surveys, nor necessarily consistent with the survey data.

Source: Guojia tongji ju, Zhongguo maoyi wujia tongji ziliao 1952-1983 [State Statistical Bureau, Trade and Price Statistics 1952-1983] (1984), p. 29, China: A Statistics Survey in 1985 (1985), p. 96; and Tongji [Statistics], Vol. 8, 1985, p. 48.

Table 42. Total and Per Capita Consumption of Fresh Eggs, by Residence: 1952 to 1984

| Year | Total consumption (in 10 thousand dan) | | | Per capita consumption (in jin) | | |
|---|---|---|---|---|---|---|
| | China | Urban | Rural | China | Urban | Rural |
| 1952..... | 1,158.9 | 243.4 | 915.5 | 2.04 | 3.51 | 1.84 |
| 1953..... | 1,243.4 | 261.1 | 982.3 | 2.14 | 3.54 | 1.94 |
| 1954..... | 1,300.1 | 286.0 | 1,014.1 | 2.19 | 3.56 | 1.97 |
| 1955..... | 1,272.5 | 286.3 | 986.2 | 2.10 | 3.42 | 1.88 |
| 1956..... | 1,470.8 | 345.6 | 1,125.2 | 2.37 | 3.66 | 2.14 |
| 1957..... | 1,597.7 | 399.4 | 1,198.3 | 2.51 | 3.99 | 2.24 |
| 1958..... | 1,660.3 | 388.4 | 1,271.9 | 2.55 | 3.33 | 2.38 |
| 1959..... | 766.2 | 120.0 | 646.2 | 1.16 | .92 | 1.21 |
| 1960..... | 644.1 | 96.6 | 547.5 | .97 | .70 | 1.04 |
| 1961..... | 655.5 | 79.9 | 575.6 | .99 | .62 | 1.09 |
| 1962..... | 1,019.0 | 164.8 | 854.2 | 1.53 | 1.42 | 1.56 |
| 1963..... | 1,404.0 | 369.5 | 1,034.5 | 2.06 | 3.28 | 1.82 |
| 1964..... | 1,876.5 | 504.8 | 1,371.7 | 2.69 | 4.32 | 2.36 |
| 1965..... | 2,043.5 | 505.5 | 1,538.0 | 2.84 | 4.12 | 2.58 |
| 1966..... | 2,532.0 | 509.5 | 2,022.5 | 3.43 | 4.26 | 3.27 |
| 1967..... | 2,314.2 | 510.5 | 1,803.7 | 3.06 | 4.11 | 2.86 |
| 1968..... | 1,760.8 | 402.0 | 1,358.8 | 2.27 | 3.20 | 2.09 |
| 1969..... | 1,912.4 | 382.0 | 1,530.4 | 2.40 | 3.00 | 3.29 |
| 1970..... | 2,158.9 | 449.0 | 1,709.9 | 2.64 | 3.36 | 2.50 |
| 1971..... | 2,723.0 | 470.0 | 2,253.0 | 3.23 | 3.35 | 3.22 |
| 1972..... | 2,638.8 | 453.5 | 2,185.3 | 3.06 | 3.23 | 3.03 |
| 1973..... | 2,864.0 | 462.5 | 2,401.5 | 3.25 | 3.25 | 3.25 |
| 1974..... | 2,838.1 | 443.0 | 2,395.1 | 3.15 | 3.06 | 3.17 |
| 1975..... | 2,989.1 | 436.0 | 2,553.1 | 3.26 | 2.96 | 3.32 |
| 1976..... | 3,282.1 | 502.0 | 2,780.1 | 3.52 | 3.31 | 3.57 |
| 1977..... | 3,491.5 | 511.9 | 2,979.6 | 3.70 | 3.16 | 3.81 |
| 1978..... | 3,766.2 | 669.7 | 3,096.5 | 3.94 | 3.93 | 3.94 |
| 1979..... | 4,025.8 | 953.1 | 3,072.7 | 4.15 | 5.43 | 3.87 |
| 1980..... | 4,458.2 | 1,066.8 | 3,391.4 | 4.54 | 5.90 | 4.23 |
| 1981..... | 4,850.0 | 1,111.0 | 3,739.0 | 4.87 | 6.00 | 4.62 |
| 1982..... | 5,089.4 | 1,220.0 | 3,869.4 | 5.05 | 6.42 | 4.73 |
| 1983..... | 6,040.1 | 1,423.0 | 4,617.1 | 5.92 | 7.34 | 5.59 |
| 1984..... | N/A | N/A | N/A | 7.81 | 14.03 | 6.35 |

NA Data not available
One dan = 50.0 kg.
One jin = 0.5 kg.

Note: Data are not from the household income and expenditure surveys, nor necessarily consistent with the survey data.

Source: Guojia tongji ju, Zhongguo maoyi wujia tongji ziliao, 1952-1983 [State Statistical Bureau, Trade and Price Statistics, 1952-1983] (1984), p. 30, China: A Statistics Survey in 1985 (1985), p. 96; and Tongji [Statistics], Vol. 8, 1985, p. 48.

Table 43. Total and Per Capita Consumption of Sugar, by Residence: 1952 to 1984

| Year | Total consumption (in 10 thousand tons) | | | Per capita consumption (in jin) | | |
|---|---|---|---|---|---|---|
| | China | Urban | Rural | China | Urban | Rural |
| 1952..... | 51.6 | 20.8 | 30.8 | 1.82 | 5.99 | 1.24 |
| 1953..... | 67.8 | 24.7 | 43.1 | 2.34 | 6.70 | 1.70 |
| 1954..... | 71.9 | 26.8 | 45.1 | 2.42 | 6.68 | 1.76 |
| 1955..... | 78.2 | 29.8 | 48.4 | 2.58 | 7.12 | 1.85 |
| 1956..... | 92.4 | 35.0 | 57.4 | 2.98 | 7.42 | 2.18 |
| 1957..... | 95.9 | 36.3 | 59.6 | 3.02 | 7.26 | 2.22 |
| 1958..... | 105.6 | 52.8 | 52.8 | 3.24 | 9.05 | 1.97 |
| 1959..... | 101.4 | 47.7 | 53.7 | 3.06 | 7.33 | 2.02 |
| 1960..... | 69.4 | 35.8 | 33.6 | 2.09 | 5.18 | 1.28 |
| 1961..... | 117.7 | 57.6 | 60.1 | 3.57 | 8.88 | 2.27 |
| 1962..... | 106.0 | 40.8 | 65.2 | 3.19 | 7.04 | 2.38 |
| 1963..... | 92.0 | 36.1 | 55.9 | 2.70 | 6.41 | 1.97 |
| 1964..... | 102.6 | 41.9 | 60.7 | 2.94 | 7.17 | 2.09 |
| 1965..... | 120.7 | 43.4 | 77.3 | 3.36 | 7.08 | 2.59 |
| 1966..... | 144.7 | 45.5 | 99.2 | 3.92 | 7.61 | 3.21 |
| 1967..... | 170.8 | 49.4 | 121.4 | 4.52 | 7.95 | 3.85 |
| 1968..... | 183.5 | 55.2 | 128.3 | 4.73 | 8.79 | 3.95 |
| 1969..... | 200.3 | 59.1 | 141.2 | 5.03 | 9.28 | 4.22 |
| 1970..... | 168.3 | 57.9 | 110.4 | 4.11 | 8.68 | 3.22 |
| 1971..... | 176.7 | 64.6 | 112.1 | 4.20 | 9.21 | 3.20 |
| 1972..... | 183.5 | 66.8 | 116.7 | 4.26 | 9.50 | 3.23 |
| 1973..... | 199.2 | 78.3 | 120.9 | 4.52 | 11.00 | 3.27 |
| 1974..... | 211.4 | 82.2 | 129.2 | 4.69 | 11.35 | 3.42 |
| 1975..... | 207.2 | 83.2 | 124.0 | 4.52 | 11.31 | 3.22 |
| 1976..... | 216.5 | 78.8 | 137.7 | 4.65 | 10.39 | 3.53 |
| 1977..... | 275.8 | 121.3 | 154.5 | 5.84 | 14.98 | 3.95 |
| 1978..... | 327.2 | 138.9 | 188.3 | 6.84 | 16.29 | 4.79 |
| 1979..... | 345.0 | 149.0 | 196.0 | 7.11 | 16.97 | 4.94 |
| 1980..... | 376.0 | 161.5 | 214.5 | 7.66 | 17.87 | 5.35 |
| 1981..... | 407.2 | 169.0 | 238.2 | 8.19 | 18.25 | 5.88 |
| 1982..... | 445.0 | 181.0 | 264.0 | 8.83 | 19.05 | 6.45 |
| 1983..... | 455.9 | 185.0 | 270.9 | 8.94 | 19.07 | 6.56 |
| 1984..... | N/A | N/A | N/A | 9.76 | 20.95 | 7.12 |

NA Data not available
On jin = 0.5 kg.

Note: Data are not from household income and expenditure surveys, nor necessarily consistent with the surveys data.

Source: Guojia tongji ju, Zhongguo maoyi wujia tongji ziliao 1952-1983 [State Statistical Bureau, Trade and Price Statistics 1952-1983] (1984), p. 31, China: A Statistics Survey in 1985 (1985), p. 96; and Tongji [Statistics], Vol. 8, 1985, p. 48.

Table 44. Total and Per Capita Consumption of Salt, by Residence: 1952 to 1984

| Year | Total consumption (in 10 thousand tons) | | | Per capita consumption (in jin) | | |
|---|---|---|---|---|---|---|
| | China | Urban | Rural | China | Urban | Rural |
| 1952..... | 314.1 | 50.3 | 263.8 | 10.07 | 14.47 | 10.59 |
| 1953..... | 363.7 | 58.2 | 305.5 | 12.54 | 15.78 | 12.07 |
| 1954..... | 371.6 | 59.5 | 312.1 | 12.51 | 14.82 | 12.15 |
| 1955..... | 378.4 | 60.5 | 317.9 | 12.46 | 14.45 | 12.14 |
| 1956..... | 389.4 | 62.7 | 326.7 | 12.56 | 13.29 | 12.43 |
| 1957..... | 398.1 | 63.7 | 334.4 | 12.52 | 12.74 | 12.47 |
| 1958..... | 455.0 | 75.1 | 379.9 | 13.96 | 12.88 | 14.19 |
| 1959..... | 504.8 | 85.3 | 419.5 | 15.24 | 13.11 | 15.76 |
| 1960..... | 662.3 | 132.5 | 529.8 | 19.96 | 19.17 | 20.17 |
| 1961..... | 616.7 | 123.3 | 493.4 | 18.71 | 19.00 | 18.64 |
| 1962..... | 507.2 | 76.1 | 431.1 | 15.26 | 13.13 | 15.71 |
| 1963..... | 383.7 | 57.6 | 326.1 | 11.27 | 10.23 | 11.47 |
| 1964..... | 458.4 | 69.0 | 389.4 | 13.15 | 11.80 | 13.42 |
| 1965..... | 494.2 | 74.1 | 420.1 | 13.74 | 12.09 | 14.08 |
| 1966..... | 521.8 | 78.3 | 443.5 | 14.15 | 13.09 | 14.35 |
| 1967..... | 555.0 | 83.2 | 471.8 | 14.69 | 13.39 | 14.95 |
| 1968..... | 550.0 | 82.5 | 467.5 | 14.19 | 13.14 | 14.39 |
| 1969..... | 610.0 | 91.5 | 518.5 | 15.31 | 14.37 | 15.48 |
| 1970..... | 639.9 | 95.5 | 541.4 | 15.56 | 14.31 | 15.80 |
| 1971..... | 632.0 | 94.8 | 537.2 | 15.03 | 13.51 | 15.34 |
| 1972..... | 631.3 | 94.7 | 536.6 | 14.65 | 13.47 | 14.87 |
| 1973..... | 608.9 | 91.3 | 517.6 | 13.80 | 12.82 | 13.99 |
| 1974..... | 662.9 | 99.4 | 563.5 | 14.72 | 13.72 | 14.91 |
| 1975..... | 741.1 | 111.2 | 629.9 | 16.17 | 15.11 | 16.37 |
| 1976..... | 735.0 | 110.3 | 624.7 | 15.79 | 14.55 | 16.03 |
| 1977..... | 860.0 | 129.0 | 731.0 | 18.22 | 15.93 | 18.69 |
| 1978..... | 798.7 | 119.8 | 678.9 | 16.69 | 14.05 | 17.26 |
| 1979..... | 785.0 | 117.0 | 668.0 | 16.19 | 13.33 | 16.82 |
| 1980..... | 780.0 | 118.0 | 662.0 | 15.09 | 13.06 | 16.52 |
| 1981..... | 773.0 | 116.0 | 657.0 | 15.54 | 12.53 | 16.23 |
| 1982..... | 765.0 | 114.0 | 651.0 | 15.18 | 12.00 | 15.91 |
| 1983..... | 809.5 | 117.4 | 692.1 | 15.87 | 12.10 | 16.75 |
| 1984..... | N/A | N/A | N/A | 16.62 | 12.60 | 17.56 |

NA Data not available
One jin = 0.5 kg.

Note: Data are not from the household income and expenditure surveys, nor necessarily consistent with the survey data.

Source: Guojia tongji ju, Zhongguo maoyi wujia tongji ziliao 1952-1983 [State Statistical Bureau, Trade and Price Statistics 1952-1983] (1984), p. 32; and Tongji [Statistics], Vol. 8, 1985, p. 48.

Table 45. Total and Per Capita Consumption of Cigarettes, by Residence: 1952 to 1984

| Year | Total consumption (in 10 thousand cases) | | | Per capita consumption (in boxes) | | |
|---|---|---|---|---|---|---|
| | China | Urban | Rural | China | Urban | Rural |
| 1952..... | 246.5 | 103.5 | 143.0 | 10.90 | 37.30 | 7.20 |
| 1953..... | 345.9 | 138.4 | 207.5 | 14.90 | 46.90 | 10.20 |
| 1954..... | 377.0 | 144.0 | 233.0 | 15.90 | 44.90 | 11.30 |
| 1955..... | 355.8 | 136.8 | 219.0 | 14.60 | 40.90 | 10.50 |
| 1956..... | 365.5 | 145.0 | 220.5 | 14.70 | 38.40 | 10.50 |
| 1957..... | 430.8 | 171.0 | 259.8 | 16.90 | 42.80 | 12.10 |
| 1958..... | 470.4 | 202.7 | 267.7 | 18.00 | 43.50 | 12.50 |
| 1959..... | 553.2 | 217.4 | 335.8 | 20.90 | 41.80 | 15.80 |
| 1960..... | 525.2 | 266.8 | 258.4 | 19.80 | 48.30 | 12.30 |
| 1961..... | 245.5 | 148.0 | 97.5 | 9.30 | 28.50 | 4.60 |
| 1962..... | 257.2 | 133.7 | 123.5 | 9.70 | 28.80 | 5.60 |
| 1963..... | 325.3 | 165.9 | 159.4 | 11.90 | 36.80 | 7.00 |
| 1964..... | 391.5 | 187.1 | 204.4 | 14.00 | 40.00 | 8.80 |
| 1965..... | 464.6 | 180.0 | 284.6 | 16.15 | 36.72 | 11.92 |
| 1966..... | 510.6 | 188.9 | 321.7 | 17.30 | 39.48 | 13.01 |
| 1967..... | 532.0 | 208.9 | 323.1 | 17.61 | 42.04 | 12.80 |
| 1968..... | 491.5 | 212.4 | 279.1 | 15.85 | 42.28 | 10.74 |
| 1969..... | 653.6 | 246.2 | 407.4 | 20.50 | 48.34 | 15.21 |
| 1970..... | 672.0 | 229.8 | 442.2 | 20.52 | 43.04 | 16.13 |
| 1971..... | 719.0 | 256.9 | 462.1 | 21.38 | 45.77 | 16.49 |
| 1972..... | 805.9 | 289.6 | 516.3 | 23.37 | 51.49 | 17.89 |
| 1973..... | 881.8 | 321.0 | 560.8 | 24.99 | 56.35 | 18.95 |
| 1974..... | 866.3 | 383.9 | 482.4 | 24.05 | 66.24 | 15.96 |
| 1975..... | 961.5 | 420.4 | 541.1 | 26.22 | 71.43 | 17.57 |
| 1976..... | 1,056.4 | 473.5 | 582.9 | 28.36 | 78.06 | 18.69 |
| 1977..... | 1,149.2 | 518.4 | 630.8 | 30.43 | 80.04 | 20.16 |
| 1978..... | 1,179.8 | 529.0 | 650.8 | 30.82 | 77.57 | 20.66 |
| 1979..... | 1,352.2 | 556.0 | 796.2 | 34.86 | 79.18 | 25.06 |
| 1980..... | 1,593.2 | 630.0 | 963.2 | 40.56 | 87.16 | 30.05 |
| 1981..... | 1,750.0 | 682.5 | 1,067.5 | 43.97 | 92.13 | 32.96 |
| 1982..... | 1,759.3 | 677.3 | 1,082.0 | 43.63 | 89.12 | 33.06 |
| 1983..... | 2,004.3 | 701.5 | 1,302.8 | 49.12 | 90.40 | 39.41 |
| 1984..... | N/A | N/A | N/A | 55.47 | 93.24 | 46.57 |

NA Data not available

Note: Data are not from the household income and expenditure surveys, nor necessarily consistent with the survey data.

Source: Guojia tongji ju, Zhongguo maoyi wujia tongji ziliao 1952-1983 [State Statistical Bureau, Trade and Price Statistics 1952-1983] (1984), p.33; and Tongji [Statistics], Vol. 8, 1985, p. 48.

Table 46. Total and Per Capita Consumption of Liquor, by Residence: 1952 to 1984

| Year | Total consumption (in 10 thousand tons) | | | Per capita consumption (in jin) | | |
|---|---|---|---|---|---|---|
| | China | Urban | Rural | China | Urban | Rural |
| 1952..... | 64.6 | 30.1 | 34.5 | 2.28 | 8.67 | 1.38 |
| 1953..... | 75.8 | 35.7 | 40.1 | 2.65 | 9.68 | 1.58 |
| 1954..... | 72.1 | 33.3 | 38.8 | 2.42 | 8.30 | 1.51 |
| 1955..... | 64.8 | 29.4 | 35.4 | 2.13 | 7.02 | 1.35 |
| 1956..... | 76.0 | 32.5 | 43.5 | 2.45 | 6.89 | 1.65 |
| 1957..... | 86.7 | 38.0 | 48.7 | 2.73 | 7.60 | 1.82 |
| 1958..... | 92.7 | 38.6 | 54.1 | 2.84 | 6.62 | 2.02 |
| 1959..... | 122.3 | 50.5 | 71.8 | 3.69 | 7.76 | 2.70 |
| 1960..... | 128.2 | 66.2 | 62.0 | 3.86 | 9.58 | 2.36 |
| 1961..... | 73.3 | 45.2 | 28.1 | 2.22 | 6.97 | 1.06 |
| 1962..... | 75.9 | 41.7 | 34.2 | 2.28 | 7.19 | 1.25 |
| 1963..... | 81.4 | 44.0 | 37.4 | 2.39 | 7.81 | 1.32 |
| 1964..... | 86.0 | 44.7 | 41.3 | 2.47 | 7.65 | 1.42 |
| 1965..... | 93.7 | 43.6 | 50.1 | 2.60 | 7.12 | 1.68 |
| 1966..... | 99.4 | 42.5 | 56.9 | 2.69 | 7.11 | 1.84 |
| 1967..... | 108.2 | 49.5 | 58.7 | 2.86 | 7.97 | 1.86 |
| 1968..... | 98.9 | 51.9 | 47.0 | 2.55 | 8.27 | 1.45 |
| 1969..... | 115.0 | 56.8 | 58.2 | 2.89 | 8.92 | 1.74 |
| 1970..... | 123.3 | 58.0 | 65.3 | 3.01 | 8.69 | 1.91 |
| 1971..... | 139.9 | 65.1 | 74.8 | 3.33 | 9.28 | 2.14 |
| 1972..... | 157.4 | 71.8 | 85.6 | 3.65 | 10.21 | 2.37 |
| 1973..... | 163.0 | 81.3 | 81.7 | 3.70 | 11.42 | 2.21 |
| 1974..... | 179.6 | 85.7 | 93.9 | 3.99 | 11.83 | 2.48 |
| 1975..... | 199.5 | 106.3 | 93.2 | 4.35 | 14.45 | 2.42 |
| 1976..... | 232.8 | 114.0 | 118.8 | 5.00 | 15.04 | 3.05 |
| 1977..... | 236.7 | 111.9 | 124.8 | 5.01 | 13.82 | 3.19 |
| 1978..... | 246.0 | 114.0 | 132.0 | 5.14 | 13.38 | 3.36 |
| 1979..... | 289.2 | 130.0 | 159.2 | 5.96 | 14.81 | 4.09 |
| 1980..... | 334.2 | 140.0 | 194.2 | 6.81 | 16.49 | 4.85 |
| 1981..... | 439.2 | 177.9 | 261.3 | 8.83 | 19.21 | 6.45 |
| 1982..... | 528.8 | 206.2 | 322.6 | 10.49 | 21.71 | 7.89 |
| 1983..... | 592.7 | 214.0 | 378.7 | 11.62 | 22.06 | 9.17 |
| 1984..... | N/A | N/A | N/A | 13.19 | 25.16 | 10.36 |

NA Data not available
One jin = 0.5 kg.

Note: Data are not from the household income and expenditure surveys, nor necessarily consistent with the survey data.

Source: Guojia tongji ju, Zhongguo maoyi wujia tongji ziliao 1952-1983 [State Statistical Bureau, Trade and Price Statistics 1952-1983] (1984), p. 34; and Tongji [Statistics], Vol. 8, 1985, p. 48.

Table 47. Total and Per Capita Consumption of Cloth Material, by Residence: 1952 to 1984

| Year | Total consumption (in 100 million meters) | | | Per capita consumption (in chi) | | |
|---|---|---|---|---|---|---|
| | China | Urban | Rural | China | Urban | Rural |
| 1952..... | 32.4 | 9.3 | 23.1 | 17.12 | 40.19 | 13.91 |
| 1953..... | 42.6 | 11.8 | 30.8 | 22.03 | 48.00 | 18.25 |
| 1954..... | 44.1 | 12.1 | 32.0 | 22.27 | 45.22 | 18.69 |
| 1955..... | 41.6 | 10.5 | 31.1 | 20.55 | 37.63 | 17.82 |
| 1956..... | 53.6 | 13.9 | 39.7 | 25.93 | 44.18 | 22.65 |
| 1957..... | 43.4 | 11.4 | 32.0 | 20.47 | 34.20 | 17.91 |
| 1958..... | 54.6 | 15.6 | 39.0 | 25.12 | 40.13 | 21.86 |
| 1959..... | 64.4 | 17.7 | 46.7 | 29.17 | 40.81 | 26.32 |
| 1960..... | 55.4 | 18.0 | 37.4 | 25.05 | 39.06 | 21.36 |
| 1961..... | 18.9 | 6.6 | 12.3 | 8.60 | 15.26 | 6.97 |
| 1962..... | 24.6 | 8.0 | 16.6 | 11.10 | 21.47 | 9.01 |
| 1963..... | 27.8 | 9.0 | 18.8 | 12.24 | 23.84 | 9.92 |
| 1964..... | 35.8 | 11.6 | 24.2 | 15.40 | 29.62 | 12.52 |
| 1965..... | 44.4 | 14.3 | 30.1 | 18.51 | 35.00 | 15.13 |
| 1966..... | 48.9 | 15.2 | 33.7 | 19.89 | 38.12 | 16.36 |
| 1967..... | 53.6 | 16.8 | 36.8 | 21.33 | 40.57 | 17.50 |
| 1968..... | 40.1 | 12.7 | 27.4 | 15.51 | 30.34 | 12.65 |
| 1969..... | 57.4 | 17.9 | 39.5 | 21.60 | 42.18 | 17.68 |
| 1970..... | 66.4 | 20.9 | 45.5 | 24.33 | 46.97 | 19.92 |
| 1971..... | 63.4 | 18.8 | 44.6 | 22.62 | 40.19 | 19.10 |
| 1972..... | 63.1 | 19.0 | 44.1 | 21.96 | 40.53 | 18.34 |
| 1973..... | 63.6 | 19.9 | 43.7 | 21.62 | 41.92 | 17.72 |
| 1974..... | 70.6 | 22.5 | 48.1 | 23.52 | 46.58 | 19.10 |
| 1975..... | 69.8 | 22.4 | 47.4 | 22.84 | 45.67 | 18.47 |
| 1976..... | 73.1 | 23.4 | 49.7 | 23.55 | 46.29 | 19.12 |
| 1977..... | 73.2 | 23.1 | 50.1 | 23.26 | 41.80 | 19.21 |
| 1978..... | 76.9 | 24.4 | 52.5 | 24.11 | 42.93 | 20.03 |
| 1979..... | 86.8 | 27.1 | 59.7 | 26.85 | 46.31 | 22.54 |
| 1980..... | 98.4 | 29.5 | 68.9 | 30.06 | 48.97 | 25.79 |
| 1981..... | 102.5 | 30.5 | 72.0 | 30.91 | 49.41 | 26.68 |
| 1982..... | 100.8 | 29.0 | 71.8 | 30.00 | 45.79 | 26.33 |
| 1983..... | 105.4 | 29.5 | 75.9 | 30.99 | 45.62 | 27.56 |
| 1984..... | N/A | N/A | N/A | 32.52 | 47.04 | 29.09 |

NA Data not available
One chi = 1/3 meter

Note: Data are not from the household income and expenditure surveys, nor necessarily consistent with the survey data.

Source: Guojia tongji ju, Zhongguo maoyi wujia tongji ziliao 1952-1983 [State Statistical Bureau, Trade and Price Statistics 1952-1983] (1984), p. 35; China: A Statistics Survey in 1985 (1985), p. 96, and Tongji [Statistics], Vol. 8, 1985, p. 48.

Table 48. Total and Per Capita Consumption of Cotton Cloth, by Residence 1952 to 1984

| Year | Total consumption (in 100 million meters) | | | Per capita consumption (in chi) | | |
|---|---|---|---|---|---|---|
| | China | Urban | Rural | China | Urban | Rural |
| 1952..... | 32.4 | 9.3 | 23.1 | 17.12 | 40.19 | 13.91 |
| 1953..... | 42.6 | 11.8 | 30.8 | 22.03 | 48.00 | 18.25 |
| 1954..... | 44.1 | 12.1 | 32.0 | 22.27 | 45.22 | 18.69 |
| 1955..... | 41.6 | 10.5 | 31.1 | 20.55 | 37.63 | 17.82 |
| 1956..... | 53.6 | 13.9 | 39.7 | 25.93 | 44.18 | 22.65 |
| 1957..... | 43.4 | 11.4 | 32.0 | 20.47 | 34.20 | 17.91 |
| 1958..... | 54.6 | 15.6 | 39.0 | 25.12 | 40.13 | 21.86 |
| 1959..... | 64.4 | 17.7 | 46.7 | 29.17 | 40.81 | 26.32 |
| 1960..... | 55.4 | 18.0 | 37.4 | 25.05 | 39.06 | 21.36 |
| 1961..... | 18.9 | 6.6 | 12.3 | 8.60 | 15.26 | 6.97 |
| 1962..... | 24.2 | 7.8 | 16.4 | 10.92 | 20.93 | 8.90 |
| 1963..... | 26.8 | 8.4 | 18.4 | 11.80 | 22.25 | 9.71 |
| 1964..... | 33.8 | 10.5 | 23.3 | 14.54 | 26.81 | 12.05 |
| 1965..... | 41.9 | 13.0 | 28.9 | 17.47 | 31.82 | 14.53 |
| 1966..... | 46.0 | 13.7 | 32.3 | 18.71 | 34.36 | 15.68 |
| 1967..... | 49.7 | 14.8 | 34.9 | 19.74 | 35.74 | 16.59 |
| 1968..... | 37.0 | 11.1 | 25.9 | 14.31 | 26.52 | 11.96 |
| 1969..... | 54.2 | 16.2 | 38.0 | 20.40 | 38.17 | 17.02 |
| 1970..... | 62.2 | 18.7 | 43.5 | 22.79 | 42.03 | 19.04 |
| 1971..... | 59.1 | 16.6 | 42.5 | 21.09 | 35.49 | 18.20 |
| 1972..... | 57.7 | 16.2 | 41.5 | 20.08 | 34.56 | 17.26 |
| 1973..... | 55.5 | 15.7 | 39.8 | 18.87 | 33.07 | 16.14 |
| 1974..... | 61.6 | 17.8 | 43.8 | 20.52 | 36.85 | 17.39 |
| 1975..... | 60.2 | 17.5 | 42.7 | 19.70 | 35.68 | 16.64 |
| 1976..... | 62.6 | 18.0 | 44.6 | 20.17 | 35.61 | 17.16 |
| 1977..... | 61.2 | 16.9 | 44.3 | 19.45 | 31.31 | 16.99 |
| 1978..... | 63.7 | 17.8 | 45.9 | 19.97 | 31.32 | 17.51 |
| 1979..... | 66.8 | 18.1 | 48.7 | 20.66 | 30.93 | 18.39 |
| 1980..... | 71.9 | 19.3 | 52.6 | 21.96 | 32.04 | 19.69 |
| 1981..... | 71.0 | 19.0 | 52.0 | 21.41 | 30.78 | 19.27 |
| 1982..... | 67.0 | 16.8 | 50.2 | 19.94 | 26.53 | 18.41 |
| 1983..... | 61.0 | 14.8 | 46.2 | 17.94 | 22.89 | 16.78 |
| 1984..... | N/A | N/A | N/A | 18.56 | 23.52 | 17.39 |

NA Data not available
One chi = 1/3 meter

Note: Data are not from the household income and expenditure surveys, nor necessarily consistent with the survey data.

Source: Guojia tongji ju, Zhongguo maoyi wujia tongji ziliao 1952-1983 [State Statistical Bureau, Trade and Price Statistics 1952-1983] (1984), p. 36; and Tongji [Statistics], Vol. 8, 1985, p. 48.

Table 49. Total and Per Capita Consumption of Chemical Fiber Cloth, by Residence: 1952 to 1984

| Year | Total consumption (in 100 million meters) | | | Per capita consumption (in chi) | | |
|---|---|---|---|---|---|---|
| | China | Urban | Rural | China | Urban | Rural |
| 1952..... | N/A | N/A | N/A | N/A | N/A | N/A |
| 1953..... | N/A | N/A | N/A | N/A | N/A | N/A |
| 1954..... | N/A | N/A | N/A | N/A | N/A | N/A |
| 1955..... | N/A | N/A | N/A | N/A | N/A | N/A |
| 1956..... | N/A | N/A | N/A | N/A | N/A | N/A |
| 1957..... | N/A | N/A | N/A | N/A | N/A | N/A |
| 1958..... | N/A | N/A | N/A | N/A | N/A | N/A |
| 1959..... | N/A | N/A | N/A | N/A | N/A | N/A |
| 1960..... | N/A | N/A | N/A | N/A | N/A | N/A |
| 1961..... | N/A | N/A | N/A | N/A | N/A | N/A |
| 1962..... | .4 | .2 | .2 | .18 | .54 | .11 |
| 1963..... | 1.0 | .6 | .4 | .44 | 1.59 | .21 |
| 1964..... | 2.0 | 1.1 | .9 | .86 | 2.81 | .47 |
| 1965..... | 2.5 | 1.3 | 1.2 | 1.04 | 3.18 | .60 |
| 1966..... | 2.9 | 1.5 | 1.4 | 1.18 | 3.76 | .68 |
| 1967..... | 3.9 | 2.0 | 1.9 | 1.59 | 4.83 | .91 |
| 1968..... | 3.1 | 1.6 | 1.5 | 1.20 | 3.82 | .69 |
| 1969..... | 3.2 | 1.7 | 1.5 | 1.20 | 4.01 | .66 |
| 1970..... | 4.2 | 2.2 | 2.0 | 1.54 | 4.94 | .88 |
| 1971..... | 4.3 | 2.2 | 2.1 | 1.53 | 4.70 | .90 |
| 1972..... | 5.4 | 2.8 | 2.6 | 1.88 | 5.97 | 1.08 |
| 1973..... | 8.1 | 4.2 | 3.9 | 2.75 | 8.85 | 1.58 |
| 1974..... | 9.0 | 4.7 | 4.3 | 3.00 | 9.73 | 1.71 |
| 1975..... | 9.6 | 4.9 | 4.7 | 3.14 | 9.99 | 1.83 |
| 1976..... | 10.5 | 5.4 | 5.1 | 3.38 | 10.68 | 1.96 |
| 1977..... | 12.0 | 6.2 | 5.8 | 3.81 | 11.49 | 2.22 |
| 1978..... | 13.2 | 6.6 | 6.6 | 4.14 | 11.61 | 2.52 |
| 1979..... | 20.0 | 9.0 | 11.0 | 6.19 | 15.38 | 4.15 |
| 1980..... | 26.5 | 10.2 | 16.3 | 8.10 | 16.93 | 6.10 |
| 1981..... | 31.5 | 11.5 | 20.0 | 9.50 | 18.63 | 7.41 |
| 1982..... | 33.8 | 12.2 | 21.6 | 10.06 | 19.26 | 7.92 |
| 1983..... | 44.4 | 14.7 | 29.7 | 13.05 | 22.73 | 10.78 |
| 1984..... | N/A | N/A | N/A | 13.96 | 23.52 | 11.70 |

NA Data not available
One chi = 1/3 meter

Note: Data are not from the household income and expenditure surveys, nor necessarily consistent with the survey data.

Data include cotton and chemical fiber blends, and chemical fiber cloth.

Source: Guojia tongji ju, Zhongguo maoyi wujia tongji ziliao 1952-1983 [State Statistical Bureau, Trade and Price Statistics 1952-1983] (1984), p. 37; and Tongji [Statistics], Vol. 8, 1985, p. 48.

Table 50. Total and Per Capita Consumption of Knitted Underwear by Residence: 1952 to 1984

| Year | Total consumption (in 10 thousand pieces) | | | Per capita consumption (in pieces) | | |
|---|---|---|---|---|---|---|
| | China | Urban | Rural | China | Urban | Rural |
| 1952..... | 2,900.4 | 1,012.2 | 1,888.2 | .05 | .15 | .04 |
| 1953..... | 4,838.4 | 1,683.8 | 3,154.6 | .08 | .24 | .06 |
| 1954..... | 9,777.6 | 3,441.6 | 6,336.0 | .16 | .43 | .12 |
| 1955..... | 9,636.0 | 3,372.6 | 6,263.4 | .16 | .40 | .12 |
| 1956..... | 16,711.2 | 5,681.8 | 11,029.4 | .27 | .60 | .21 |
| 1957..... | 20,253.6 | 6,683.7 | 13,569.9 | .32 | .67 | .25 |
| 1958..... | 28,230.0 | 9,598.2 | 18,631.8 | .43 | .82 | .35 |
| 1959..... | 44,683.2 | 15,862.5 | 28,820.7 | .67 | 1.22 | .54 |
| 1960..... | 50,774.4 | 18,278.8 | 32,495.6 | .77 | 1.32 | .62 |
| 1961..... | 10,130.9 | 4,275.2 | 5,855.7 | .15 | .33 | .11 |
| 1962..... | 12,865.2 | 5,068.9 | 7,796.3 | .19 | .45 | .14 |
| 1963..... | 18,247.2 | 6,660.2 | 11,587.0 | .27 | .59 | .20 |
| 1964..... | 15,718.6 | 5,690.1 | 10,028.5 | .23 | .48 | .17 |
| 1965..... | 23,199.6 | 8,375.1 | 14,824.5 | .32 | .68 | .25 |
| 1966..... | 29,427.5 | 10,593.9 | 18,833.6 | .40 | .89 | .30 |
| 1967..... | 34,096.1 | 12,240.5 | 21,855.6 | .45 | .99 | .35 |
| 1968..... | 27,656.3 | 9,873.3 | 17,783.0 | .36 | .79 | .27 |
| 1969..... | 40,255.6 | 14,290.7 | 25,964.9 | .51 | 1.12 | .39 |
| 1970..... | 42,384.4 | 14,961.7 | 27,422.7 | .52 | 1.12 | .40 |
| 1971..... | 43,947.8 | 15,381.7 | 28,566.1 | .52 | 1.10 | .41 |
| 1972..... | 46,753.1 | 16,223.3 | 30,529.8 | .54 | 1.15 | .42 |
| 1973..... | 47,058.7 | 16,188.2 | 30,870.5 | .53 | 1.14 | .42 |
| 1974..... | 57,238.4 | 19,518.3 | 37,720.1 | .64 | 1.34 | .50 |
| 1975..... | 60,283.7 | 20,375.9 | 39,907.8 | .66 | 1.38 | .52 |
| 1976..... | 61,604.0 | 20,637.3 | 40,966.7 | .66 | 1.36 | .53 |
| 1977..... | 64,819.2 | 21,390.0 | 43,429.2 | .69 | 1.32 | .56 |
| 1978..... | 69,535.5 | 22,950.0 | 46,585.5 | .73 | 1.35 | .59 |
| 1979..... | 90,928.0 | 30,437.0 | 60,491.0 | .94 | 1.73 | .76 |
| 1980..... | 96,676.0 | 30,940.0 | 65,736.0 | .98 | 1.71 | .82 |
| 1981..... | 107,592.6 | 33,229.6 | 74,363.0 | 1.08 | 1.79 | .92 |
| 1982..... | 117,069.0 | 35,251.0 | 81,818.0 | 1.16 | 1.86 | 1.00 |
| 1983..... | 121,245.1 | 35,381.1 | 85,864.0 | 1.19 | 1.82 | 1.04 |
| 1984..... | N/A | N/A | N/A | 1.27 | 1.93 | 1.12 |

NA Data not available

Note: Data are not from the household income and expenditure surveys, nor necessarily consistent with the survey data.

Data include sleeveless undershirts, knitted shirts, and pants, sweatshirts, and sweatpants.

Source: Guojia tongji ju, Zhongguo maoyi wujia tongji ziliao 1952-1983 [State Statistical Bureau, Trade and Price Statistics 1952-1983] (1984), p. 38; and Tongji [Statistics], Vol. 8, 1985, p. 48.

Table 51. Total and Per Capita Consumption of Shoes, by Residence: 1952 to 1984

| Year | Total consumption (in 10 thousand pairs) | | | Per capita consumption (in pairs) | | |
|---|---|---|---|---|---|---|
| | China | Urban | Rural | China | Urban | Rural |
| 1952..... | 10,330.8 | 7,231.4 | 3,099.4 | .18 | 1.04 | .06 |
| 1953..... | 12,448.1 | 8,388.1 | 4,060.0 | .21 | 1.14 | .08 |
| 1954..... | 15,663.0 | 9,424.5 | 6,238.5 | .26 | 1.17 | .12 |
| 1955..... | 13,504.7 | 10,198.2 | 3,306.5 | .22 | 1.22 | .06 |
| 1956..... | 18,212.8 | 11,839.8 | 6,373.0 | .29 | 1.25 | .12 |
| 1957..... | 20,231.8 | 13,075.4 | 7,156.4 | .32 | 1.31 | .13 |
| 1958..... | 28,216.1 | 16,589.9 | 11,626.2 | .43 | 1.42 | .22 |
| 1959..... | 31,564.3 | 18,734.5 | 12,829.8 | .48 | 1.44 | .24 |
| 1960..... | 34,649.5 | 21,785.9 | 12,863.6 | .52 | 1.58 | .24 |
| 1961..... | 27,211.7 | 17,814.2 | 9,397.5 | .41 | 1.37 | .18 |
| 1962..... | 29,201.4 | 15,290.3 | 13,911.1 | .44 | 1.37 | .25 |
| 1963..... | 29,082.7 | 15,856.1 | 13,226.6 | .43 | 1.40 | .23 |
| 1964..... | 31,759.5 | 17,207.2 | 14,552.3 | .46 | 1.46 | .25 |
| 1965..... | 32,768.0 | 17,350.0 | 15,418.0 | .46 | 1.42 | .26 |
| 1966..... | 36,942.1 | 19,205.0 | 17,737.1 | .50 | 1.61 | .29 |
| 1967..... | 38,955.7 | 19,865.0 | 19,090.7 | .52 | 1.60 | .30 |
| 1968..... | 39,682.0 | 19,838.0 | 19,844.0 | .51 | 1.58 | .31 |
| 1969..... | 43,222.0 | 21,178.0 | 22,044.0 | .54 | 1.66 | .33 |
| 1970..... | 48,755.1 | 23,158.0 | 25,597.1 | .60 | 1.73 | .37 |
| 1971..... | 50,396.9 | 23,182.0 | 27,214.9 | .60 | 1.65 | .39 |
| 1972..... | 55,822.3 | 25,120.0 | 30,702.3 | .65 | 1.79 | .43 |
| 1973..... | 64,305.3 | 28,294.0 | 36,011.3 | .73 | 1.99 | .49 |
| 1974..... | 65,686.1 | 28,245.0 | 37,441.1 | .73 | 1.95 | .50 |
| 1975..... | 70,810.3 | 29,740.0 | 41,070.3 | .77 | 2.02 | .53 |
| 1976..... | 75,046.0 | 30,768.0 | 44,278.0 | .81 | 2.03 | .57 |
| 1977..... | 77,505.7 | 31,002.0 | 46,503.7 | .82 | 1.91 | .59 |
| 1978..... | 86,929.9 | 33,903.0 | 53,026.9 | .91 | 1.99 | .67 |
| 1979..... | 93,284.2 | 35,448.0 | 57,836.2 | .96 | 2.02 | .73 |
| 1980..... | 105,632.0 | 39,132.0 | 66,500.0 | 1.08 | 2.17 | .83 |
| 1981..... | 112,405.0 | 43,838.0 | 68,567.0 | 1.13 | 2.37 | .85 |
| 1982..... | 115,454.5 | 42,718.0 | 72,736.5 | 1.15 | 2.25 | .89 |
| 1983..... | 118,582.4 | 42,503.8 | 76,078.6 | 1.16 | 2.19 | .92 |
| 1984..... | N/A | N/A | N/A | 1.30 | 2.12 | 1.11 |

NA Data not available

Note: Data are not from the household income and expenditure surveys, nor necessarily consistent with the survey data.

Data include leather shoes, rubber shoes (galoshes, sneakers, etc.), cloth shoes, and plastic shoes.

Source: Guojia tongji ju, Zhongguo maoyi wujia tongji ziliao 1952-1983 [State Statistical Bureau, Trade and Price Statistics 1952-1983] (1984), p. 39; and Tongji [Statistics], Vol. 8, 1985, p. 48.

Table 52. Total and Per Capita Consumption of Matches, by Residence: 1952 to 1984

| Year | Total consumption (in 10 thousand cases) | | | Per capita consumption (in boxes) | | |
|---|---|---|---|---|---|---|
| | China | Urban | Rural | China | Urban | Rural |
| 1952..... | 816.0 | 154.2 | 661.8 | 14.40 | 22.20 | 13.30 |
| 1953..... | 865.4 | 169.1 | 696.3 | 14.90 | 22.90 | 15.80 |
| 1954..... | 994.6 | 184.4 | 810.2 | 16.70 | 23.00 | 13.80 |
| 1955..... | 1,025.9 | 191.6 | 834.3 | 16.90 | 22.90 | 15.90 |
| 1956..... | 1,081.6 | 204.8 | 876.8 | 17.40 | 21.70 | 16.70 |
| 1957..... | 1,100.0 | 210.0 | 890.0 | 17.30 | 21.00 | 16.60 |
| 1958..... | 1,191.4 | 278.8 | 912.6 | 18.30 | 23.90 | 17.20 |
| 1959..... | 1,240.1 | 287.7 | 952.4 | 18.70 | 22.10 | 17.90 |
| 1960..... | 1,430.5 | 432.0 | 998.5 | 21.60 | 31.30 | 19.00 |
| 1961..... | 1,024.7 | 333.0 | 619.7 | 15.50 | 25.70 | 13.10 |
| 1962..... | 1,070.3 | 267.6 | 802.7 | 16.10 | 23.10 | 14.60 |
| 1963..... | 1,105.2 | 223.0 | 882.2 | 16.20 | 19.80 | 15.50 |
| 1964..... | 1,158.3 | 219.0 | 939.3 | 16.60 | 18.70 | 16.20 |
| 1965..... | 1,266.0 | 229.9 | 1,036.1 | 17.60 | 18.76 | 17.36 |
| 1966..... | 1,376.0 | 223.6 | 1,152.4 | 18.65 | 18.69 | 18.64 |
| 1967..... | 1,501.0 | 275.5 | 1,225.5 | 19.87 | 22.17 | 19.42 |
| 1968..... | 1,021.0 | 250.9 | 770.1 | 13.17 | 19.98 | 11.85 |
| 1969..... | 1,198.0 | 281.5 | 916.5 | 15.03 | 22.11 | 13.68 |
| 1970..... | 1,393.4 | 296.7 | 1,096.7 | 17.02 | 22.23 | 16.00 |
| 1971..... | 1,364.3 | 264.2 | 1,100.1 | 16.23 | 18.83 | 15.70 |
| 1972..... | 1,406.1 | 275.0 | 1,131.1 | 16.31 | 19.56 | 15.68 |
| 1973..... | 1,554.4 | 303.9 | 1,250.5 | 17.62 | 21.34 | 16.90 |
| 1974..... | 1,599.6 | 340.4 | 1,259.2 | 17.76 | 23.49 | 16.66 |
| 1975..... | 1,631.5 | 369.6 | 1,261.9 | 17.79 | 25.12 | 16.39 |
| 1976..... | 1,717.0 | 404.0 | 1,313.0 | 18.44 | 26.64 | 16.84 |
| 1977..... | 1,729.0 | 437.0 | 1,292.0 | 18.31 | 26.99 | 16.52 |
| 1978..... | 1,784.4 | 447.5 | 1,336.9 | 18.65 | 26.25 | 17.00 |
| 1979..... | 1,937.6 | 469.0 | 1,468.6 | 19.98 | 26.71 | 18.49 |
| 1980..... | 2,134.0 | 545.0 | 1,589.0 | 21.73 | 30.16 | 19.83 |
| 1981..... | 2,364.0 | 590.0 | 1,774.0 | 23.76 | 31.86 | 21.91 |
| 1982..... | 2,265.4 | 579.2 | 1,686.2 | 22.47 | 30.48 | 20.61 |
| 1983..... | 2,530.5 | 645.3 | 1,885.2 | 24.80 | 33.26 | 22.82 |
| 1984..... | N/A | N/A | N/A | 26.08 | 34.53 | 24.08 |

NA Data not available

Note: Data are not from the household income and expenditure surveys, nor necessarily consistent with the survey data.

Source: Guojia tongji ju, Zhongguo maoyi wujia tongji ziliao 1952-1983 [State Statistical Bureau, Trade and Price Statistics 1952-1983] (1984), p. 40; and Tongji [Statistics], Vol. 8, 1985, p. 48.

Table 53. Total and Per Capita Consumption of Soap, by Residence: 1952 to 1984

| Year | Total consumption (in 10 thousand cases) | | | Per capita consumption (in pieces) | | |
|---|---|---|---|---|---|---|
| | China | Urban | Rural | China | Urban | Rural |
| 1952..... | 630.0 | 410.0 | 220.0 | 1.33 | 7.03 | .53 |
| 1953..... | 684.5 | 434.5 | 250.0 | 1.42 | 7.07 | .59 |
| 1954..... | 772.9 | 472.9 | 300.0 | 1.56 | 7.07 | .70 |
| 1955..... | 837.1 | 502.8 | 334.3 | 1.65 | 7.33 | .77 |
| 1956..... | 950.0 | 562.9 | 387.1 | 1.84 | 7.16 | .88 |
| 1957..... | 1,165.0 | 665.0 | 500.0 | 2.20 | 7.89 | 1.12 |
| 1958..... | 1,555.5 | 962.9 | 592.6 | 2.86 | 9.91 | 1.33 |
| 1959..... | 1,940.9 | 1,183.9 | 757.0 | 3.52 | 10.92 | 1.52 |
| 1960..... | 1,918.9 | 1,191.6 | 727.3 | 3.47 | 10.34 | 1.66 |
| 1961..... | 1,165.0 | 736.3 | 428.7 | 2.12 | 6.81 | .97 |
| 1962..... | 799.5 | 511.7 | 287.8 | 1.44 | 5.30 | .63 |
| 1963..... | 1,077.3 | 592.9 | 484.4 | 1.90 | 6.32 | 1.02 |
| 1964..... | 1,155.3 | 622.5 | 532.8 | 1.99 | 6.39 | 1.10 |
| 1965..... | 1,357.0 | 805.2 | 551.8 | 2.26 | 7.88 | 1.11 |
| 1966..... | 1,947.0 | 945.3 | 1,001.7 | 3.17 | 9.48 | 1.94 |
| 1967..... | 2,311.0 | 1,153.4 | 1,157.6 | 3.67 | 11.14 | 2.21 |
| 1968..... | 1,978.0 | 1,274.2 | 703.8 | 3.06 | 12.18 | 1.30 |
| 1969..... | 2,439.0 | 1,385.8 | 1,053.8 | 3.67 | 13.06 | 1.89 |
| 1970..... | 2,330.4 | 1,502.4 | 828.0 | 3.42 | 13.51 | 1.45 |
| 1971..... | 2,456.6 | 1,464.5 | 992.1 | 3.51 | 12.53 | 1.70 |
| 1972..... | 2,712.3 | 1,700.1 | 1,012.2 | 3.78 | 14.51 | 1.68 |
| 1973..... | 2,857.1 | 1,718.0 | 1,139.1 | 3.89 | 14.48 | 1.85 |
| 1974..... | 2,885.5 | 1,805.0 | 1,080.5 | 3.84 | 14.95 | 1.72 |
| 1975..... | 3,224.1 | 2,005.0 | 1,219.1 | 4.22 | 16.35 | 1.90 |
| 1976..... | 3,151.1 | 2,083.2 | 1,067.9 | 4.06 | 16.49 | 1.64 |
| 1977..... | 2,956.6 | 2,045.3 | 911.3 | 3.76 | 15.16 | 1.40 |
| 1978..... | 3,204.2 | 2,090.0 | 1,114.2 | 4.02 | 14.71 | 1.70 |
| 1979..... | 3,676.0 | 2,184.0 | 1,492.0 | 4.55 | 14.93 | 2.25 |
| 1980..... | 4,043.0 | 2,245.0 | 1,798.0 | 4.94 | 14.91 | 2.69 |
| 1981..... | 4,700.0 | 2,397.0 | 2,303.0 | 5.67 | 15.53 | 3.41 |
| 1982..... | 4,850.0 | 2,376.5 | 2,473.5 | 5.77 | 15.01 | 3.63 |
| 1983..... | 5,403.4 | 2,508.0 | 2,895.4 | 6.36 | 15.51 | 4.21 |
| 1984..... | N/A | N/A | N/A | 6.84 | 15.95 | 4.69 |

NA Data not available

Note: Data are not from the household income and expenditure surveys, nor necessarily consistent with the survey data.

Source: Guojia tongji ju, Zhongguo maoyi wujia tongji ziliao 1952-1983 [State Statistical Bureau, Trade and Price Statistics 1952-1983] (1984), p. 41; and Tongji [Statistics], Vol. 8, 1985, p. 48.

Table 54. Total and Per Capita Consumption of Coal, by Residence: 1952 to 1984

| Year | Total consumption (in 10 thousand tons) | | | Per capita consumption (in jin) | | |
|---|---|---|---|---|---|---|
| | China | Urban | Rural | China | Urban | Rural |
| 1952..... | 2,361.1 | 1,253.8 | 1,107.3 | 83.19 | 361.22 | 44.45 |
| 1953..... | 2,997.8 | 1,724.7 | 1,273.1 | 103.35 | 467.72 | 50.28 |
| 1954..... | 3,566.0 | 1,963.5 | 1,602.5 | 120.06 | 489.22 | 62.38 |
| 1955..... | 3,966.7 | 2,152.2 | 1,814.5 | 130.61 | 514.14 | 69.30 |
| 1956..... | 5,218.8 | 2,605.8 | 2,613.0 | 168.29 | 552.22 | 99.39 |
| 1957..... | 5,413.4 | 2,800.6 | 2,612.8 | 170.19 | 560.12 | 97.47 |
| 1958..... | 5,834.5 | 3,561.4 | 2,273.1 | 178.98 | 610.72 | 84.92 |
| 1959..... | 6,311.2 | 3,968.4 | 2,342.8 | 190.57 | 609.96 | 88.04 |
| 1960..... | 7,202.9 | 4,861.4 | 2,341.5 | 217.12 | 703.28 | 89.16 |
| 1961..... | 7,195.0 | 4,820.6 | 2,374.4 | 218.29 | 743.00 | 89.69 |
| 1962..... | 7,299.0 | 4,212.0 | 3,087.0 | 219.65 | 726.71 | 112.52 |
| 1963..... | 6,664.0 | 3,940.7 | 2,723.3 | 195.67 | 699.57 | 95.81 |
| 1964..... | 7,114.0 | 4,060.8 | 3,053.2 | 204.10 | 694.51 | 105.25 |
| 1965..... | 7,500.0 | 4,140.0 | 3,360.0 | 208.51 | 675.64 | 112.59 |
| 1966..... | 7,700.0 | 4,146.0 | 3,554.0 | 208.75 | 693.14 | 115.00 |
| 1967..... | 7,770.0 | 4,179.0 | 3,591.0 | 205.72 | 672.73 | 113.79 |
| 1968..... | 7,550.0 | 4,054.0 | 3,496.0 | 194.75 | 645.64 | 107.61 |
| 1969..... | 7,900.0 | 4,246.0 | 3,654.0 | 198.23 | 666.88 | 109.12 |
| 1970..... | 8,120.0 | 4,313.0 | 3,807.0 | 198.34 | 646.24 | 111.10 |
| 1971..... | 8,420.0 | 4,566.0 | 3,854.0 | 200.29 | 650.84 | 110.04 |
| 1972..... | 8,863.0 | 4,720.0 | 4,143.0 | 205.61 | 671.36 | 114.84 |
| 1973..... | 8,998.0 | 4,783.0 | 4,215.0 | 203.98 | 671.68 | 113.95 |
| 1974..... | 8,899.0 | 4,972.0 | 3,927.0 | 197.62 | 686.27 | 103.92 |
| 1975..... | 9,350.0 | 5,212.0 | 4,138.0 | 203.95 | 708.44 | 107.51 |
| 1976..... | 8,900.0 | 4,975.0 | 3,925.0 | 191.15 | 656.16 | 100.70 |
| 1977..... | 9,627.0 | 5,367.0 | 4,260.0 | 203.94 | 662.92 | 108.92 |
| 1978..... | 10,063.0 | 5,479.0 | 4,584.0 | 210.31 | 642.74 | 116.57 |
| 1979..... | 10,600.0 | 5,723.0 | 4,877.0 | 218.60 | 661.97 | 122.81 |
| 1980..... | 12,574.0 | 6,200.0 | 6,374.0 | 256.08 | 686.18 | 159.09 |
| 1981..... | 13,388.8 | 6,400.0 | 6,988.8 | 269.13 | 691.11 | 172.62 |
| 1982..... | 14,756.5 | 6,785.0 | 7,971.5 | 292.74 | 714.21 | 194.86 |
| 1983..... | 15,494.3 | 7,007.4 | 8,486.9 | 303.76 | 722.41 | 205.45 |
| 1984..... | N/A | N/A | N/A | 329.82 | 759.05 | 228.65 |

NA Data not available
One jin = 0.5 kg.

Note: Data are not from the household income and expenditure surveys, nor necessarily consistent with the survey data.

Source: Guojia tongji ju, Zhongguo maoyi wujia tongji ziliao 1952-1983 [State Statistical Bureau, Trade and Price Statistics 1952-1983] (1984), p. 49; and Tongji [Statistics], Vol. 8, 1985, p. 48.

Table 55. Total and Consumption Per 100 Persons of Thermos Bottles, by Residence: 1952 to 1984

| Year | Total consumption (in 10 thousand bottles) | | | Consumption per 100 persons (in bottles) | | |
|---|---|---|---|---|---|---|
| | China | Urban | Rural | China | Urban | Rural |
| 1952..... | 840.0 | 660.0 | 180.0 | 1.48 | 9.51 | .36 |
| 1953..... | 1,347.6 | 888.0 | 459.6 | 2.32 | 12.04 | .91 |
| 1954..... | 1,474.2 | 932.4 | 541.8 | 2.48 | 11.62 | 1.05 |
| 1955..... | 1,659.8 | 942.8 | 717.0 | 2.73 | 11.26 | 1.37 |
| 1956..... | 1,912.8 | 1,095.9 | 816.9 | 3.08 | 11.61 | 1.55 |
| 1957..... | 2,770.8 | 1,618.1 | 1,152.7 | 4.36 | 16.18 | 2.15 |
| 1958..... | 3,694.5 | 1,954.4 | 1,740.1 | 5.67 | 16.76 | 3.25 |
| 1959..... | 3,327.8 | 1,760.4 | 1,567.4 | 5.02 | 13.53 | 2.94 |
| 1960..... | 4,418.8 | 2,421.5 | 1,997.3 | 6.66 | 17.52 | 3.80 |
| 1961..... | 3,761.1 | 1,993.4 | 1,767.7 | 5.71 | 15.36 | 3.34 |
| 1962..... | 3,094.2 | 1,547.0 | 1,547.2 | 4.66 | 13.35 | 2.82 |
| 1963..... | 2,763.8 | 1,462.1 | 1,301.7 | 4.06 | 12.98 | 2.29 |
| 1964..... | 2,778.1 | 1,470.1 | 1,308.0 | 3.99 | 12.58 | 2.25 |
| 1965..... | 3,277.0 | 1,526.9 | 1,750.1 | 4.56 | 12.46 | 2.93 |
| 1966..... | 3,954.0 | 1,539.0 | 2,415.0 | 5.36 | 12.86 | 3.91 |
| 1967..... | 4,002.0 | 1,656.4 | 2,345.6 | 5.30 | 13.33 | 3.72 |
| 1968..... | 3,072.0 | 1,504.8 | 1,567.2 | 3.96 | 11.98 | 2.41 |
| 1969..... | 3,239.0 | 1,756.2 | 1,482.8 | 4.06 | 13.79 | 2.21 |
| 1970..... | 4,256.8 | 2,134.3 | 2,122.5 | 5.20 | 15.99 | 3.10 |
| 1971..... | 4,676.5 | 2,263.6 | 2,412.9 | 5.56 | 16.13 | 3.44 |
| 1972..... | 5,015.2 | 2,268.6 | 2,746.6 | 5.82 | 16.13 | 3.81 |
| 1973..... | 5,155.3 | 2,435.9 | 2,719.4 | 5.84 | 17.10 | 3.68 |
| 1974..... | 4,706.1 | 2,549.8 | 2,156.3 | 5.23 | 17.60 | 2.85 |
| 1975..... | 4,594.6 | 2,913.0 | 1,681.6 | 5.01 | 19.80 | 2.18 |
| 1976..... | 4,919.9 | 2,963.9 | 1,956.0 | 5.28 | 19.55 | 2.51 |
| 1977..... | 6,560.0 | 4,103.0 | 2,457.0 | 6.95 | 25.34 | 3.14 |
| 1978..... | 8,169.2 | 4,901.5 | 3,267.7 | 8.54 | 28.75 | 4.15 |
| 1979..... | 9,112.0 | 5,110.0 | 4,002.0 | 9.40 | 29.11 | 5.04 |
| 1980..... | 10,051.0 | 5,220.0 | 4,831.0 | 10.23 | 28.89 | 6.03 |
| 1981..... | 10,812.5 | 5,190.0 | 5,622.5 | 10.87 | 28.02 | 6.94 |
| 1982..... | 11,015.3 | 4,626.4 | 6,388.9 | 10.93 | 24.35 | 7.81 |
| 1983..... | 11,820.9 | 4,865.7 | 6,955.2 | 11.59 | 25.08 | 8.42 |
| 1984..... | N/A | N/A | N/A | N/A | N/A | N/A |

NA Data not available

Note: Data are not from the household income and expenditure surveys, nor necessarily consistent with the survey data.

Source: Guojia tongji ju, Zhongguo maoyi wujia tongji ziliao 1952-1983 [State Statistical Bureau, Trade and Price Statistics 1952-1983] (1984), p. 42.

Table 56. Total and Consumption Per 100 Persons of Enamel Mugs, by Residence: 1952 to 1984

| Year | Total consumption (in 10 thousand mugs) | | | Consumption per 100 persons (in mugs) | | |
|---|---|---|---|---|---|---|
| | China | Urban | Rural | China | Urban | Rural |
| 1952..... | 1,500.0 | 960.0 | 540.0 | 2.64 | 13.83 | 1.08 |
| 1953..... | 1,589.8 | 962.0 | 627.8 | 2.74 | 13.04 | 1.23 |
| 1954..... | 1,973.6 | 1,192.1 | 781.5 | 3.32 | 14.85 | 1.52 |
| 1955..... | 1,618.2 | 1,017.5 | 600.7 | 2.66 | 12.15 | 1.15 |
| 1956..... | 2,884.7 | 1,768.3 | 1,116.4 | 4.65 | 18.74 | 2.12 |
| 1957..... | 2,500.0 | 1,500.0 | 1,000.0 | 3.93 | 15.00 | 1.87 |
| 1958..... | 3,790.5 | 1,990.0 | 1,800.5 | 5.81 | 17.06 | 3.36 |
| 1959..... | 5,076.0 | 2,576.0 | 2,500.0 | 7.66 | 19.80 | 4.70 |
| 1960..... | 5,986.8 | 3,269.9 | 2,716.9 | 9.02 | 23.65 | 5.17 |
| 1961..... | 3,039.5 | 1,592.7 | 1,446.8 | 4.61 | 12.27 | 2.73 |
| 1962..... | 2,585.6 | 1,293.0 | 1,292.6 | 3.89 | 11.15 | 2.36 |
| 1963..... | 2,695.6 | 1,279.8 | 1,415.8 | 3.96 | 11.36 | 2.49 |
| 1964..... | 2,739.1 | 1,394.1 | 1,345.0 | 3.93 | 11.92 | 2.32 |
| 1965..... | 2,749.0 | 1,306.2 | 1,442.8 | 3.82 | 10.66 | 2.42 |
| 1966..... | 3,432.0 | 1,400.7 | 2,031.3 | 4.65 | 11.71 | 3.39 |
| 1967..... | 3,707.0 | 1,337.5 | 2,369.5 | 4.91 | 10.77 | 3.75 |
| 1968..... | 4,922.0 | 1,558.0 | 3,364.0 | 6.35 | 12.41 | 5.18 |
| 1969..... | 4,695.0 | 1,533.0 | 3,162.0 | 5.89 | 12.04 | 4.72 |
| 1970..... | 4,764.0 | 1,543.7 | 3,220.3 | 5.82 | 11.57 | 4.70 |
| 1971..... | 5,350.8 | 1,754.7 | 3,596.1 | 6.36 | 12.51 | 5.13 |
| 1972..... | 6,265.7 | 2,483.5 | 3,782.2 | 7.27 | 17.66 | 5.24 |
| 1973..... | 6,234.1 | 2,777.2 | 3,456.9 | 7.07 | 19.50 | 4.67 |
| 1974..... | 5,554.4 | 2,619.9 | 2,934.5 | 6.17 | 18.08 | 3.88 |
| 1975..... | 6,373.0 | 2,670.2 | 3,702.8 | 6.95 | 18.15 | 4.81 |
| 1976..... | 7,095.5 | 2,682.0 | 4,413.5 | 7.62 | 17.69 | 5.66 |
| 1977..... | 8,392.0 | 3,241.0 | 5,151.0 | 8.89 | 20.02 | 6.59 |
| 1978..... | 8,831.0 | 3,350.0 | 5,481.0 | 9.23 | 19.65 | 6.97 |
| 1979..... | 9,655.0 | 3,572.0 | 6,083.0 | 9.96 | 20.35 | 7.66 |
| 1980..... | 9,300.0 | 3,150.0 | 6,150.0 | 9.47 | 17.43 | 7.67 |
| 1981..... | 10,455.0 | 3,345.6 | 7,109.4 | 10.51 | 18.06 | 8.78 |
| 1982..... | 9,938.9 | 3,180.0 | 6,758.9 | 9.86 | 16.74 | 8.26 |
| 1983..... | 10,117.8 | 3,197.2 | 6,920.6 | 9.92 | 16.48 | 8.38 |
| 1984..... | N/A | N/A | N/A | N/A | N/A | N/A |

NA Data not available

Note: Data are not from the household income and expenditure surveys, nor necessarily consistent with the survey data.

Source: Guojia tongji ju, Zhongguo maoyi wujia tongji ziliao 1952-1983 [State Statistical Bureau, Trade and Price Statistics 1952-1983] (1984), p. 43.

Table 57. Total and Consumption Per 100 Persons of Enamel Bowls, by Residence: 1952 to 1984

| Year | Total consumption (in 10 thousand bowls) | | | Consumption per 100 persons (in bowls) | | |
|---|---|---|---|---|---|---|
| | China | Urban | Rural | China | Urban | Rural |
| 1952..... | 800.0 | 550.0 | 250.0 | 1.41 | 7.92 | .50 |
| 1953..... | 1,202.7 | 802.7 | 400.0 | 2.07 | 10.88 | .79 |
| 1954..... | 1,383.1 | 833.1 | 550.0 | 2.33 | 10.38 | 1.07 |
| 1955..... | 1,277.1 | 777.1 | 500.0 | 2.10 | 9.28 | .95 |
| 1956..... | 1,940.0 | 1,120.0 | 820.0 | 3.13 | 11.87 | 1.56 |
| 1957..... | 1,800.0 | 1,000.0 | 800.0 | 2.83 | 10.00 | 1.49 |
| 1958..... | 2,514.7 | 1,415.7 | 1,099.0 | 3.86 | 12.14 | 2.05 |
| 1959..... | 3,592.9 | 2,012.0 | 1,580.9 | 5.12 | 15.46 | 2.97 |
| 1960..... | 5,011.2 | 2,726.2 | 2,285.0 | 7.55 | 19.72 | 4.35 |
| 1961..... | 1,951.0 | 1,034.0 | 917.0 | 2.96 | 7.97 | 1.73 |
| 1962..... | 2,600.4 | 1,300.4 | 1,300.0 | 3.91 | 11.22 | 2.37 |
| 1963..... | 2,701.5 | 1,228.5 | 1,473.0 | 3.97 | 10.90 | 2.59 |
| 1964..... | 1,988.1 | 995.1 | 993.0 | 2.85 | 8.51 | 1.71 |
| 1965..... | 1,995.0 | 887.9 | 1,107.1 | 2.77 | 7.25 | 1.85 |
| 1966..... | 2,631.0 | 975.3 | 1,655.7 | 3.57 | 8.15 | 2.68 |
| 1967..... | 3,043.0 | 1,113.0 | 1,930.0 | 4.03 | 8.96 | 3.06 |
| 1968..... | 4,850.0 | 1,704.3 | 3,145.7 | 6.26 | 13.57 | 4.84 |
| 1969..... | 5,446.0 | 1,780.7 | 3,665.3 | 6.83 | 13.98 | 5.47 |
| 1970..... | 4,485.4 | 1,550.1 | 2,935.3 | 5.48 | 11.61 | 4.28 |
| 1971..... | 3,933.3 | 1,495.5 | 2,437.8 | 4.68 | 10.66 | 3.48 |
| 1972..... | 4,768.3 | 1,668.8 | 3,099.5 | 5.53 | 11.87 | 4.30 |
| 1973..... | 5,571.1 | 1,970.7 | 3,600.4 | 6.31 | 13.84 | 4.87 |
| 1974..... | 5,533.4 | 1,880.1 | 3,653.3 | 6.14 | 12.98 | 4.83 |
| 1975..... | 6,260.0 | 2,104.9 | 4,155.1 | 6.83 | 14.31 | 5.40 |
| 1976..... | 6,669.6 | 2,128.2 | 4,541.4 | 7.16 | 14.03 | 5.83 |
| 1977..... | 7,675.0 | 2,516.0 | 5,159.0 | 8.13 | 15.54 | 6.60 |
| 1978..... | 7,527.0 | 2,484.0 | 5,043.0 | 7.87 | 14.57 | 6.41 |
| 1979..... | 7,696.0 | 2,585.0 | 5,111.0 | 7.94 | 14.72 | 6.44 |
| 1980..... | 8,761.0 | 2,800.0 | 5,961.0 | 8.92 | 15.49 | 7.44 |
| 1981..... | 9,350.0 | 2,805.0 | 6,545.0 | 9.40 | 15.14 | 8.08 |
| 1982..... | 8,585.7 | 2,575.7 | 6,010.0 | 8.52 | 13.56 | 7.35 |
| 1983..... | 8,628.6 | 2,562.7 | 6,065.9 | 8.46 | 13.21 | 7.34 |
| 1984..... | N/A | N/A | N/A | N/A | N/A | N/A |

NA Data not available

Note: Data are not from the household income and expenditure surveys, nor necessarily consistent with the survey data.

Source: Guojia tongji ju, Zhongguo maoyi wujia tongji ziliao 1952-1983 [State Statistical Bureau, Trade and Price Statistics 1952-1983] (1984), p. 44.

Table 58. Total and Consumption Per 100 Persons of Sewing Machines, by Residence: 1952 to 1984

| Year | Total consumption (in 10 thousand machines) | | | Consumption per 100 persons (in machines) | | |
|---|---|---|---|---|---|---|
| | China | Urban | Rural | China | Urban | Rural |
| 1952..... | 10.0 | 9.4 | .6 | .02 | .14 | N/A |
| 1953..... | 13.7 | 12.8 | .9 | .02 | .17 | N/A |
| 1954..... | 19.6 | 18.4 | 1.2 | .03 | .23 | N/A |
| 1955..... | 12.3 | 10.9 | 1.4 | .02 | .13 | N/A |
| 1956..... | 22.6 | 19.2 | 3.4 | .04 | .20 | .01 |
| 1957..... | 25.1 | 19.4 | 5.7 | .04 | .19 | .01 |
| 1958..... | 32.0 | 21.5 | 10.5 | .05 | .18 | .02 |
| 1959..... | 34.1 | 22.4 | 11.7 | .05 | .17 | .02 |
| 1960..... | 48.2 | 34.1 | 14.1 | .07 | .25 | .03 |
| 1961..... | 61.3 | 40.0 | 21.3 | .09 | .31 | .04 |
| 1962..... | 62.8 | 37.7 | 25.1 | .09 | .33 | .05 |
| 1963..... | 79.0 | 46.0 | 33.0 | .12 | .41 | .06 |
| 1964..... | 87.8 | 52.4 | 35.4 | .13 | .45 | .06 |
| 1965..... | 89.7 | 56.3 | 33.4 | .12 | .46 | .06 |
| 1966..... | 120.6 | 67.7 | 52.9 | .16 | .57 | .09 |
| 1967..... | 119.1 | 58.5 | 60.6 | .16 | .47 | .10 |
| 1968..... | 103.9 | 50.7 | 53.2 | .13 | .40 | .08 |
| 1969..... | 165.6 | 109.8 | 55.8 | .21 | .86 | .08 |
| 1970..... | 218.7 | 142.4 | 76.3 | .27 | 1.07 | .11 |
| 1971..... | 235.9 | 185.4 | 50.5 | .28 | 1.32 | .07 |
| 1972..... | 234.0 | 173.2 | 60.8 | .27 | 1.23 | .08 |
| 1973..... | 251.1 | 194.6 | 56.5 | .28 | 1.37 | .08 |
| 1974..... | 267.3 | 194.3 | 73.0 | .30 | 1.34 | .10 |
| 1975..... | 302.7 | 188.5 | 114.2 | .33 | 1.28 | .15 |
| 1976..... | 322.9 | 157.2 | 165.7 | .35 | 1.04 | .21 |
| 1977..... | 380.7 | 204.6 | 176.1 | .40 | 1.26 | .23 |
| 1978..... | 439.8 | 228.0 | 211.8 | .46 | 1.34 | .27 |
| 1979..... | 540.0 | 274.0 | 266.0 | .56 | 1.56 | .33 |
| 1980..... | 665.0 | 315.0 | 350.0 | .68 | 1.74 | .44 |
| 1981..... | 926.6 | 417.0 | 509.6 | .93 | 2.25 | .63 |
| 1982..... | 1,141.8 | 491.8 | 650.0 | 1.13 | 2.58 | .79 |
| 1983..... | 1,021.2 | 422.9 | 598.3 | 1.00 | 2.18 | .72 |
| 1984..... | N/A | N/A | N/A | N/A | N/A | N/A |

NA Data not available

Note: Data are not from the household income and expenditure surveys, nor necessarily consistent with the survey data.

Source: Guojia tongji ju, Zhongguo maoyi wujia tongji ziliao 1952-1983 [State Statistical Bureau, Trade and Price Statistics 1952-1983] (1984), p. 45.

Table 59. Total and Consumption Per 100 Persons of Wrist Watches, by Residence: 1952 to 1984

| Year | Total consumption (in 10 thousand watches) | | | Consumption per 100 persons (in watches) | | |
|---|---|---|---|---|---|---|
| | China | Urban | Rural | China | Urban | Rural |
| 1952..... | 38.5 | 38.5 | N/A | .07 | .55 | N/A |
| 1953..... | 103.4 | 103.4 | N/A | .18 | 1.40 | N/A |
| 1954..... | 35.9 | 35.9 | N/A | .06 | .45 | N/A |
| 1955..... | 38.3 | 38.3 | N/A | .06 | .46 | N/A |
| 1956..... | 120.3 | 120.3 | N/A | .19 | 1.27 | N/A |
| 1957..... | 107.6 | 103.0 | 4.6 | .17 | 1.03 | .01 |
| 1958..... | 80.3 | 77.2 | 3.1 | .12 | .66 | .01 |
| 1959..... | 66.7 | 63.8 | 2.9 | .10 | .49 | .01 |
| 1960..... | 50.0 | 47.6 | 2.4 | .08 | .34 | |
| 1961..... | 75.1 | 71.2 | 3.9 | .11 | .55 | .01 |
| 1962..... | 99.1 | 93.1 | 6.0 | .15 | .80 | .01 |
| 1963..... | 109.8 | 103.2 | 6.6 | .16 | .92 | .01 |
| 1964..... | 172.5 | 162.2 | 10.3 | .25 | 1.39 | .02 |
| 1965..... | 189.1 | 175.9 | 13.2 | .26 | 1.44 | .02 |
| 1966..... | 237.4 | 219.6 | 17.8 | .32 | 1.84 | .03 |
| 1967..... | 193.5 | 179.2 | 14.3 | .26 | 1.44 | .02 |
| 1968..... | 173.0 | 160.4 | 12.6 | .22 | 1.28 | .02 |
| 1969..... | 184.2 | 170.4 | 13.8 | .23 | 1.34 | .02 |
| 1970..... | 254.1 | 234.8 | 19.3 | .31 | 1.76 | .03 |
| 1971..... | 434.3 | 399.6 | 34.7 | .52 | 2.85 | .05 |
| 1972..... | 546.0 | 494.1 | 51.9 | .63 | 3.51 | .07 |
| 1973..... | 650.4 | 585.4 | 65.0 | .74 | 4.11 | .09 |
| 1974..... | 758.4 | 678.8 | 79.6 | .84 | 4.68 | .11 |
| 1975..... | 819.9 | 729.7 | 90.2 | .89 | 4.96 | .12 |
| 1976..... | 1,051.7 | 917.1 | 134.6 | 1.13 | 6.05 | .17 |
| 1977..... | 1,149.7 | 928.0 | 221.7 | 1.22 | 5.73 | .38 |
| 1978..... | 1,388.1 | 1,007.8 | 380.3 | 1.45 | 5.91 | .48 |
| 1979..... | 1,944.4 | 1,264.0 | 680.4 | 2.00 | 7.20 | .86 |
| 1980..... | 2,534.0 | 1,520.0 | 1,014.0 | 2.58 | 8.41 | 1.27 |
| 1981..... | 2,944.0 | 1,708.0 | 1,236.0 | 2.96 | 9.22 | 1.53 |
| 1982..... | 3,595.4 | 1,078.2 | 2,517.2 | 3.57 | 5.67 | 3.08 |
| 1983..... | 3,917.3 | 1,140.8 | 2,776.5 | 3.84 | 5.88 | 3.36 |
| 1984..... | N/A | N/A | N/A | N/A | N/A | N/A |

NA Data not available

Note: Data are not from the household income and expenditure surveys, nor necessarily consistent with the survey data.

Source: Guojia tongji ju, Zhongguo maoyi wujia tongji ziliao 1952-1983 [State Statistical Bureau, Trade and Price Statistics 1952-1983] (1984), p. 46.

Table 60. Total and Consumption Per 100 Persons of Bicycles, by Residence: 1952 to 1984

| Year | Total consumption (in 10 thousand bicycles) | | | Consumption per 100 persons (in bicycles) | | |
|---|---|---|---|---|---|---|
| | China | Urban | Rural | China | Urban | Rural |
| 1952..... | 33.5 | 31.7 | 1.8 | .06 | .45 | N/A |
| 1953..... | 38.9 | 37.0 | 1.9 | .06 | .48 | N/A |
| 1954..... | 38.4 | 34.4 | 4.0 | .06 | .41 | .01 |
| 1955..... | 54.1 | 46.1 | 8.0 | .08 | .49 | .01 |
| 1956..... | 71.4 | 55.4 | 16.0 | .10 | .50 | .03 |
| 1957..... | 84.7 | 59.4 | 25.3 | .11 | .50 | .04 |
| 1958..... | 100.4 | 71.1 | 29.3 | .13 | .51 | .05 |
| 1959..... | 132.4 | 95.8 | 36.6 | .17 | .61 | .06 |
| 1960..... | 160.0 | 122.8 | 37.2 | .21 | .77 | .06 |
| 1961..... | 74.9 | 56.4 | 18.5 | .09 | .36 | .02 |
| 1962..... | 83.2 | 58.1 | 25.1 | .11 | .45 | .04 |
| 1963..... | 139.5 | 97.9 | 41.6 | .19 | .81 | .06 |
| 1964..... | 147.1 | 103.5 | 43.6 | .19 | .82 | .07 |
| 1965..... | 176.2 | 106.4 | 69.8 | .24 | .87 | .12 |
| 1966..... | 217.8 | 131.0 | 86.8 | .30 | 1.10 | .14 |
| 1967..... | 180.1 | 96.3 | 83.8 | .24 | .78 | .13 |
| 1968..... | 145.7 | 69.0 | 76.7 | .19 | .55 | .12 |
| 1969..... | 248.6 | 149.6 | 99.0 | .31 | 1.17 | .15 |
| 1970..... | 335.2 | 215.1 | 120.1 | .41 | 1.61 | .18 |
| 1971..... | 356.7 | 232.6 | 124.1 | .42 | 1.66 | .18 |
| 1972..... | 452.2 | 309.5 | 115.7 | .49 | 2.20 | .16 |
| 1973..... | 443.2 | 294.0 | 149.2 | .50 | 2.06 | .20 |
| 1974..... | 453.1 | 303.9 | 149.2 | .50 | 2.10 | .20 |
| 1975..... | 561.4 | 349.3 | 212.1 | .61 | 2.37 | .28 |
| 1976..... | 620.0 | 309.3 | 310.7 | .67 | 2.04 | .40 |
| 1977..... | 682.1 | 352.0 | 330.1 | .72 | 2.17 | .42 |
| 1978..... | 809.6 | 404.0 | 405.6 | .85 | 2.37 | .52 |
| 1979..... | 954.5 | 468.0 | 486.5 | .98 | 2.67 | .61 |
| 1980..... | 1,186.0 | 540.0 | 646.0 | 1.21 | 2.99 | .81 |
| 1981..... | 1,592.2 | 716.0 | 876.2 | 1.60 | 3.87 | 1.08 |
| 1982..... | 2,220.4 | 766.4 | 1,454.0 | 2.20 | 4.03 | 1.78 |
| 1983..... | 2,626.1 | 889.0 | 1,737.1 | 2.57 | 4.58 | 2.10 |
| 1984..... | N/A | N/A | N/A | N/A | N/A | N/A |

NA Data not available

Note: Data are not from the household income and expenditure surveys, nor necessarily consistent with the survey data.

Source: Guojia tongji ju, Zhongguo maoyi wujia tongji ziliao 1952-1983 [State Statistical Bureau, Trade and Price Statistics 1952-1983] (1984), p. 47.

Table 61. Total and Consumption Per 100 Persons of Radios, by Residence: 1952 to 1984

| Year | Total consumption (in 10 thousand radios) | | | Consumption per 100 persons (in radios) | | |
|---|---|---|---|---|---|---|
| | China | Urban | Rural | China | Urban | Rural |
| 1952..... | 2.0 | 2.0 | N/A | N/A | .03 | N/A |
| 1953..... | 2.8 | 2.8 | N/A | N/A | .04 | N/A |
| 1954..... | 4.0 | 4.0 | N/A | .01 | .05 | N/A |
| 1955..... | 9.7 | 9.6 | .1 | .01 | .11 | N/A |
| 1956..... | 15.2 | 14.7 | .5 | .02 | .14 | N/A |
| 1957..... | 26.4 | 25.5 | .9 | .04 | .22 | N/A |
| 1958..... | 68.8 | 66.7 | 2.1 | .09 | .46 | N/A |
| 1959..... | 77.9 | 74.0 | 3.9 | .09 | .45 | .01 |
| 1960..... | 98.1 | 90.2 | 7.9 | .12 | .52 | .02 |
| 1961..... | 174.5 | 155.0 | 19.5 | .25 | 1.10 | .04 |
| 1962..... | 94.3 | 83.9 | 10.4 | .13 | .66 | .02 |
| 1963..... | 39.1 | 34.8 | 4.3 | .05 | .28 | .01 |
| 1964..... | 95.4 | 81.1 | 14.3 | .13 | .65 | .02 |
| 1965..... | 83.6 | 62.7 | 20.9 | .12 | .51 | .04 |
| 1966..... | 102.1 | 76.0 | 26.1 | .14 | .64 | .04 |
| 1967..... | 83.4 | 52.4 | 31.0 | .11 | .42 | .05 |
| 1968..... | 86.6 | 45.2 | 41.4 | .11 | .36 | .06 |
| 1969..... | 151.4 | 81.7 | 69.7 | .19 | .64 | .10 |
| 1970..... | 170.1 | 97.9 | 72.2 | .21 | .73 | .11 |
| 1971..... | 179.9 | 135.9 | 44.0 | .21 | .97 | .06 |
| 1972..... | 357.3 | 272.2 | 85.1 | .41 | 1.94 | .12 |
| 1973..... | 425.3 | 259.4 | 165.9 | .48 | 1.82 | .22 |
| 1974..... | 487.2 | 270.7 | 216.5 | .54 | 1.87 | .29 |
| 1975..... | 714.4 | 409.1 | 305.3 | .78 | 2.78 | .40 |
| 1976..... | 840.7 | 428.2 | 412.5 | .90 | 2.82 | .53 |
| 1977..... | 994.1 | 443.3 | 550.8 | 1.05 | 2.74 | .70 |
| 1978..... | 1,388.9 | 611.0 | 777.9 | 1.45 | 3.58 | .99 |
| 1979..... | 1,639.5 | 689.0 | 950.5 | 1.69 | 3.92 | 1.20 |
| 1980..... | 2,722.0 | 1,088.0 | 1,634.0 | 2.77 | 6.02 | 2.04 |
| 1981..... | 3,074.9 | 1,168.5 | 1,906.4 | 3.09 | 6.31 | 2.35 |
| 1982..... | 3,625.0 | 1,232.5 | 2,392.5 | 3.60 | 6.49 | 2.92 |
| 1983..... | 3,074.5 | 1,106.0 | 1,968.5 | 3.01 | 5.70 | 2.38 |
| 1984..... | N/A | N/A | N/A | N/A | N/A | N/A |

NA Data not available

Note: Data are not from the household income and expenditure surveys, nor necessarily consistent with the survey data.

Source: Guojia tongji ju, Zhongguo maoyi wujia tongji ziliao 1952-1983 [State Statistical Bureau, Trade and Price Statistics 1952-1983] (1984), p. 48.

Table 62. Retail Sales of Social Commodities by Residence, and Function: 1952 to 1984
(In 100 million yuan)

| Year | Total value of retail sales | Function: Consumer goods | Function: Means of agricultural production | Residence: Urban | Residence: Rural |
|---|---|---|---|---|---|
| 1952....... | 276.8 | 262.7 | 14.1 | 125.6 | 151.2 |
| 1953....... | 348.0 | 328.8 | 19.2 | 168.2 | 179.8 |
| 1954....... | 381.1 | 356.1 | 25.0 | 178.6 | 202.5 |
| 1955....... | 392.2 | 364.0 | 28.2 | 183.2 | 209.0 |
| 1956....... | 461.0 | 424.0 | 37.0 | 227.0 | 234.0 |
| 1957....... | 474.2 | 441.6 | 32.6 | 238.4 | 235.8 |
| 1958....... | 548.0 | 481.2 | 66.8 | 255.9 | 292.1 |
| 1959....... | 638.0 | 556.5 | 81.5 | 322.8 | 315.2 |
| 1960....... | 696.9 | 595.4 | 101.5 | 370.1 | 326.8 |
| 1961....... | 607.7 | 537.7 | 70.0 | 351.1 | 256.6 |
| 1962....... | 604.0 | 543.7 | 60.3 | 318.5 | 285.5 |
| 1963....... | 604.5 | 544.8 | 59.7 | 304.9 | 299.6 |
| 1964....... | 638.2 | 572.7 | 65.5 | 323.0 | 315.2 |
| 1965....... | 670.3 | 590.1 | 80.2 | 338.9 | 331.4 |
| 1966....... | 732.8 | 632.8 | 100.0 | 362.8 | 370.0 |
| 1967....... | 770.5 | 679.1 | 91.4 | 382.0 | 388.5 |
| 1968....... | 737.3 | 649.2 | 88.1 | 373.2 | 364.1 |
| 1969....... | 801.5 | 698.2 | 103.3 | 393.5 | 408.0 |
| 1970....... | 858.0 | 728.8 | 129.2 | 400.0 | 458.0 |
| 1971....... | 929.2 | 776.9 | 152.3 | 436.7 | 492.5 |
| 1972....... | 1,023.3 | 853.5 | 169.8 | 495.6 | 527.7 |
| 1973....... | 1,106.7 | 917.7 | 189.0 | 531.3 | 575.4 |
| 1974....... | 1,163.6 | 967.4 | 196.2 | 560.2 | 603.4 |
| 1975....... | 1,271.1 | 1,046.4 | 224.7 | 606.9 | 664.2 |
| 1976....... | 1,339.4 | 1,099.0 | 240.4 | 645.4 | 694.0 |
| 1977....... | 1,432.8 | 1,174.3 | 258.5 | 678.9 | 744.9 |
| 1978....... | 1,558.6 | 1,264.9 | 293.7 | 748.2 | 810.4 |
| 1979....... | 1,800.0 | 1,476.0 | 324.0 | 815.2 | 984.8 |
| 1980....... | 2,140.0 | 1,794.0 | 346.0 | 950.3 | 1,189.7 |
| 1981....... | 2,350.0 | 2,002.5 | 347.5 | 1,026.0 | 1,324.0 |
| 1982....... | 2,570.0 | 2,181.5 | 388.5 | 1,090.0 | 1,480.0 |
| 1983....... | 2,849.4 | 2,426.1 | 423.3 | 1,179.4 | 1,670.0 |
| 1984....... | 3,376.4 | 2,899.2 | 477.2 | 1,377.1 | 1,999.3 |

Source: Guojia tongji ju, Tongji nianjian 1984 [State Statistical Bureau, Statistical Yearbook of China 1984] (1984), p. 345; and State Statistical Bureau, China: A Statistics Survey in 1985 (1985), p. 80.

Table 63. Retail Sales of Consumer Goods, by Residence and Type of Consumer: 1952 to 1983
(In 100 million yuan)

| | Total retail sales | | | Sales to individuals | | | Sales to collectives | | |
|---|---|---|---|---|---|---|---|---|---|
| | Total | Urban | Rural | Total | Urban | Rural | Total | Urban | Rural |
| 1952....... | 262.7 | 125.6 | 137.1 | 237.9 | 100.8 | 137.1 | 24.8 | 24.8 | .0 |
| 1953....... | 328.8 | 168.2 | 160.6 | 294.0 | 133.4 | 160.6 | 34.8 | 34.8 | .0 |
| 1954....... | 356.1 | 178.6 | 177.5 | 317.5 | 140.3 | 177.2 | 38.6 | 38.3 | .3 |
| 1955....... | 364.0 | 183.2 | 180.8 | 325.1 | 145.4 | 179.7 | 38.9 | 37.8 | 1.1 |
| 1956....... | 424.0 | 227.0 | 197.0 | 371.0 | 177.2 | 193.8 | 53.0 | 49.8 | 3.2 |
| 1957....... | 441.6 | 238.4 | 203.2 | 395.3 | 195.7 | 199.6 | 46.3 | 42.7 | 3.6 |
| 1958....... | 481.2 | 255.9 | 225.3 | 425.2 | 206.0 | 219.2 | 56.0 | 49.9 | 6.1 |
| 1959....... | 556.5 | 322.8 | 233.7 | 488.0 | 260.8 | 227.2 | 68.5 | 62.0 | 6.5 |
| 1960....... | 595.4 | 370.1 | 225.3 | 513.6 | 294.8 | 218.8 | 81.8 | 75.3 | 6.5 |
| 1961....... | 537.7 | 351.1 | 186.6 | 483.7 | 301.7 | 182.0 | 54.0 | 49.4 | 4.6 |
| 1962....... | 543.7 | 318.5 | 225.2 | 500.4 | 278.7 | 221.7 | 43.3 | 39.8 | 3.5 |
| 1963....... | 544.8 | 304.9 | 239.9 | 501.6 | 265.2 | 236.4 | 43.2 | 39.7 | 3.5 |
| 1964....... | 572.7 | 323.0 | 249.7 | 522.4 | 276.5 | 245.9 | 50.3 | 46.5 | 3.8 |
| 1965....... | 590.1 | 338.9 | 251.2 | 537.1 | 289.9 | 247.2 | 53.0 | 49.0 | 4.0 |
| 1966....... | 632.8 | 362.8 | 270.0 | 574.8 | 307.3 | 267.5 | 58.0 | 55.5 | 2.5 |
| 1967....... | 679.1 | 382.0 | 297.1 | 615.6 | 324.0 | 291.6 | 63.5 | 58.0 | 5.5 |
| 1968....... | 649.2 | 373.2 | 276.0 | 595.0 | 323.0 | 272.0 | 54.2 | 50.2 | 4.0 |
| 1969....... | 698.2 | 393.5 | 304.7 | 634.2 | 335.5 | 298.7 | 64.0 | 58.0 | 6.0 |
| 1970....... | 728.8 | 400.0 | 328.8 | 666.7 | 343.9 | 322.8 | 62.1 | 56.1 | 6.0 |
| 1971....... | 776.9 | 436.7 | 340.2 | 692.7 | 359.0 | 333.7 | 84.2 | 77.7 | 6.5 |
| 1972....... | 853.5 | 495.6 | 357.9 | 754.8 | 403.9 | 350.9 | 98.7 | 91.7 | 7.0 |
| 1973....... | 917.7 | 531.3 | 386.4 | 810.1 | 431.3 | 378.8 | 107.6 | 100.0 | 7.6 |
| 1974....... | 967.4 | 560.2 | 407.0 | 859.2 | 460.0 | 399.2 | 108.2 | 100.2 | 8.0 |
| 1975....... | 1,046.4 | 606.9 | 439.5 | 922.8 | 494.7 | 428.1 | 123.6 | 112.2 | 11.4 |
| 1976....... | 1,099.0 | 645.4 | 453.6 | 965.9 | 525.2 | 440.7 | 133.1 | 120.2 | 12.9 |
| 1977....... | 1,174.3 | 687.9 | 486.4 | 1,036.6 | 566.4 | 470.2 | 137.7 | 121.5 | 16.2 |
| 1978....... | 1,264.9 | 748.2 | 516.7 | 1,121.2 | 621.5 | 499.7 | 143.7 | 126.7 | 17.0 |
| 1979....... | 1,476.0 | 815.2 | 660.8 | 1,311.7 | 673.1 | 638.6 | 164.3 | 142.1 | 22.2 |
| 1980....... | 1,794.0 | 950.3 | 843.7 | 1,608.0 | 789.3 | 818.7 | 186.0 | 161.0 | 25.0 |
| 1981....... | 2,002.5 | 1,026.0 | 976.5 | 1,798.5 | 848.0 | 950.5 | 204.0 | 178.0 | 26.0 |
| 1982....... | 2,181.5 | 1,090.0 | 1,091.5 | 1,956.1 | 892.6 | 1,063.5 | 225.4 | 197.4 | 28.0 |
| 1983....... | 2,426.1 | 1,179.4 | 1,246.7 | 2,169.5 | 952.2 | 1,217.3 | 256.6 | 227.2 | 29.4 |

Source: Guojia tongji ju, Zhongguo maoyi wujia tongji ziliao 1952-1983 [ State Statistical Bureau, Trade and Price Statistics of China 1952-1983] (1984), pp. 70-71.

Table 64. Retail Sales of Consumer Goods, by Major Commodity Group: 1952 to 1984
(In 100 million yuan)

| Year | Retail sales of consumer goods | Food | Clothing | Goods for daily use | Cultural and educational articles | Books, newspapers, and magazines | Medicine and medical products | Fuel |
|---|---|---|---|---|---|---|---|---|
| 1952.... | 262.7 | 148.3 | 50.8 | 39.5 | 6.7 | 2.0 | 6.8 | 8.6 |
| 1953.... | 328.8 | 177.9 | 69.5 | 51.1 | 7.6 | 2.6 | 9.1 | 11.0 |
| 1954.... | 356.1 | 197.3 | 71.6 | 52.1 | 8.3 | 3.0 | 10.8 | 13.0 |
| 1955.... | 364.0 | 202.6 | 71.9 | 50.7 | 9.8 | 3.5 | 11.4 | 14.1 |
| 1956.... | 424.0 | 219.3 | 94.1 | 60.5 | 11.9 | 4.8 | 14.6 | 18.8 |
| 1957.... | 441.6 | 241.0 | 82.6 | 65.3 | 12.7 | 4.9 | 16.7 | 18.4 |
| 1958.... | 481.2 | 250.1 | 102.0 | 65.7 | 16.8 | 6.8 | 18.9 | 20.9 |
| 1959.... | 556.5 | 274.6 | 132.0 | 75.7 | 18.3 | 6.7 | 28.2 | 21.0 |
| 1960.... | 595.4 | 286.7 | 129.0 | 90.1 | 21.5 | 6.9 | 36.2 | 25.0 |
| 1961.... | 537.7 | 291.7 | 62.8 | 101.1 | 20.8 | 4.5 | 28.2 | 28.6 |
| 1962.... | 543.7 | 280.7 | 79.9 | 106.4 | 17.9 | 4.2 | 26.1 | 28.5 |
| 1963.... | 544.8 | 283.1 | 90.1 | 98.6 | 16.7 | 5.2 | 25.2 | 25.9 |
| 1964.... | 572.7 | 301.8 | 99.6 | 91.9 | 18.4 | 6.1 | 26.1 | 28.8 |
| 1965.... | 590.1 | 327.1 | 112.5 | 68.7 | 17.3 | 6.4 | 27.8 | 30.3 |
| 1966.... | 632.8 | 347.9 | 126.7 | 67.5 | 21.6 | 7.0 | 30.9 | 31.2 |
| 1967.... | 679.1 | 367.8 | 142.0 | 78.9 | 19.8 | 3.7 | 34.6 | 32.3 |
| 1968.... | 649.2 | 358.5 | 119.7 | 83.4 | 18.9 | 4.6 | 31.1 | 33.0 |
| 1969.... | 698.2 | 373.7 | 149.6 | 80.5 | 20.4 | 4.1 | 36.6 | 33.3 |
| 1970.... | 728.8 | 389.0 | 170.2 | 76.4 | 18.5 | 3.2 | 36.5 | 35.0 |
| 1971.... | 776.9 | 413.5 | 165.5 | 90.2 | 21.3 | 5.7 | 42.5 | 38.2 |
| 1972.... | 853.5 | 459.8 | 170.6 | 105.1 | 23.5 | 6.3 | 46.2 | 42.0 |
| 1973.... | 917.7 | 493.2 | 188.3 | 108.0 | 25.2 | 8.2 | 49.8 | 45.0 |
| 1974.... | 967.4 | 511.2 | 207.8 | 114.5 | 27.1 | 8.7 | 52.9 | 45.2 |
| 1975.... | 1,046.4 | 554.2 | 219.4 | 127.0 | 29.3 | 9.8 | 57.1 | 49.6 |
| 1976.... | 1,099.0 | 577.9 | 237.1 | 134.2 | 30.3 | 10.4 | 60.1 | 49.0 |
| 1977.... | 1,174.3 | 618.5 | 255.9 | 140.3 | 31.9 | 10.7 | 64.9 | 52.1 |
| 1978.... | 1,264.9 | 655.8 | 278.5 | 156.3 | 42.2 | 12.1 | 64.7 | 55.3 |
| 1979.... | 1,476.0 | 760.2 | 339.2 | 187.2 | 55.4 | 16.4 | 58.5 | 59.1 |
| 1980.... | 1,794.0 | 918.1 | 413.7 | 231.8 | 73.5 | 23.1 | 65.8 | 68.0 |
| 1981.... | 2,002.5 | 1,022.3 | 463.0 | 264.4 | 85.5 | 25.0 | 70.8 | 71.5 |
| 1982.... | 2,181.5 | 1,153.0 | 465.9 | 290.5 | 97.2 | 27.6 | 73.0 | 74.3 |
| 1983.... | 2,426.1 | 1,307.5 | 491.5 | 323.6 | 107.4 | 29.8 | 86.0 | 80.3 |
| 1984.... | 2,899.2 | 1,546.6 | 570.3 | 690.4 | | | | 91.9 |

Source: Guojia tongji ju, Zhongguo maoyi wujia tongji ziliao 1952-1983 (State Statistical Bureau, Chinese Trade and Price Statistics 1952-1983] (1984), p. 72; and State Statistical Bureau, China: A Statistics Survey in 1985 (1985), p. 82.

Table 65. Retail Sales of Consumer Goods, by Major Commodity Group: 1952 to 1984 (In percent)

| Year | Retail sales of consumer goods | Food | Clothing | Goods for daily use | Cultural and educational articles | Books, newspapers, and magazines | Medicine and medical products | Fuel |
|---|---|---|---|---|---|---|---|---|
| 1952....... | 100.0 | 56.4 | 19.3 | 15.0 | 2.6 | .8 | 2.6 | 3.3 |
| 1953....... | 100.0 | 54.1 | 21.1 | 15.5 | 2.3 | .8 | 2.8 | 3.4 |
| 1954....... | 100.0 | 55.4 | 20.1 | 14.7 | 2.3 | .8 | 3.0 | 3.7 |
| 1955....... | 100.0 | 55.6 | 19.8 | 13.9 | 2.7 | 1.0 | 3.1 | 3.9 |
| 1956....... | 100.0 | 51.7 | 22.2 | 14.3 | 2.8 | 1.1 | 3.5 | 4.4 |
| 1957....... | 100.0 | 54.5 | 18.7 | 14.8 | 2.9 | 1.1 | 3.8 | 4.2 |
| 1958....... | 100.0 | 52.0 | 21.2 | 13.7 | 3.5 | 1.4 | 3.9 | 4.3 |
| 1959....... | 100.0 | 49.3 | 23.7 | 13.6 | 3.3 | 1.2 | 5.1 | 3.8 |
| 1960....... | 100.0 | 48.2 | 21.7 | 15.1 | 3.6 | 1.1 | 6.1 | 4.2 |
| 1961....... | 100.0 | 54.3 | 11.7 | 18.8 | 3.9 | .8 | 5.2 | 5.3 |
| 1962....... | 100.0 | 51.6 | 14.7 | 19.6 | 3.3 | .8 | 4.8 | 5.2 |
| 1963....... | 100.0 | 52.0 | 16.5 | 18.1 | 3.1 | 1.0 | 4.6 | 4.7 |
| 1964....... | 100.0 | 52.7 | 17.4 | 16.0 | 3.2 | 1.1 | 4.6 | 5.0 |
| 1965....... | 100.0 | 55.4 | 19.1 | 11.7 | 2.9 | 1.1 | 4.7 | 5.1 |
| 1966....... | 100.0 | 55.0 | 19.9 | 10.7 | 3.4 | 1.1 | 4.9 | 5.0 |
| 1967....... | 100.0 | 54.2 | 20.9 | 11.6 | 2.9 | .5 | 5.1 | 4.8 |
| 1968....... | 100.0 | 55.2 | 18.4 | 12.9 | 2.9 | .7 | 4.8 | 5.1 |
| 1969....... | 100.0 | 53.5 | 21.4 | 11.5 | 2.9 | .6 | 5.3 | 4.8 |
| 1970....... | 100.0 | 53.4 | 23.4 | 10.5 | 2.5 | .4 | 5.0 | 4.8 |
| 1971....... | 100.0 | 53.2 | 21.3 | 11.6 | 2.8 | .7 | 5.5 | 4.9 |
| 1972....... | 100.0 | 53.9 | 20.0 | 12.3 | 2.8 | .7 | 5.4 | 4.9 |
| 1973....... | 100.0 | 53.7 | 20.5 | 11.8 | 2.8 | .9 | 5.4 | 4.9 |
| 1974....... | 100.0 | 52.8 | 21.5 | 11.8 | 2.8 | .9 | 5.5 | 4.7 |
| 1975....... | 100.0 | 53.0 | 21.0 | 12.1 | 2.8 | .9 | 5.5 | 4.7 |
| 1976....... | 100.0 | 52.6 | 21.6 | 12.2 | 2.7 | .9 | 5.5 | 4.5 |
| 1977....... | 100.0 | 52.7 | 21.8 | 12.0 | 2.7 | .9 | 5.5 | 4.4 |
| 1978....... | 100.0 | 51.8 | 22.0 | 12.4 | 3.3 | 1.0 | 5.1 | 4.4 |
| 1979....... | 100.0 | 51.5 | 23.0 | 12.7 | 3.7 | 1.1 | 4.0 | 4.0 |
| 1980....... | 100.0 | 51.2 | 23.0 | 12.9 | 4.1 | 1.3 | 3.7 | 3.8 |
| 1981....... | 100.0 | 51.1 | 23.1 | 13.2 | 4.3 | 1.2 | 3.5 | 3.6 |
| 1982....... | 100.0 | 52.9 | 21.3 | 13.3 | 4.5 | 1.3 | 3.3 | 3.4 |
| 1983....... | 100.0 | 53.9 | 20.3 | 13.3 | 4.4 | 1.2 | 3.6 | 3.3 |
| 1984....... | 100.0 | 53.3 | 19.7 | 23.8 | | | | 3.2 |

Source: Guojia tongji ju, Zhongguo maoyi wujia tongji ziliao 1952-1983 [State Statistical Bureau, Chinese Trade and Price Statistics 1952-1983] (1984), p. 73; and State Statistical Bureau, China: A Statistics Survey in 1985 (1985), p. 82.

Table 66. Retail Sales of Selected Foods, Beverages, and Tobacco: 1952 to 1983
(In 100 million yuan)

| Year | Grain | Edible vege-table oil | Hogs | Beef cattle | Mutton and sheep | Fowl | Fresh eggs | Aquatic pro-ducts | Dried and fresh vege-tables |
|---|---|---|---|---|---|---|---|---|---|
| 1952......... | 58.6 | 6.6 | 17.2 | 1.0 | .5 | 1.6 | 1.0 | 3.6 | 6.5 |
| 1953......... | 63.2 | 7.6 | 19.9 | 1.2 | .7 | 2.0 | 1.1 | 4.9 | 8.6 |
| 1954......... | 71.8 | 8.5 | 20.8 | 1.4 | .8 | 2.0 | 1.3 | 6.6 | 9.6 |
| 1955......... | 74.9 | 10.4 | 18.8 | 2.0 | .9 | 1.7 | 1.5 | 6.5 | 10.4 |
| 1956......... | 75.5 | 12.7 | 17.8 | 2.3 | 1.1 | 2.3 | 1.9 | 6.9 | 12.8 |
| 1957......... | 81.9 | 11.7 | 20.9 | 2.2 | 1.1 | 2.5 | 2.7 | 8.9 | 15.7 |
| 1958......... | 93.9 | 11.9 | 19.5 | 1.2 | .9 | 2.2 | 3.6 | 8.2 | 20.5 |
| 1959......... | 102.3 | 10.7 | 11.5 | 1.5 | 1.0 | 1.8 | 1.7 | 8.6 | 25.6 |
| 1960......... | 111.0 | 10.5 | 6.9 | 1.4 | 1.2 | 2.5 | 1.6 | 8.8 | 35.7 |
| 1961......... | 92.8 | 8.4 | 6.2 | 1.1 | 2.0 | 2.3 | 3.3 | 10.4 | 43.7 |
| 1962......... | 77.7 | 5.7 | 13.3 | .6 | 2.1 | 2.6 | 4.1 | 10.8 | 32.3 |
| 1963......... | 80.6 | 8.0 | 28.8 | .7 | 2.5 | 2.4 | 6.2 | 13.2 | 27.5 |
| 1964......... | 92.6 | 10.4 | 37.5 | .8 | 2.2 | 1.8 | 5.9 | 11.4 | 24.4 |
| 1965......... | 87.4 | 12.1 | 47.8 | 1.1 | 2.0 | 1.2 | 5.6 | 10.3 | 24.6 |
| 1966......... | 88.9 | 12.7 | 54.9 | 1.3 | 1.7 | 1.4 | 5.5 | 10.5 | 26.3 |
| 1967......... | 91.2 | 12.5 | 53.0 | 1.3 | 1.6 | 1.0 | 5.5 | 8.9 | 28.1 |
| 1968......... | 88.6 | 11.6 | 52.8 | 1.1 | 1.5 | .8 | 4.3 | 7.8 | 26.8 |
| 1969......... | 96.1 | 11.9 | 46.9 | 1.7 | 1.9 | .8 | 4.1 | 7.7 | 21.0 |
| 1970......... | 95.1 | 11.6 | 47.3 | 1.7 | 1.8 | .8 | 4.9 | 10.2 | 22.0 |
| 1971......... | 98.7 | 12.1 | 51.5 | 1.8 | 1.8 | 1.1 | 5.1 | 12.6 | 23.4 |
| 1972......... | 109.2 | 12.5 | 62.4 | 1.7 | 1.6 | 1.3 | 4.9 | 12.5 | 25.7 |
| 1973......... | 114.9 | 12.2 | 63.9 | 1.7 | 1.5 | 1.3 | 5.1 | 14.4 | 27.5 |
| 1974......... | 113.2 | 12.7 | 63.6 | 1.5 | 1.5 | 1.1 | 5.0 | 19.0 | 31.1 |
| 1975......... | 120.9 | 13.6 | 68.5 | 1.7 | 1.7 | 1.3 | 4.9 | 18.5 | 34.5 |
| 1976......... | 128.1 | 14.3 | 67.6 | 1.6 | 1.8 | 1.2 | 5.6 | 20.4 | 33.4 |
| 1977......... | 136.7 | 13.6 | 64.6 | 1.5 | 1.7 | 1.4 | 5.8 | 18.5 | 37.4 |
| 1978......... | 145.8 | 15.1 | 77.7 | 1.9 | 2.4 | 3.4 | 8.6 | 23.3 | 40.9 |
| 1979......... | 154.6 | 18.6 | 108.4 | 1.9 | 2.7 | 4.4 | 14.8 | 23.7 | 43.8 |
| 1980......... | 179.5 | 23.0 | 141.2 | 2.5 | 3.5 | 5.3 | 18.9 | 29.4 | 49.5 |
| 1981......... | 205.9 | 33.9 | 150.7 | 2.2 | 3.1 | 6.0 | 17.8 | 27.2 | 55.2 |
| 1982......... | 235.6 | 43.6 | 160.1 | 2.9 | 4.4 | 7.7 | 19.7 | 31.0 | 61.6 |
| 1983......... | 256.1 | 53.2 | 171.1 | 3.8 | 5.8 | 12.0 | 27.7 | 37.8 | 65.5 |

Table 66. Retail Sales of Selected Foods, Beverages, and Tobacco: 1952 to 1983--continued
(In 100 million yuan)

| Year | Dried and fresh fruit | Sugar | Sweets | Confect-ionary | Cigar-ettes | Liquors | Salt | Tea |
|---|---|---|---|---|---|---|---|---|
| 1952......... | 5.1 | 4.5 | N/A | N/A | 9.3 | 7.6 | 8.6 | .8 |
| 1953......... | 6.0 | 6.0 | N/A | N/A | 14.3 | 9.5 | 10.0 | 1.3 |
| 1954......... | 6.6 | 6.9 | N/A | N/A | 15.7 | 10.0 | 10.0 | 1.6 |
| 1955......... | 7.2 | 8.2 | N/A | N/A | 15.7 | 8.9 | 10.3 | 1.8 |
| 1956......... | 8.6 | 9.7 | N/A | N/A | 15.8 | 9.6 | 10.6 | 2.5 |
| 1957......... | 9.6 | 10.0 | 6.1 | 5.9 | 19.1 | 10.9 | 12.3 | 2.2 |
| 1958......... | 8.5 | 11.2 | 6.6 | 6.9 | 20.8 | 11.7 | 14.1 | 1.8 |
| 1959......... | 7.0 | 10.8 | 7.5 | 8.5 | 21.7 | 15.4 | 15.7 | 1.5 |
| 1960......... | 6.5 | 8.2 | 9.2 | 13.8 | 19.7 | 16.2 | 20.5 | 1.7 |
| 1961......... | 7.9 | 14.6 | 17.6 | 31.2 | 9.6 | 10.0 | 17.9 | 2.0 |
| 1962......... | 8.1 | 14.3 | 11.0 | 24.4 | 11.1 | 15.0 | 14.8 | 2.0 |
| 1963......... | 9.5 | 12.3 | 4.0 | 12.0 | 15.6 | 17.0 | 11.2 | 1.9 |
| 1964......... | 7.6 | 12.8 | 3.5 | 10.5 | 20.4 | 12.9 | 13.6 | 2.2 |
| 1965......... | 7.7 | 15.5 | 5.1 | 9.0 | 23.2 | 13.6 | 14.6 | 2.0 |
| 1966......... | 8.2 | 18.8 | 6.9 | 8.2 | 24.5 | 14.9 | 15.4 | 2.1 |
| 1967......... | 8.8 | 22.4 | 7.0 | 9.1 | 26.6 | 16.8 | 16.4 | 2.2 |
| 1968......... | 8.4 | 24.2 | 6.2 | 9.2 | 24.6 | 15.8 | 16.3 | 2.0 |
| 1969......... | 12.7 | 26.8 | 9.5 | 14.3 | 32.7 | 19.6 | 18.1 | 2.6 |
| 1970......... | 13.3 | 22.5 | 10.5 | 14.4 | 33.6 | 21.6 | 18.9 | 2.8 |
| 1971......... | 14.1 | 23.8 | 12.1 | 14.4 | 36.0 | 25.2 | 18.7 | 3.6 |
| 1972......... | 15.5 | 24.8 | 12.4 | 16.8 | 40.3 | 28.3 | 18.7 | 3.9 |
| 1973......... | 16.6 | 27.3 | 14.2 | 17.1 | 51.4 | 31.9 | 17.5 | 6.3 |
| 1974......... | 19.6 | 29.0 | 16.0 | 19.4 | 52.5 | 35.2 | 19.3 | 6.4 |
| 1975......... | 17.5 | 28.4 | 16.3 | 19.7 | 59.8 | 38.7 | 21.6 | 6.5 |
| 1976......... | 17.5 | 30.4 | 15.9 | 20.6 | 65.2 | 48.6 | 21.3 | 7.4 |
| 1977......... | 19.4 | 38.5 | 15.0 | 23.7 | 72.4 | 48.8 | 25.3 | 7.5 |
| 1978......... | 14.7 | 45.8 | 13.4 | 24.0 | 74.2 | 51.1 | 23.4 | 7.6 |
| 1979......... | 16.7 | 50.1 | 16.2 | 26.0 | 93.1 | 58.2 | 22.7 | 10.8 |
| 1980......... | 18.2 | 55.3 | 18.0 | 28.1 | 107.2 | 68.1 | 22.6 | 13.3 |
| 1981......... | 22.0 | 58.9 | 20.7 | 28.3 | 135.6 | 98.0 | 22.2 | 14.3 |
| 1982......... | 27.1 | 63.9 | 20.2 | 28.2 | 149.3 | 132.1 | 22.0 | 15.7 |
| 1983......... | 31.0 | 66.2 | 22.8 | 33.4 | 178.9 | 148.1 | 23.5 | 16.8 |

NA Data not available

Source: Guojia tongji ju, Zhongguo maoyi wujia tongji ziliao 1952-1983 [State Statistical Bureau, Trade and Price Statistics of China 1952-1983] (1984), pp. 90-95.

Table 67. Retail Sales of Selected Textiles, Clothing, and Footwear: 1952 to 1983
(In 100 million yuan)

| Year | Total cotton and cotton blended cloth | Cotton cloth | Blended cotton and chemical cloth | Chemical fibre cloth | Silk and satins | Under-wear | Woolen fabrics | Towels | Socks | Bed sheets |
|---|---|---|---|---|---|---|---|---|---|---|
| 1952......... | 31.2 | 31.2 | N/A | .6 | .8 | .9 | .5 | 1.1 | 2.0 | .2 |
| 1953......... | 41.9 | 41.9 | N/A | .8 | 1.3 | 1.6 | 1.0 | 1.2 | 2.5 | .3 |
| 1954......... | 45.3 | 45.3 | N/A | 1.1 | 1.4 | 3.1 | 1.2 | 1.3 | 2.5 | .5 |
| 1955......... | 43.4 | 43.4 | N/A | 1.3 | 1.6 | 2.6 | 1.2 | 1.4 | 2.7 | .4 |
| 1956......... | 56.2 | 56.2 | N/A | 1.8 | 2.4 | 4.6 | 1.8 | 1.7 | 3.2 | .4 |
| 1957......... | 46.3 | 46.3 | N/A | 1.6 | 2.4 | 5.2 | 1.7 | 1.7 | 3.1 | .5 |
| 1958......... | 59.3 | 59.3 | N/A | 2.1 | 2.9 | 8.1 | 2.2 | 2.6 | 3.7 | .5 |
| 1959......... | 69.6 | 69.6 | N/A | 3.6 | 3.6 | 11.5 | 2.4 | 2.9 | 4.5 | .8 |
| 1960......... | 64.2 | 64.2 | N/A | 2.9 | 3.0 | 10.9 | 2.3 | 4.4 | 6.1 | .8 |
| 1961......... | 24.0 | 24.0 | N/A | 2.3 | 2.2 | 2.4 | 1.0 | 1.7 | 2.6 | .3 |
| 1962......... | 36.8 | 35.9 | .9 | 3.7 | 3.1 | 3.3 | 1.5 | 1.0 | 1.6 | .4 |
| 1963......... | 41.8 | 39.5 | 2.3 | 6.6 | 3.5 | 4.7 | 1.9 | 1.3 | 2.9 | .5 |
| 1964......... | 54.0 | 49.4 | 4.6 | 5.4 | 3.5 | 3.9 | 2.6 | 1.1 | 2.4 | .5 |
| 1965......... | 65.8 | 60.0 | 5.8 | 3.7 | 3.5 | 5.9 | 2.2 | 1.4 | 3.1 | .7 |
| 1966......... | 72.4 | 65.7 | 6.7 | 3.7 | 4.9 | 7.4 | 2.4 | 1.8 | 4.8 | .8 |
| 1967......... | 80.6 | 71.6 | 9.0 | 4.4 | 7.1 | 8.6 | 2.6 | 3.2 | 5.8 | .9 |
| 1968......... | 60.1 | 53.0 | 7.1 | 4.0 | 6.4 | 7.0 | 2.1 | 3.2 | 6.2 | 1.0 |
| 1969......... | 85.6 | 78.2 | 7.4 | 4.4 | 5.3 | 10.1 | 3.6 | 3.1 | 6.5 | 1.2 |
| 1970......... | 99.7 | 90.0 | 9.7 | 4.6 | 6.8 | 11.5 | 4.8 | 3.3 | 7.4 | 1.2 |
| 1971......... | 94.5 | 84.6 | 9.9 | 4.6 | 6.4 | 11.9 | 4.4 | 2.7 | 7.7 | 1.1 |
| 1972......... | 94.8 | 82.4 | 12.4 | 5.2 | 7.0 | 12.1 | 4.9 | 3.0 | 8.0 | 1.2 |
| 1973......... | 107.5 | 84.6 | 22.9 | 6.3 | 7.2 | 11.9 | 5.5 | 3.9 | 8.1 | 1.3 |
| 1974......... | 121.1 | 93.9 | 27.2 | 7.1 | 6.6 | 14.9 | 5.7 | 3.7 | 9.1 | 1.5 |
| 1975......... | 124.0 | 91.7 | 32.3 | 8.8 | 7.2 | 15.7 | 5.6 | 4.0 | 9.9 | 1.7 |
| 1976......... | 132.7 | 95.2 | 37.5 | 9.6 | 7.6 | 16.1 | 7.3 | 4.3 | 11.2 | 1.7 |
| 1977......... | 137.4 | 92.8 | 44.6 | 12.6 | 9.1 | 17.2 | 7.6 | 4.9 | 10.7 | 1.9 |
| 1978......... | 147.8 | 96.8 | 51.0 | 13.5 | 9.4 | 20.9 | 8.2 | 4.9 | 9.9 | 1.9 |
| 1979......... | 176.1 | 105.5 | 70.6 | 18.1 | 12.0 | 25.0 | 11.3 | 5.5 | 11.0 | 2.3 |
| 1980......... | 213.4 | 113.6 | 99.8 | 25.7 | 15.3 | 27.3 | 15.0 | 5.8 | 11.2 | 2.9 |
| 1981......... | 224.6 | 113.8 | 110.8 | 31.6 | 17.2 | 30.7 | 16.0 | 6.7 | 13.2 | 4.5 |
| 1982......... | 217.2 | 106.5 | 110.7 | 34.2 | 17.7 | 32.6 | 16.6 | 6.7 | 11.6 | 4.6 |
| 1983......... | 224.1 | 103.7 | 120.4 | 35.6 | 20.4 | 36.4 | 16.8 | 6.9 | 11.6 | 5.3 |

Table 67. Retail Sales of Selected Textiles, Clothing, and Footwear: 1952 to 1983--continued
(In 100 million yuan)

| Year | Cotton wadding | Leather shoes | Rubber shoes | Cloth shoes | All-plastic shoes |
|---|---|---|---|---|---|
| 1952......... | 1.8 | 1.4 | 2.7 | .6 | N/A |
| 1953......... | 2.7 | 1.9 | 3.1 | .8 | N/A |
| 1954......... | 2.6 | 2.0 | 3.4 | 1.0 | N/A |
| 1955......... | 2.3 | 2.1 | 3.0 | 1.3 | N/A |
| 1956......... | 4.0 | 2.3 | 4.4 | 1.5 | N/A |
| 1957......... | 4.0 | 2.4 | 5.4 | 1.7 | N/A |
| 1958......... | 3.5 | 2.4 | 8.4 | 2.0 | N/A |
| 1959......... | 3.8 | 3.4 | 8.3 | 2.7 | N/A |
| 1960......... | 3.1 | 5.0 | 7.8 | 4.1 | N/A |
| 1961......... | 1.2 | 4.1 | 4.4 | 5.2 | N/A |
| 1962......... | 1.1 | 3.1 | 7.6 | 4.2 | .8 |
| 1963......... | 1.6 | 2.9 | 8.6 | 2.2 | 1.0 |
| 1964......... | 2.4 | 2.0 | 7.9 | 2.1 | .8 |
| 1965......... | 3.0 | 1.6 | 8.2 | 2.6 | 1.0 |
| 1966......... | 3.4 | 1.9 | 9.8 | 2.8 | 1.3 |
| 1967......... | 4.1 | 2.0 | 10.4 | 2.7 | 1.4 |
| 1968......... | 3.5 | 2.1 | 9.4 | 2.7 | 1.1 |
| 1969......... | 3.8 | 2.8 | 11.4 | 2.5 | 1.9 |
| 1970......... | 3.4 | 5.0 | 12.1 | 3.2 | 1.9 |
| 1971......... | 2.7 | 4.8 | 12.0 | 3.3 | 2.2 |
| 1972......... | 2.9 | 4.3 | 12.7 | 3.8 | 2.5 |
| 1973......... | 3.4 | 4.7 | 14.3 | 4.2 | 3.0 |
| 1974......... | 4.3 | 5.0 | 15.1 | 4.5 | 3.2 |
| 1975......... | 4.3 | 5.7 | 15.9 | 4.7 | 3.6 |
| 1976......... | 4.8 | 7.3 | 16.6 | 5.3 | 3.9 |
| 1977......... | 4.9 | 8.8 | 16.7 | 5.9 | 4.1 |
| 1978......... | 4.8 | 10.5 | 16.1 | 6.6 | 4.2 |
| 1979......... | 5.2 | 14.0 | 16.9 | 7.5 | 5.2 |
| 1980......... | 5.7 | 20.2 | 19.8 | 8.5 | 6.3 |
| 1981......... | 6.2 | 24.1 | 20.6 | 9.5 | 6.9 |
| 1982......... | 5.9 | 28.5 | 20.6 | 9.7 | 6.9 |
| 1983......... | 6.9 | 29.7 | 21.8 | 9.7 | 6.2 |

NA Data not available

Source: Guojia tongji ju, Zhongguo maoyi wujia tongji ziliao 1952-1983 [State Statistical Bureau, Trade and Price Statistics of China 1952-1983] (1984), pp. 95-100.

Table 68. Retail Sales of Selected Articles for Daily Use: 1952 to 1983
(In 100 million yuan)

| Year | Aluminium pots and pans | Enamel mugs | Enamel basins | Iron pots | Pottery and porcelain for daily use | Clocks | Wrist watches | Flash-lights | Batteries |
|---|---|---|---|---|---|---|---|---|---|
| 1952......... | .04 | .1 | .2 | N/A | .7 | .03 | .4 | .2 | .5 |
| 1953......... | .1 | .1 | .4 | N/A | 1.0 | .1 | .9 | .2 | .6 |
| 1954......... | .1 | .2 | .4 | N/A | 1.2 | .1 | .4 | .3 | .6 |
| 1955......... | .1 | .2 | .4 | N/A | 1.4 | .1 | .5 | .2 | .7 |
| 1956......... | .1 | .3 | .6 | N/A | 1.6 | .3 | 1.6 | .3 | .7 |
| 1957......... | .2 | .2 | .5 | .8 | 1.8 | .3 | 1.3 | .3 | .9 |
| 1958......... | .2 | .3 | .7 | .6 | 2.6 | .4 | .9 | .3 | 1.0 |
| 1959......... | .2 | .4 | 1.1 | .6 | 2.7 | .6 | .5 | .5 | 1.2 |
| 1960......... | .2 | .5 | 1.7 | .4 | 3.7 | 1.0 | .4 | .6 | 1.4 |
| 1961......... | .2 | .3 | .7 | .9 | 4.2 | 1.1 | .6 | .3 | .7 |
| 1962......... | .4 | .3 | 1.1 | 1.4 | 4.2 | .7 | 1.5 | .3 | .9 |
| 1963......... | .4 | .3 | 1.1 | 1.0 | 3.5 | .4 | 1.5 | .3 | 1.2 |
| 1964......... | .3 | .3 | .7 | 1.1 | 3.3 | .5 | 2.0 | .3 | 1.2 |
| 1965......... | .4 | .2 | .6 | 1.2 | 3.6 | .3 | 2.0 | .3 | 1.2 |
| 1966......... | .4 | .3 | .7 | 1.1 | 3.6 | .4 | 2.5 | .4 | 1.6 |
| 1967......... | .5 | .3 | .9 | 1.2 | 4.4 | .4 | 2.0 | .4 | 1.6 |
| 1968......... | .5 | .4 | 1.4 | 1.1 | 4.4 | .4 | 1.8 | .4 | 1.0 |
| 1969......... | .6 | .4 | 1.5 | 1.1 | 4.0 | .5 | 1.9 | .6 | 1.6 |
| 1970......... | .7 | .4 | 1.3 | 1.2 | 4.3 | .6 | 2.7 | .7 | 2.0 |
| 1971......... | .7 | .4 | 1.1 | 1.1 | 4.9 | .8 | 4.6 | .8 | 2.2 |
| 1972......... | .9 | .5 | 1.3 | 1.3 | 5.1 | .9 | 6.3 | .7 | 2.6 |
| 1973......... | .9 | .5 | 1.6 | 1.4 | 5.1 | .9 | 8.7 | .7 | 2.7 |
| 1974......... | 1.1 | .5 | 1.5 | 1.3 | 4.9 | 1.0 | 10.2 | .6 | 2.6 |
| 1975......... | 1.3 | .5 | 1.8 | 1.3 | 5.1 | 1.2 | 10.6 | .8 | 2.9 |
| 1976......... | 1.4 | .6 | 1.9 | 1.4 | 5.0 | 1.3 | 13.8 | .9 | 2.9 |
| 1977......... | 1.5 | .7 | 2.1 | 1.5 | 5.2 | 1.5 | 14.6 | .8 | 3.3 |
| 1978......... | 1.5 | .7 | 2.1 | 1.7 | 5.2 | 1.6 | 17.3 | .8 | 4.0 |
| 1979......... | 1.6 | .8 | 2.2 | 1.7 | 5.8 | 2.0 | 23.9 | 1.0 | 4.8 |
| 1980......... | 1.8 | .8 | 2.6 | 1.8 | 5.9 | 2.4 | 31.1 | 1.1 | 6.8 |
| 1981......... | 2.0 | .9 | 2.8 | 1.8 | 6.1 | 2.9 | 32.3 | 1.2 | 7.8 |
| 1982......... | 2.0 | .9 | 2.6 | 1.7 | 6.1 | 3.0 | 33.6 | 1.4 | 9.2 |
| 1983......... | 2.1 | .9 | 2.6 | 1.9 | 6.5 | 3.5 | 33.6 | 1.6 | 9.8 |

Table 68. Retail Sales of Selected Articles for Daily Use: 1952 to 1983--continued
(In 100 million yuan)

| Year | Matches | Soap | Deter-gent | Thermos bottle | Sewing machine | Electric bulbs | Valve radio sets | Trans-istor radio sets | Tele-vision sets |
|---|---|---|---|---|---|---|---|---|---|
| 1952......... | 1.2 | 1.2 | N/A | .2 | .2 | .1 | .03 | N/A | N/A |
| 1953......... | 1.2 | 1.5 | N/A | .3 | .2 | .2 | .04 | N/A | N/A |
| 1954......... | 1.3 | 1.5 | N/A | .4 | .3 | .2 | .1 | N/A | N/A |
| 1955......... | 1.4 | 1.6 | N/A | .4 | .2 | .2 | .1 | N/A | N/A |
| 1956......... | 1.5 | 1.9 | N/A | .5 | .3 | .3 | .2 | N/A | N/A |
| 1957......... | 1.5 | 2.3 | N/A | .6 | .4 | .3 | .4 | N/A | N/A |
| 1958......... | 1.7 | 3.1 | N/A | .9 | .5 | .3 | .8 | N/A | N/A |
| 1959......... | 1.9 | 3.8 | N/A | .8 | .5 | .6 | .9 | N/A | N/A |
| 1960......... | 2.3 | 3.8 | N/A | 1.1 | .7 | .5 | 1.2 | N/A | N/A |
| 1961......... | 1.7 | 2.2 | N/A | 1.1 | .8 | .6 | 2.0 | N/A | N/A |
| 1962......... | 2.1 | 1.8 | .2 | 1.4 | .9 | .7 | 1.3 | N/A | N/A |
| 1963......... | 2.4 | 2.8 | .2 | 1.1 | 1.3 | .7 | .6 | N/A | N/A |
| 1964......... | 2.3 | 3.2 | .2 | 1.0 | 1.3 | .7 | 1.0 | N/A | N/A |
| 1965......... | 2.5 | 3.8 | .3 | 1.0 | 1.3 | .4 | .4 | .4 | N/A |
| 1966......... | 2.8 | 5.2 | .3 | 1.3 | 1.8 | .8 | .4 | .5 | N/A |
| 1967......... | 3.0 | 6.0 | .4 | 1.3 | 1.7 | .6 | .2 | .5 | N/A |
| 1968......... | 2.0 | 5.1 | .4 | 1.0 | 1.5 | .4 | .2 | .5 | N/A |
| 1969......... | 2.4 | 6.3 | .6 | 1.1 | 2.4 | .6 | .2 | 1.1 | N/A |
| 1970......... | 2.8 | 6.1 | .9 | 1.4 | 3.2 | .9 | .1 | 1.3 | N/A |
| 1971......... | 2.7 | 6.4 | .9 | 1.6 | 3.4 | 1.0 | .1 | 1.1 | .1 |
| 1972......... | 2.8 | 7.1 | 1.3 | 1.8 | 3.4 | 1.1 | .2 | 2.0 | .1 |
| 1973......... | 3.1 | 7.3 | 1.7 | 1.8 | 3.7 | 1.2 | .2 | 2.0 | .3 |
| 1974......... | 3.2 | 7.4 | 1.9 | 1.7 | 3.9 | 1.1 | .2 | 2.1 | .4 |
| 1975......... | 3.3 | 8.3 | 2.3 | 1.7 | 4.4 | 1.2 | .3 | 2.9 | .4 |
| 1976......... | 3.4 | 8.3 | 2.4 | 1.9 | 4.7 | 1.1 | .3 | 3.2 | .8 |
| 1977......... | 3.5 | 7.6 | 2.5 | 2.5 | 5.6 | 1.1 | .3 | 3.7 | 1.0 |
| 1978......... | 3.6 | 8.3 | 3.5 | 3.3 | 6.4 | 1.4 | .5 | 4.6 | 2.1 |
| 1979......... | 3.9 | 9.6 | 4.3 | 3.8 | 8.0 | 2.8 | .7 | 6.2 | 9.9 |
| 1980......... | 4.3 | 10.5 | 4.9 | 4.3 | 9.8 | 3.4 | .9 | 10.8 | 20.1 |
| 1981......... | 4.9 | 12.3 | 6.2 | 5.0 | 13.8 | 4.3 | 1.6 | 12.2 | 31.9 |
| 1982......... | 4.8 | 12.7 | 7.6 | 5.0 | 16.9 | 6.3 | 1.8 | 13.3 | 35.4 |
| 1983......... | 5.7 | 14.4 | 9.8 | 5.4 | 15.2 | 7.0 | 1.2 | 11.0 | 39.0 |

NA Data not available

Source: Guojia tongji ju, Zhongguo maoyi wujia tongji ziliao 1952-1983 [State Statistical Bureau, Trade and Price Statistics of China 1952-1983] (1984), pp. 100-106.

Table 68. Retail Sales of Selected Articles for Daily Use: 1952 to 1983--continued
(In 100 million yuan)

| Year | Cultural and education articles | | | | Fuels | |
|---|---|---|---|---|---|---|
| | Machine-made thin paper | Indig-enous paper | Pens | Pencils | Kerosene | Coal |
| 1952........ | 2.9 | 1.4 | .2 | .1 | 1.7 | 4.7 |
| 1953........ | 3.3 | 1.6 | .3 | .2 | 2.5 | 5.9 |
| 1954........ | 3.8 | 1.6 | .3 | .2 | 3.3 | 7.2 |
| 1955........ | 4.6 | 2.2 | .3 | .2 | 3.2 | 8.4 |
| 1956........ | 5.6 | 2.1 | .4 | .2 | 4.6 | 11.3 |
| 1957........ | 4.9 | 2.0 | .4 | .2 | 4.6 | 10.4 |
| 1958........ | 6.0 | 2.9 | .5 | .2 | 5.9 | 11.2 |
| 1959........ | 6.7 | 4.1 | .6 | .4 | 6.1 | 12.1 |
| 1960........ | 6.6 | 3.4 | .9 | .6 | 6.0 | 14.4 |
| 1961........ | 4.5 | 2.1 | 1.0 | .5 | 5.3 | 18.2 |
| 1962........ | 5.5 | 2.0 | .8 | .5 | 6.8 | 18.5 |
| 1963........ | 6.8 | 2.3 | .5 | .4 | 6.4 | 16.7 |
| 1964........ | 7.3 | 2.7 | .9 | .5 | 6.8 | 19.6 |
| 1965........ | 4.3 | 2.5 | .9 | .5 | 6.1 | 21.3 |
| 1966........ | 5.8 | 2.5 | .8 | .4 | 6.5 | 21.6 |
| 1967........ | 4.0 | 2.5 | .6 | .2 | 6.6 | 21.0 |
| 1968........ | 2.8 | 2.5 | .7 | .2 | 4.8 | 20.4 |
| 1969........ | 3.8 | 2.1 | .9 | .3 | 7.1 | 21.3 |
| 1970........ | 4.5 | 2.3 | .8 | .4 | 6.6 | 21.9 |
| 1971........ | 4.8 | 2.4 | .9 | .6 | 6.1 | 22.7 |
| 1972........ | 4.8 | 2.8 | 1.1 | .7 | 6.3 | 24.8 |
| 1973........ | 5.4 | 2.7 | 1.3 | .8 | 6.7 | 26.1 |
| 1974........ | 5.9 | 2.8 | 1.4 | .6 | 6.6 | 25.4 |
| 1975........ | 6.0 | 3.0 | 1.5 | .7 | 7.3 | 27.9 |
| 1976........ | 6.0 | 3.1 | 1.6 | .7 | 6.9 | 26.1 |
| 1977........ | 5.8 | 2.9 | 1.8 | .8 | 7.0 | 28.5 |
| 1978........ | 7.2 | 3.6 | 1.9 | 1.1 | 6.9 | 31.0 |
| 1979........ | 8.0 | 3.6 | 2.2 | 1.2 | 6.7 | 33.2 |
| 1980........ | 7.4 | 3.5 | 2.1 | 1.3 | 6.9 | 39.5 |
| 1981........ | 5.5 | 3.0 | 2.2 | 1.3 | 8.1 | 43.7 |
| 1982........ | 5.9 | 3.0 | 2.2 | 1.3 | 7.0 | 47.1 |
| 1983........ | 6.7 | 3.1 | 2.3 | 1.3 | 8.7 | 48.5 |

Source: Guojia tongji ju, Zhongguo maooyi wujia tongji ziliao 1952-1983 [State Statistical Bureau, Trade and Price Statistics of China 1952-1983] (1984), pp. 107-108.

Table 69. Durable Goods Possessed Per 100 Staff and Workers' Households: 1980 to 1984 (At yearend)

| Commodity | 1980 | 1981 | 1982 | 1983 | 1984 |
|---|---|---|---|---|---|
| Bicycles............ | 126.77 | 135.90 | 146.65 | 159.93 | 162.67 |
| Sewing machines..... | 65.57 | 70.41 | 73.60 | 76.21 | 77.52 |
| Wrist watches....... | 223.89 | 240.76 | 248.89 | 268.24 | 282.95 |
| Electric fans....... | 21.86 | 42.62 | 53.17 | 63.61 | 66.41 |
| Washing machines.... | N/A | 6.34 | 16.09 | 29.08 | 40.13 |
| Refrigerators....... | N/A | .22 | .67 | 1.65 | 3.22 |
| Wardrobes........... | N/A | 86.09 | 94.63 | 101.48 | 102.91 |
| Sofas............... | N/A | 89.33 | 109.49 | 123.77 | 131.63 |
| Writing desks....... | N/A | 55.17 | 63.37 | 70.67 | 74.41 |
| Radio sets.......... | 84.90 | 100.52 | 103.04 | 104.55 | 103.11 |
| Record players...... | N/A | N/A | N/A | 9.08 | 9.96 |
| Television sets..... | N/A | 57.65 | 73.31 | 83.15 | 85.36 |
| Black and white... | 32.29 | 57.06 | 72.21 | 80.58 | 79.98 |
| Color............. | N/A | .59 | 1.10 | 2.57 | 5.38 |
| Valve radios........ | N/A | 37.45 | 34.71 | 32.23 | 32.74 |
| Transistor radios... | N/A | 63.07 | 68.33 | 72.32 | 70.37 |
| Tape recorders...... | 5.45 | 12.97 | 17.99 | 27.11 | 34.17 |
| Cameras............. | 2.84 | 4.29 | 5.57 | 7.28 | 8.92 |

NA Data not available

Note: Data are from sample surveys of household income and expenditure of urban staff and workers in state-owned and collective units.

Data for ownership of refrigerators and sofas in 1983 and ownership of black and white televisions in 1984 differ slightly between Tongji yuebao and China: A Statistics Survey in 1985. Where there were differences, the latter reference was used.

Source: Guojia tongji ju, Guanghui de sanshiwu nian 1949-1984 [State Statistical Bureau, Thirty-five Glorious Years 1949-1984] (1984), p. 168; State Statistical Bureau, Statistical Yearbook of China 1984 (1984), p. 466; China: A Statistics Survey in 1985 (1985), p. 101; and Tongji yuebao [Statistics Monthly], No. 1, July 1985, p. 85.

Table 70. Durable Goods Possessed Per 100 Urban Staff and Workers' Households, by Income Group: 1982 (At yearend)

| Commodity | | Per Capita Monthly Income Group (in Yuan) | | | | | |
|---|---|---|---|---|---|---|---|
| | Average | 20 and below | 20.01-25.00 | 25.01-35.00 | 35.01-50.00 | 50.01-60.00 | 60.01 and above |
| Bicycles............... | 146.65 | 102.49 | 106.49 | 130.46 | 146.51 | 171.58 | 173.21 |
| Sewing machines........ | 73.60 | 62.17 | 51.69 | 72.15 | 72.68 | 80.50 | 81.55 |
| Wrist watches.......... | 248.89 | 146.11 | 173.52 | 210.80 | 246.25 | 302.64 | 311.88 |
| Electric fans.......... | 53.17 | 10.53 | 15.98 | 39.41 | 54.89 | 64.80 | 67.53 |
| Wardrobes.............. | 94.63 | 62.62 | 70.29 | 87.95 | 94.92 | 103.49 | 108.33 |
| Sofas.................. | 109.49 | 34.75 | 72.16 | 88.69 | 109.71 | 139.09 | 141.30 |
| Writing desks.......... | 63.37 | 28.90 | 53.34 | 59.68 | 63.66 | 70.38 | 76.29 |
| Radio sets............. | 103.04 | 76.69 | 78.86 | 95.86 | 102.07 | 112.76 | 131.41 |
| Television sets........ | 73.31 | 21.88 | 40.75 | 65.30 | 75.95 | 84.39 | 85.81 |
| Tape recorders......... | 17.99 | N/A | 7.18 | 9.00 | 17.22 | 25.20 | 32.22 |

NA Data not available

Note: Data are from sample surveys of household income and expenditure of urban staff and workers in state-owned and collective units.

Source: State Statistical Bureau, Statistical Yearbook of China 1983 (1983), p. 497.

Table 71. Durable Goods Possessed Per 100 Urban Staff and Workers' Households, by Income Group: 1983 (At yearend)

| Commodity | Average | Per Capita Monthly Income Group (in Yuan) | | | | | |
|---|---|---|---|---|---|---|---|
| | | 20 and below | 20.01-25.00 | 25.01-35.00 | 35.01-50.00 | 50.01-60.00 | 60.01 and above |
| Bicycles............... | 159.93 | 124.69 | 141.49 | 144.85 | 156.34 | 175.48 | 188.96 |
| Sewing machines........ | 76.21 | 72.59 | 68.02 | 74.58 | 74.18 | 80.47 | 85.17 |
| Wrist watches.......... | 268.24 | 185.51 | 193.61 | 229.39 | 262.28 | 300.82 | 327.55 |
| Electric fans.......... | 63.61 | 27.48 | 30.05 | 44.01 | 59.41 | 74.62 | 82.53 |
| Washing machines....... | 29.08 | N/A | 17.65 | 23.93 | 28.39 | 35.81 | 40.25 |
| Refrigerators.......... | 1.65 | N/A | N/A | .09 | .64 | 1.76 | 7.42 |
| Wardrobes.............. | 101.48 | 67.62 | 81.67 | 93.33 | 100.81 | 109.57 | 117.49 |
| Sofas.................. | 123.77 | 76.90 | 88.19 | 104.37 | 125.31 | 133.47 | 153.28 |
| Writing desks.......... | 70.67 | 56.28 | 61.59 | 66.19 | 70.05 | 73.01 | 84.58 |
| Radio sets............. | 104.55 | 84.75 | 94.12 | 99.46 | 100.51 | 114.86 | 126.59 |
| Television sets........ | 83.15 | N/A | N/A | 74.00 | 84.88 | 89.38 | 95.95 |
| Black and white...... | 80.58 | 53.29 | 58.58 | 73.44 | 83.10 | 86.42 | 86.77 |
| Color................ | 2.57 | N/A | N/A | .56 | 1.78 | 2.96 | 9.18 |
| Tape recorders......... | 27.11 | 5.16 | 7.59 | 13.31 | 25.00 | 37.14 | 52.81 |
| Cameras................ | 7.28 | N/A | N/A | 2.72 | 6.54 | 10.33 | 16.03 |

NA Data not available

Note: Data are from sample surveys of household income and expenditure of urban staff and workers in state-owned and collective units.

Source: State Statistical Bureau, Statistical Yearbook of China 1984 (1984), p. 470.

Table 72. Durable Goods Possessed Per 100 Peasant Households: 1978 to 1984 (At yearend)

| Commodity | 1978 | 1979 | 1980 | 1981 | 1982 | 1983 | 1984 |
|---|---|---|---|---|---|---|---|
| Bicycles......... | 30.73 | 36.20 | 36.87 | 44.41 | 51.50 | 63.41 | 74.48 |
| Sewing machines.. | 19.80 | 22.62 | 23.31 | 27.68 | 32.76 | 38.07 | 42.57 |
| Clocks and watches......... | 51.75 | 55.14 | 68.53 | 89.03 | 104.35 | 132.09 | 151.54 |
| Clocks......... | 24.33 | 27.31 | 30.95 | 33.94 | 36.26 | 40.65 | 42.10 |
| Wrist watches.. | 27.42 | 27.83 | 37.58 | 55.09 | 68.09 | 91.44 | 109.44 |
| Electric fans.... | N/A | N/A | N/A | N/A | 2.29 | 4.42 | N/A |
| Radio sets....... | 17.44 | 26.13 | 33.54 | 42.25 | 50.46 | 56.82 | 61.13 |
| Television sets.. | N/A | N/A | .39 | .87 | 1.68 | 3.99 | 7.24 |
| Tape recorders... | N/A | N/A | N/A | N/A | .66 | 1.51 | N/A |

NA Data not available

Note: Data are from sample surveys of household income and expenditure of peasants.

Source: Guojia tongji ju, Woguo nongmin shenghuo de juda bianhua [State Statistical Bureau, Great Changes in the Lives of China's Peasants] (1984), p. 86; and State Statistical Bureau, China: A Statistics Survey in 1985 (1985), p. 104.

Table 73. Ownership of Durable Goods Per 100 Persons, by Residence: 1978 to 1984
(At yearend)

| Commodity and residence | 1978 | 1979 | 1980 | 1981 | 1982 | 1983 | 1984 |
|---|---|---|---|---|---|---|---|
| Sewing machine: | | | | | | | |
| China........... | 3.5 | 4.0 | 4.7 | 5.5 | 6.6 | 7.5 | 8.4 |
| Urban........... | 8.6 | 9.8 | 11.2 | 13.0 | 14.8 | 16.6 | 18.6 |
| Rural........... | 2.4 | 2.7 | 3.2 | 3.8 | 4.7 | 5.3 | 6.1 |
| Wrist watch: | | | | | | | |
| China........... | 8.5 | 10.4 | 12.9 | 15.7 | 18.8 | 22.2 | 29.1 |
| Urban........... | 29.3 | 35.2 | 44.4 | 52.2 | 55.8 | 59.5 | 69.2 |
| Rural........... | 4.0 | 4.8 | 5.8 | 7.3 | 10.2 | 13.5 | 19.7 |
| Bicycle: | | | | | | | |
| China........... | 7.7 | 8.6 | 9.7 | 11.2 | 13.1 | 15.4 | 18.8 |
| Urban........... | 23.3 | 25.0 | 27.9 | 30.9 | 33.9 | 37.4 | 41.2 |
| Rural........... | 4.3 | 4.9 | 5.6 | 6.6 | 8.3 | 10.2 | 13.5 |
| Radio: | | | | | | | |
| China........... | 7.8 | 9.4 | 12.1 | 14.9 | 18.2 | 20.9 | 21.6 |
| Urban........... | 20.2 | 23.3 | 29.6 | 31.8 | 32.8 | 36.3 | 35.0 |
| Rural........... | 5.1 | 6.3 | 8.1 | 11.0 | 14.8 | 17.3 | 18.5 |
| Television: | | | | | | | |
| China........... | .3 | .5 | .9 | 1.6 | 2.7 | 3.5 | 4.6 |
| Urban........... | 1.3 | 2.0 | 3.5 | 5.6 | 10.2 | 12.6 | 19.4 |
| Rural........... | .1 | .2 | .3 | .6 | 1.0 | 1.4 | 1.1 |
| Fan: | | | | | | | |
| China........... | N/A | N/A | N/A | N/A | N/A | N/A | 4.2 |
| Urban........... | N/A | N/A | N/A | N/A | N/A | N/A | 17.0 |
| Rural........... | N/A | N/A | N/A | N/A | N/A | N/A | 1.2 |
| Washing machine: | | | | | | | |
| China........... | N/A | N/A | N/A | N/A | N/A | N/A | 1.9 |
| Urban........... | N/A | N/A | N/A | N/A | N/A | N/A | 8.4 |
| Rural........... | N/A | N/A | N/A | N/A | N/A | N/A | .3 |
| Refrigerator: | | | | | | | |
| China........... | N/A | N/A | N/A | N/A | N/A | N/A | .2 |
| Urban........... | N/A | N/A | N/A | N/A | N/A | N/A | .7 |
| Rural........... | N/A | N/A | N/A | N/A | N/A | N/A | .1 |
| Tape Recorder: | | | | | | | |
| China........... | N/A | N/A | N/A | N/A | N/A | N/A | 2.2 |
| Urban........... | N/A | N/A | N/A | N/A | N/A | N/A | 9.0 |
| Rural........... | N/A | N/A | N/A | N/A | N/A | N/A | .6 |
| Camera: | | | | | | | |
| China........... | N/A | N/A | N/A | N/A | N/A | N/A | .9 |
| Urban........... | N/A | N/A | N/A | N/A | N/A | N/A | 4.2 |
| Rural........... | N/A | N/A | N/A | N/A | N/A | N/A | .2 |

NA Data not available

Note: Data are not from the household income and expenditure surveys, nor necessarily consistent with the survey data.

Source: Guojia tongji ju, Zhongguo maoyi wujia tongji ziliao 1952-1983 [State Statistical Bureau, Trade and Price Statistics of China 1952-1983] (1984), p. 59; and China: A Statistics Survey in 1985 (1985), p. 96.

Table 74. Housing Statistics for Urban Households: 1978 to 1984

| Year | Living Space Per Capita at Yearend (Square meter) |
|---|---|
| 1978.......... | 4.2 |
| 1979.......... | 4.4 |
| 1980.......... | N/A 5.0 |
| 1981.......... | 5.3 |
| 1982.......... | 5.6 |
| 1983.......... | 5.9 |
| 1984.......... | 7.6 |
| 1985 | 7.0 |

NA Data not available

Note: Data are from sample survey of worker and staff households.

Source: State Statistical Bureau, Statistical Yearbook of China 1981 (1982), p. 429; Statistical Yearbook of China 1983 (1983), p. 483; and China: A Statistics Survey in 1985 (1985), p. 94.

Table 75. Housing Statistics For Rural Households: Selected Years, 1957 to 1984

| Item | 1957 | 1978 | 1979 | 1980 | 1981 | 1982 | 1983 | 1984 |
|---|---|---|---|---|---|---|---|---|
| Households with new residential construction as a percent of total households surveyed......... | N/A | N/A | 7.80 | 8.90 | 11.60 | 8.70 | 11.20 | N/A |
| Average number of rooms built by each household per year.................... | .08 | .11 | .22 | .23 | .27 | .29 | .31 | .25 |
| Average number of rooms available for each household at year end.................. | 3.98 | 3.64 | 3.84 | 4.06 | 4.28 | 4.56 | 4.81 | 5.07 |
| Average floor space per capita at yearend (sq. meters)................. | 11.30 | 10.17 | 11.03 | 11.59 | 12.47 | 13.41 | 14.25 | 15.38 |
| of which living space (sq. meters)................ | N/A | 8.10 | 8.40 | 9.40 | 10.16 | 10.73 | 11.63 | 13.60 |

NA Data not available

Note: Data are from sample surveys of household income and expenditure of peasants.

Source: Guojia tongji ju, Woguo nongmin shenghuo de juda bianhua [State Statistical Bureau, Great Changes in the Lives of China's Peasants] (1984), p. 87; State Statistical Bureau, Statistical Yearbook of China 1984 (1984), p. 471; and China: A Statistics Survey in 1985 (1985), p. 102.

Table 76. Per Capita Income Available for Living Expenses, for Staff and Worker Households, by Province: 1978, 1982 and 1983 (In yuan)

| Province | 1978 | 1982 | 1983 |
|---|---|---|---|
| China.......... | 315.60 | 494.52 | 525.96 |
| North | | | |
| Beijing....... | 365.40 | 561.10 | 590.50 |
| Tianjin....... | N/A | 529.20 | 552.00 |
| Hebei......... | N/A | 462.36 | 479.16 |
| Shanxi........ | 260.40 | 403.20 | 415.20 |
| Neimenggu..... | N/A | 439.20 | 439.80 |
| Northeast | | | |
| Liaoning...... | 343.30 | 493.20 | 510.90 |
| Jilin......... | N/A | 431.00 | 466.60 |
| Heilongjiang.. | N/A | 443.50 | 487.40 |
| East | | | |
| Shanghai...... | N/A | 608.00 | 641.00 |
| Jiangsu....... | N/A | 482.20 | 498.00 |
| Zhejiang...... | 303.84 | 480.60 | 505.32 |
| Anhui......... | N/A | 420.80 | 453.51 |
| Fujian........ | N/A | 481.30 | 525.24 |
| Jiangxi....... | N/A | 401.64 | 413.52 |
| Shandong...... | 322.44 | 489.12 | 500.88 |
| South | | | |
| Henan......... | | | |
| Hubei......... | N/A | 488.53 | 502.49 |
| Hunan......... | N/A | N/A | 501.48 |
| Guangdong..... | N/A | 651.72 | 734.52 |
| Guangxi....... | 289.20 | 468.72 | 482.61 |
| Southwest | | | |
| Sichuan....... | N/A | 440.88 | 481.58 |
| Guizhou....... | N/A | 413.70 | 442.90 |
| Yunnan........ | N/A | 473.88 | 494.52 |
| Xizang........ | N/A | N/A | N/A |
| Northwest | | | |
| Shaanxi....... | 290.30 | 420.60 | 452.80 |
| Gansu......... | N/A | 474.00 | 491.00 |
| Qinghai....... | N/A | 462.98 | 499.56 |
| Ningxia....... | 320.40 | 478.80 | 500.40 |
| Xinjiang...... | N/A | N/A | N/A |

NA Data not available

Note: Data are from urban staff and worker household income and expenditure sample surveys. 1982 and 1983 data for Ningxia are from a survey of 80 households in Xining city.

Source: Gu Shutang, et al., Tianjin jingji gaikuang [General Economic Conditions in Tianjin] (1984), p. 498; Hu Qiaomu, et al., eds., Zhongguo baike nianjian 1984 [Encyclopedic Yearbook of China 1984], (1984), pp. 86 and 94; JPRS-CEA-84-054, July 21, 1984, p. 78; and Xue Muqiao, et al., eds, Zhongguo jingji nianjian, 1984 [Economic Yearbook of China, 1984] (1984), pp. VI.1-239.

Table 77. Average Wage, for Urban Staff and Workers, by Type of Ownership System and Province: Selected Years, 1978 to 1983
(In yuan)

| Province | Average wage | | | | State-owned units | | | Collective-owned units in cities and towns | | |
|---|---|---|---|---|---|---|---|---|---|---|
| | 1978 | 1981 | 1982 | 1983 | 1981 | 1982 | 1983 | 1981 | 1982 | 1983 |
| China.......... | 614 | 772 | 798 | 826 | 812 | 836 | 865 | 642 | 671 | 698 |
| North | | | | | | | | | | |
| Beijing....... | N/A | 837 | 863 | 931 | 880 | 896 | 964 | 649 | 716 | 787 |
| Tianjin....... | 710 | 805 | 820 | 868 | 845 | 865 | 916 | 674 | 672 | 721 |
| Hebei......... | 597 | 744 | 772 | 796 | 771 | 800 | 824 | 617 | 648 | 668 |
| Shanxi........ | 634 | 764 | 786 | 827 | 802 | 830 | 868 | 593 | 600 | 649 |
| Neimenggu..... | 710 | 807 | 825 | 862 | 851 | 868 | 902 | 643 | 670 | 714 |
| Northeast | | | | | | | | | | |
| Liaoning...... | 650 | 777 | 784 | 806 | 822 | 828 | 852 | 667 | 675 | 704 |
| Jilin......... | 651 | 776 | 799 | 823 | 840 | 863 | 881 | 611 | 637 | 679 |
| Heilongjiang.. | 676 | 831 | 855 | 869 | 889 | 908 | 930 | 670 | 703 | 719 |
| East | | | | | | | | | | |
| Shanghai...... | 672 | 870 | 883 | 897 | 910 | 920 | 935 | 727 | 750 | 763 |
| Jiangsu....... | 513 | 672 | 702 | 723 | 718 | 748 | 768 | 594 | 626 | 643 |
| Zhejiang...... | 565 | 709 | 740 | 760 | 769 | 783 | 797 | 625 | 671 | 697 |
| Anhui......... | 555 | 690 | 717 | 733 | 749 | 772 | 791 | 538 | 575 | 584 |
| Fujian........ | 567 | 716 | 765 | 827 | 746 | 793 | 861 | 637 | 691 | 730 |
| Jiangxi....... | 550 | 719 | 732 | 747 | 745 | 758 | 774 | 613 | 625 | 640 |
| Shandong...... | 564 | 754 | 769 | 789 | 782 | 797 | 818 | 667 | 679 | 696 |
| South | | | | | | | | | | |
| Henan......... | N/A | 742 | 754 | 768 | 772 | 789 | 805 | 604 | 604 | 606 |
| Hubei......... | 586 | 717 | 739 | 759 | 739 | 760 | 781 | 633 | 657 | 677 |
| Hunan......... | 567 | 725 | 750 | 780 | 748 | 772 | 803 | 643 | 670 | 700 |
| Guangdong..... | 611 | 854 | 938 | 992 | 883 | 967 | 1,022 | 769 | 845 | 898 |
| Guangxi....... | 551 | 721 | 759 | 787 | 748 | 781 | 810 | 591 | 647 | 670 |
| Southwest | | | | | | | | | | |
| Sichuan....... | 591 | 748 | 761 | 788 | 788 | 798 | 827 | 613 | 633 | 652 |
| Guizhou....... | 610 | 767 | 784 | 801 | 804 | 815 | 830 | 589 | 632 | 655 |
| Yunnan........ | 606 | 780 | 806 | 840 | 800 | 825 | 857 | 639 | 676 | 719 |
| Xizang........ | N/A | 1,114 | 1,301 | 1,395 | 1,132 | 1,319 | 1,397 | 870 | 1,134 | 1,379 |
| Northwest | | | | | | | | | | |
| Shaanxi....... | 642 | 780 | 797 | 824 | 812 | 831 | 857 | 609 | 619 | 652 |
| Gansu......... | 732 | 877 | 906 | 944 | 904 | 936 | 973 | 647 | 649 | 702 |
| Qinghai....... | 908 | 1,056 | 1,111 | 1,246 | 1,091 | 1,155 | 1,302 | 828 | 848 | 933 |
| Ningxia....... | 731 | 874 | 894 | 922 | 910 | 932 | 970 | 633 | 646 | 706 |
| Xinjiang...... | N/A | 915 | 941 | 972 | 935 | 968 | 998 | 744 | 722 | 767 |

NA Data not available

Source: State Statistical Bureau, Statistical Yearbook of China 1981 (1982), p. 434; Statistical Yearbook of China 1983 (1983), p. 488; Statistical Yearbook of China 1984 (1984), p. 457, Xue Muqiao, et al., eds., Zhongguo jingji nianjian, 1983 [Economic Yearbook of China, 1983] (1983), pp. V-4 and V-9; and Zhongguo jingji nianjian, 1984 [Economic Yearbook of China 1984] (1984), pp. VI-1 to VI-252.

Table 78. Peasant Net Income, by Province: Selected Years, 1978 to 1983
(In yuan)

| Province | 1978 | 1982 | 1983 |
|---|---|---|---|
| China............ | 133.6 | 270.1 | 309.8 |
| North: | | | |
| Beijing......... | 224.8 | 433.0 | 519.0 |
| Tianjin......... | 178.4 | 326.0 | 412.0 |
| Hebei........... | 91.5 | 236.0 | 298.0 |
| Shanxi.......... | N/A | 227.0 | 276.0 |
| Neimenggu....... | 100.3 | 273.0 | 294.0 |
| Northeast: | | | |
| Liaoning........ | 165.2 | 334.0 | 452.0 |
| Jilin........... | 179.2 | 333.0 | 462.0 |
| Heilongjiang.... | 167.9 | 250.0 | 388.0 |
| East: | | | |
| Shanghai........ | 290.0 | 530.0 | 563.0 |
| Jiangsu......... | 152.1 | 309.0 | 357.0 |
| Zhejiang........ | N/A | 346.0 | 359.0 |
| Anhui........... | 101.7 | 269.0 | 305.0 |
| Fujian.......... | 134.9 | 268.0 | 301.0 |
| Jiangxi......... | N/A | 270.0 | 302.0 |
| Shandong........ | 101.2 | 304.0 | 368.0 |
| South: | | | |
| Henan........... | 101.4 | 217.0 | 272.0 |
| Hubei........... | 106.5 | 286.0 | 299.0 |
| Hunan........... | 134.4 | 284.0 | 316.0 |
| Guangdong....... | 182.3 | 382.0 | 396.0 |
| Guangxi......... | N/A | 235.0 | 262.0 |
| Southwest: | | | |
| Sichuan......... | 116.7 | 256.0 | 258.0 |
| Guizhou......... | 108.0 | 223.0 | 225.0 |
| Yunnan.......... | 123.9 | 232.0 | 267.0 |
| Xizang (Tibet).. | N/A | N/A | N/A |
| Northwest: | | | |
| Shaanxi......... | N/A | 218.0 | 236.0 |
| Gansu........... | 98.4 | 174.0 | 213.0 |
| Qinghai......... | N/A | 201.0 | 252.0 |
| Ningxia......... | N/A | 229.0 | 289.0 |
| Xinjiang........ | N/A | 277.0 | 307.0 |

NA Data not available

Source: State Statistical Bureau, Statistical Yearbook of China 1984 (1984), p. 475.

Table 79. Per Capita Total Living Expenditure of Peasants, by Province: 1981
(In yuan)

| Province | Total | Consumer goods | Food | | | Clothes | Fuel | Housing | Daily articles and others | | Culture and service |
|---|---|---|---|---|---|---|---|---|---|---|---|
| | | | Total | Staple | Non-staple | | | | Total | of which furniture | |
| China............ | 190.81 | 186.17 | 113.83 | 61.07 | 41.50 | 23.57 | 10.59 | 18.67 | 19.51 | 3.46 | 4.64 |
| North | | | | | | | | | | | |
| Beijing........ | 312.99 | 298.65 | 163.11 | 76.04 | 57.15 | 36.00 | 9.19 | 49.24 | 41.11 | 5.31 | 14.34 |
| Tianjin........ | 249.17 | 245.30 | 126.42 | 64.64 | 43.77 | 37.49 | 10.06 | 41.44 | 29.89 | 5.25 | 3.87 |
| Hebei.......... | 164.66 | 162.19 | 85.93 | 52.77 | 25.79 | 23.48 | 8.66 | 19.41 | 24.71 | 4.60 | 2.47 |
| Shanxi......... | 147.78 | 145.43 | 85.86 | 56.79 | 20.80 | 23.88 | 5.55 | 12.15 | 17.99 | 2.32 | 2.35 |
| Neimenggu...... | 177.12 | 173.29 | 110.74 | 57.86 | 42.65 | 24.77 | 7.62 | 8.46 | 21.70 | 1.88 | 3.83 |
| Northeast | | | | | | | | | | | |
| Liaoning....... | 258.50 | 253.60 | 139.06 | 61.94 | 64.82 | 35.88 | 16.44 | 25.16 | 37.06 | 5.73 | 4.90 |
| Jilin.......... | 246.07 | 242.89 | 152.39 | 74.88 | 57.58 | 34.04 | 15.24 | 13.70 | 27.52 | 3.93 | 3.18 |
| Heilongjiang.... | 175.23 | 168.60 | 101.98 | 61.41 | 32.54 | 29.97 | 10.52 | 8.56 | 17.57 | 2.96 | 6.63 |
| East | | | | | | | | | | | |
| Shanghai....... | 389.85 | 384.02 | 198.10 | 67.78 | 87.65 | 43.25 | 12.43 | 83.43 | 46.81 | 11.28 | 5.83 |
| Jiangsu........ | 225.54 | 219.54 | 128.22 | 66.22 | 44.01 | 25.80 | 9.49 | 33.15 | 22.88 | 3.99 | 6.00 |
| Zhejiang....... | 266.46 | 261.61 | 147.01 | 61.67 | 59.96 | 31.75 | 11.81 | 43.15 | 27.89 | 3.70 | 4.85 |
| Anhui.......... | 193.26 | 187.21 | 117.90 | 68.37 | 38.49 | 21.49 | 11.12 | 19.67 | 17.03 | 4.04 | 6.05 |
| Fujian......... | 199.25 | 193.52 | 123.50 | 62.32 | 51.83 | 19.98 | 16.52 | 14.82 | 18.70 | 2.65 | 5.73 |
| Jiangxi........ | 194.17 | 189.38 | 117.99 | 66.57 | 43.00 | 20.52 | 15.35 | 21.00 | 14.52 | 3.77 | 4.79 |
| Shandong....... | 178.95 | 174.88 | 89.56 | 53.07 | 28.09 | 27.03 | 7.69 | 24.00 | 26.60 | 5.03 | 4.07 |
| South | | | | | | | | | | | |
| Henan.......... | 165.57 | 161.40 | 89.08 | 58.10 | 20.89 | 24.51 | 8.68 | 19.96 | 19.17 | 3.67 | 4.17 |
| Hubei.......... | 183.78 | 178.27 | 114.75 | 65.36 | 40.46 | 22.58 | 10.34 | 15.56 | 15.04 | 3.72 | 5.51 |
| Hunan.......... | 207.59 | 202.88 | 135.98 | 65.06 | 59.55 | 23.06 | 14.28 | 13.59 | 15.97 | 3.33 | 4.71 |
| Guangdong...... | 266.05 | 257.66 | 157.72 | 61.23 | 77.25 | 21.32 | 17.01 | 33.25 | 28.36 | 5.25 | 8.39 |
| Guangxi........ | 171.45 | 168.41 | 115.93 | 58.43 | 49.87 | 14.93 | 10.72 | 9.50 | 17.33 | .68 | 3.04 |
| Southwest | | | | | | | | | | | |
| Sichuan........ | 184.07 | 179.53 | 121.21 | 61.48 | 50.11 | 20.65 | 9.13 | 13.38 | 15.16 | 1.86 | 4.54 |
| Guizhou........ | 162.51 | 157.07 | 105.16 | 54.33 | 42.96 | 18.93 | 14.29 | 9.19 | 9.50 | 2.16 | 5.44 |
| Yunnan......... | 137.75 | 135.09 | 91.83 | 49.43 | 33.65 | 15.90 | 7.71 | 9.04 | 10.61 | 1.88 | 2.66 |
| Xizang......... | N/A | N/A | N/A | N/A | N/A | N/A | N/A | N/A | N/A | N/A | N/A |
| Northwest | | | | | | | | | | | |
| Shaanxi........ | 148.46 | 145.39 | 92.10 | 61.45 | 22.80 | 18.82 | 9.75 | 9.13 | 15.59 | 2.40 | 3.07 |
| Gansu.......... | 135.23 | 131.11 | 92.99 | 66.32 | 21.15 | 16.37 | 5.17 | 7.11 | 9.47 | 2.43 | 4.12 |
| Qinghai........ | 153.48 | 140.55 | 103.43 | 63.19 | 28.58 | 18.90 | 7.67 | 7.24 | 9.31 | 1.73 | 6.93 |
| Ningxia........ | 141.68 | 139.05 | 89.06 | 61.62 | 23.48 | 20.11 | 5.80 | 7.42 | 16.66 | 4.95 | 2.63 |
| Xinjiang....... | 168.58 | 163.83 | 98.98 | 55.33 | 33.31 | 35.08 | 10.22 | 4.99 | 14.56 | 3.79 | 4.75 |

NA Data not available

Source: State Statistical Bureau, Statistical Yearbook of China 1981 (1981), pp.445-446.

Table 80. Per Capita Total Living Expenditure of Peasants, by Province: 1982
(In yuan)

| Province | Total | Consumer goods | Food: Total | Food: Staple | Food: Non-staple | Food: Other | Clothes | Fuel | Housing | Daily articles and other | Culture and services |
|---|---|---|---|---|---|---|---|---|---|---|---|
| China............ | 220.23 | 215.30 | 133.20 | 70.74 | 47.85 | 14.61 | 24.77 | 12.36 | 22.58 | 22.39 | 4.93 |
| North | | | | | | | | | | | |
| Beijing......... | 362.42 | 353.38 | 190.33 | 92.91 | 61.22 | 36.20 | 43.77 | 9.73 | 60.54 | 49.01 | 9.04 |
| Tianjin......... | 266.66 | 262.72 | 135.20 | 65.92 | 40.12 | 29.16 | 36.40 | 10.47 | 44.16 | 36.49 | 3.94 |
| Hebei........... | 175.39 | 172.59 | 95.21 | 58.93 | 27.02 | 9.26 | 22.83 | 9.30 | 22.44 | 22.81 | 2.80 |
| Shanxi.......... | 167.66 | 164.41 | 104.78 | 71.42 | 24.11 | 9.25 | 25.11 | 6.46 | 9.89 | 18.17 | 3.25 |
| Neimenggu....... | 204.82 | 201.55 | 128.41 | 70.07 | 46.23 | 12.11 | 27.63 | 8.94 | 12.58 | 23.99 | 3.27 |
| Northeast | | | | | | | | | | | |
| Liaoning........ | 266.15 | 262.68 | 145.68 | 64.00 | 68.99 | 12.69 | 32.83 | 17.79 | 27.29 | 39.09 | 3.47 |
| Jilin........... | 253.44 | 248.22 | 159.37 | 76.34 | 63.75 | 19.28 | 33.38 | 18.37 | 11.81 | 25.29 | 5.22 |
| Heilongjiang.... | 200.58 | 194.54 | 116.22 | 65.53 | 40.01 | 10.68 | 29.57 | 13.24 | 13.76 | 21.75 | 6.04 |
| East | | | | | | | | | | | |
| Shanghai........ | 444.64 | 438.75 | 221.11 | 73.65 | 94.36 | 53.10 | 38.64 | 12.53 | 115.65 | 50.82 | 5.89 |
| Jiangsu......... | 261.41 | 255.67 | 144.98 | 69.32 | 55.36 | 20.30 | 29.12 | 11.67 | 42.60 | 27.30 | 5.74 |
| Zhejiang........ | 301.86 | 296.86 | 169.92 | 70.99 | 68.45 | 30.48 | 32.75 | 12.72 | 47.12 | 34.35 | 5.00 |
| Anhui........... | 239.93 | 233.54 | 153.11 | 84.98 | 49.09 | 19.04 | 23.09 | 15.62 | 23.54 | 18.18 | 6.39 |
| Fujian.......... | 231.14 | 224.41 | 144.92 | 68.47 | 59.98 | 16.47 | 21.26 | 16.96 | 19.52 | 21.75 | 6.73 |
| Jiangxi......... | 219.87 | 214.93 | 140.54 | 77.43 | 50.55 | 12.56 | 21.59 | 17.64 | 19.19 | 15.97 | 4.94 |
| Shandong........ | 230.03 | 226.18 | 115.84 | 67.37 | 34.51 | 13.96 | 30.76 | 12.20 | 33.61 | 33.77 | 3.85 |
| South | | | | | | | | | | | |
| Henan........... | 177.90 | 173.60 | 101.18 | 66.44 | 23.55 | 11.19 | 23.26 | 8.46 | 20.20 | 20.50 | 4.30 |
| Hubei........... | 226.96 | 220.73 | 140.64 | 78.44 | 47.62 | 14.58 | 28.26 | 12.35 | 18.53 | 20.95 | 6.23 |
| Hunan........... | 248.69 | 242.65 | 164.02 | 78.71 | 70.57 | 14.74 | 24.74 | 13.63 | 22.20 | 18.06 | 6.04 |
| Guangdong....... | 312.44 | 300.76 | 182.55 | 71.98 | 89.14 | 21.43 | 20.52 | 18.32 | 42.40 | 36.97 | 11.68 |
| Guangxi......... | 210.15 | 206.30 | 139.08 | 68.86 | 59.14 | 11.08 | 18.47 | 14.68 | 13.41 | 20.66 | 3.86 |
| Southwest | | | | | | | | | | | |
| Sichuan......... | 208.23 | 203.84 | 137.80 | 72.69 | 51.51 | 13.60 | 20.74 | 11.07 | 17.74 | 16.49 | 4.39 |
| Guizhou......... | 187.02 | 182.45 | 121.67 | 59.25 | 51.10 | 11.32 | 21.53 | 12.58 | 14.49 | 12.18 | 4.57 |
| Yunnan.......... | 185.75 | 182.72 | 124.27 | 61.65 | 48.99 | 13.63 | 19.81 | 8.89 | 14.22 | 15.53 | 3.03 |
| Xizang (Tibet).. | NA | NA | NA | NA | NA | NA | NA | NA | NA | NA | NA |
| Northwest | | | | | | | | | | | |
| Shaanxi......... | 168.92 | 165.63 | 106.02 | 69.86 | 26.17 | 9.99 | 20.56 | 10.94 | 10.11 | 18.00 | 3.29 |
| Gansu........... | 141.05 | 136.56 | 95.65 | 67.97 | 22.21 | 5.47 | 16.82 | 5.70 | 6.03 | 12.36 | 4.49 |
| Qinghai......... | 152.66 | 146.73 | 107.12 | 79.69 | 19.71 | 7.72 | 16.45 | 8.98 | 5.4 | 8.78 | 5.93 |
| Ningxia......... | 179.37 | 176.84 | 113.74 | 76.66 | 28.69 | 8.39 | 24.11 | 6.46 | 9.61 | 22.92 | 2.53 |
| Xinjiang........ | 203.12 | 197.37 | 123.24 | 64.56 | 44.88 | 13.80 | 38.00 | 13.72 | 4.64 | 17.77 | 5.75 |

NA Data not available

Source: State Statistical Bureau, Statistical Yearbook of China 1983 (1983), pp. 503-504; and He kang, et al., eds., Zhongguo nongye nianjian 1983 [Agricultural Yearbook of China 1983] (1984), pp. 141-142.

Table 81. Per Capita Total Living Expenditure of Peasants, by Province: 1983
(In yuan)

| Province | Total | Consumer goods | Food: Total | Food: Staple | Food: Non-staple | Food: Other | Food: Outside meals | Clothes |
|---|---|---|---|---|---|---|---|---|
| China.......... | 248.29 | 242.81 | 147.24 | 75.04 | 53.69 | 15.81 | 2.70 | 27.65 |
| North: | | | | | | | | |
| Beijing....... | 384.41 | 376.96 | 193.22 | 78.15 | 71.09 | 36.87 | 7.11 | 48.75 |
| Tianjin....... | 336.49 | 332.12 | 164.05 | 78.95 | 49.48 | 29.36 | 6.26 | 42.39 |
| Hebei......... | 224.65 | 220.94 | 120.23 | 72.23 | 34.63 | 11.14 | 2.23 | 28.97 |
| Shanxi........ | 203.35 | 199.08 | 117.42 | 75.45 | 26.63 | 13.29 | 2.05 | 27.92 |
| Neimenggu..... | 226.55 | 220.55 | 136.08 | 74.13 | 46.23 | 13.59 | 2.13 | 28.53 |
| Northeast: | | | | | | | | |
| Liaoning...... | 307.37 | 301.63 | 162.89 | 72.72 | 71.20 | 15.93 | 3.04 | 37.79 |
| Jilin......... | 274.97 | 269.71 | 174.23 | 86.96 | 68.22 | 16.85 | 2.20 | 31.17 |
| Heilongjiang.. | 213.73 | 204.48 | 115.26 | 60.18 | 38.13 | 15.50 | 1.45 | 31.49 |
| East: | | | | | | | | |
| Shanghai...... | 511.60 | 504.05 | 241.48 | 75.07 | 105.12 | 53.54 | 7.75 | 45.86 |
| Jiangsu....... | 322.15 | 316.00 | 178.16 | 85.81 | 64.27 | 24.75 | 3.33 | 33.68 |
| Zhejiang...... | 325.85 | 320.22 | 183.07 | 77.16 | 71.26 | 30.93 | 3.72 | 35.57 |
| Anhui......... | 258.42 | 252.06 | 153.55 | 82.49 | 51.05 | 17.69 | 2.32 | 26.70 |
| Fujian........ | 261.27 | 254.60 | 167.41 | 76.38 | 72.23 | 16.10 | 2.70 | 22.26 |
| Jiangxi....... | 252.26 | 246.80 | 157.78 | 80.88 | 60.96 | 13.29 | 2.65 | 23.30 |
| Shandong...... | 264.42 | 260.58 | 134.16 | 75.57 | 39.59 | 16.79 | 2.21 | 34.60 |
| South: | | | | | | | | |
| Henan......... | 196.21 | 191.93 | 113.71 | 75.65 | 25.89 | 10.46 | 1.71 | 24.32 |
| Hubei......... | 252.47 | 246.18 | 156.03 | 79.18 | 57.10 | 17.59 | 2.16 | 30.02 |
| Hunan......... | 273.86 | 267.74 | 175.62 | 81.16 | 75.49 | 16.08 | 2.89 | 26.71 |
| Guangdong..... | 328.76 | 319.10 | 198.23 | 72.93 | 101.12 | 18.95 | 5.23 | 20.11 |
| Guangxi....... | 224.05 | 219.46 | 148.31 | 66.81 | 67.32 | 10.66 | 3.52 | 18.14 |
| Southwest: | | | | | | | | |
| Sichuan....... | 231.12 | 226.55 | 150.63 | 74.52 | 59.04 | 14.11 | 2.96 | 24.50 |
| Guizhou....... | 185.11 | 180.68 | 125.88 | 60.84 | 52.63 | 10.67 | 1.74 | 18.40 |
| Yunnan........ | 223.81 | 220.06 | 144.63 | 65.05 | 59.24 | 16.42 | 3.92 | 25.19 |
| Xizang........ | NA | NA | NA | NA | NA | NA | NA | NA |
| Northwest: | | | | | | | | |
| Shaanxi....... | 203.41 | 199.37 | 122.24 | 77.20 | 32.50 | 10.60 | 1.94 | 22.73 |
| Gansu......... | 162.68 | 158.64 | 103.62 | 74.72 | 21.04 | 7.07 | 0.79 | 21.56 |
| Qinghai....... | 201.99 | 193.64 | 124.86 | 76.01 | 32.98 | 14.71 | 1.16 | 32.74 |
| Ningxia....... | 208.88 | 205.36 | 126.54 | 80.88 | 34.05 | 9.87 | 1.74 | 28.83 |
| Xinjiang...... | 227.96 | 222.00 | 132.40 | 73.10 | 42.71 | 14.90 | 1.69 | 43.32 |

Table 81. Per Capita Total Living Expenditure of Peasants, by Province: 1983--continued
(In yuan)

| Province | Fuel | Housing | Articles for daily use | Articles for culture and rec. | Books, newspap., and mags. | Medicine, and med. articles | Other articles | Culture and services |
|---|---|---|---|---|---|---|---|---|
| China.......... | 13.47 | 27.56 | 18.43 | 2.17 | 0.81 | 3.65 | 1.83 | 5.48 |
| North: | | | | | | | | |
| Beijing....... | 12.20 | 64.73 | 39.01 | 12.37 | 0.17 | 5.04 | 1.47 | 7.45 |
| Tianjin....... | 12.86 | 60.39 | 41.17 | 2.20 | 0.26 | 3.77 | 5.03 | 4.37 |
| Hebei......... | 10.99 | 31.79 | 21.72 | 1.73 | 0.58 | 3.44 | 1.49 | 3.71 |
| Shanxi........ | 7.65 | 19.46 | 18.32 | 3.65 | 0.87 | 2.86 | 0.93 | 4.27 |
| Neimenggu..... | 10.29 | 13.74 | 20.74 | 4.21 | 0.72 | 4.95 | 1.29 | 6.00 |
| Northeast: | | | | | | | | |
| Liaoning...... | 19.70 | 40.71 | 26.25 | 7.29 | .80 | 3.14 | 3.06 | 5.74 |
| Jilin......... | 15.19 | 18.05 | 19.13 | 5.66 | 0.35 | 4.68 | 1.25 | 5.26 |
| Heilongjiang.. | 11.67 | 15.77 | 19.23 | 2.34 | 0.23 | 1.78 | 6.71 | 9.25 |
| East: | | | | | | | | |
| Shanghai...... | 12.77 | 152.50 | 43.27 | 4.13 | 0.99 | 2.44 | 0.61 | 7.55 |
| Jiangsu....... | 15.78 | 54.71 | 24.18 | 2.24 | 0.81 | 3.43 | 3.01 | 6.15 |
| Zhejiang...... | 13.91 | 49.90 | 28.99 | 0.99 | 0.73 | 5.37 | 1.69 | 5.63 |
| Anhui......... | 16.21 | 29.55 | 18.11 | 0.91 | 0.81 | 4.43 | 1.79 | 6.36 |
| Fujian........ | 17.62 | 23.53 | 15.60 | 2.21 | 1.22 | 3.78 | 0.97 | 6.67 |
| Jiangxi....... | 19.12 | 25.76 | 13.77 | 1.00 | 0.97 | 3.93 | 1.17 | 5.46 |
| Shandong...... | 13.49 | 40.36 | 30.69 | 1.08 | 0.86 | 3.50 | 1.84 | 3.84 |
| South: | | | | | | | | |
| Henan......... | 10.23 | 22.10 | 13.78 | 1.05 | 0.85 | 4.76 | 1.13 | 4.28 |
| Hubei......... | 13.54 | 19.03 | 18.93 | 1.96 | 0.76 | 3.80 | 2.11 | 6.29 |
| Hunan......... | 13.49 | 28.13 | 16.27 | 1.14 | 1.35 | 3.92 | 1.11 | 6.12 |
| Guangdong..... | 20.36 | 45.71 | 20.36 | 3.24 | 1.31 | 5.87 | 3.91 | 9.66 |
| Guangxi....... | 14.87 | 15.26 | 16.57 | 1.45 | 0.96 | 2.60 | 1.30 | 4.59 |
| Southwest: | | | | | | | | |
| Sichuan....... | 10.99 | 20.13 | 12.72 | 1.85 | 1.35 | 3.45 | 0.93 | 4.57 |
| Guizhou....... | 11.02 | 12.75 | 8.47 | 0.84 | 0.69 | 1.69 | 0.94 | 4.43 |
| Yunnan........ | 11.27 | 17.49 | 14.97 | 1.66 | 0.32 | 3.45 | 1.08 | 3.75 |
| Xizang........ | | | | | | | | |
| Northwest: | | | | | | | | |
| Shaanxi....... | 12.40 | 18.70 | 16.10 | 1.50 | 0.65 | 4.26 | 0.79 | 4.04 |
| Gansu......... | 9.29 | 8.08 | 10.58 | 0.88 | 0.52 | 2.81 | 1.30 | 4.04 |
| Qinghai....... | 15.25 | 6.63 | 10.22 | 0.09 | 0.07 | 0.50 | 3.28 | 8.35 |
| Ningxia....... | 10.73 | 12.58 | 15.72 | 5.72 | 0.48 | 3.78 | 0.98 | 3.52 |
| Xinjiang...... | 17.43 | 8.14 | 15.07 | 1.33 | 0.29 | 2.93 | 1.09 | 5.96 |

NA Data not available

Source: Guojia tongji ju, Woguo nongmin shenghuo de juda bianhua
[State Statistical Bureau, Great Changes in the Lives of China's Peasants]
(1984), pp. 72-74.

Table 82. Distribution of Per Capita Total Living Expenditure of Peasants, by Province: 1981
(In percent)

| Province | Total | Consumer goods | Food | | | Clothes | Fuel | Housing | Daily articles and others | | Culture and service |
|---|---|---|---|---|---|---|---|---|---|---|---|
| | | | Total | Staple | Non-staple | | | | Total | of which furniture | |
| China............ | 100.00 | 97.57 | 59.66 | 32.01 | 21.75 | 12.35 | 5.55 | 9.78 | 10.22 | 1.81 | 2.43 |
| North | | | | | | | | | | | |
| Beijing......... | 100.00 | 95.42 | 52.11 | 24.29 | 18.26 | 11.50 | 2.94 | 15.73 | 13.13 | 1.70 | 4.58 |
| Tianjin......... | 100.00 | 98.45 | 50.74 | 25.94 | 17.57 | 15.05 | 4.04 | 16.63 | 12.00 | 2.11 | 1.55 |
| Hebei........... | 100.00 | 98.50 | 52.19 | 32.05 | 15.66 | 14.26 | 5.26 | 11.79 | 15.01 | 2.79 | 1.50 |
| Shanxi.......... | 100.00 | 98.41 | 58.10 | 38.43 | 14.07 | 16.16 | 3.76 | 8.22 | 12.17 | 1.57 | 1.59 |
| Neimenggu....... | 100.00 | 97.84 | 62.52 | 32.67 | 24.08 | 13.98 | 4.30 | 4.78 | 12.25 | 1.06 | 2.16 |
| Northeast | | | | | | | | | | | |
| Liaoning........ | 100.00 | 98.10 | 53.79 | 23.96 | 25.08 | 13.88 | 6.36 | 9.73 | 14.34 | 2.22 | 1.90 |
| Jilin........... | 100.00 | 98.71 | 61.93 | 30.43 | 23.40 | 13.83 | 6.19 | 5.57 | 11.18 | 1.60 | 1.29 |
| Heilongjiang.... | 100.00 | 96.22 | 58.20 | 35.05 | 18.57 | 17.10 | 6.00 | 4.89 | 10.03 | 1.69 | 3.78 |
| East | | | | | | | | | | | |
| Shanghai........ | 100.00 | 98.50 | 50.81 | 17.39 | 22.48 | 11.09 | 3.19 | 21.40 | 12.01 | 2.89 | 1.50 |
| Jiangsu......... | 100.00 | 97.34 | 56.86 | 29.36 | 19.51 | 11.44 | 4.21 | 14.70 | 10.14 | 1.77 | 2.66 |
| Zhejiang........ | 100.00 | 98.18 | 55.17 | 23.14 | 22.50 | 11.92 | 4.43 | 16.19 | 10.47 | 1.39 | 1.82 |
| Anhui........... | 100.00 | 96.87 | 61.01 | 35.38 | 19.92 | 11.12 | 5.75 | 10.18 | 8.81 | 2.09 | 3.13 |
| Fujian.......... | 100.00 | 97.12 | 61.98 | 31.28 | 26.01 | 10.03 | 8.29 | 7.44 | 9.39 | 1.33 | 2.88 |
| Jiangxi......... | 100.00 | 97.53 | 60.77 | 34.28 | 22.15 | 10.57 | 7.91 | 10.82 | 7.48 | 1.94 | 2.47 |
| Shandong........ | 100.00 | 97.73 | 50.05 | 29.66 | 15.70 | 15.10 | 4.30 | 13.41 | 14.86 | 2.81 | 2.27 |
| South | | | | | | | | | | | |
| Henan........... | 100.00 | 97.48 | 53.80 | 35.09 | 12.62 | 14.80 | 5.24 | 12.06 | 11.58 | 2.22 | 2.52 |
| Hubei........... | 100.00 | 97.00 | 62.44 | 35.56 | 22.02 | 12.29 | 5.63 | 8.47 | 8.18 | 2.02 | 3.00 |
| Hunan........... | 100.00 | 97.73 | 65.50 | 31.34 | 28.69 | 11.11 | 6.88 | 6.55 | 7.69 | 1.60 | 2.27 |
| Guangdong....... | 100.00 | 96.86 | 59.28 | 23.01 | 29.04 | 8.01 | 6.39 | 12.50 | 10.66 | 1.97 | 3.15 |
| Guangxi......... | 100.00 | 98.23 | 67.62 | 34.08 | 29.09 | 8.71 | 6.25 | 5.54 | 10.11 | .40 | 1.77 |
| Southwest | | | | | | | | | | | |
| Sichuan......... | 100.00 | 97.53 | 65.86 | 33.40 | 27.22 | 11.22 | 4.96 | 7.27 | 8.24 | 1.01 | 2.47 |
| Guizhou......... | 100.00 | 96.65 | 64.71 | 33.43 | 26.44 | 11.65 | 8.79 | 5.66 | 5.86 | 1.33 | 3.35 |
| Yunnan.......... | 100.00 | 98.07 | 66.66 | 35.88 | 24.43 | 11.54 | 5.60 | 6.56 | 7.70 | 1.36 | 1.93 |
| Xizang.......... | 100.00 | N/A | N/A | N/A | N/A | N/A | N/A | N/A | N/A | N/A | N/A |
| Northwest | | | | | | | | | | | |
| Shaanxi......... | 100.00 | 97.93 | 62.04 | 41.39 | 15.36 | 12.68 | 6.57 | 6.15 | 10.50 | 1.62 | 2.07 |
| Gansu........... | 100.00 | 96.95 | 68.76 | 49.04 | 15.64 | 12.11 | 3.82 | 5.26 | 7.00 | 1.80 | 3.05 |
| Qinghai......... | 100.00 | 95.48 | 67.39 | 41.17 | 18.62 | 12.31 | 5.00 | 4.72 | 6.07 | 1.13 | 4.52 |
| Ningxia......... | 100.00 | 98.14 | 62.86 | 43.49 | 16.57 | 14.19 | 4.09 | 5.24 | 11.76 | 3.49 | 1.86 |
| Xinjiang........ | 100.00 | 97.18 | 58.71 | 32.82 | 19.76 | 20.81 | 6.06 | 2.96 | 8.64 | 2.25 | 2.82 |

NA Data not available

Source: State Statistical Bureau, Statistical Yearbook of China 1981 (1981), pp.445-446.

Table 83. Distribution of Per Capita Total Living Expenditure of Peasants, by Province: 1982
(In percent)

| Province | Total | Consumer goods | Food: Total | Food: Staple | Food: Non-staple | Food: Other | Clothes | Fuel | Housing | Daily articles and other | Culture and services |
|---|---|---|---|---|---|---|---|---|---|---|---|
| China............ | 100.00 | 97.76 | 60.48 | 32.12 | 21.73 | 6.63 | 11.25 | 5.61 | 10.25 | 10.17 | 2.24 |
| North | | | | | | | | | | | |
| Beijing........ | 100.00 | 97.51 | 52.52 | 25.64 | 16.89 | 9.99 | 12.08 | 2.68 | 16.70 | 13.52 | 2.49 |
| Tianjin........ | 100.00 | 98.52 | 50.70 | 24.72 | 15.05 | 10.94 | 13.65 | 3.93 | 16.56 | 13.68 | 1.48 |
| Hebei.......... | 100.00 | 98.40 | 54.28 | 33.60 | 15.41 | 5.28 | 13.02 | 5.30 | 12.79 | 13.01 | 1.60 |
| Shanxi......... | 100.00 | 98.06 | 62.50 | 42.60 | 14.38 | 5.52 | 14.98 | 3.85 | 5.90 | 10.84 | 1.94 |
| Neimenggu....... | 100.00 | 98.40 | 62.69 | 34.21 | 22.57 | 5.91 | 13.49 | 4.36 | 6.14 | 11.71 | 1.60 |
| Northeast | | | | | | | | | | | |
| Liaoning....... | 100.00 | 98.70 | 54.74 | 24.05 | 25.92 | 4.77 | 12.34 | 6.68 | 10.25 | 14.69 | 1.30 |
| Jilin.......... | 100.00 | 97.94 | 62.88 | 30.12 | 25.15 | 7.61 | 13.17 | 7.25 | 4.66 | 9.98 | 2.06 |
| Heilongjiang.... | 100.00 | 96.99 | 57.94 | 32.67 | 19.95 | 5.32 | 14.74 | 6.60 | 6.86 | 10.84 | 3.01 |
| East | | | | | | | | | | | |
| Shanghai........ | 100.00 | 98.68 | 49.73 | 16.56 | 21.22 | 11.94 | 8.69 | 2.82 | 26.01 | 11.43 | 1.32 |
| Jiangsu........ | 100.00 | 97.80 | 55.46 | 26.52 | 21.18 | 7.77 | 11.14 | 4.46 | 16.30 | 10.44 | 2.20 |
| Zhejiang....... | 100.00 | 98.34 | 56.29 | 23.52 | 22.68 | 10.10 | 10.85 | 4.21 | 15.61 | 11.38 | 1.66 |
| Anhui.......... | 100.00 | 97.34 | 63.81 | 35.42 | 20.46 | 7.94 | 9.62 | 6.51 | 9.81 | 7.58 | 2.66 |
| Fujian......... | 100.00 | 97.09 | 62.70 | 29.62 | 25.95 | 7.13 | 9.20 | 7.34 | 8.45 | 9.41 | 2.91 |
| Jiangxi........ | 100.00 | 97.75 | 63.92 | 35.22 | 22.99 | 5.71 | 9.82 | 8.02 | 8.73 | 7.26 | 2.25 |
| Shandong....... | 100.00 | 98.33 | 50.36 | 29.29 | 15.00 | 6.07 | 13.37 | 5.30 | 14.61 | 14.68 | 1.67 |
| South | | | | | | | | | | | |
| Henan.......... | 100.00 | 97.58 | 56.87 | 37.35 | 13.24 | 6.29 | 13.07 | 4.76 | 11.35 | 11.52 | 2.42 |
| Hubei.......... | 100.00 | 97.26 | 61.97 | 34.56 | 20.98 | 6.42 | 12.45 | 5.44 | 8.16 | 9.23 | 2.74 |
| Hunan.......... | 100.00 | 97.57 | 65.95 | 31.65 | 28.38 | 5.82 | 9.95 | 5.48 | 8.93 | 7.26 | 2.43 |
| Guangdong....... | 100.00 | 96.26 | 58.43 | 23.04 | 28.53 | 6.86 | 6.57 | 5.86 | 13.57 | 11.83 | 3.74 |
| Guangxi......... | 100.00 | 98.17 | 66.18 | 32.77 | 28.14 | 5.27 | 8.79 | 6.99 | 6.38 | 9.83 | 1.83 |
| Southwest | | | | | | | | | | | |
| Sichuan........ | 100.00 | 97.89 | 66.18 | 34.91 | 24.74 | 6.53 | 9.96 | 5.32 | 8.52 | 7.92 | 2.11 |
| Guizhou........ | 100.00 | 97.56 | 65.06 | 31.68 | 27.32 | 6.05 | 11.51 | 6.73 | 7.75 | 6.51 | 2.44 |
| Yunnan......... | 100.00 | 98.37 | 66.90 | 33.19 | 26.37 | 7.34 | 10.66 | 4.79 | 7.66 | 8.36 | 1.63 |
| Xizang (Tibet).. | N/A | N/A | N/A | N/A | N/A | N/A | N/A | N/A | N/A | N/A | N/A |
| Northwest | | | | | | | | | | | |
| Shaanxi........ | 100.00 | 98.05 | 62.76 | 41.36 | 15.49 | 5.91 | 12.17 | 6.48 | 5.99 | 10.66 | 1.95 |
| Gansu.......... | 100.00 | 96.82 | 67.81 | 48.19 | 15.75 | 3.88 | 11.92 | 4.04 | 4.28 | 8.76 | 3.18 |
| Qinghai........ | 100.00 | 96.12 | 70.17 | 52.20 | 12.91 | 5.06 | 10.78 | 5.88 | 3.54 | 5.75 | 3.88 |
| Ningxia........ | 100.00 | 98.59 | 63.41 | 42.74 | 15.99 | 4.68 | 13.44 | 3.60 | 5.36 | 12.78 | 1.41 |
| Xinjiang....... | 100.00 | 97.17 | 60.67 | 31.78 | 22.10 | 6.79 | 18.71 | 6.75 | 2.28 | 8.75 | 2.83 |

NA Data not available

Source: State Statistical Bureau, Statistical Yearbook of China 1983 (1983), pp. 503-504; and He Kang, et al., eds., Zhongguo nongye nianjian 1983 [Agricultural Yearbook of China 1983] (1984), pp. 143-144.

Table 84. Distribution of Per Capita Total Living Expenditure of Peasants, by Province: 1983
(In percent)

| Province | Total | Consumer goods | Food: Total | Food: Staple | Food: Non-staple | Food: Other | Food: Outside meals | Clothes |
|---|---|---|---|---|---|---|---|---|
| China.......... | 100 | 97.79 | 59.30 | 30.22 | 21.62 | 6.37 | 1.09 | 11.14 |
| North | | | | | | | | |
| Beijing....... | 100 | 98.06 | 50.26 | 20.33 | 18.49 | 9.59 | 1.85 | 12.68 |
| Tianjin....... | 100 | 98.70 | 48.75 | 23.46 | 14.70 | 8.73 | 1.86 | 12.60 |
| Hebei......... | 100 | 98.35 | 53.52 | 32.15 | 15.42 | 4.96 | .99 | 12.90 |
| Shanxi........ | 100 | 97.90 | 57.74 | 37.10 | 13.10 | 6.54 | 1.01 | 13.73 |
| Neimenggu..... | 100 | 97.35 | 60.07 | 32.72 | 20.41 | 6.00 | .94 | 12.59 |
| Northeast | | | | | | | | |
| Liaoning...... | 100 | 98.13 | 52.99 | 23.66 | 23.16 | 5.18 | .99 | 12.29 |
| Jilin......... | 100 | 98.09 | 63.36 | 31.63 | 24.81 | 6.13 | .80 | 11.34 |
| Heilongjiang.. | 100 | 95.67 | 53.93 | 28.16 | 17.84 | 7.25 | .68 | 14.73 |
| East | | | | | | | | |
| Shanghai...... | 100 | 98.52 | 47.20 | 14.67 | 20.55 | 10.47 | 1.51 | 8.96 |
| Jiangsu....... | 100 | 98.09 | 55.30 | 26.64 | 19.95 | 7.68 | 1.03 | 10.45 |
| Zhejiang...... | 100 | 98.27 | 56.18 | 23.68 | 21.87 | 9.49 | 1.14 | 10.92 |
| Anhui......... | 100 | 97.54 | 59.42 | 31.92 | 19.75 | 6.85 | .90 | 10.33 |
| Fujian........ | 100 | 97.45 | 64.08 | 29.23 | 27.65 | 6.16 | 1.03 | 8.52 |
| Jiangxi....... | 100 | 97.84 | 62.55 | 32.06 | 24.17 | 5.27 | 1.05 | 9.24 |
| Shandong...... | 100 | 98.55 | 50.74 | 28.58 | 14.97 | 6.35 | .84 | 13.09 |
| South | | | | | | | | |
| Henan......... | 100 | 97.82 | 57.95 | 38.56 | 13.20 | 5.33 | .87 | 12.39 |
| Hubei......... | 100 | 97.51 | 61.80 | 31.36 | 22.62 | 6.97 | .86 | 11.89 |
| Hunan......... | 100 | 97.77 | 64.13 | 29.64 | 27.57 | 5.87 | 1.06 | 9.75 |
| Guangdong..... | 100 | 97.06 | 60.30 | 22.18 | 30.76 | 5.76 | 1.59 | 6.12 |
| Guangxi....... | 100 | 97.95 | 66.20 | 29.82 | 30.05 | 4.76 | 1.57 | 8.10 |
| Southwest | | | | | | | | |
| Sichuan....... | 100 | 98.02 | 65.17 | 32.24 | 25.55 | 6.11 | 1.28 | 10.60 |
| Guizhou....... | 100 | 97.61 | 68.00 | 32.87 | 28.43 | 5.76 | .94 | 9.94 |
| Yunnan........ | 100 | 98.32 | 64.62 | 29.06 | 26.47 | 7.34 | 1.75 | 11.26 |
| Xizang........ | N/A | N/A | N/A | N/A | N/A | N/A | N/A | N/A |
| Northwest | | | | | | | | |
| Shaanxi....... | 100 | 98.01 | 60.10 | 37.95 | 15.98 | 5.21 | .95 | 11.17 |
| Gansu......... | 100 | 97.52 | 63.70 | 45.93 | 12.93 | 4.35 | .49 | 13.25 |
| Qinghai....... | 100 | 95.87 | 61.81 | 37.63 | 16.33 | 7.28 | .57 | 16.21 |
| Ningxia....... | 100 | 98.31 | 60.58 | 38.72 | 16.30 | 4.73 | .83 | 13.80 |
| Xinjiang...... | 100 | 97.39 | 58.08 | 32.07 | 18.74 | 6.54 | .74 | 19.00 |

Table 84. Distribution of Per Capita Total Living Expenditure of Peasants, by Province: 1983--continued (In percent)

| Province | Fuel | Housing | Articles for daily use | Articles for culture and recreation | Books, news-papers, and magazines | Medicine and medical articles | Other articles | Culture and services |
|---|---|---|---|---|---|---|---|---|
| China.......... | 5.43 | 11.10 | 7.42 | .87 | .33 | 1.47 | .74 | 2.21 |
| North | | | | | | | | |
| Beijing....... | 3.17 | 16.84 | 10.15 | 3.22 | .04 | 1.31 | .38 | 1.94 |
| Tianjin....... | 3.82 | 17.95 | 12.24 | .65 | .08 | 1.12 | 1.49 | 1.30 |
| Hebei......... | 4.89 | 14.15 | 9.67 | .77 | .26 | 1.53 | .66 | 1.65 |
| Shanxi........ | 3.76 | 9.57 | 9.01 | 1.79 | .43 | 1.41 | .46 | 2.10 |
| Neimenggu..... | 4.54 | 6.06 | 9.15 | 1.86 | .32 | 2.18 | .57 | 2.65 |
| Northeast | | | | | | | | |
| Liaoning...... | 6.41 | 13.24 | 8.54 | 2.37 | .26 | 1.02 | 1.00 | 1.87 |
| Jilin......... | 5.52 | 6.56 | 6.96 | 2.06 | .13 | 1.70 | .45 | 1.91 |
| Heilongjiang.. | 5.46 | 7.38 | 9.00 | 1.09 | .11 | .83 | 3.14 | 4.33 |
| East | | | | | | | | |
| Shanghai...... | 2.50 | 29.81 | 8.46 | .81 | .19 | .48 | .12 | 1.48 |
| Jiangsu....... | 4.90 | 16.98 | 7.51 | .70 | .25 | 1.06 | .93 | 1.91 |
| Zhejiang...... | 4.27 | 15.31 | 8.90 | .30 | .22 | 1.65 | .52 | 1.73 |
| Anhui......... | 6.27 | 11.43 | 7.01 | .35 | .31 | 1.71 | .69 | 2.46 |
| Fujian........ | 6.74 | 9.01 | 5.97 | .85 | .47 | 1.45 | .37 | 2.55 |
| Jiangxi....... | 7.58 | 10.21 | 5.46 | .40 | .38 | 1.56 | .46 | 2.16 |
| Shandong...... | 5.10 | 15.26 | 11.61 | .41 | .33 | 1.32 | .70 | 1.45 |
| South | | | | | | | | |
| Henan......... | 5.21 | 11.26 | 7.02 | .54 | .43 | 2.43 | .58 | 2.18 |
| Hubei......... | 5.36 | 7.54 | 7.50 | .78 | .30 | 1.51 | .84 | 2.49 |
| Hunan......... | 4.93 | 10.27 | 5.94 | .42 | .49 | 1.43 | .41 | 2.23 |
| Guangdong..... | 6.19 | 13.90 | 6.19 | .99 | .40 | 1.79 | 1.19 | 2.94 |
| Guangxi....... | 6.64 | 6.81 | 7.40 | .65 | .43 | 1.16 | .58 | 2.05 |
| Southwest | | | | | | | | |
| Sichuan....... | 4.76 | 8.71 | 5.50 | .80 | .58 | 1.49 | .40 | 1.98 |
| Guizhou....... | 5.95 | 6.89 | 4.58 | .45 | .37 | .91 | .51 | 2.39 |
| Yunnan........ | 5.04 | 7.81 | 6.69 | .74 | .14 | 1.54 | .48 | 1.68 |
| Xizang........ | N/A | N/A | N/A | N/A | N/A | N/A | N/A | N/A |
| Northwest | | | | | | | | |
| Shaanxi....... | 6.10 | 9.19 | 7.92 | .74 | .32 | 2.09 | .39 | 1.99 |
| Gansu......... | 5.71 | 4.97 | 6.50 | .54 | .32 | 1.73 | .80 | 2.48 |
| Qinghai....... | 7.55 | 3.28 | 5.06 | .04 | .03 | .25 | 1.62 | 4.13 |
| Ningxia....... | 5.14 | 6.02 | 7.53 | 2.74 | .23 | 1.81 | .47 | 1.69 |
| Xinjiang...... | 7.65 | 3.57 | 6.61 | .58 | .13 | 1.29 | .48 | 2.61 |

NA Data not available

Source: Guojia tongji ju, Woguo nongmin shenghuo de juda bianhua [State Statistical Bureau, Great Changes in the Lives of China's Peasants] (1984), pp. 72-74.

Table 85. Purchased Portion of Per Capita Living Expenditures of Peasants, by Province: 1981
(In yuan)

| Province | Total expenditure | Expenditure on consumer goods | Food | Clothes | Fuel | Housing | Daily articles and others | Expenditure on means of production |
|---|---|---|---|---|---|---|---|---|
| China.......... | 132.90 | 104.35 | 41.70 | 23.25 | 2.66 | 17.59 | 19.15 | 28.55 |
| North | | | | | | | | |
| Beijing....... | 229.55 | 217.04 | 93.57 | 35.82 | 7.04 | 42.22 | 38.39 | 12.51 |
| Tianjin....... | 201.68 | 182.75 | 73.62 | 37.21 | 3.86 | 39.40 | 28.66 | 18.93 |
| Hebei......... | 121.81 | 103.75 | 34.72 | 23.00 | 3.65 | 18.21 | 24.17 | 18.06 |
| Shanxi........ | 104.55 | 86.64 | 30.92 | 23.02 | 3.65 | 11.21 | 17.84 | 17.91 |
| Neimenggu..... | 117.60 | 86.31 | 29.18 | 24.77 | 3.13 | 7.53 | 21.70 | 31.29 |
| Northeast | | | | | | | | |
| Liaoning...... | 175.83 | 155.06 | 55.58 | 35.78 | 2.75 | 24.13 | 36.82 | 20.77 |
| Jilin......... | 130.84 | 109.46 | 35.99 | 33.88 | .61 | 12.19 | 26.79 | 21.38 |
| Heilongjiang.. | 102.41 | 86.63 | 28.30 | 29.64 | 8.58 | 2.58 | 17.26 | 15.78 |
| East | | | | | | | | |
| Shanghai...... | 232.57 | 297.79 | 131.76 | 40.95 | 3.64 | 76.11 | 45.33 | 25.78 |
| Jiangsu....... | 165.25 | 136.22 | 56.11 | 25.35 | 1.31 | 31.00 | 22.45 | 29.03 |
| Zhejiang...... | 207.37 | 172.52 | 70.92 | 31.58 | 1.73 | 40.30 | 26.99 | 34.85 |
| Anhui......... | 155.13 | 98.60 | 41.02 | 21.17 | 1.65 | 18.22 | 16.54 | 56.53 |
| Fujian........ | 149.19 | 107.94 | 53.48 | 19.96 | 1.47 | 14.47 | 18.56 | 41.25 |
| Jiangxi....... | 117.73 | 90.66 | 34.84 | 20.19 | 2.47 | 19.07 | 14.09 | 27.07 |
| Shandong...... | 152.02 | 117.88 | 38.57 | 26.23 | 3.30 | 23.63 | 26.15 | 34.14 |
| South | | | | | | | | |
| Henan......... | 139.82 | 98.84 | 32.07 | 23.96 | 4.13 | 19.70 | 18.98 | 40.98 |
| Hubei......... | 99.60 | 86.27 | 33.28 | 22.06 | 1.48 | 14.91 | 14.54 | 13.33 |
| Hunan......... | 125.22 | 97.68 | 44.14 | 22.92 | 2.43 | 12.38 | 15.81 | 27.54 |
| Guangdong..... | 214.23 | 160.44 | 75.70 | 21.31 | 2.28 | 32.85 | 28.30 | 53.79 |
| Guangxi....... | 118.05 | 81.65 | 39.87 | 14.90 | .31 | 9.25 | 17.32 | 36.40 |
| Southwest | | | | | | | | |
| Sichuan....... | 120.52 | 91.47 | 41.99 | 20.54 | 2.46 | 11.59 | 14.89 | 29.05 |
| Guizhou....... | 105.64 | 72.09 | 31.37 | 18.61 | 3.81 | 9.12 | 9.18 | 33.55 |
| Yunnan........ | 86.10 | 65.01 | 29.44 | 15.80 | .74 | 8.62 | 10.41 | 21.09 |
| Xizang........ | N/A | N/A | N/A | N/A | N/A | N/A | N/A | N/A |
| Northwest | | | | | | | | |
| Shaanxi....... | 90.33 | 72.40 | 27.25 | 18.49 | 2.88 | 8.30 | 15.48 | 17.93 |
| Gansu......... | 75.15 | 55.43 | 20.43 | 16.28 | 2.54 | 6.87 | 9.31 | 19.72 |
| Qinghai....... | 72.54 | 58.32 | 19.80 | 18.90 | 3.48 | 7.19 | 8.95 | 14.22 |
| Ningxia....... | 95.25 | 69.18 | 21.42 | 20.03 | 3.92 | 7.42 | 16.39 | 26.07 |
| Xinjiang...... | 126.05 | 98.51 | 38.28 | 34.46 | 7.74 | 4.17 | 13.86 | 27.54 |

NA Data not available

Source: State Statistical Bureau, Statistical Yearbook of China 1981 (1981), pp. 447-448.

Table 86. Purchased Portion of Per Capita Living Expenditures of Peasants, by Province: 1982
(In yuan)

| Province | Total expenditure on commodities | Expenditure on consumer goods | Food | Clothes | Fuel | Housing | Daily articles and others | Expenditure on means of production |
|---|---|---|---|---|---|---|---|---|
| China.......... | 153.97 | 121.57 | 50.61 | 24.36 | 2.80 | 21.70 | 22.10 | 32.40 |
| North | | | | | | | | |
| Beijing....... | 273.42 | 252.62 | 104.45 | 43.58 | 6.92 | 50.20 | 47.47 | 20.80 |
| Tianjin....... | 234.49 | 202.05 | 86.76 | 36.24 | 3.50 | 41.53 | 34.02 | 32.44 |
| Hebei......... | 140.61 | 109.19 | 38.75 | 21.85 | 4.10 | 21.85 | 22.64 | 31.42 |
| Shanxi........ | 115.65 | 89.79 | 32.94 | 24.21 | 4.71 | 9.85 | 18.08 | 25.86 |
| Neimenggu..... | 143.88 | 99.18 | 32.17 | 27.61 | 3.65 | 11.76 | 23.99 | 44.70 |
| Northeast | | | | | | | | |
| Liaoning...... | 200.83 | 164.32 | 62.24 | 32.79 | 3.16 | 27.07 | 39.06 | 36.51 |
| Jilin......... | 149.20 | 111.26 | 43.82 | 33.23 | .28 | 9.40 | 24.53 | 37.94 |
| Heilongjiang.. | 122.24 | 103.12 | 35.46 | 29.10 | 4.03 | 13.03 | 21.50 | 19.12 |
| East | | | | | | | | |
| Shanghai...... | 377.82 | 342.43 | 144.06 | 37.08 | 3.74 | 109.46 | 48.09 | 35.39 |
| Jiangsu....... | 201.24 | 163.88 | 66.73 | 28.42 | 1.35 | 40.47 | 26.91 | 37.36 |
| Zhejiang...... | 227.47 | 193.77 | 80.22 | 32.46 | 1.45 | 45.74 | 33.90 | 33.70 |
| Anhui......... | 149.70 | 121.67 | 57.64 | 22.66 | 1.29 | 22.25 | 17.83 | 28.03 |
| Fujian........ | 162.52 | 128.94 | 64.89 | 21.26 | 1.79 | 19.24 | 21.76 | 33.58 |
| Jiangxi....... | 132.70 | 103.03 | 44.97 | 21.28 | 2.30 | 18.66 | 15.82 | 29.67 |
| Shandong...... | 188.74 | 150.02 | 50.75 | 29.24 | 3.80 | 32.99 | 33.24 | 38.72 |
| South | | | | | | | | |
| Henan......... | 133.30 | 103.72 | 36.88 | 22.93 | 3.76 | 19.74 | 20.41 | 29.58 |
| Hubei......... | 136.62 | 113.09 | 45.31 | 27.69 | 1.29 | 17.99 | 20.81 | 23.53 |
| Hunan......... | 153.33 | 118.96 | 52.25 | 24.43 | 3.15 | 21.15 | 17.98 | 34.37 |
| Guangdong..... | 248.80 | 193.69 | 94.17 | 20.32 | 1.48 | 41.36 | 36.36 | 55.11 |
| Guangxi....... | 141.59 | 106.51 | 53.98 | 18.41 | .52 | 13.00 | 20.60 | 35.08 |
| Southwest | | | | | | | | |
| Sichuan....... | 142.60 | 105.73 | 49.51 | 20.68 | 2.36 | 16.83 | 16.35 | 36.87 |
| Guizhou....... | 119.72 | 89.48 | 37.47 | 21.38 | 4.22 | 14.28 | 12.13 | 30.24 |
| Yunnan........ | 118.28 | 89.78 | 40.04 | 19.69 | 1.03 | 13.74 | 15.28 | 28.50 |
| Xizang........ | N/A | N/A | N/A | N/A | N/A | N/A | N/A | N/A |
| Northwest | | | | | | | | |
| Shaanxi....... | 109.20 | 82.69 | 31.84 | 19.95 | 2.99 | 10.01 | 17.90 | 26.51 |
| Gansu......... | 82.80 | 65.52 | 28.48 | 16.72 | 2.63 | 5.72 | 11.97 | 17.28 |
| Qinghai....... | 80.92 | 53.34 | 19.37 | 16.44 | 3.39 | 5.40 | 8.74 | 27.58 |
| Ningxia....... | 121.07 | 92.60 | 31.20 | 24.11 | 5.07 | 9.38 | 22.84 | 28.47 |
| Xinjiang...... | 137.48 | 115.71 | 48.95 | 37.76 | 7.38 | 4.30 | 17.32 | 21.77 |

NA Data not available

Source: State Statistical Bureau, Statistical Yearbook of China 1983 (1983), pp. 505-506.

Table 87. Purchased Portion of Per Capita Total Living Expenditure of Peasants, by Province: 1983
(In yuan)

| Province | Total | Consumer goods | Food: Total | Food: Staple | Food: Non-staple | Food: Other | Food: Outside meals | Clothes |
|---|---|---|---|---|---|---|---|---|
| China.......... | 148.30 | 142.87 | 59.14 | 11.97 | 29.84 | 14.36 | 2.70 | 27.14 |
| North: | | | | | | | | |
| Beijing....... | 308.42 | 302.29 | 129.84 | 30.75 | 55.76 | 36.22 | 7.11 | 48.59 |
| Tianjin....... | 274.70 | 270.70 | 113.79 | 33.34 | 45.08 | 29.11 | 6.26 | 42.19 |
| Hebei......... | 144.20 | 140.53 | 48.68 | 13.99 | 21.73 | 10.73 | 2.23 | 27.37 |
| Shanxi........ | 129.69 | 125.42 | 47.50 | 16.03 | 16.62 | 12.80 | 2.05 | 27.36 |
| Neimenggu..... | 122.94 | 116.97 | 39.54 | 11.36 | 12.93 | 13.12 | 2.13 | 28.53 |
| Northeast: | | | | | | | | |
| Liaoning...... | 201.92 | 196.18 | 75.76 | 25.09 | 32.29 | 15.34 | 3.04 | 37.45 |
| Jilin......... | 132.39 | 127.13 | 46.20 | 10.97 | 20.20 | 12.84 | 2.19 | 31.17 |
| Heilongjiang.. | 142.06 | 132.82 | 52.58 | 14.21 | 22.41 | 14.51 | 1.45 | 31.47 |
| East: | | | | | | | | |
| Shanghai...... | 421.20 | 414.58 | 169.02 | 17.93 | 90.20 | 53.14 | 7.75 | 44.90 |
| Jiangsu....... | 209.82 | 203.74 | 82.40 | 12.91 | 41.97 | 24.19 | 3.33 | 32.78 |
| Zhejiang...... | 219.05 | 213.42 | 89.77 | 11.47 | 45.82 | 28.76 | 3.72 | 35.23 |
| Anhui......... | 147.12 | 140.78 | 59.02 | 9.69 | 29.92 | 17.09 | 2.32 | 26.08 |
| Fujian........ | 154.28 | 147.62 | 76.36 | 9.69 | 49.09 | 14.88 | 2.70 | 22.26 |
| Jiangxi....... | 127.38 | 121.92 | 51.20 | 7.44 | 30.57 | 10.54 | 2.65 | 23.05 |
| Shandong...... | 181.60 | 177.80 | 64.61 | 14.49 | 32.00 | 15.91 | 2.21 | 32.52 |
| South: | | | | | | | | |
| Henan......... | 113.47 | 109.20 | 38.31 | 7.94 | 18.60 | 10.06 | 1.71 | 23.36 |
| Hubei......... | 136.53 | 130.26 | 54.27 | 10.11 | 25.12 | 16.88 | 2.16 | 29.06 |
| Hunan......... | 149.50 | 143.39 | 62.46 | 9.12 | 36.60 | 13.85 | 2.89 | 26.39 |
| Guangdong..... | 216.53 | 206.91 | 105.37 | 10.40 | 72.08 | 17.66 | 5.23 | 19.86 |
| Guangxi....... | 120.33 | 115.74 | 59.18 | 7.91 | 38.72 | 9.03 | 3.52 | 18.10 |
| Southwest: | | | | | | | | |
| Sichuan....... | 123.69 | 119.14 | 52.66 | 11.22 | 25.22 | 13.27 | 2.95 | 24.35 |
| Guizhou....... | 95.50 | 91.09 | 42.73 | 10.43 | 21.57 | 9.00 | 1.73 | 18.31 |
| Yunnan........ | 125.72 | 121.97 | 56.72 | 11.03 | 27.13 | 14.64 | 3.92 | 25.07 |
| Xizang........ | NA | NA | NA | NA | NA | NA | NA | NA |
| Northwest: | | | | | | | | |
| Shaanxi....... | 102.84 | 98.80 | 32.48 | 6.70 | 14.15 | 9.69 | 1.94 | 22.14 |
| Gansu......... | 80.09 | 76.06 | 27.62 | 10.15 | 9.93 | 6.75 | 0.79 | 21.40 |
| Qinghai....... | 98.23 | 89.88 | 32.27 | 8.64 | 10.19 | 12.28 | 1.16 | 32.55 |
| Ningxia....... | 115.36 | 111.84 | 39.18 | 14.34 | 13.35 | 9.75 | 1.74 | 28.47 |
| Xinjiang...... | 127.12 | 121.36 | 45.24 | 15.99 | 17.36 | 10.20 | 1.69 | 42.82 |

Table 87. Purchased Portion of Per Capita Total Living Expenditure of Peasants, by Province: 1983--continued
(In yuan)

| Province | Fuel | Housing | Articles for daily use | Articles for culture and rec. | Books, newspap., and mags. | Medicine, and med. articles | Other articles | Culture and services |
|---|---|---|---|---|---|---|---|---|
| China.......... | 3.01 | 26.95 | 18.27 | 2.16 | 0.81 | 3.63 | 1.76 | 5.43 |
| North: | | | | | | | | |
| Beijing....... | 8.67 | 58.82 | 38.58 | 12.37 | 0.17 | 5.04 | 0.21 | 6.13 |
| Tianjin....... | 4.61 | 59.36 | 41.15 | 2.17 | 0.25 | 3.75 | 3.43 | 4.00 |
| Hebei......... | 4.26 | 31.33 | 21.66 | 1.72 | 0.58 | 3.44 | 1.49 | 3.67 |
| Shanxi........ | 4.73 | 19.28 | 18.25 | 3.65 | 0.87 | 2.86 | 0.92 | 4.27 |
| Neimenggu..... | 3.65 | 13.64 | 20.74 | 4.20 | 0.72 | 4.93 | 1.02 | 5.97 |
| Northeast: | | | | | | | | |
| Liaoning...... | 2.74 | 39.96 | 26.03 | 7.29 | 0.80 | 3.12 | 3.03 | 5.74 |
| Jilin......... | 0.67 | 18.00 | 19.13 | 5.66 | 0.35 | 4.68 | 1.27 | 5.26 |
| Heilongjiang.. | 3.36 | 15.48 | 19.08 | 2.31 | 0.23 | 1.71 | 6.60 | 9.24 |
| East: | | | | | | | | |
| Shanghai...... | 4.08 | 145.99 | 42.91 | 4.01 | 0.99 | 2.03 | 0.65 | 6.62 |
| Jiangsu....... | 1.24 | 53.92 | 24.01 | 2.24 | 0.81 | 3.38 | 2.96 | 6.08 |
| Zhejiang...... | 1.67 | 49.43 | 28.54 | 0.99 | 0.73 | 5.37 | 1.69 | 5.63 |
| Anhui......... | 1.06 | 28.79 | 17.97 | 0.89 | 0.81 | 4.42 | 1.74 | 6.34 |
| Fujian........ | 1.78 | 23.51 | 15.53 | 2.21 | 1.22 | 3.78 | 0.97 | 6.66 |
| Jiangxi....... | 2.16 | 24.90 | 13.56 | 0.99 | 0.97 | 3.92 | 1.17 | 5.46 |
| Shandong...... | 3.53 | 39.45 | 30.43 | 1.03 | 0.86 | 3.49 | 1.88 | 3.80 |
| South: | | | | | | | | |
| Henan......... | 4.15 | 21.94 | 13.69 | 1.03 | 0.85 | 4.75 | 1.12 | 4.27 |
| Hubei......... | 1.22 | 18.43 | 18.69 | 1.96 | 0.76 | 3.79 | 2.08 | 6.27 |
| Hunan......... | 3.49 | 27.37 | 16.16 | 1.13 | 1.35 | 3.91 | 1.13 | 6.11 |
| Guangdong..... | 2.05 | 45.60 | 19.82 | 3.22 | 1.31 | 5.87 | 3.81 | 9.62 |
| Guangxi....... | 0.54 | 15.06 | 16.57 | 1.44 | 0.95 | 2.60 | 1.30 | 4.59 |
| Southwest: | | | | | | | | |
| Sichuan....... | 2.61 | 19.43 | 12.59 | 1.84 | 1.35 | 3.45 | 0.86 | 4.55 |
| Guizhou....... | 4.87 | 12.58 | 8.45 | 0.84 | 0.69 | 1.68 | 0.94 | 4.41 |
| Yunnan........ | 1.53 | 17.44 | 14.76 | 1.64 | 0.32 | 3.45 | 1.04 | 3.75 |
| Xizang........ | NA | NA | NA | NA | NA | NA | NA | NA |
| Northwest: | | | | | | | | |
| Shaanxi....... | 2.77 | 18.27 | 15.95 | 1.49 | 0.65 | 4.26 | 0.79 | 4.04 |
| Gansu......... | 3.13 | 7.87 | 10.54 | 0.88 | 0.52 | 2.80 | 1.30 | 4.03 |
| Qinghai....... | 4.69 | 6.42 | 10.05 | 0.09 | 0.07 | 0.50 | 3.24 | 8.35 |
| Ningxia....... | 5.69 | 11.88 | 15.67 | 5.72 | 0.48 | 3.78 | 0.97 | 3.52 |
| Xinjiang...... | 6.15 | 6.64 | 15.05 | 1.33 | 0.29 | 2.77 | 1.07 | 5.76 |

NA Data not available

Source: Guojia tongji ju, Woguo nongmin shenghuo de juda bianhua [State Statistical Bureau, Great Changes in the Lives of China's Peasants] (1984), pp. 78-80.

Table 88. Purchases as a Percent of Per Capita Expenditure of Peasants, by Province: 1981
(In percent)

| Province | Total | Consumer goods | Food | Clothes | Fuel | Housing | Daily articles and others |
|---|---|---|---|---|---|---|---|
| China............ | 69.65 | 56.05 | 36.63 | 98.64 | 25.12 | 94.22 | 98.15 |
| North | | | | | | | |
| Beijing......... | 73.34 | 72.67 | 57.37 | 99.50 | 76.61 | 85.74 | 93.38 |
| Tianjin......... | 80.94 | 74.50 | 58.23 | 99.25 | 38.37 | 95.08 | 95.88 |
| Hebei........... | 73.98 | 63.97 | 40.40 | 97.96 | 42.15 | 93.82 | 97.81 |
| Shanxi.......... | 70.75 | 59.58 | 36.01 | 96.40 | 65.77 | 92.26 | 99.17 |
| Neimenggu....... | 66.40 | 49.81 | 26.35 | 100.00 | 41.08 | 89.01 | 100.00 |
| Northeast | | | | | | | |
| Liaoning........ | 68.02 | 61.14 | 39.97 | 99.72 | 16.73 | 95.91 | 99.35 |
| Jilin........... | 53.17 | 45.07 | 23.62 | 99.53 | 4.00 | 88.98 | 97.35 |
| Heilongjiang.... | 58.44 | 51.38 | 27.75 | 98.90 | 81.56 | 30.14 | 98.24 |
| East | | | | | | | |
| Shanghai........ | 59.66 | 77.55 | 66.51 | 94.68 | 29.28 | 91.23 | 96.84 |
| Jiangsu......... | 73.27 | 62.05 | 43.76 | 98.26 | 13.80 | 93.51 | 98.12 |
| Zhejiang........ | 77.82 | 65.95 | 48.24 | 99.46 | 14.65 | 93.40 | 96.77 |
| Anhui........... | 80.27 | 52.67 | 34.79 | 98.51 | 14.84 | 92.63 | 97.12 |
| Fujian.......... | 74.88 | 55.78 | 43.30 | 99.90 | 8.90 | 97.64 | 99.25 |
| Jiangxi......... | 60.63 | 47.87 | 29.53 | 98.39 | 16.09 | 90.81 | 97.04 |
| Shandong........ | 84.95 | 67.41 | 43.07 | 97.04 | 42.91 | 98.46 | 98.31 |
| South | | | | | | | |
| Henan........... | 84.45 | 61.24 | 36.00 | 97.76 | 47.58 | 98.70 | 99.01 |
| Hubei........... | 54.20 | 48.39 | 29.00 | 97.70 | 14.31 | 95.82 | 96.68 |
| Hunan........... | 60.32 | 48.15 | 32.46 | 99.39 | 17.02 | 91.10 | 99.00 |
| Guangdong....... | 80.52 | 62.27 | 48.00 | 99.95 | 13.40 | 98.80 | 99.79 |
| Guangxi......... | 68.85 | 48.48 | 34.39 | 99.80 | 2.89 | 97.37 | 99.94 |
| Southwest | | | | | | | |
| Sichuan......... | 65.48 | 50.95 | 34.64 | 99.47 | 26.94 | 86.62 | 98.22 |
| Guizhou......... | 65.01 | 45.90 | 29.83 | 98.31 | 26.66 | 99.24 | 96.63 |
| Yunnan.......... | 62.50 | 48.12 | 32.06 | 99.37 | 9.60 | 95.35 | 98.11 |
| Xizang.......... | N/A | N/A | N/A | N/A | N/A | N/A | N/A |
| Northwest | | | | | | | |
| Shaanxi......... | 60.84 | 49.80 | 29.59 | 98.25 | 29.54 | 90.91 | 99.29 |
| Gansu........... | 55.57 | 42.28 | 21.97 | 99.45 | 49.13 | 96.62 | 98.31 |
| Qinghai......... | 47.26 | 39.80 | 19.14 | 100.00 | 45.37 | 99.31 | 96.13 |
| Ningxia......... | 67.23 | 49.75 | 24.05 | 99.60 | 67.59 | 100.00 | 98.38 |
| Xinjiang........ | 74.77 | 60.13 | 38.67 | 98.23 | 75.73 | 83.57 | 95.19 |

NA Data not available

Source: State Statistical Bureau, Statistical Yearbook of China 1981 (1981), pp.445-446, and 447-448.

Table 89. Purchases as a Percent of Per Capita Living Expenditures of Peasants, by Province: 1982
(In percent)

| Province | Total expenditure on commodities | Expenditure on consumer goods | Food | Clothes | Fuel | Housing | Daily articles and others |
|---|---|---|---|---|---|---|---|
| China.......... | 69.91 | 56.47 | 38.00 | 98.34 | 22.65 | 96.10 | 98.70 |
| North | | | | | | | |
| Beijing....... | 75.44 | 71.49 | 54.88 | 99.57 | 71.12 | 82.92 | 96.86 |
| Tianjin....... | 87.94 | 76.91 | 64.17 | 99.56 | 33.43 | 94.04 | 93.23 |
| Hebei......... | 80.17 | 63.27 | 40.70 | 95.71 | 44.09 | 97.37 | 99.25 |
| Shanxi........ | 68.98 | 54.61 | 31.44 | 96.42 | 72.91 | 99.60 | 99.50 |
| Neimenggu..... | 70.25 | 49.21 | 25.05 | 99.93 | 40.83 | 93.48 | 100.00 |
| Northeast | | | | | | | |
| Liaoning...... | 75.46 | 62.56 | 42.72 | 99.88 | 17.76 | 99.19 | 99.92 |
| Jilin......... | 58.87 | 44.82 | 27.50 | 99.55 | 1.52 | 79.59 | 96.99 |
| Heilongjiang.. | 60.94 | 53.01 | 30.51 | 98.41 | 30.44 | 94.69 | 98.85 |
| East | | | | | | | |
| Shanghai...... | 84.97 | 78.05 | 65.15 | 95.96 | 29.85 | 94.65 | 94.63 |
| Jiangsu....... | 76.98 | 64.10 | 46.03 | 97.60 | 11.57 | 95.00 | 98.57 |
| Zhejiang...... | 75.36 | 65.27 | 47.21 | 99.11 | 11.40 | 97.07 | 98.69 |
| Anhui......... | 62.39 | 52.10 | 37.65 | 98.14 | 8.26 | 94.52 | 98.07 |
| Fujian........ | 70.31 | 57.46 | 44.78 | 100.00 | 10.55 | 98.57 | 100.05 |
| Jiangxi....... | 60.35 | 47.94 | 32.00 | 98.56 | 13.04 | 97.24 | 99.06 |
| Shandong...... | 82.05 | 66.33 | 43.81 | 95.06 | 31.15 | 98.16 | 98.43 |
| South | | | | | | | |
| Henan......... | 74.93 | 59.75 | 36.45 | 98.58 | 44.44 | 97.72 | 99.56 |
| Hubei......... | 60.20 | 51.23 | 32.22 | 97.98 | 10.45 | 97.09 | 99.33 |
| Hunan......... | 61.66 | 49.03 | 31.86 | 98.75 | 23.11 | 95.27 | 99.56 |
| Guangdong..... | 79.63 | 64.40 | 51.59 | 99.03 | 8.08 | 97.55 | 98.35 |
| Guangxi....... | 67.38 | 51.63 | 38.81 | 99.68 | 3.54 | 96.94 | 99.71 |
| Southwest | | | | | | | |
| Sichuan....... | 68.48 | 51.87 | 35.93 | 99.71 | 21.32 | 94.87 | 99.15 |
| Guizhou....... | 64.01 | 49.04 | 30.80 | 99.30 | 33.55 | 98.55 | 99.59 |
| Yunnan........ | 63.68 | 49.14 | 32.22 | 99.39 | 11.59 | 96.62 | 98.39 |
| Xizang........ | N/A | N/A | N/A | N/A | N/A | N/A | N/A |
| Northwest | | | | | | | |
| Shaanxi....... | 64.65 | 49.92 | 30.03 | 97.03 | 27.33 | 99.01 | 99.44 |
| Gansu......... | 58.70 | 47.98 | 29.78 | 99.41 | 46.14 | 94.86 | 96.84 |
| Qinghai....... | 53.01 | 36.35 | 18.08 | 99.94 | 37.75 | 100.00 | 99.54 |
| Ningxia....... | 67.50 | 52.36 | 27.43 | 100.00 | 78.48 | 97.61 | 99.65 |
| Xinjiang...... | 67.68 | 58.63 | 39.72 | 99.37 | 53.79 | 92.67 | 97.47 |

NA Data not available

Source: State Statistical Bureau, Statistical Yearbook of China 1983 (1983), pp. 503-504, and 505-506.

Table 90. Purchases as a Percent of Per Capita Total Living Expenditure of Peasants, by Province: 1983
(In percent)

| Province | Total | Consumer goods | Food: Total | Food: Staple | Food: Non-staple | Food: Other | Outside meals | Clothes |
|---|---|---|---|---|---|---|---|---|
| China.......... | 59.73 | 58.84 | 40.17 | 15.95 | 55.58 | 90.83 | 100.00 | 98.16 |
| North: | | | | | | | | |
| Beijing....... | 80.23 | 80.19 | 67.20 | 39.35 | 78.44 | 98.24 | 100.00 | 99.67 |
| Tianjin....... | 81.64 | 81.51 | 69.36 | 42.23 | 91.11 | 99.15 | 100.00 | 99.53 |
| Hebei......... | 64.19 | 63.61 | 40.49 | 19.37 | 62.75 | 96.32 | 100.00 | 94.48 |
| Shanxi........ | 63.78 | 63.00 | 40.45 | 21.25 | 62.41 | 96.31 | 100.00 | 97.99 |
| Neimenggu..... | 54.27 | 53.04 | 29.06 | 15.32 | 27.97 | 96.54 | 100.00 | 100.00 |
| Northeast: | | | | | | | | |
| Liaoning...... | 65.69 | 65.04 | 46.51 | 34.50 | 45.35 | 96.30 | 100.00 | 99.10 |
| Jilin......... | 48.15 | 47.14 | 26.52 | 12.61 | 29.61 | 76.20 | 99.55 | 100.00 |
| Heilongjiang.. | 66.47 | 64.96 | 45.62 | 23.61 | 58.77 | 93.61 | 100.00 | 99.94 |
| East: | | | | | | | | |
| Shanghai...... | 82.33 | 82.25 | 69.99 | 23.88 | 85.81 | 99.25 | 100.00 | 97.91 |
| Jiangsu....... | 65.13 | 64.47 | 46.25 | 15.04 | 65.30 | 97.74 | 100.00 | 97.33 |
| Zhejiang...... | 67.22 | 66.65 | 49.04 | 14.87 | 64.30 | 92.98 | 100.00 | 99.04 |
| Anhui......... | 56.93 | 55.85 | 38.44 | 11.75 | 58.61 | 96.61 | 100.00 | 97.68 |
| Fujian........ | 59.05 | 57.98 | 45.61 | 12.69 | 67.96 | 92.42 | 100.00 | 100.00 |
| Jiangxi....... | 50.50 | 49.40 | 32.45 | 9.20 | 50.15 | 79.31 | 100.00 | 98.93 |
| Shandong...... | 68.68 | 68.23 | 48.16 | 19.17 | 80.83 | 94.76 | 100.00 | 93.99 |
| South: | | | | | | | | |
| Henan......... | 68.68 | 56.90 | 33.69 | 10.50 | 71.84 | 96.18 | 100.00 | 96.05 |
| Hubei......... | 54.08 | 52.91 | 34.78 | 12.77 | 43.99 | 95.96 | 100.00 | 96.80 |
| Hunan......... | 54.59 | 53.56 | 35.57 | 11.24 | 48.48 | 86.13 | 100.00 | 98.80 |
| Guangdong..... | 65.86 | 64.84 | 53.16 | 14.26 | 71.28 | 93.19 | 100.00 | 98.76 |
| Guangxi....... | 53.71 | 52.74 | 39.90 | 11.84 | 57.52 | 84.71 | 100.00 | 99.78 |
| Southwest: | | | | | | | | |
| Sichuan....... | 53.52 | 52.59 | 34.96 | 15.06 | 42.72 | 94.05 | 99.66 | 99.39 |
| Guizhou....... | 51.59 | 50.42 | 33.95 | 17.14 | 40.98 | 84.35 | 99.43 | 99.51 |
| Yunnan........ | 56.17 | 55.43 | 39.22 | 16.96 | 45.80 | 89.16 | 100.00 | 99.52 |
| Xizang........ | N/A | N/A | N/A | N/A | N/A | N/A | N/A | N/A |
| Northwest: | | | | | | | | |
| Shaanxi....... | 50.56 | 49.56 | 26.57 | 8.68 | 43.54 | 91.42 | 100.00 | 97.40 |
| Gansu......... | 49.23 | 47.95 | 26.66 | 13.58 | 47.20 | 95.47 | 100.00 | 99.26 |
| Qinghai....... | 48.63 | 46.42 | 25.84 | 11.37 | 30.90 | 83.48 | 100.00 | 99.42 |
| Ningxia....... | 55.23 | 54.46 | 30.96 | 17.73 | 39.21 | 98.78 | 100.00 | 98.75 |
| Xinjiang...... | 55.76 | 54.67 | 34.17 | 21.87 | 40.65 | 68.46 | 100.00 | 98.85 |

Table 90. Purchases as a Percent of Per Capita Living Expenditure of Peasants, by Province: 1983--continued
(In percent)

| Province | Fuel | Housing | Articles for daily use | Articles for culture and rec. | Books, newspap., and mags. | Medicine, and med. articles | Other articles | Culture and services |
|---|---|---|---|---|---|---|---|---|
| China.......... | 22.35 | 97.79 | 99.13 | 99.54 | 100.00 | 99.45 | 96.17 | 99.09 |
| North: | | | | | | | | |
| Beijing....... | 71.07 | 90.87 | 98.90 | 100.00 | 100.00 | 100.00 | 14.29 | 82.28 |
| Tianjin....... | 35.85 | 98.29 | 99.95 | 98.64 | 96.15 | 99.47 | 68.19 | 91.53 |
| Hebei......... | 38.76 | 98.55 | 99.72 | 99.42 | 100.00 | 100.00 | 100.00 | 98.92 |
| Shanxi........ | 61.83 | 99.08 | 99.62 | 100.00 | 100.00 | 100.00 | 98.92 | 100.00 |
| Neimenggu..... | 35.47 | 99.27 | 100.00 | 99.76 | 100.00 | 99.60 | 79.07 | 99.50 |
| Northeast: | | | | | | | | |
| Liaoning...... | 13.91 | 98.16 | 99.16 | 100.00 | 100.00 | 99.36 | 99.02 | 100.00 |
| Jilin......... | 4.41 | 99.72 | 100.00 | 100.00 | 100.00 | 100.00 | 101.60 | 100.00 |
| Heilongjiang.. | 28.79 | 98.16 | 99.22 | 98.72 | 100.00 | 96.07 | 98.36 | 99.89 |
| East: | | | | | | | | |
| Shanghai...... | 31.95 | 95.73 | 99.17 | 97.09 | 100.00 | 83.20 | 106.56 | 87.68 |
| Jiangsu....... | 7.86 | 98.56 | 99.30 | 100.00 | 100.00 | 98.54 | 98.34 | 98.86 |
| Zhejiang...... | 12.01 | 99.06 | 98.45 | 100.00 | 100.00 | 100.00 | 100.00 | 100.00 |
| Anhui......... | 6.54 | 97.43 | 99.23 | 97.80 | 100.00 | .00 | 97.21 | 99.69 |
| Fujian........ | 10.10 | 99.92 | 99.55 | 100.00 | 100.00 | 100.00 | 100.00 | 99.85 |
| Jiangxi....... | 11.30 | 96.66 | 98.47 | 99.00 | 100.00 | 99.75 | 100.00 | 100.00 |
| Shandong...... | 26.17 | 97.75 | 99.15 | 95.37 | 100.00 | 99.71 | 102.17 | 98.96 |
| South: | | | | | | | | |
| Henan......... | 40.57 | 99.28 | 99.35 | 98.10 | 100.00 | 99.79 | 99.12 | 99.77 |
| Hubei......... | 9.01 | 96.85 | 98.73 | 100.00 | 100.00 | 99.74 | 98.58 | 99.68 |
| Hunan......... | 25.87 | 97.30 | 99.32 | 99.12 | 100.00 | 99.74 | 101.80 | 99.84 |
| Guangdong..... | 10.07 | 99.76 | 97.35 | 99.38 | 100.00 | 100.00 | 97.44 | 99.59 |
| Guangxi....... | 3.63 | 98.69 | 100.00 | 99.31 | 98.96 | 100.00 | 100.00 | 100.00 |
| Southwest: | | | | | | | | |
| Sichuan....... | 23.75 | 96.52 | 98.98 | 99.46 | 100.00 | 100.00 | 92.47 | 99.56 |
| Guizhou....... | 44.19 | 98.67 | 99.76 | 100.00 | 100.00 | 99.41 | 100.00 | 99.55 |
| Yunnan........ | 13.58 | 99.71 | 98.60 | 98.80 | 100.00 | 100.00 | 96.30 | 100.00 |
| Xizang........ | N/A | N/A | N/A | N/A | N/A | N/A | N/A | N/A |
| Northwest: | | | | | | | | |
| Shaanxi....... | 22.34 | 97.70 | 99.07 | 99.33 | 100.00 | 100.00 | 100.00 | 100.00 |
| Gansu......... | 33.69 | 97.40 | 99.62 | 100.00 | 100.00 | 99.64 | 100.00 | 99.75 |
| Qinghai....... | 30.75 | 96.83 | 98.34 | 100.00 | 100.00 | 100.00 | 98.78 | 100.00 |
| Ningxia....... | 53.03 | 94.44 | 99.68 | 100.00 | 100.00 | 100.00 | 98.98 | 100.00 |
| Xinjiang...... | 35.28 | 81.57 | 99.87 | 100.00 | 100.00 | 94.54 | 98.17 | 96.64 |

NA Data not available

Source: Guojia tongji ju, Woguo nongmin shenghuo de juda bianhua [State Statistical Bureau, Great Changes in the Lives of China's Peasants] (1984), pp. 72-74, and 78-80.

Table 91. Peasant Per Capita Consumption of Major Consumer Goods, by Province: 1982

| Province | Grain | | | | | Vermicelli, bean noodles and other bean products | Edible Oil | |
|---|---|---|---|---|---|---|---|---|
| | Total | Wheat | Rice | Coarse | Vegetables | | Vegetable | Animal |
| (Unit) | jin | jin | jin | jin | jin | jin | jin | jin |
| China.......... | 519.95 | 118.04 | 265.64 | 136.27 | 264.08 | 4.40 | 4.14 | 2.72 |
| North | | | | | | | | |
| Beijing...... | 512.23 | 278.31 | 74.20 | 159.72 | 430.35 | 1.61 | 3.03 | 5.29 |
| Tianjin...... | 436.51 | 177.91 | 82.08 | 176.52 | 184.28 | 2.04 | 3.24 | 2.59 |
| Hebei........ | 412.73 | 129.36 | 11.49 | 271.88 | 234.80 | 4.88 | 2.38 | 1.53 |
| Shanxi....... | 473.98 | 146.70 | 4.05 | 323.23 | 182.86 | 6.15 | 3.32 | 1.05 |
| Neimenggu.... | 494.85 | 164.57 | 8.81 | 321.47 | 237.65 | 6.14 | 3.71 | 3.63 |
| Northeast | | | | | | | | |
| Liaoning..... | 483.60 | 32.78 | 81.64 | 369.18 | 428.71 | 3.93 | 2.88 | 4.84 |
| Jilin........ | 555.28 | 21.94 | 85.82 | 447.52 | 480.23 | 5.25 | 3.05 | 2.36 |
| Heilongjiang. | 500.94 | 155.72 | 53.26 | 291.96 | 292.11 | 5.39 | 6.57 | 2.32 |
| East | | | | | | | | |
| Shanghai..... | 553.65 | 32.83 | 499.21 | 21.61 | 234.87 | 4.21 | 8.27 | .97 |
| Jiangsu...... | 597.67 | 129.75 | 374.42 | 93.50 | 245.12 | 5.70 | 7.15 | 1.01 |
| Zhejiang..... | 604.24 | 46.60 | 487.97 | 69.67 | 286.75 | 4.44 | 4.20 | 1.41 |
| Anhui........ | 596.84 | 202.62 | 338.28 | 55.94 | 226.51 | 10.90 | 5.96 | 3.93 |
| Fujian....... | 568.46 | 5.27 | 532.43 | 30.76 | 261.58 | 5.44 | 1.22 | 3.26 |
| Jiangxi...... | 639.83 | 3.55 | 621.30 | 14.98 | 332.39 | 4.60 | 5.69 | 2.48 |
| Shandong..... | 432.57 | 161.19 | 2.96 | 268.42 | 236.48 | 6.95 | 5.76 | 1.37 |
| South | | | | | | | | |
| Henan........ | 454.86 | 268.19 | 54.47 | 132.20 | 219.20 | 5.52 | 2.80 | 1.17 |
| Hubei........ | 606.12 | 81.24 | 457.99 | 66.89 | 369.16 | 4.08 | 6.72 | 2.65 |
| Hunan........ | 634.77 | 8.40 | 600.78 | 25.59 | 333.27 | 5.32 | 5.27 | 5.66 |
| Guangdong.... | 548.43 | 2.88 | 519.65 | 25.90 | 242.72 | 4.12 | 4.39 | 1.86 |
| Guangxi...... | 527.87 | 1.34 | 469.67 | 56.86 | 268.68 | .90 | 2.25 | 3.92 |
| Southwest | | | | | | | | |
| Sichuan...... | 517.80 | 90.84 | 313.85 | 113.11 | 308.91 | 1.28 | 2.55 | 3.85 |
| Guizhou...... | 445.64 | 24.26 | 304.52 | 116.86 | 285.88 | 4.13 | 1.78 | 4.46 |
| Yunnan....... | 459.57 | 36.94 | 276.51 | 146.12 | 303.40 | 2.81 | 1.04 | 3.39 |
| Xizang....... | N/A | N/A | N/A | N/A | N/A | N/A | N/A | N/A |
| Northwest | | | | | | | | |
| Shaanxi...... | 493.21 | 254.18 | 38.06 | 200.97 | 136.55 | 3.42 | 2.95 | 1.55 |
| Gansu........ | 446.58 | 298.77 | 8.95 | 138.86 | 70.55 | 1.35 | 3.04 | 2.58 |
| Qinghai...... | 498.09 | 343.24 | .45 | 154.40 | 152.99 | .66 | 7.74 | .31 |
| Ningxia...... | 501.23 | 266.80 | 125.49 | 108.94 | 203.84 | 1.83 | 6.32 | 1.64 |
| Xinjiang..... | 431.60 | 276.79 | 9.15 | 145.66 | 158.46 | 1.07 | 5.40 | 1.99 |

Table 91. Peasant Per Capita Consumption of Major Consumer Goods, by Province: 1982--continued

| Province | Pork | Beef and mutton | Fowl | Eggs | Fish and shrimp | Sugar | Cigar-ettes | Liquor | Tea |
|---|---|---|---|---|---|---|---|---|---|
| (Unit) | jin | jin | jin | jin | jin | jin | packs | jin | jin |
| China.......... | 16.72 | 1.39 | 1.56 | 2.85 | 2.63 | 2.37 | 18.87 | 5.46 | .43 |
| North | | | | | | | | | |
| Beijing....... | 16.60 | 1.03 | .57 | 5.38 | 2.31 | 2.79 | 17.75 | 7.84 | 1.36 |
| Tianjin....... | 11.36 | 2.02 | .40 | 3.73 | 5.87 | 2.72 | 17.00 | 4.48 | .20 |
| Hebei......... | 9.75 | .72 | .17 | 2.29 | .58 | .97 | 13.61 | 2.15 | .14 |
| Shanxi........ | 6.03 | 2.19 | .10 | 2.11 | .09 | 1.13 | 19.44 | 1.17 | .21 |
| Neimenggu..... | 23.64 | 3.36 | .24 | 2.66 | .26 | 1.26 | 10.97 | 2.91 | .42 |
| Northeast | | | | | | | | | |
| Liaoning...... | 21.22 | .65 | .60 | 5.84 | 3.41 | 1.24 | 5.48 | 4.65 | .10 |
| Jilin......... | 20.98 | .42 | 1.43 | 5.02 | 1.74 | 1.02 | 3.09 | 5.20 | .16 |
| Heilongjiang.. | 15.51 | .40 | .64 | 4.59 | 1.18 | 1.63 | 4.14 | 4.25 | .11 |
| East | | | | | | | | | |
| Shanghai...... | 32.85 | .80 | 2.42 | 8.35 | 11.18 | 6.52 | 50.15 | 10.97 | .31 |
| Jiangsu....... | 16.34 | .26 | 1.94 | 4.74 | 4.73 | 2.57 | 26.79 | 5.60 | .09 |
| Zhejiang...... | 22.20 | .35 | 2.81 | 4.82 | 11.47 | 5.12 | 33.98 | 16.51 | .45 |
| Anhui......... | 15.31 | .92 | 2.98 | 3.42 | 3.18 | 2.81 | 36.80 | 5.26 | .48 |
| Fujian........ | 14.23 | .52 | 2.84 | 2.26 | 8.23 | 5.28 | 19.20 | 11.66 | .56 |
| Jiangxi....... | 15.10 | .26 | 1.82 | 2.47 | 3.30 | 2.17 | 18.53 | 7.40 | .34 |
| Shandong...... | 9.67 | .97 | .77 | 4.37 | 2.25 | 1.61 | 25.87 | 5.69 | .49 |
| South | | | | | | | | | |
| Henan......... | 8.67 | .63 | .52 | 3.10 | .43 | 1.54 | 22.96 | 1.79 | .03 |
| Hubei......... | 17.38 | .43 | 1.25 | 3.79 | 4.09 | 2.28 | 32.67 | 5.95 | .33 |
| Hunan......... | 26.21 | .37 | 3.01 | 3.12 | 3.10 | 2.52 | 24.57 | 9.04 | .54 |
| Guangdong..... | 18.81 | .28 | 5.30 | 1.79 | 12.31 | 8.77 | 19.20 | 4.09 | .49 |
| Guangxi....... | 16.67 | .29 | 3.95 | .91 | 1.70 | 1.89 | 9.72 | 7.20 | .04 |
| Southwest | | | | | | | | | |
| Sichuan....... | 29.28 | .62 | 1.29 | 2.65 | .37 | 2.21 | 16.34 | 5.81 | .34 |
| Guizhou....... | 24.29 | .37 | .89 | 1.12 | .53 | 1.84 | 14.49 | 9.84 | .45 |
| Yunnan........ | 20.34 | .64 | 1.77 | 1.46 | .53 | 3.06 | 7.77 | 5.79 | .56 |
| Xizang........ | N/A | N/A | N/A | N/A | N/A | N/A | N/A | N/A | N/A |
| Northwest | | | | | | | | | |
| Shaanxi....... | 10.21 | .44 | .20 | 1.23 | .02 | 1.02 | 13.33 | 3.91 | .43 |
| Gansu......... | 9.07 | 6.16 | .15 | .81 | N/A | .79 | 7.25 | .88 | .96 |
| Qinghai....... | 16.36 | .89 | .11 | 1.33 | .02 | .35 | 9.17 | 1.93 | 2.27 |
| Ningxia....... | 9.13 | 5.04 | .38 | 1.31 | .09 | 1.67 | 14.78 | .80 | .75 |
| Xinjiang...... | 3.82 | 25.07 | .41 | 1.06 | .13 | 1.66 | 2.18 | 1.57 | 2.83 |

NA Data not available
One jin = 0.5 kg.

Source: He Kang, et al., eds., Zhongguo nongye nianjian 1983 [Agricultural Yearbook of China 1983] (1983), pp. 147-148.

Table 92. Peasant Per Capita Consumption of Major Consumer Goods, by Province: 1983

| Province | Grain | | | | | | Edible Oil | | Meat | | |
|---|---|---|---|---|---|---|---|---|---|---|---|
| | Total | Refined | Wheat | Rice | Coarse | Vege-tables | Vege-table | Animal | Total | Pork | Beef and mutton |
| (Unit) | jin | jin | jin | jin | jin | jin | jin | jin | jin | jin | jin |
| China.......... | 519.81 | 392.51 | 132.14 | 260.37 | 127.30 | 261.90 | 4.38 | 2.67 | 19.93 | 18.59 | 1.34 |
| North: | | | | | | | | | | | |
| Beijing....... | 475.36 | 342.79 | 259.60 | 83.19 | 132.57 | 401.50 | 3.89 | 5.57 | 18.18 | 16.78 | 1.40 |
| Tianjin....... | 449.40 | 288.78 | 215.94 | 72.84 | 160.62 | 191.08 | 3.62 | 3.69 | 15.01 | 12.29 | 2.72 |
| Hebei......... | 433.96 | 182.78 | 169.58 | 13.20 | 251.18 | 240.05 | 3.30 | 1.73 | 12.48 | 11.68 | .80 |
| Shanxi........ | 438.79 | 194.57 | 191.65 | 2.92 | 244.22 | 192.31 | 4.01 | .60 | 7.96 | 5.66 | 2.30 |
| Neimenggu..... | 493.45 | 175.38 | 173.06 | 2.32 | 318.07 | 312.46 | 3.34 | 3.25 | 27.68 | 23.82 | 3.86 |
| Northeast: | | | | | | | | | | | |
| Liaoning...... | 496.47 | 134.36 | 36.70 | 97.66 | 362.11 | 407.59 | 3.27 | 4.10 | 23.41 | 22.99 | .42 |
| Jilin......... | 565.68 | 114.87 | 23.97 | 90.90 | 450.81 | 441.06 | 3.33 | 2.24 | 22.15 | 21.96 | .18 |
| Heilongjiang.. | 473.89 | 181.89 | 124.84 | 57.05 | 292.00 | 385.91 | 11.43 | 2.66 | 21.29 | 20.48 | .81 |
| East: | | | | | | | | | | | |
| Shanghai...... | 541.47 | 516.91 | 14.97 | 501.94 | 24.56 | 247.48 | 8.96 | .74 | 35.82 | 34.59 | 1.23 |
| Jiangsu....... | 612.62 | 520.72 | 121.83 | 398.89 | 91.90 | 239.70 | 7.48 | .96 | 19.05 | 18.77 | .28 |
| Zhejiang...... | 592.42 | 551.22 | 38.38 | 512.84 | 41.20 | 230.91 | 4.02 | 1.53 | 24.08 | 23.65 | .43 |
| Anhui......... | 568.29 | 525.56 | 190.28 | 335.28 | 42.73 | 210.50 | 5.68 | 2.92 | 16.03 | 15.43 | .60 |
| Fujian........ | 590.76 | 541.43 | 2.83 | 538.60 | 49.33 | 271.26 | 1.21 | 3.23 | 16.44 | 16.19 | .25 |
| Jiangxi....... | 658.68 | 638.72 | 2.58 | 636.14 | 19.96 | 357.50 | 5.95 | 2.74 | 18.95 | 18.60 | .35 |
| Shandong...... | 445.95 | 262.21 | 255.05 | 7.16 | 183.74 | 239.81 | 5.90 | 1.29 | 12.29 | 11.47 | .82 |
| South: | | | | | | | | | | | |
| Henan......... | 481.78 | 361.83 | 312.23 | 49.60 | 119.95 | 167.09 | 3.20 | .98 | 8.81 | 8.30 | .51 |
| Hubei......... | 598.31 | 531.33 | 57.92 | 473.41 | 66.98 | 391.95 | 6.55 | 2.69 | 22.37 | 21.99 | .38 |
| Hunan......... | 654.36 | 629.42 | 5.46 | 623.96 | 24.94 | 328.46 | 5.12 | 2.52 | 29.49 | 29.12 | .37 |
| Guangdong..... | 539.46 | 514.60 | 1.34 | 513.26 | 24.86 | 226.00 | 4.12 | 2.02 | 22.83 | 22.43 | .40 |
| Guangxi....... | 531.25 | 486.56 | 2.78 | 483.78 | 44.69 | 272.32 | 2.48 | 3.57 | 20.90 | 20.42 | .48 |
| Southwest: | | | | | | | | | | | |
| Sichuan....... | 530.33 | 441.62 | 97.12 | 344.50 | 88.71 | 318.87 | 2.31 | 4.13 | 32.36 | 31.66 | .70 |
| Guizhou....... | 445.60 | 327.22 | 27.44 | 299.78 | 118.38 | 285.75 | 2.17 | 4.90 | 25.57 | 25.22 | .35 |
| Yunnan........ | 463.43 | 359.19 | 43.08 | 316.11 | 104.24 | 208.17 | .85 | 4.30 | 25.85 | 25.17 | .68 |
| Xizang........ | N/A | N/A | N/A | N/A | N/A | N/A | N/A | N/A | N/A | N/A | N/A |
| Northwest: | | | | | | | | | | | |
| Shaanxi....... | 503.85 | 300.28 | 260.61 | 39.67 | 203.57 | 138.95 | 3.58 | 1.91 | 12.62 | 12.09 | .53 |
| Gansu......... | 460.25 | 349.96 | 346.65 | 3.31 | 110.29 | 100.60 | 2.64 | 1.19 | 9.52 | 8.58 | .94 |
| Qinghai....... | 444.84 | 338.44 | 338.42 | .02 | 106.40 | 79.92 | 7.79 | 2.74 | 25.18 | 11.33 | 14.44 |
| Ningxia....... | 493.79 | 386.82 | 287.10 | 99.72 | 106.97 | 196.65 | 6.01 | 1.63 | 13.73 | 9.11 | 4.62 |
| Xinjiang...... | 410.57 | 302.90 | 288.99 | 13.91 | 107.67 | 154.73 | 6.30 | 2.04 | 19.59 | 3.60 | 15.99 |

NA Data not available
One jin = 0.5 kg.

Table 92. Peasant Per-Capita Consumption of Major Consumer Goods, by Province: 1983—continued

| Province | Cows and goats milk | Fowl | Eggs | Fish and shrimp | Sugar | Cigar-ettes | Liquor | Tea | Candy | Fruit |
|---|---|---|---|---|---|---|---|---|---|---|
| (Unit) | jin | jin | jin | jin | jin | packs | jin | jin | jin | jin |
| China.......... | 1.33 | 1.63 | 3.14 | 3.17 | 2.51 | 19.89 | 6.39 | .44 | 1.61 | 6.04 |
| North: | | | | | | | | | | |
| Beijing...... | .43 | .53 | 9.07 | 2.18 | 3.33 | 18.00 | 9.33 | .61 | 6.30 | 18.28 |
| Tianjin...... | N/A | .56 | 4.75 | 7.10 | 2.76 | 20.48 | 5.02 | .17 | 4.99 | 9.69 |
| Hebei........ | .03 | .23 | 3.13 | .68 | 1.18 | 16.40 | 2.44 | .11 | 1.74 | 5.27 |
| Shanxi....... | .24 | .12 | 2.03 | .05 | 1.23 | 26.52 | 1.45 | .23 | 1.10 | 4.19 |
| Neimenggu.... | .35 | .25 | 2.89 | .31 | 1.21 | 11.49 | 3.33 | .52 | .98 | 2.94 |
| Northeast: | | | | | | | | | | |
| Liaoning..... | N/A | .55 | 6.17 | 3.06 | 1.11 | 7.19 | 5.75 | .22 | 1.48 | 6.79 |
| Jilin........ | N/A | .80 | 6.54 | 1.65 | 1.13 | 3.70 | 5.54 | .09 | 1.81 | 2.85 |
| Heilongjiang. | .66 | .93 | 6.70 | 2.91 | 2.08 | 5.48 | 5.87 | .09 | 1.34 | 2.42 |
| East: | | | | | | | | | | |
| Shanghai..... | .26 | 2.70 | 8.58 | 9.55 | 7.78 | 53.74 | 13.53 | .37 | 5.35 | 5.03 |
| Jiangsu...... | N/A | 1.96 | 6.10 | 5.95 | 3.22 | 29.89 | 8.52 | .09 | 3.64 | 3.12 |
| Zhejiang..... | N/A | 2.05 | 4.80 | 11.27 | 5.79 | 37.92 | 25.43 | .45 | .91 | 6.45 |
| Anhui........ | .02 | 3.15 | 3.51 | 3.04 | 3.49 | 29.96 | 4.94 | .42 | 1.50 | 1.85 |
| Fujian....... | N/A | 3.57 | 2.16 | 8.18 | 6.41 | 22.26 | 12.57 | .53 | .99 | 1.64 |
| Jiangxi...... | .01 | 2.02 | 2.69 | 3.95 | 2.27 | 22.23 | 9.00 | .33 | 1.70 | 2.03 |
| Shandong..... | .16 | .87 | 4.08 | 2.50 | 1.60 | 27.90 | 6.26 | .47 | 3.06 | 8.14 |
| South: | | | | | | | | | | |
| Henan........ | .02 | .82 | 2.48 | .46 | 1.63 | 23.99 | 1.81 | .04 | 1.60 | 5.74 |
| Hubei........ | .02 | 1.55 | 3.48 | 4.70 | 2.53 | 34.86 | 7.91 | .36 | 1.70 | 4.16 |
| Hunan........ | .01 | 3.09 | 2.97 | 3.60 | 2.58 | 27.11 | 10.31 | .51 | 2.13 | 5.69 |
| Guangdong.... | .05 | 6.02 | 1.89 | 15.92 | 7.95 | 13.79 | 6.58 | .63 | 1.86 | 2.98 |
| Guangxi...... | N/A | 4.45 | 1.19 | 2.62 | 2.35 | 13.45 | 8.68 | .04 | .57 | 3.08 |
| Southwest: | | | | | | | | | | |
| Sichuan...... | .34 | 1.31 | 2.63 | .39 | 2.51 | 19.71 | 6.38 | .30 | .81 | 4.75 |
| Guizhou...... | .02 | .85 | 1.12 | .60 | 1.61 | 15.05 | 8.63 | .39 | .65 | 4.21 |
| Yunnan....... | .01 | 2.35 | 1.88 | .77 | 3.58 | 13.01 | 7.48 | .77 | 1.54 | 11.73 |
| Xizang....... | N/A | N/A | N/A | N/A | N/A | N/A | N/A | N/A | N/A | N/A |
| Northwest: | | | | | | | | | | |
| Shaanxi...... | .13 | .30 | 1.58 | .03 | 1.17 | 16.56 | 3.52 | .73 | .85 | 5.72 |
| Gansu........ | .03 | .12 | 1.47 | N/A | .63 | 8.71 | 1.20 | .66 | .31 | 3.99 |
| Qinghai...... | 38.55 | .08 | .58 | .05 | .67 | 7.56 | 2.00 | 3.63 | 1.05 | 2.53 |
| Ningxia...... | .13 | .54 | 1.18 | .06 | 1.84 | 12.99 | .75 | .60 | .69 | 3.01 |
| Xinjiang..... | 22.25 | .40 | 1.58 | .11 | 1.32 | 1.59 | 1.20 | 1.99 | .87 | N/A |

NA Data not available
One jin = 0.5 kg.

Source: Guojia tongji ju, Woguo nongmin shenghuo de juda bianhua
[State Statistical Bureau, Great Changes in the Lives of China's Peasants] (1984),
pp. 88–91.

Table 93. Total Value of Retail Sales, by Province: 1980 to 1983
(In 100 million Yuan)

| Province | Total value of retail sales | | | | Percent increase from 1980 to 1983 |
|---|---|---|---|---|---|
| | 1980 | 1981 | 1982 | 1983 | |
| North | | | | | |
| Beijing....... | 61.32 | 68.82 | 73.31 | 83.57 | 36 |
| Tianjin....... | 37.75 | 42.07 | 43.14 | 47.36 | 25 |
| Hebei......... | 103.93 | 111.95 | 121.11 | 138.05 | 33 |
| Shanxi........ | 51.73 | 56.51 | 61.34 | 69.42 | 34 |
| Neimenggu..... | 44.31 | 47.36 | 52.12 | 57.65 | 30 |
| Northeast | | | | | |
| Liaoning...... | 120.06 | 136.98 | 145.50 | 160.89 | 34 |
| Jilin......... | 60.25 | 67.55 | 76.25 | 85.92 | 43 |
| Heilongjiang.. | 94.12 | 105.55 | 115.11 | 124.11 | 32 |
| East | | | | | |
| Shanghai...... | 88.15 | 95.27 | 97.33 | 108.87 | 24 |
| Jiangsu....... | 154.48 | 167.84 | 186.31 | 207.48 | 34 |
| Zhejiang...... | 92.64 | 103.80 | 112.96 | 125.35 | 35 |
| Anhui......... | 75.38 | 82.54 | 92.82 | 102.68 | 36 |
| Fujian........ | 54.20 | 60.65 | 66.12 | 72.33 | 33 |
| Jiangxi....... | 54.86 | 62.87 | 68.04 | 73.04 | 33 |
| Shandong...... | 146.88 | 168.29 | 183.11 | 209.11 | 42 |
| South | | | | | |
| Henan......... | 121.93 | 135.23 | 144.11 | 156.56 | 28 |
| Hubei......... | 100.55 | 107.89 | 120.08 | 133.20 | 32 |
| Hunan......... | 95.50 | 104.17 | 112.40 | 124.91 | 31 |
| Guangdong..... | 148.08 | 176.19 | 203.19 | 225.25 | 52 |
| Guangxi....... | 54.83 | 59.09 | 65.22 | 71.06 | 30 |
| Southwest | | | | | |
| Sichuan....... | 151.88 | 165.46 | 175.44 | 192.47 | 27 |
| Guizhou....... | 30.02 | 34.00 | 38.43 | 42.58 | 42 |
| Yunnan........ | 43.08 | 46.72 | 53.39 | 62.10 | 44 |
| Xizang........ | N/A | N/A | 4.15 | 4.34 | N/A |
| Northwest | | | | | |
| Shaanxi....... | 51.25 | 54.80 | 59.11 | 64.64 | 26 |
| Gansu......... | 30.42 | 32.79 | 35.75 | 38.72 | 27 |
| Qinghai....... | 9.20 | 9.93 | 10.55 | 11.70 | 27 |
| Ningxia....... | 8.02 | 8.68 | 9.78 | 11.10 | 38 |
| Xinjiang...... | 32.36 | 36.96 | 39.61 | 44.98 | 39 |

NA Data not available

Source: Guojia tongji ju, Zhongguo maoyi wujia tongji ziliao [State Statistical Bureau, Trade and Price Statistical Bureau], (1984), pp. 86-89.

Table 94. Total Value of Retail Sales, by Province: 1980
(In 100 million Yuan)

| Province | Total value of retail sales | Retail sales of social commodities: Sub-total | To individuals and collectives: Total | Individual | Collective | Agricultural means of production | Retail sales to non-agricultural residents |
|---|---|---|---|---|---|---|---|
| North | | | | | | | |
| Beijing | 61.32 | 60.89 | 57.25 | 48.83 | 8.42 | 3.64 | .42 |
| Tianjin | 37.75 | 37.25 | 34.39 | 29.73 | 4.66 | 2.86 | .50 |
| Hebei | 103.93 | 102.40 | 79.68 | 71.54 | 8.14 | 22.73 | 1.53 |
| Shanxi | 51.73 | 50.87 | 41.80 | 36.27 | 5.53 | 9.07 | .86 |
| Neimenggu | 44.31 | 43.13 | 38.31 | 33.03 | 5.28 | 4.83 | 1.17 |
| Northeast | | | | | | | |
| Liaoning | 120.06 | 116.47 | 101.82 | 89.90 | 11.92 | 14.65 | 3.58 |
| Jilin | 60.25 | 58.30 | 50.88 | 45.00 | 5.88 | 7.42 | 1.95 |
| Heilongjiang | 94.12 | 92.68 | 80.98 | 71.59 | 9.39 | 11.70 | 1.44 |
| East | | | | | | | |
| Shanghai | 88.15 | 87.29 | 79.57 | 72.04 | 7.53 | 7.72 | .87 |
| Jiangsu | 154.48 | 149.66 | 117.74 | 106.27 | 11.47 | 31.92 | 4.82 |
| Zhejiang | 92.64 | 89.40 | 71.63 | 64.68 | 6.96 | 17.76 | 3.24 |
| Anhui | 75.38 | 72.09 | 59.20 | 54.18 | 5.02 | 12.88 | 3.29 |
| Fujian | 54.20 | 51.76 | 43.04 | 39.16 | 3.88 | 8.72 | 2.44 |
| Jiangxi | 54.86 | 52.31 | 42.93 | 38.39 | 4.54 | 9.38 | 2.55 |
| Shandong | 146.88 | 143.50 | 110.63 | 98.41 | 12.22 | 32.87 | 3.38 |
| South | | | | | | | |
| Henan | 121.93 | 118.49 | 92.61 | 80.71 | 11.89 | 25.89 | 3.44 |
| Hubei | 100.55 | 97.13 | 78.49 | 68.60 | 9.88 | 18.64 | 3.42 |
| Hunan | 95.50 | 92.32 | 72.02 | 63.87 | 8.15 | 20.30 | 3.18 |
| Guangdong | 148.08 | 140.72 | 120.19 | 109.76 | 10.43 | 20.53 | 7.37 |
| Guangxi | 54.83 | 50.50 | 41.39 | 37.73 | 3.66 | 9.11 | 4.33 |
| Southwest | | | | | | | |
| Sichuan | 151.88 | 145.62 | 122.10 | 110.78 | 11.31 | 23.53 | 6.25 |
| Guizhou | 30.02 | 27.92 | 24.61 | 22.20 | 2.41 | 3.31 | 2.12 |
| Yunnan | 43.08 | 41.23 | 36.11 | 33.10 | 3.01 | 5.12 | 1.86 |
| Xizang | N/A | N/A | N/A | N/A | N/A | N/A | N/A |
| Northwest | | | | | | | |
| Shaanxi | 51.25 | 49.60 | 41.73 | 35.35 | 6.38 | 7.87 | 1.65 |
| Gansu | 30.42 | 29.59 | 25.65 | 22.06 | 3.59 | 3.94 | .83 |
| Qinghai | 9.20 | 9.06 | 8.15 | 7.02 | 1.13 | .90 | .14 |
| Ningxia | 8.02 | 7.85 | 6.57 | 5.74 | .83 | 1.28 | .17 |
| Xinjiang | 32.36 | 30.95 | 27.44 | 24.56 | 2.89 | 3.50 | 1.42 |

NA Data not available

Source: Guojia tongji ju, Zhongguo maoyi wujia tongji ziliao
[State Statistical Bureau, Trade and Price Statistics] (1984), p. 86.

Table 95. Total Value of Retail Sales, by Province: 1981
(In 100 million yuan)

| Province | Total value of retail sales | Retail sales of social commodities | | | | | | Retail sales by peasants to non-agricultural residents |
|---|---|---|---|---|---|---|---|---|
| | | Sub-total | To individuals and collectives | | | Agricultural means of production | |
| | | | Total | Individuals | Collectives | | |
| North: | | | | | | | |
| Beijing....... | 68.82 | 68.16 | 64.19 | 53.76 | 10.43 | 3.97 | .66 |
| Tianjin....... | 42.07 | 41.35 | 38.36 | 32.94 | 5.42 | 2.98 | .72 |
| Hebei......... | 111.95 | 109.79 | 87.92 | 79.46 | 8.46 | 21.87 | 2.16 |
| Shanxi........ | 56.51 | 54.97 | 47.23 | 41.39 | 5.84 | 7.75 | 1.53 |
| Neimenggu..... | 47.36 | 46.09 | 42.11 | 36.37 | 5.74 | 3.98 | 1.26 |
| Northeast: | | | | | | | |
| Liaoning...... | 136.98 | 131.51 | 115.50 | 102.6 | 12.89 | 16.01 | 5.47 |
| Jilin......... | 67.55 | 64.97 | 56.68 | 50.35 | 6.33 | 8.29 | 2.58 |
| Heilongjiang.. | 105.55 | 103.48 | 91.48 | 80.93 | 10.55 | 12.00 | 2.07 |
| East: | | | | | | | |
| Shanghai...... | 95.27 | 93.72 | 87.18 | 78.79 | 8.39 | 6.54 | 1.55 |
| Jiangsu....... | 167.84 | 162.02 | 128.97 | 115.9 | 13.07 | 33.05 | 5.83 |
| Zhejiang...... | 103.80 | 98.68 | 80.87 | 72.78 | 8.09 | 17.81 | 5.12 |
| Anhui......... | 82.54 | 78.64 | 64.15 | 59 | 5.16 | 14.49 | 3.90 |
| Fujian........ | 60.65 | 56.84 | 48.25 | 44.27 | 3.97 | 8.59 | 3.81 |
| Jiangxi....... | 62.87 | 58.76 | 49.64 | 44.37 | 5.27 | 9.13 | 4.11 |
| Shandong...... | 168.29 | 164.78 | 127.94 | 115.04 | 12.9 | 36.84 | 3.51 |
| South: | | | | | | | |
| Henan......... | 135.23 | 131.07 | 102.96 | 90.56 | 12.39 | 28.12 | 4.16 |
| Hubei......... | 107.89 | 103.66 | 85.67 | 75 | 10.67 | 17.99 | 4.23 |
| Hunan......... | 104.17 | 99.82 | 81.11 | 72.35 | 8.76 | 18.71 | 4.34 |
| Guangdong..... | 176.19 | 166.58 | 143.81 | 131.04 | 12.77 | 22.77 | 9.61 |
| Guangxi....... | 59.09 | 53.97 | 44.80 | 40.85 | 3.95 | 9.18 | 5.12 |
| Southwest: | | | | | | | |
| Sichuan....... | 165.46 | 157.90 | 134.60 | 122.68 | 11.92 | 23.29 | 7.57 |
| Guizhou....... | 34.00 | 31.55 | 28.03 | 25.45 | 2.58 | 3.52 | 2.45 |
| Yunnan........ | 46.72 | 44.37 | 39.58 | 36.49 | 3.1 | 4.79 | 2.35 |
| Xizang........ | N/A | N/A | N/A | N/A | N/A | N/A | N/A |
| Northwest: | | | | | | | |
| Shaanxi....... | 54.80 | 52.63 | 45.34 | 38.79 | 6.54 | 7.29 | 2.17 |
| Gansu......... | 32.79 | 31.70 | 28.05 | 24.06 | 3.99 | 3.66 | 1.08 |
| Qinghai....... | 9.93 | 9.73 | 8.99 | 7.89 | 1.1 | .74 | .20 |
| Ningxia....... | 8.68 | 8.46 | 7.18 | 6.36 | .82 | 1.28 | .22 |
| Xinjiang...... | 36.96 | 35.41 | 32.53 | 29.44 | 3.09 | 2.88 | 1.54 |

NA Data not available

Source: Guojia tongji ju, Zhongguo maoyi wujia tongji ziliao
[State Statistical Bureau, Trade and Price Statistics] (1984), p. 87.

Table 96. Total Value of Retail Sales, by Province: 1982
(In 100 million yuan)

| Province | Total value of retail sales | Retail sales of social commodities: Sub-total | To individuals and collectives: Total | To individuals and collectives: Individuals | To individuals and collectives: Collectives | Agricultural means of production | Retail sales by peasants to non-agricultural residents |
|---|---|---|---|---|---|---|---|
| North: | | | | | | | |
| Beijing..... | 73.31 | 72.57 | 67.40 | 55.80 | 11.60 | 5.17 | .74 |
| Tianjin..... | 43.14 | 42.30 | 39.04 | 32.92 | 6.12 | 3.26 | .84 |
| Hebei....... | 121.11 | 117.69 | 93.07 | 84.22 | 8.85 | 24.62 | 3.42 |
| Shanxi...... | 61.34 | 59.56 | 50.72 | 44.38 | 6.34 | 8.84 | 1.78 |
| Neimenggu... | 52.12 | 50.52 | 45.80 | 39.38 | 6.42 | 4.72 | 1.60 |
| Northeast: | | | | | | | |
| Liaoning.... | 145.50 | 139.05 | 121.46 | 106.79 | 14.67 | 17.59 | 6.45 |
| Jilin....... | 76.25 | 72.77 | 63.54 | 56.16 | 7.38 | 9.23 | 3.48 |
| Heilongjiang | 115.11 | 112.44 | 100.09 | 87.10 | 12.99 | 12.35 | 2.67 |
| East: | | | | | | | |
| Shanghai.... | 97.33 | 95.75 | 88.22 | 78.65 | 9.57 | 7.53 | 1.58 |
| Jiangsu..... | 186.31 | 179.34 | 143.04 | 128.54 | 14.50 | 36.30 | 6.97 |
| Zhejiang.... | 112.96 | 106.64 | 87.45 | 78.90 | 8.55 | 19.19 | 6.32 |
| Anhui....... | 92.82 | 87.82 | 70.68 | 65.14 | 5.54 | 17.14 | 5.00 |
| Fujian...... | 66.12 | 61.93 | 52.57 | 48.17 | 4.40 | 9.36 | 4.19 |
| Jiangxi..... | 68.04 | 63.48 | 53.09 | 47.04 | 6.05 | 10.39 | 4.56 |
| Shandong.... | 183.11 | 178.29 | 136.67 | 123.67 | 13.00 | 41.62 | 4.82 |
| South: | | | | | | | |
| Henan....... | 144.11 | 139.09 | 108.89 | 95.94 | 12.95 | 30.20 | 5.02 |
| Hubei....... | 120.08 | 113.52 | 94.07 | 82.49 | 11.58 | 19.45 | 6.56 |
| Hunan....... | 112.40 | 107.10 | 88.15 | 78.64 | 9.51 | 18.95 | 5.30 |
| Guangdong... | 203.19 | 191.25 | 165.27 | 151.73 | 13.54 | 25.98 | 11.94 |
| Guangxi..... | 65.22 | 59.37 | 48.73 | 44.66 | 4.07 | 10.64 | 5.85 |
| Southwest: | | | | | | | |
| Sichuan..... | 175.44 | 166.68 | 142.57 | 129.48 | 13.09 | 24.11 | 8.76 |
| Guizhou..... | 38.43 | 35.02 | 31.15 | 28.38 | 2.77 | 3.87 | 3.41 |
| Yunnan...... | 53.39 | 50.39 | 44.64 | 40.88 | 3.76 | 5.75 | 3.00 |
| Xizang...... | 4.15 | 3.98 | 3.71 | 3.19 | .52 | .27 | .17 |
| Northwest: | | | | | | | |
| Shaanxi..... | 59.11 | 56.69 | 48.23 | 40.94 | 7.29 | 8.46 | 2.42 |
| Gansu....... | 35.75 | 34.14 | 30.11 | 25.85 | 4.26 | 4.03 | 1.61 |
| Qinghai..... | 10.55 | 10.22 | 9.46 | 8.24 | 1.22 | .76 | .33 |
| Ningxia..... | 9.78 | 9.40 | 8.08 | 7.06 | 1.02 | 1.32 | .38 |
| Xinjiang.... | 39.61 | 37.95 | 34.75 | 30.95 | 3.80 | 3.20 | 1.66 |

NA Data not available

Source: Guojia tongji ju, Zhongguo maoyi wujia tongji ziliao [State Statistical Bureau, Trade and Price Statistics] (1984), p. 88.

Table 97. Total Value of Retail Sales, by Province: 1983
(In 100 million Yuan)

| Province | Total value of retail sales | Retail Sales: Sub-total | To individuals and collectives: Total | Individuals | Collectives | Agricultural means of production | Retail sales by peasants to non-agricultural residents |
|---|---|---|---|---|---|---|---|
| **North** | | | | | | | |
| Beijing | 83.57 | 82.72 | 76.94 | 63.08 | 13.86 | 5.78 | .86 |
| Tianjin | 47.36 | 46.63 | 43.07 | 36.06 | 7.01 | 3.55 | .73 |
| Hebei | 138.05 | 134.19 | 104.55 | 94.75 | 9.80 | 29.64 | 3.86 |
| Shanxi | 69.42 | 67.19 | 56.09 | 49.07 | 7.02 | 11.10 | 2.23 |
| Neimenggu | 57.65 | 55.81 | 50.31 | 42.91 | 7.40 | 5.50 | 1.84 |
| **Northeast** | | | | | | | |
| Liaoning | 160.89 | 153.38 | 134.32 | 117.29 | 17.03 | 19.06 | 7.50 |
| Jilin | 85.92 | 81.31 | 70.93 | 62.45 | 8.48 | 10.37 | 4.61 |
| Heilongjiang | 124.11 | 120.38 | 107.95 | 93.28 | 14.67 | 12.43 | 3.73 |
| **East** | | | | | | | |
| Shanghai | 108.87 | 106.63 | 98.44 | 85.64 | 12.80 | 8.20 | 2.24 |
| Jiangsu | 207.48 | 199.57 | 161.20 | 144.89 | 16.31 | 38.36 | 7.92 |
| Zhejiang | 125.35 | 118.07 | 96.95 | 87.28 | 9.67 | 21.12 | 7.29 |
| Anhui | 102.68 | 96.58 | 77.13 | 70.90 | 6.22 | 19.45 | 6.11 |
| Fujian | 72.33 | 66.98 | 57.24 | 52.35 | 4.88 | 9.74 | 5.35 |
| Jiangxi | 73.04 | 67.31 | 56.25 | 49.73 | 6.52 | 11.05 | 5.73 |
| Shandong | 209.11 | 203.95 | 156.98 | 142.28 | 14.70 | 46.97 | 5.16 |
| **South** | | | | | | | |
| Henan | 156.56 | 150.26 | 116.75 | 103.27 | 13.47 | 33.51 | 6.30 |
| Hubei | 133.20 | 125.52 | 104.77 | 91.23 | 13.53 | 20.76 | 7.68 |
| Hunan | 124.91 | 118.43 | 98.69 | 88.49 | 10.20 | 19.74 | 6.48 |
| Guangdong | 225.25 | 210.45 | 183.08 | 167.03 | 16.05 | 27.37 | 14.80 |
| Guangxi | 71.06 | 65.05 | 53.77 | 49.20 | 4.57 | 11.27 | 6.01 |
| **Southwest** | | | | | | | |
| Sichuan | 192.47 | 181.68 | 155.20 | 140.40 | 14.81 | 26.48 | 10.79 |
| Guizhou | 42.58 | 38.16 | 34.03 | 31.12 | 2.91 | 4.13 | 4.43 |
| Yunnan | 62.10 | 58.53 | 51.61 | 47.45 | 4.16 | 6.91 | 3.57 |
| Xizang | 4.34 | 4.27 | 3.94 | 3.38 | .56 | .33 | .07 |
| **Northwest** | | | | | | | |
| Shaanxi | 64.64 | 61.96 | 52.22 | 44.00 | 8.22 | 9.74 | 2.68 |
| Gansu | 38.72 | 36.86 | 32.43 | 27.59 | 4.84 | 4.43 | 1.86 |
| Qinghai | 11.70 | 11.27 | 10.36 | 9.02 | 1.34 | .90 | .43 |
| Ningxia | 11.10 | 10.59 | 8.83 | 7.76 | 1.07 | 1.76 | .51 |
| Xinjiang | 44.98 | 42.76 | 39.12 | 34.63 | 4.49 | 3.65 | 2.22 |

Source: Guojia tongji ju, Zhongguo maoyi wujia tongji ziliao
[State Statistical Bureau, Trade and Price Statistics] (1984), p.89.

Table 98. Rural Ownership of Durable Goods Per 100 Persons, by Commodity, and Province: 1982

| Province | Bicycle | Sewing machine | Radio | Clocks and watches: Total | Clocks | Watches | Tele-vision | Tape recorder | Electric fan |
|---|---|---|---|---|---|---|---|---|---|
| China.......... | 9.43 | 6.00 | 9.24 | 19.11 | 6.64 | 12.47 | .31 | .12 | .42 |
| North | | | | | | | | | |
| Beijing....... | 30.44 | 11.66 | 20.98 | 52.07 | 17.10 | 34.97 | 6.87 | N/A | 1.94 |
| Tianjin....... | 25.00 | 11.78 | 18.07 | 41.68 | 18.98 | 22.70 | 3.48 | .18 | 1.10 |
| Hebei......... | 18.31 | 9.82 | 15.26 | 23.95 | 12.23 | 11.72 | .15 | .03 | .04 |
| Shanxi........ | 14.54 | 10.77 | 9.55 | 22.77 | 9.19 | 13.58 | .10 | N/A | N/A |
| Neimenggu..... | 13.38 | 10.45 | 11.51 | 20.67 | 8.81 | 11.86 | .16 | .08 | N/A |
| Northeast | | | | | | | | | |
| Liaoning...... | 16.88 | 11.55 | 14.79 | 38.67 | 16.64 | 22.03 | 1.89 | .24 | .08 |
| Jilin......... | 9.81 | 9.51 | 15.15 | 29.50 | 12.75 | 16.75 | .49 | .19 | N/A |
| Heilongjiang.. | 9.78 | 9.92 | 14.03 | 25.99 | 8.77 | 17.22 | .14 | .08 | .03 |
| East | | | | | | | | | |
| Shanghai...... | 22.13 | 14.02 | 13.62 | 58.14 | 16.41 | 41.73 | 3.06 | .40 | 4.58 |
| Jiangsu....... | 11.25 | 4.69 | 11.47 | 28.07 | 8.83 | 19.24 | .10 | .02 | .29 |
| Zhejiang...... | 7.02 | 6.39 | 5.34 | 36.22 | 11.31 | 24.91 | .16 | .04 | 1.29 |
| Anhui......... | 5.00 | 3.90 | 10.78 | 11.71 | 3.26 | 8.45 | .04 | N/A | .24 |
| Fujian........ | 3.30 | 6.04 | 5.66 | 26.96 | 8.05 | 18.91 | .08 | .15 | .46 |
| Jiangxi....... | 2.91 | 1.80 | 8.52 | 16.52 | 4.95 | 11.57 | N/A | .03 | .13 |
| Shandong...... | 18.78 | 7.80 | 14.09 | 21.35 | 9.50 | 11.85 | .10 | .01 | .03 |
| South | | | | | | | | | |
| Henan......... | 9.65 | 7.50 | 11.64 | 10.44 | 3.28 | 7.16 | .02 | .02 | N/A |
| Hubei......... | 4.36 | 3.99 | 8.48 | 12.39 | 2.55 | 9.84 | .04 | .04 | .11 |
| Hunan......... | 2.99 | 2.99 | 4.60 | 15.20 | 2.78 | 12.42 | .04 | .01 | .11 |
| Guangdong..... | 15.90 | 8.60 | 9.94 | 33.13 | 10.95 | 22.18 | .77 | 1.34 | 4.91 |
| Guangxi....... | 12.11 | 5.78 | 3.99 | 15.00 | 4.68 | 10.32 | .08 | .10 | .47 |
| Southwest | | | | | | | | | |
| Sichuan....... | 2.71 | 1.50 | 5.73 | 13.30 | 3.98 | 9.32 | .13 | .09 | .06 |
| Guizhou....... | 1.32 | 2.16 | 1.96 | 8.09 | 1.68 | 6.41 | .07 | .11 | .02 |
| Yunnan........ | 2.56 | 2.29 | 3.94 | 8.71 | 1.52 | 7.19 | .08 | .25 | N/A |
| Xizang........ | N/A | N/A | N/A | N/A | N/A | N/A | N/A | N/A | N/A |
| Northwest | | | | | | | | | |
| Shaanxi....... | 8.19 | 6.61 | 8.64 | 10.45 | 4.63 | 5.82 | .06 | .02 | N/A |
| Gansu......... | 7.32 | 4.77 | 5.21 | 10.95 | 4.68 | 6.27 | .04 | .04 | N/A |
| Qinghai....... | 5.63 | 5.18 | 4.28 | 9.57 | 4.50 | 5.07 | N/A | N/A | N/A |
| Ningxia....... | 15.37 | 7.57 | 9.63 | 17.52 | 4.57 | 12.95 | .69 | .03 | N/A |
| Xinjiang...... | 8.76 | 8.80 | 8.49 | 14.70 | 4.60 | 10.10 | .20 | .24 | N/A |

NA Data not available

Source: Hu Qiaomu, et al., eds., Zhongguo nongye nianjian 1984 [Agricultural Yearbook of China 1984] (1984), p. 149.

Table 99. Rural Ownership of Durable Goods Per 100 Persons, by Commodity, and Province: 1983

| Province | Bicycle | Sewing machine | Radio | Clocks and watches: Total | Clocks | Watches | Tele-vision | Tape recorder | Electric fan |
|---|---|---|---|---|---|---|---|---|---|
| China.......... | 11.68 | 7.01 | 10.47 | 24.34 | 7.49 | 16.85 | .74 | .28 | .81 |
| North | | | | | | | | | |
| Beijing....... | 35.57 | 11.69 | 20.90 | 59.98 | 19.07 | 40.91 | 8.85 | 1.42 | 3.69 |
| Tianjin....... | 32.49 | 14.63 | 19.43 | 52.88 | 20.51 | 32.37 | 6.49 | .73 | 2.96 |
| Hebei......... | 21.18 | 11.23 | 17.19 | 30.30 | 14.12 | 16.18 | .47 | .08 | .13 |
| Shanxi........ | 16.88 | 12.60 | 12.44 | 29.89 | 10.32 | 19.57 | .82 | .23 | .02 |
| Neimenggu..... | 15.78 | 11.42 | 13.32 | 26.21 | 10.19 | 16.02 | .59 | .28 | .04 |
| Northeast | | | | | | | | | |
| Liaoning...... | 19.73 | 12.76 | 14.73 | 43.03 | 17.11 | 25.92 | 3.20 | .44 | .05 |
| Jilin......... | 12.08 | 10.08 | 15.62 | 34.77 | 13.43 | 21.34 | .78 | .55 | .05 |
| Heilongjiang.. | 11.88 | 9.65 | 13.71 | 26.78 | 8.16 | 18.62 | 1.66 | .45 | .04 |
| East | | | | | | | | | |
| Shanghai...... | 26.00 | 15.46 | 14.79 | 63.40 | 17.76 | 45.64 | 3.71 | .61 | 6.14 |
| Jiangsu....... | 15.54 | 5.69 | 14.70 | 34.99 | 9.74 | 25.25 | .43 | .10 | 1.24 |
| Zhejiang...... | 10.52 | 7.74 | 5.62 | 41.58 | 12.21 | 29.37 | .20 | .28 | 2.44 |
| Anhui......... | 7.06 | 4.57 | 12.69 | 15.02 | 3.85 | 11.17 | .19 | .07 | .52 |
| Fujian........ | 5.29 | 7.44 | 6.08 | 32.72 | 8.66 | 24.06 | .26 | .23 | 1.32 |
| Jiangxi....... | 4.30 | 2.34 | 10.30 | 20.50 | 5.59 | 14.91 | .01 | .06 | .35 |
| Shandong...... | 22.51 | 8.45 | 18.61 | 28.15 | 12.33 | 15.82 | .25 | .03 | .10 |
| South | | | | | | | | | |
| Henan......... | 12.74 | 8.64 | 12.99 | 14.32 | 4.24 | 10.08 | .13 | .07 | .11 |
| Hubei......... | 7.12 | 4.89 | 9.51 | 18.66 | 2.84 | 15.82 | .35 | .16 | .28 |
| Hunan......... | 4.42 | 3.83 | 5.69 | 18.90 | 3.17 | 15.73 | .05 | .08 | .18 |
| Guangdong..... | 18.31 | 9.07 | 9.52 | 36.11 | 11.57 | 24.54 | .87 | 1.32 | 6.72 |
| Guangxi....... | 14.02 | 7.20 | 4.87 | 18.71 | 4.99 | 13.72 | .21 | .19 | .89 |
| Southwest | | | | | | | | | |
| Sichuan....... | 2.91 | 2.03 | 6.43 | 17.07 | 3.94 | 13.13 | .20 | .04 | .04 |
| Guizhou....... | 1.53 | 2.19 | 2.66 | 10.95 | 1.53 | 9.42 | .17 | .16 | .05 |
| Yunnan........ | 4.89 | 3.34 | 6.33 | 14.99 | 1.74 | 13.25 | .33 | .73 | .05 |
| Xizang........ | N/A | N/A | N/A | N/A | N/A | N/A | N/A | N/A | N/A |
| Northwest | | | | | | | | | |
| Shaanxi....... | 10.04 | 7.52 | 10.11 | 15.19 | 5.88 | 9.31 | .27 | .11 | N/A |
| Gansu......... | 9.05 | 5.89 | 7.33 | 15.58 | 5.10 | 10.48 | .23 | .07 | N/A |
| Qinghai....... | 6.87 | 5.83 | 5.00 | 16.27 | 6.40 | 9.87 | .05 | .25 | .05 |
| Ningxia....... | 16.72 | 8.75 | 10.43 | 21.35 | 4.92 | 16.43 | 1.61 | .44 | N/A |
| Xinjiang...... | 9.39 | 8.64 | 7.88 | 17.21 | 3.87 | 13.34 | .27 | .38 | N/A |

NA Data not available

Source: Hu Qiaomu, et al., Zhongguo nongye nianjian 1984 [Agricultural Yearbook of China 1984] (1984), pp. 207-208.

Table 100. Selected Price and Cost of Living Indexes: 1951 to 1984 (1950 = 100)

| Year | General retail price index | General index of cost of living of staff and workers | General index of retail prices of industrial products in rural areas |
|---|---|---|---|
| 1950....... | 100.0 | 100.0 | 100.0 |
| 1951....... | 112.2 | 112.5 | 110.2 |
| 1952....... | 111.8 | 115.5 | 109.7 |
| 1953....... | 115.6 | 121.4 | 108.2 |
| 1954....... | 118.3 | 123.1 | 110.3 |
| 1955....... | 119.5 | 123.5 | 111.9 |
| 1956....... | 119.5 | 123.4 | 110.8 |
| 1957....... | 121.3 | 126.6 | 112.1 |
| 1958....... | 121.6 | 125.2 | 111.4 |
| 1959....... | 122.7 | 125.6 | 112.4 |
| 1960....... | 126.5 | 128.8 | 115.5 |
| 1961....... | 147.0 | 149.6 | 121.2 |
| 1962....... | 152.6 | 155.3 | 126.6 |
| 1963....... | 143.6 | 146.1 | 125.3 |
| 1964....... | 138.3 | 140.7 | 122.9 |
| 1965....... | 134.6 | 139.0 | 118.4 |
| 1966....... | 134.2 | 137.3 | 115.0 |
| 1967....... | 133.2 | 136.4 | 114.1 |
| 1968....... | 133.3 | 136.5 | 113.8 |
| 1969....... | 131.8 | 137.8 | 112.1 |
| 1970....... | 131.5 | 137.8 | 111.9 |
| 1971....... | 130.5 | 137.7 | 110.2 |
| 1972....... | 130.2 | 137.9 | 109.6 |
| 1973....... | 131.0 | 138.0 | 109.6 |
| 1974....... | 131.7 | 138.9 | 109.6 |
| 1975....... | 131.9 | 139.5 | 109.6 |
| 1976....... | 132.3 | 139.9 | 109.7 |
| 1977....... | 135.0 | 143.7 | 109.8 |
| 1978....... | 135.9 | 144.7 | 109.8 |
| 1979....... | 138.6 | 147.4 | 109.9 |
| 1980....... | 146.9 | 158.5 | 110.8 |
| 1981....... | 150.4 | 162.5 | 111.9 |
| 1982....... | 153.3 | 165.8 | 113.7 |
| 1983....... | 155.6 | 169.1 | 114.8 |
| 1984....... | 160.0 | 173.7 | 118.4 |

Source: State Statistical Bureau, Statistical Yearbook of China 1984 (1984), p. 425; and China: A Statistics Survey in 1985 (1985), p. 93.

Table 101. Official Period Average Chinese Exchange Rates: 1957 to 1984 (Yuan per U.S. dollar)

| | Exchange Rate (yuan per dollar) |
|---|---|
| 1957........... | 2.4618 |
| 1958........... | 2.4618 |
| 1959........... | 2.4618 |
| 1960........... | 2.4618 |
| 1961........... | 2.4618 |
| 1962........... | 2.4618 |
| 1963........... | 2.4618 |
| 1964........... | 2.4618 |
| 1965........... | 2.4618 |
| 1966........... | 2.4618 |
| 1967........... | 2.4618 |
| 1968........... | 2.4618 |
| 1969........... | 2.4618 |
| 1970........... | 2.4618 |
| 1971........... | 2.4618 |
| 1972........... | 2.2451 |
| 1973........... | 1.9894 |
| 1974........... | 1.9612 |
| 1975........... | 1.8598 |
| 1976........... | 1.9414 |
| 1977........... | 1.8578 |
| 1978........... | 1.6836 |
| 1979........... | 1.5550 |
| 1980........... | 1.4984 |
| 1981........... | 1.7045 |
| 1982........... | 1.8925 |
| 1983........... | 1.9757 |
| 1984........... | 2.3200 |

Source: International Monetary Fund, International Financial Statistics Yearbook 1985 (1985), pp. 240-241.

# BIBLIOGRAPHY


Blecher, M. "Income Distribution in Small Rural Chinese Communities," The China Quarterly, December 1976.

Berney, Karen. "China's Growing Consumer Market," China Business Review, Vol. 24, No. 40, October 1981.

Chen, Nai-Ruenn. Chinese Economic Statistics: A Handbook for Mainland China. Chicago: Social Science Research Council, 1967.

Chinn, D. L. "Basic Commodity Distribution in the People's Republic of China," The China Quarterly, December 1980.

Griffin, K. "Income Differentials in Rural China," The China Quarterly, December 1982.

Griffin, K. "Institutional Change and Income Distribution in the Chinese Countryside," Oxford Bulletin of Economics and Statistics, August 1983.

Griffin, K. and A. Saith. Growth and Equality in Rural China. Geneva: International Labour Office, Asian Employment Programme, 1981.

Griffin, K. and A. Saith. "The Pattern Of Income Inequality in Rural China," Oxford Economic Papers, March 1982.

Gu Shutang, et al., eds. Tianjin jingji gaikuang [General Economic Conditions in Tianjin]. Tianjin: Tianjin renmin chubanshe, 1984.

Guojia tongji ju [State Statistical Bureau]. Guanghui de sanshiwunian, 1949-1984 [Thirty-five Glorious Years, 1949-1984]. Beijing: Zhongguo tongji chubanshe, 1984.

__________. Woguo nongmin shenghuo de juda bianhua [Great Changes in the Lives of China's Peasants]. Beijing: Zhongguo tongji chubanshe, 1984.

__________. Zhongguo gongye de fazhan [The Development of China's Industry]. Beijing: Zhongguo tongji chubanshe, 1985.

__________. Zhongguo maoyi wujia tongji ziliao, 1952-1983 [China Trade and Price Statistics, 1952-1983]. Beijing: Zhongguo tongji chubanshe, 1984.

______________. Zhongguo tongji zhaiyao, 1983 [Statistical Abstract of China, 1983]. Beijing: Zhongguo tongji chubanshe, 1983.

______________. Zhongguo tongji zhaiyao, 1984 [Statistical Abstract of China, 1984]. Beijing: Zhongguo tongji chubanshe, 1984.

He Kang, et al., eds. Zhongguo nongye nianjian, 1983 [Agricultural Yearbook of China, 1983]. Beijing: Zhongguo nongye chubanshe, 1984.

______________. Zhongguo nongye nianjian, 1984 [Agricultural Yearbook of China, 1984]. Beijing: Zhongguo nongye chubanshe, 1984.

Howe, Christopher. "Wages, Prices, and the Standard of Living of Urban Workers in the PRC," China Business Review, July 1978.

Hu Qiaomu, et al., eds. Zhongguo baike nianjian, 1981 [Encyclopedic Yearbook of China, 1981]. Beijing: Zhongguo da baike quanshu chubanshe, 1981.

______________. Zhongguo baike nianjian, 1984 [Encyclopedic Yearbook of China, 1984]. Beijing: Zhongguo da baike quanshu chubanshe, 1984.

International Monetary Fund. International Financial Statistics Yearbook, 1985. Washington, D.C.: International Monetary Fund, 1985.

JPRS-CEA-84-054 [Joint Publications Research Service, China Economic Affairs, Number 54, 1984], July 21, 1984, p. 78.

Klatt, W. "The Staff of Life: Living Standards in China, 1977-81," The China Quarterly, March 1983.

Lardy, Nicholas R. Agriculture in China's Modern Economic Development. Cambridge: Cambridge University Press, 1983.

Li Chengrui. "Economic Reform Brings Better Life," Beijing Review, Vol. 28, No. 29, July 22, 1985, pp. 15-22.

______________. "Statistical Reporting on the Impact of China's Economic Policies of Recent Years on People's Income and Consumption." Proceedings of the International Statistical Institute. Amsterdam: International Statistical Institute, 1985.

Long, Jing. "San zhong quanhui yilai nongmin yu zhigong shenghuo chaju suoxiao" [Reduction in the Disparity between Peasant and Worker and Staff Living Standards Since the Third Party Plenum], Tongji, [Statistics], No. 10, October 17, pp. 9-11.

Ma Hong. Zhongguo jingji shidian [Economic Events in Modern China]. Beijing: Zhongguo shehui kexue chubanshe, 1982.

Nickum, J. E. and D. C. Schak. "Living Standards and Economic Development in Shanghai and Taiwan," The China Quarterly, March 1979.

Rada, E. "Food Policy in China: Recent Efforts to Balance Supplies and Consumption Requirements," Asian Survey, April 1983.

Renmin ribao [People's Daily], December 31, 1980, p. 1.

__________, April 30, 1982, p. 4.

Schran, Peter. The Development of Chinese Agriculture, 1950-1959. Urbana: University of Illinois Press, 1969.

Song Min and Liu Anping. "Woguo xiaofei pin de shouru tanxing fenxi ji xiaofei jiegou yusuan," ["Income Elasticity Analysis of Consumer Goods and Forecast of Chinese Consumption Structure"], Shuliang jingji jishu jingji yanjiu [Quantitative and Technical Economics Research], No. 1, 1984, pp. 27-35,and 80.

State Statistical Bureau. Statistical Yearbook of China, 1981. Hong Kong: Economic Information & Agency, 1982.

__________. Statistical Yearbook of China, 1983. Hong Kong: Economic Information & Agency, 1983.

__________. Statistical Yearbook of China, 1984. Hong Kong: Economic Information & Agency, 1984.

__________. China: A Statistics Survey in 1985. Beijing: New World Press and China Statistical Information and Consultancy Service Centre, 1985.

__________. The Present Conditions of the Statistical Work in China. Beijing: State Statistical Bureau, 1985.

Summary of World Broadcasts. FE/6616/C/1, January 1, 1981.

Surls, Fredric M. "Dramatic Growth of Rural Income," in U.S. Department of Agriculture, China: Outlook and Situation Report. Washington, D.C.: U.S. Department of Agriculture, Economic Research Service, June 1984.

Tan Yi. "Wei zhigong jiaji diaocha guodu dao chengzhen zhuhu diaocha da hao jichu" [Lay a Good Foundation for Moving from the Survey of Worker and Staff Households to the Survey of Urban Residents], Tongji [Statistics], No. 7, July 1984, p. 3.

Taylor, Jeffrey R. Employment and Unemployment in China. Foreign Economic Report No. 23. Washington, D.C.: U.S. Bureau of the Census, 1985.

Tongji [Statistics], No. 8, August 1985, p. 48.

Tongji yuebao [Statistics Monthly], No. 1, July 1985.

Tuan, Francis C. "China's Feed Industry: Recent Development and Future Plans," in U. S. Department of Agriculture, China Outlook and Situation Report. Washington, D.C.: U.S. Department of Agriculture, Economic Research Service, June 1984.

Tuan, Francis C., and Frederick W. Crook. Planning and Statistical Systems in China's Agriculture. Washington, D.C. U.S. Department of Agriculture, 1983.

United Nations. Industrial Statistics Yearbook, 1981. Vol. I. New York: United Nations, 1984.

____________. Industrial Statistics Yearbook, 1982. Vol. I. New York: United Nations, 1985.

U.S. Department of Agriculture. China: Outlook and Economic Situation. Washington, D.C.: U.S. Department of Agriculture, Economic Research Service, July 1985.

Van Der Gaag, Jacques. Private Household Consumption in China: A Study of People's Livelihood. World Bank Staff Working Paper No. 701. Washington, D.C.: The World Bank, 1984.

Vermeer, E. B. "Income Differentials in Rural China," The China Quarterly, March 1982.

Walker, Kenneth R. Food Grain Procurement and Consumption in China. Cambridge: Cambridge University Press, 1984.

Whyte, M. T. "Inequality and Stratification in China,"The China Quarterly, December 1975.

World Bank. China: Long-Term Issues and Options. Washington, D.C.: The World Bank, 1985.

Wortzel, H. V. "Equity and Efficiency in the Distribution of Non-Food Consumer Goods in China: Shanghai as an Example," Asian Survey, July 1983.

Xue Muqiao, et al., eds. Zhongguo jingji nianjian, 1981 [Economic Yearbook of China, 1981]. Beijing: Jingji guanli zazhishe, 1981.

________. *Zhongguo jingji nianjian, 1982* [Economic Yearbook of China, 1982]. Beijing: Jingji guanli zazhishe, 1982.

________. *Zhongguo jingji nianjian, 1983* [Economic Yearbook of China, 1983]. Beijing: Jingji guanli zazhishe, 1983.

________. *Zhongguo jingji nianjian, 1984* [Economic Yearbook of China, 1984]. Beijing: Jingji guanli zazhishe, 1984.